LIBRARY OF NEW TESTAMENT STUDIES

614

formerly the Journal for the Study of the New Testament Supplement series

Editor
Chris Keith

Editorial Board
Dale C. Allison, John M.G. Barclay, Lynn H. Cohick, R. Alan Culpepper,
Craig A. Evans, Robert Fowler, Simon J. Gathercole, Juan Hernandez Jr., John
S. Kloppenborg, Michael Labahn, Love L. Sechrest, Robert Wall, Catrin H. Williams,
Brittany Wilson

Gospel Women and the Long Ending of Mark

Kara J. Lyons-Pardue

LONDON • NEW YORK • OXFORD • NEW DELHI • SYDNEY

T&T CLARK
Bloomsbury Publishing Plc
50 Bedford Square, London, WC1B 3DP, UK
1385 Broadway, New York, NY 10018, USA
29 Earlsfort Terrace, Dublin 2, Ireland

BLOOMSBURY, T&T CLARK and the T&T Clark logo are trademarks of
Bloomsbury Publishing Plc

First published in Great Britain 2020
This paperback edition published in 2021

Copyright © Kara J. Lyons-Pardue, 2020

Kara J. Lyons-Pardue has asserted her right under the Copyright, Designs and Patents Act,
1988, to be identified as Author of this work.

For legal purposes the Acknowledgments on p. xi constitute an extension
of this copyright page.

All rights reserved. No part of this publication may be reproduced or transmitted
in any form or by any means, electronic or mechanical, including photocopying,
recording, or any information storage or retrieval system, without prior permission
in writing from the publishers.

Bloomsbury Publishing Plc does not have any control over, or responsibility for, any
third-party websites referred to or in this book. All internet addresses given in this
book were correct at the time of going to press. The author and publisher regret any
inconvenience caused if addresses have changed or sites have ceased to exist, but can
accept no responsibility for any such changes.

A catalogue record for this book is available from the British Library.

A catalog record for this book is available from the Library of Congress.

ISBN: HB: 978-0-5676-9240-5
PB: 978-0-5677-0213-5
ePDF: 978-0-5676-9241-2
eBook: 978-0-5676-9243-6

Series: Library of New Testament Studies, volume 614
ISSN 2513–8790

Typeset by Newgen KnowledgeWorks Pvt. Ltd., Chennai, India

To find out more about our authors and books visit www.bloomsbury.com
and sign up for our newsletters.

Contents

List of Tables	vii
List of Abbreviations	viii
List of Abbreviations of Ancient Sources	x
Acknowledgments	xi
Introduction	1

1 Scholarly Inquiry into the Long Ending as a Conclusion to Mark's Gospel 5
    1. In Defense of Mark's Ending at 16:20: Burgon as Paradigm 10
    2. Preoccupation with "Originality" in Studies of Mk 16:9-20: Following Burgon 14
    3. Reading Mk 16:8 as the Ending of the Second Gospel 26
    4. Reading through to Mk 16:20 as *an* Ending of the Second Gospel 39
    5. Conclusion 46

2 Mary Magdalene in the Long Ending and Mark 49
    1. Mary Magdalene's Role in Mk 16:9-14 51
    2. Mary Magdalene's Place in Resurrection Narratives: The Long Ending's Derivation and Innovation 52
    3. Mary Magdalene's Anonymous Female Predecessors in Mark's Gospel 75
    4. Conclusion 87

3 Unfaithful Disciples in the Long Ending and Mark 89
    1. The Eleven Disciples' Role in Mk 16:9-14 91
    2. The Disciples' Place in Canonical and Noncanonical Resurrection Narratives: The Long Ending's Derivation and Innovation 94
    3. The Eleven when They Were Twelve: Disciples in Mark's Gospel 114

4 Being Disciples Like Mary Magdalene: Implications of the Long Ending's Reading of Mark 119
    1. The Commission and Success of Jesus's Followers 120
    2. A Woman as the Primary Example of Faithful, Post-Resurrection Discipleship 122

3.	Implications of This Second-Century Continuation of Mark	134
4.	Conclusion: The Long Ending Canonizes Mary Magdalene's Witness	143

Appendix: The Many Endings to Mark's Gospel: Introductions, Text, and Translations   145

1.	The Shortest Ending (= at 16:8)	146
2.	The Long Ending (= Longer Ending = Mk 16:9-20)	146
3.	The Intermediate Ending (= Shorter Ending)	148
4.	Textual Obeli, Sigla, and Annotations at the Ending in the Manuscripts	150
5.	The Freer Logion within the Long Ending	151

Bibliography   159
Author Index   169
Ancient Index   172
Subject Index   184

Tables

2.1	The dependence of the LE on the canonical Gospels and Acts	54
2.2	Named/identified women in the canonical Gospel crucifixion and resurrection narratives	61
2.3	Appearance, report, and rejection in 16:9-11 and 16:12-13	73
2.4	Successive descriptions of the hemorrhaging woman in Mark	80
3.1	References to recipients of news of Jesus's resurrection	91
3.2	References to disbelief in the LE	92
3.3	The *Epistula Apostolorum*: outline and relevant excerpts	98
4.1	*Going* and *telling* in the LE	121
4.2	*Flight* and *silence* in the Gethsemane and empty tomb narratives	122
A.1	Synoptic table of the Greek text of Markan endings	153
A.2	Synoptic table of the author's English translation of Markan endings	155

Abbreviations

ABR	*Australian Biblical Review*
AGJU	Arbeiten zur Geschichte des antiken Judentums und des Urchristentums
ANTC	Abingdon New Testament Commentaries
AT	Author's translation
AThR	*Anglican Theological Review*
AYB	The Anchor Yale Bible
BBR	*Bulletin for Biblical Research*
BTB	*Biblical Theology Bulletin*
CBET	Contributions to Biblical Exegesis and Theology
CBQ	*Catholic Biblical Quarterly*
CCSL	Corpus Christianorum: Series latina. Turnhout, 1953–
CEV	Contemporary English Version
ChrCent	*Christian Century*
CurTM	*Currents in Theology and Mission*
EvQ	*Evangelical Quarterly*
EvT	*Evangelische Theologie*
ExpTim	*Expository Times*
FC	Fathers of the Church. Washington, DC, 1947–
HDR	Harvard Dissertations in Religion
HTR	*Harvard Theological Review*
HUCA	*Hebrew Union College Annual*
Int	*Interpretation*
JBL	*Journal of Biblical Literature*
JETS	*Journal of the Evangelical Theological Society*
JSHRZ	Jüdische Schriften aus hellenistisch-römischer Zeit
JSJSup	Supplements to Journal for the Study of Judaism
JSNT	*Journal for the Study of the New Testament*
JSNTSup	Journal for the Study of the New Testament: Supplement Series
JTS	*Journal of Theological Studies*
JTSA	*Journal of Theology for Southern Africa*
KJV	King James Version
LE	Long Ending
LNTS	Library of New Testament Studies
LXX	Septuagint
ms.	manuscript
NA^{27}	*Novum Testamentum Graece*, Nestle-Aland, 27th ed.
NA^{28}	*Novum Testamentum Graece*, Nestle-Aland, 28th ed.
NIBC	New International Biblical Commentary

NICNT	New International Commentary on the New Testament
NIDB	*The New Interpreter's Dictionary of the Bible*. Edited by Katharine Doob Sakenfeld. 5 vols. Nashville: Abingdon, 2006–9
NovT	*Novum Testamentum*
NovTSup	Novum Testamentum Supplements
NRSV	New Revised Standard Version
NT	New Testament
NTSup	Supplements to Novum Testamentum
OT	Old Testament
OTP	*Old Testament Pseudepigrapha*. Edited by J. H. Charlesworth. 2 vols. New York, 1983
PG	Patrologia graeca. Edited by J.-P. Migne. 162 vols. Paris, 1857–86
PTS	Patristische Texte und Studien
ResQ	*Restoration Quarterly*
SC	Sources chrétiennes. Paris: Cerf, 1943–
SemeiaSt	Semeia Studies
SNTSMS	Society for New Testament Studies Monograph Series
StPatr	Studia Patristica
TDNT	*Theological Dictionary of the New Testament*
TSK	*Theologische Studien und Kritiken*
TynBul	*Tyndale Bulletin*
TZ	*Theologische Zeitschrift*
WBC	Word Biblical Commentary
WUNT	Wissenschaftliche Untersuchungen zum Neuen Testament
WW	*Word and World*
ZNW	*Zeitschrift für die neutestamentliche Wissenschaft und die Kunde der älteren Kirche*
ZTK	*Zeitschrift für Theologie und Kirche*

Abbreviations of Ancient Sources

1 Apol.	Justin Martyr, *First Apology*
Ad Hedybiam	Jerome, *Epistula ad Hedybiam*
Ad Marinum	Eusebius, *Quaestiones ad Marinum* (in *Quaestiones et Responsiones*)
Ann.	Tacitus, *Annales*
Ant.	Josephus, *Jewish Antiquities*
Cels.	Origen, *Contra Celsum*
Cons.	Augustine, *Harmony of the Gospels*
Div.	Cicero, *De divinatione*
Enn.	Plotinus, *Enneades*
Ep.	Seneca, *Epistulae morales*
Ep. Apost.	*Epistula Apostolorum*
Eug.	*Eugnostos*
Geogr.	Strabo, *Geographica*
Gos. Mary	*Gospel of Mary*
Gos. Pet.	*Gospel of Peter*
Haer.	Irenaeus, *Adversus haereses*
Hist. eccl.	Eusebius, *Historia ecclesiastica*
Inf. Gos. Thom.	*Infancy Gospel of Thomas*
Inst.	Gaius, *Institutiones*
J.W.	Josephus, *Jewish War*
LAE	*Life of Adam and Eve*
Let. Aris.	*Letter of Aristeas*
Lucil.	Seneca, *Ad Lucilium*
Marc.	Tertullian, *Adversus Marcionem*
Metam.	Apuleius, *The Golden Ass*
Pelag.	Jerome, *Adversus Pelagianos dialogi III*
QG	Philo, *Questions and Answers on Genesis*
Sat.	Juvenal, *Satirae*
Soph. Jes. Chr.	*Sophia of Jesus Christ*
Tim.	Plato, *Timaeus*

Acknowledgments

In the process of writing a book like this one, many debts of gratitude accrue. Although I cannot mention all the people to whom appreciation is due, I shall try.

The ideas for this project developed from a mix of coursework, conversations, and lectures that intertwined during my years at Princeton Theological Seminary. Thank you to the faculty who particularly shaped the form my study took—Beverly Gaventa, Shane Berg, Loren Stuckenbruck, Dale Allison, and Lisa Bowens. A special thank you is due my faithful dissertation advisor, Clift Black, whose humor and way with words are unparalleled in our field and whose careful editorial eye benefitted this study. The deficits that remain are of my own making. I thank also my NT doctoral colleagues with whom I went through coursework—Laura Holmes, Matt Novenson, Janette Ok, Amy Peeler, Jason Sturdevant, and Brittany Wilson. They have been remarkable and inspiring conversation-partners and friends on this journey.

There are other scholars and organizations to whom I need to direct my thanks. Andy Johnson of Nazarene Theological Seminary has been a mentor and guide for years. James Kelhoffer and John Christopher Thomas met with me to discuss aspects of my project at nascent stages. Adela Yarbro Collins and Warren Gage sent me unpublished articles that assisted my thinking as well. Further, I have presented portions of this work in three different venues—a PTS Research Colloquium, the "Women in the Biblical World" Section of the Society of Biblical Literature, and the Wesleyan Theological Society—and subsequent versions of these chapters have benefitted from the feedback I received. Two libraries permitted me to use their collections for research that directly benefitted this project: Special Collections at PTS and Freer-Sackler Gallery (DC).

My colleagues and administration at Point Loma Nazarene University have encouraged me and given me time, through a Wesleyan Center Fellowship and a research sabbatical, to move this manuscript to publication. Thank you to Jessica Dunlop for her help with the indices. My students have listened patiently as I explained the Markan endings with far more enthusiasm and verbosity than could possibly have been necessary.

My biggest debt of thanks is owed to my family. My little daughters, Zoe first, then Iris, have motivated me to get work done so that I could spend time with them. My husband Charlie has been constant, calm, and supportive. His mom, Debby Pardue, traveled to care for Zoe lovingly while I wrote. My own parents, Terre and George Lyons, invested into this project encouragement, feedback, childcare, not to mention caring for me. From my earliest memory, their model of faithful Bible reading, memorization, and interpretation inspired my own. I owe them more thanks than can be expressed here. With love and gratitude, I dedicate this book to my mom and dad.

Introduction

Imagine the sensation that the discovery of a new Christian gospel fragment, dating to the early second century, would generate. In it, a female disciple—Mary Magdalene—takes center stage as the first and paradigmatic messenger of the gospel. The story continues with Jesus's closest male disciples wallowing in despair and disbelief. Finally, the resurrected Jesus appears and chides them into compliance. Such a find would be the stuff of headlines and late-night talk shows.

There *is* such a text, but it is hardly a new discovery. Instead, it is printed within brackets at the conclusion of Mark's Gospel in nearly every modern Bible. Its canonical status has been a matter of debate for more than two centuries. This debate over inclusion or exclusion, rather than the text's unexpected message, has garnered the lion's share of the scant attention afforded it. That largely irrelevant debate has led most readers of Mark to ignore its stunning narrative content. Consequently, the Long Ending of Mark (16:9-20; hereafter LE) and its unique way of completing the Second Gospel have remained in the shadows.

Once modern readers spend time scanning the LE, they are likely to be distracted by the odd mention of snake-handling and poison-drinking in 16:17-18. These were not the elements with which ancient readers wrestled.[1] Most scholars understand (correctly, I believe) that Mk 16:9-20 is a later supplement to the Second Gospel. Nevertheless, despite its strangeness to modern tastes, this passage is not a heretical encroachment, but rather a thoroughly "orthodox" addition. We can only speculate as to its author's intentions, but the evidence suggests that it aimed to secure Mark's position in the early Four-Gospel Canon[2] by providing it with the "satisfying" ending that Gospel lacked.

Modern interpreters have been perplexed by how to read Mk 16:8 as a conclusion to the Second Gospel. In comparison with the other canonical Gospels, the perceived problem is that Mark lacks a resurrection appearance of Jesus, a narrative expectation to which Mark itself has been building. The LE fills that deficit. It also redeems another

---

[1] If the exchange between Eusebius and "Marinus" (who may be a fictionalized conversation partner) reflects the concerns of real readers of the Gospels, apparent conflicts in the timing of the women's approach to the tomb were greater cause for question (*Ad Marinum* I). See Chapter 1 for more information on Eusebius's *Ad Marinum*.

[2] See Charles Horton, ed., *The Earliest Gospels: The Origins and Transmission of the Earliest Christian Gospels—The Contribution of the Chester Beatty Gospel Codex P^{45}* (JSNTSup 258; New York: T&T Clark, 2004). Brent Nongbri has recently raised some important objections to default dating found in some scholarly treatments. On the Chester Beatty Papyri, see Nongbri, *God's Library: The Archaeology of the Earliest Christian Manuscripts* (New Haven, CT: Yale University Press, 2018), 116–56. The use of "early Four-Gospel Canon" here relies on signals (some internal to the LE itself and others in patristic writings) of the preference for and deference to the four accounts about Christ that are now our canonical Gospels.

shortcoming of Mark's strange and abrupt conclusion: the women disciples who discovered the empty tomb fail to fulfill their assigned mission. The Long Ending makes clear that (1) Mary Magdalene saw Jesus (16:9), (2) she saw him *first* (16:9), and (3) she went and told others about that encounter (16:10-11).

Within the LE Jesus's inner circle of male disciples receives more narrative attention than Mary Magdalene. She exits the stage after successfully conveying news of the living Jesus to the Eleven. Nevertheless, the attention they receive is negative. In their first three appearances, the Eleven are not heroes. They are repeatedly faithless, even weeping over a Jesus who is no longer dead. This dissonance with conventional expectations of masculinity in response to Jesus's death and resurrection has some parallels in the other Gospels' endings. But here it is more extreme, despite the LE's brevity.

This study highlights exegetically the selective and complex interweaving of traditions that comprise the Long Ending's characterizations of Mary Magdalene and the Eleven. I argue that this depiction conflicts with ancient gender stereotypes in ways that are likely intentional. The bold, trustworthy female disciple turns out to be the first and best model of post-resurrection discipleship. The male insiders fail repeatedly. Only Jesus's intervention presses them into conformity with the role of true disciples—*going and telling the good news*, as Mary did first and immediately in the LE's telling.

The author of Mark's LE and the copyists and churchpersons who secured its place in the Gospel tradition almost certainly did not champion its place within canonical Mark at the behest of latent, proto-feminist impulses. Rather, they seem to have found this a fitting conclusion to Mark's Gospel. We must not forget that this story of Jesus casts many nameless women—the infirm, outsiders, and a widow—as models of faith. At the same time, Mark casts male powerbrokers—priests, rulers, Sadducees, and Pharisees—and "insiders" such as the Twelve as dimwits who repeatedly malign or misunderstand Jesus and his message.

There are good reasons justifying scholarly attention to the LE's unusual content and debates over its canonical status. But these preoccupations have obscured this material's unique presentation of Jesus's resurrection appearances. Even those who argue that the LE is the rightful (i.e., original or canonical) ending of the Second Gospel tend to divorce it from its primary function—to conclude Mark's story about Jesus. *What* the LE highlights in bringing Mark to conclusion gives us access to *how* ancient Christians read Mark's account. Among other contributions, it succeeded in protecting for posterity Mary Magdalene's model of faithful discipleship.

This study accepts the current, prevailing opinion that Mk 16:9-20 is a secondary addition to the Second Gospel. It is more likely that this satisfying ending, which seems to contain theological advancements and a more conventional conclusion, would have been added to Mark's Gospel than that an earlier one would have been removed intentionally.[3] Neither of the ancient majuscule codices of the fourth century, Sinaiticus and Vaticanus, contains any text for Mark after 16:8.[4]

---

[3] It is, of course, possible that the Long Ending was removed by accidental means. This is seldom proposed. This suggestion, that 16:9-20 is original, but removed in two major uncials (etc.) is not to be equated with the position that the original ending was lost and never (yet) recovered. (For the representatives of latter position, see Chapter 1.) The proposal that the Long Ending was the original conclusion to Mark, but lost in the *Vorlage* of two early extant codices (and in others known to Eusebius) remains in the realm of speculation, in my view. Additionally problematic is how one would account for its smooth, early, and unmentioned reintroduction into the tradition.

[4] Even these reliable manuscript witnesses do not simply trump patristic attestation of the Long Ending; their evidence is of a different order.

The LE and other endings (the Intermediate and the insertion of the Freer Logion) must have originated early. All these endings seem to have been intended to rectify a perceived deficit in Mark's earliest recoverable ending, 16:8.[5]

Eusebius and Jerome testify to the existence of various closings of the Second Gospel in manuscripts known to them. This suggests that the supplementary endings were popular well before the fourth century. It also suggests that these endings were considered neither as threats to the authority of Mark nor as challenges to its emerging canonical status.

The most plausible working hypothesis is that the LE (16:9-20) is a second-century addition to the Gospel according to Mark. It sought to repair perceived deficiencies in the Second Gospel. These repairs attempted to improve Mark's coherence within a Gospel proto-canon. The other three Gospels each concluded with resurrection narratives; by comparison, Mark appeared lacking. The LE aimed to provide for Mark a satisfactory conclusion with resurrection appearances.

I accept and survey this scholarly consensus but make no attempt to defend it. Instead, I attempt to move beyond this commonplace assumption by addressing questions few have seen fit to consider: *How* do the stories briefly recounted in the LE serve to support the emerging canonical witness? *How* do the resurrection appearances added to the empty tomb account of 16:1-8 develop and gather narrative threads already present in Mark's Gospel?

Most scholars give inadequate attention to two obvious features of the LE of Mark. First, Mary Magdalene is brought back into the storyline. Of course, she appears in the other three Gospels. But only in the Fourth Gospel and Mark's LE does she appear alone. Second, the eleven remaining male disciples disbelieve repeatedly. Their conduct serves only to compound their dismal performance in the Gospel's passion narrative—Judas's betrayal, all the disciples' desertion of Jesus, and Peter's denial. Mary's faithful witness and their stubborn faithlessness stand in sharp contrast.

Certainly the LE mentions remarkable signs expected to follow belief (16:17-18). A few scholars have investigated these to some extent. But fewer have noted what I find most remarkable—that a later addition, arising in the second century and gaining nearly universal acceptance over the centuries, brings a female witness to the resurrection "back onstage." The stress on a woman's faith, counterbalanced by an emphasis on the Eleven's stubborn lack of faith, is particularly noteworthy. In such a brief supplement, repeated insistence on their disbelief is all the more striking when viewed alongside the limited space given to their rehabilitation.

Elements of the three resurrection appearances reported in the LE strongly resemble other known Gospel conclusions. The sources of these anecdotes are likely traditions derived from or shared with Matthew, Luke, and John. But none of their endings entirely explains either the prominence assigned to Mary or the repeated incrimination of the disciples for unbelief.

---

[5] Others have spoken of this phenomenon in terms of "correction." Thus, Daniel A. Smith (*Revisiting the Empty Tomb: The Early History of Easter* [Minneapolis: Fortress, 2010]):

> In addition, just as the later canonical evangelists sought in different ways to correct the perceived deficiencies of the Markan version of the story, so also did early Christian interpreters and retellers of the story. This can be seen in both the scribal additions to the Gospel of Mark and in certain narrative expansions of the story, such as those found in the *Gospel of Peter* and in the *Epistle of the Apostles*, both of which probably were composed in the second century C.E. (155)

The LE's reliance on the other Gospels is noteworthy. But far more important is the author's reading of Mark's Gospel, whose narrative repeatedly emphasizes the faithfulness of women and the inconstancy of male disciples. These corresponding emphases have been rediscovered only within the past half-century. It is remarkable though seldom mentioned by modern scholars that an ancient reader—the scribe(s) who added the LE and, subsequently, the readers who popularized that Markan supplement—had already noticed and appreciated these emphases. The LE's way of concluding the Second Gospel develops these narrative trends from the Gospel itself.

My argument, simply put, is that Mk 16:9-20 evidences a creative reappropriation of resurrection traditions that concludes the Second Gospel in an intentionally and perceptively "Markan" way. The evidence is persuasive that whoever composed Mk 1:1–16:8 did not create this ending. The author of 16:9-20 highlights and vindicates Mary Magdalene as the first to proclaim the gospel of the risen Christ. This author does so by imitating Mark's already unfavorable depiction of the male disciples. Even if theirs is only a temporary shortcoming, it is unmistakably pronounced.

1

Scholarly Inquiry into the Long Ending as a Conclusion to Mark's Gospel

In a maze of brackets and footnotes, nestled between the Gospels According to Mark and Luke, most English versions of the New Testament (NT) have an array of endings for the Second Gospel. Typically included are the "Shorter"[1] and "Longer"[2] endings, as well as the "Freer Logion."[3] Modern readers are free either to ignore anything beyond 16:8 or proceed in a "choose-your-own-adventure" fashion, selecting their preferred ending.

From the earliest centuries of Christianity, readers of Mark have asked questions about how the Gospel should end.[4] However, due to the proliferation of the Majority Text[5] and widespread use of Latin and other translated versions, the church came to an effective—if not intentional—decision that 16:20 constituted the proper conclusion to

---

[1] This summary closing is more properly called the "Intermediate Ending" because it connects 16:8 to 16:9-20 whenever it is attested (including four uncial Greek manuscripts of the seventh, eighth, and ninth centuries, L Ψ 099 0112). There is one exception: the Intermediate Ending is found on its own in the Old Latin Codex Bobbiensis (*k*) of the fourth/fifth century. Bruce M. Metzger translates the brief summary (which appears with "trifling variations"): "But they reported briefly to Peter and those with him all that they had been told. And after these things Jesus himself sent out through them, from east to west, the sacred and imperishable proclamation of eternal salvation" (*A Textual Commentary on the Greek New Testament* [2d ed.; Stuttgart: Deutsche Bibelgesellschaft, 1994], 103).

[2] Mark 16:9-20 is referred to as the Long or Longer Ending and is abbreviated here and throughout as "LE." The LE is not found in the important, early codices Vaticanus (B) and Sinaiticus (א), but in 99 percent of the surviving Greek manuscripts and the rest of the tradition (Kurt and Barbara Aland, *The Text of the New Testament* [2d ed.; Erroll F. Rhodes, trans.; Grand Rapids, MI: Eerdmans, 1989], 292). See also Adela Yarbro Collins, *Mark* (Hermeneia; Minneapolis: Fortress, 2007), 802-7; David Parker, *The Living Text of the Gospels* (New York: Cambridge University Press, 1997), 124-47.

[3] The additional text inserted between vv. 14 and 15 is attested only in Greek in this fourth-/fifth-century manuscript variously known as Freerianus or Washingtonianus (W). The addition was known in part before its discovery in the twentieth century, due to a Latin translation in Jerome. The text softens the transition between Jesus's censure of the disciples in 16:14 and his commissioning of them in 16:15.

[4] Eusebius, *Ad Marinum* (probably dating to the first quarter of the fourth century).

[5] The term "Majority Text" refers to the widespread Byzantine text-type, mostly produced in the Middle Ages; the Majority Text comprises a great percentage of the extant Greek mss. Due to its prevalence and availability, the Majority Text formed the basis for Erasmus's edition of the Greek New Testament, the *Textus Receptus*. As Bruce Metzger and Bart Ehrman mention, the *Textus Receptus* was "only one form of several competing forms of the Byzantine text" (*The Text of the New Testament: Its Transmission, Corruption, and Restoration* [4th ed.; New York: Oxford University Press, 2005], 219).

the Second Gospel. The discovery of ancient codices with a briefer, more abrupt finale at 16:8 led eighteenth- and nineteenth-century scholars to suggest that the widely accepted and more conventionally satisfying termination of Mark in v. 20—with Jesus's ascension and the successful transmission of the gospel—might have been the work of a later interpolator. Thus began the unresolved controversy over the ending of Mark's Gospel.

Mark is widely considered the first written Gospel, a major source for at least two other canonical Gospels, Matthew and Luke, and perhaps the inventor of a new genre, "gospel."[6] It is of consequence, then, that there is significant uncertainty concerning how this landmark text originally ended.

For much of Christian history, the standard Greek and Latin copies of the NT used in churches contained the text of Mark from 1:1 through the account of Christ's ascension and the confirmation of the disciples' message with signs in 16:19-20. Access to and the eventual publication of the great fourth-century majuscule Codex Vaticanus (B) after 1845 catalyzed widespread doubts about Mark's ending at 16:20. In Vaticanus, unlike the wording in the so-called Majority Text, Mark 16 ends with the women's silence: ἐφοβοῦντο γάρ in v. 8.[7] But the recovery of Vaticanus did not *introduce* questions about the Markan ending.[8] Skepticism about the ending had emerged in learned circles in the last decades of the eighteenth century.[9] Once the contents of the great majuscule Vaticanus became known, the inquiry took on renewed fervor.

---

[6] The question of the literary genre of Mark and the other Gospels (canonical and noncanonical) has been hotly debated. See Charles H. Talbert, *What Is a Gospel? The Genre of the Canonical Gospels* (Philadelphia: Fortress, 1977). I presume that εὐαγγέλιον is similar to the Greco-Roman βίος ("life" or biography), but adapted by early believers particularly to the person of Jesus. Thus it contains an admixture of other genres, hagiography, and homiletic features. Richard Burridge, in *What Are the Gospels? A Comparison with Graeco-Roman Biography* (2d ed.; Grand Rapids: Eerdmans, 2004), 250, offers what has become a consensus:

> The four canonical gospels and Graeco-Roman βίος exhibit a clear family resemblance. The genre of βίος is flexible and diverse, with variation in the pattern of features from one βίος to another. The gospels also diverge from the pattern in some aspects, but not to any greater degree than other βίοι; in other words, they have at least as much in common with Graeco-Roman βίοι as the βίοι have with each other.

[7] For more information, see the Appendix on the Markan endings. Another unique element of Vaticanus is that at the end of its text of Mark, there is an empty column. This unusual element attests, perhaps, not only to the favored ending, but also to the uncertainty regarding the possible endings.

[8] Erasmus may have been aware of discrepancies between manuscripts in the Markan ending. He was supplied with several readings from Vaticanus, but received them "too late for use in his editions of the New Testament" (F. G. Kenyon, *Handbook to the Textual Criticism of the New Testament* [2d ed.; Grand Rapids: Eerdmans, 1912], 78).

[9] The publication dates of two pieces by J. J. Griesbach challenge James A. Kelhoffer's timeline for modern uncertainty of the LE (*Miracle and Mission: The Authentication of Missionaries and Their Message in the Longer Ending of Mark* [Tübingen: Mohr Siebeck, 2000], 6–9, 122). Griesbach raises questions regarding the Markan ending in published works that predate Andreas Birch's publication of Vaticanus by more than a decade (see n. 10). In his 1789–90 "Demonstration" (*Commentatio*), Griesbach's primary argument is the Synoptic theory for which he is famous: Mark was written after Matthew and Luke and used both as sources. In a footnote that accompanies his tables comparing the Synoptic texts, he explains Mk 16:9-20 in two ways: (1) Based on 16:9, he proposes that the Markan ending (i.e., at 16:20) is "doubtful" (*dubia*). (2) *If* one considers the LE genuine, it mainly epitomizes Matthew and Luke, adding a few lines not found in either Gospel (J. J. Griesbach, "Commentatio

The first modern text critic to posit formally that the last twelve verses of Mark may not have been original to the Gospel *on the basis of manuscript evidence* was the Danish scholar Andreas Birch.[10] Doubts regarding Mk 16:9-20, however, were more widely disseminated through the second critical edition of the Greek text edited by J. J. Griesbach a few years later.[11] The scholarly furor that followed has been well documented in the thorough, though not exhaustive, review of scholarly work on the LE undertaken by James Kelhoffer.[12] His tracing of developments and shifts in research trends on Mk 16:9-20, surveying works in English, French, and German, is unnecessary to replicate here.[13] Instead, I present some paradigmatic approaches and

---

qua Marci Evangelium totum e Matthaei et Lucae commentariis decerptum esse monstratur," in *J. J. Griesbach: Synoptic and Text-Critical Studies 1776–1976* [ed. Bernard Orchard and Thomas R. W. Longstaff; New York: Cambridge University Press, 1978], 79, 205n39). Griesbach's 1793 Pentecost sermon several times refers imprecisely to skepticism regarding "some of the verses" in the ending ("*Pentecostes festos dies pie celebrandos civibus indicit academia Ienensis*," in J. J. Griesbach, *Opuscula Academica* [ed. Johann Philip Gabler; Jena: Fr. Frommanni, 1824], 2:471–2, 484). His comments could not have been based on Vaticanus (B), which had not yet been rediscovered and disseminated. His questions regarding the LE seem to be based instead on internal considerations and knowledge of patristic dubiety (see later on Eusebius's *Ad Marinum*). In an extended discussion of the biblical warrant for the Christian confession of Jesus's ascension, Griesbach cites Mk 16:19, noting the following caveat: "Atque cum viri docti nonnulli authentiam ultimorum Evangelii Marci commatum nondum extra omnem dubitationem positam esse iudicent" ("several learned men" doubt "the authenticity of some verses at the end of the Gospel of Mark" [author's translation or AT]; ibid., 471). Griesbach's passing comments suggest that the LE was already more widely questioned before the discovery—or "reclamation"—of Vaticanus.

[10] Andreas Birch, *Variae Lectiones ad Textum IV Evangeliorum* (Copenhagen: C. G. Prost, 1801). "Vaticanus" (B) was at that time one of many manuscripts labeled "Codex Vaticanus," distinguished only by a number following; the OT and NT Greek codex was then differentiated from the others as "1209." At the time of Birch's publication, the text had been seen by few. It became widely available more than fifty years later, thanks to Cardinal Angelo Mai (1st ed. 1857; 2d ed. 1859). A facsimile was published after nearly a century (1890). In order to relate details about the otherwise unknown manuscript, Birch provides several pages of general description: e.g., the materials, use of nomina sacra, book order, and manner of titular headings (xv–xix). Birch praises the antiquity and superiority of the text (xxii). He calls the codex "the most excellent and ancient" of the codices held in the Vatican (225). He suggests that this text can be used to correct the Greek texts in use (and the Latin Vulgate). Birch notes that Codex B's Gospel of Mark ends at ἐφοβοῦντο γάρ, with the subscript κατα Μαρκον (xxiv). He points to ancient support for this reading (numerous scholia, Gregory of Nyssa, Victor of Antioch), most significantly by Jerome (in *ad Hedybiam*; ibid.). Accidents of publication, however, kept Birch's discovery and judgments from circulating broadly (see Kelhoffer, *Miracle and Mission*, 7).

[11] Although Griesbach had already questioned Mark's ending (see n. 9), the publication of his critical Greek NT provided the textual evidence for the ending at 16:8 and brought speculation on the authenticity of the LE into a broader forum (cf. Griesbach, *Novum Testamentum Graece: Cum Selecta Lectionum Varietate* [vol. 1; Leipzig: G. J. Göschen, 1803]).

[12] James Kelhoffer's monograph, *Miracle and Mission* (2000), a revised, published version of his University of Chicago dissertation, is the most extensive recent treatment of the LE. His subtitle, "The Authentication of Missionaries and Their Message in the Longer Ending of Mark," identifies 16:15-20 as his particular focus. In his fifth chapter, Kelhoffer turns to the expectation of signs to authenticate belief; "taking up" serpents (16:18a) occupies the sixth chapter; drinking poison (16:18b), the seventh. He summarizes his findings in his Epilogue (473–80). The first four chapters (half of the study) are concerned with general matters pertaining to the entire LE.

[13] Kelhoffer's history of scholarship, the most comprehensive to date, spans two centuries of hypotheses pertaining to the interpretation of the LE. His is not the first *Forschungsbericht* on the famous textual variant, but it is arguably the most successful. Kelhoffer notes that at least "six such reviews of scholarship" were undertaken between 1973 and 2000 (ibid., 5). His review did "not seek to repeat unnecessarily what these and other scholars have noted in their respective reviews of the scholarly literature, but rather to build upon past insights, to explore certain hypotheses not

otherwise consider only treatments of the LE that have appeared since the publication of Kelhoffer's study.[14]

Kelhoffer's study examined a neglected issue in the LE—the function of the snake-handling and poison-drinking signs of Mk 16:18 as authentication of the second-century Christian mission—and alerted us to others.[15] A nearly exclusive focus on establishing the *origins* of Mk 16:9-20, whether original to Mark or a later

---

discussed elsewhere and to offer a more complete picture of scholarly views, in particular over the past two centuries" (ibid.). It is difficult to overstate the importance of Kelhoffer's achievement: his survey proceeds chronologically by dividing scholarly contributions to the subject into periods: A. Birch to J. W. Burgon (1801–71); F. C. Conybeare to C. R. Williams (1891–1915); G. Hartmann to E. Helzle (1936–59); and E. Linnemann to S. L. Cox (1969–93). Kelhoffer explains his approach and the periodization of researchers (ibid., 5).

[14] What follows is a chronological list of many of the books and articles that treat or demonstrate a significant interest in the Markan ending at 16:8 and, especially, the LE published since 2000. Specifically concerning the LE: John Christopher Thomas and Kimberly Ervin Alexander, "'And the Signs Are Following': Mark 16:9-20—A Journey into Pentecostal Hermeneutics," *Journal of Pentecostal Theology* 11 (2003): 147–70; Matthew D. McDill, "A Textual and Structural Analysis of Mark 16:9-20," *Filologia Neotestamentica* 27 (2004): 27–43; Delbert Burkett, *Rethinking the Gospel Sources: From Proto-Mark to Mark* (New York: T&T Clark, 2004); David P. Kuske, "Textual Criticism Brief: Mark 16:9-20," *Wisconsin Lutheran Quarterly* 102 (2005): 58–9; Carl B. Bridges, "The Canonical Status of the Longer Ending of Mark," *Stone-Campbell Journal* 9 (2006): 231–42; Bridget Gilfillan Upton, *Hearing Mark's Endings: Listening to Ancient Popular Texts through Speech Act Theory* (Boston: Brill, 2006); David Alan Black, ed., *Perspectives on the Ending of Mark* (Nashville: Broadman and Holman, 2008), which includes chapters by Darrell Bock, Keith Elliott, Maurice Robinson, and Daniel Wallace; Christine E. Joynes, "Wombs and Tombs: The Reception History of Mark 16:1-20," in *From the Margins 2: Women of the New Testament and Their Afterlives* (ed. Christine E. Joynes and Christopher C. Rowland; Sheffield: Sheffield Phoenix, 2009), 226–43; Thomas R. Shepherd, "Narrative Analysis as a Text Critical Tool: Mark 16 in Codex W as a Test Case," *JSNT* (2009): 77–98; Philip Oakeshott, "The Wrong Conclusion: Mark 16:1-8 and Literary Theory," *Theology* 113 (2010): 105–13; Travis B. Williams, "Bringing Method to the Madness: Examining the Style of the Longer Ending of Mark," *BBR* 20 (2010): 397–418. Generally concerned with the ending of Mark (esp. the ending at 16:8): Craig A. Evans, *Mark 8:27–16:20* (WBC, vol. 34b; Nashville: Thomas Nelson Publishers, 2001); N. Clayton Croy, *The Mutilation of Mark's Gospel* (Nashville: Abingdon, 2003); Burkett, *Rethinking Gospel Sources*, esp. 252–66; Beverly Roberts Gaventa and Patrick D. Miller, eds., *The Ending of Mark and the Ends of God: Essays in Memory of Donald Harrisville Juel* (Louisville: Westminster John Knox, 2005); Nicholas Denyer, "Mark 16:8 and Plato, *Protagoras* 328D," *Tyndale Bulletin* 57 (2006): 149–50; Kelly R. Iverson, "A Further Word on Final Γάρ (Mark 16:8)," *CBQ* 68 (2006): 79–94; Lars Hartman, "Mark 16:1-8: The Ending of a Biography-Like Narrative and of a Gospel," *Theology & Life* 30 (2007): 31–47; Matthijs J. de Jong, "Mark 16:8 as a Satisfying Ending to the Gospel," in *Jesus, Paul, and Early Christianity: Studies in Honour of Henk Jan de Jonge* (ed. Rieuwerd Buitenwerf et al.; NovTSup 130; Boston: Brill, 2008), 123–49; Stanley E. Porter, "Verbal Aspect and Discourse Function in Mark 16:1-8: Three Significant Instances," in *Studies in the Greek Bible: Essays in Honor of Francis T. Gignac, S.J.* (ed. Jeremy Corley and Vincent Skemp; Washington, DC: Catholic Biblical Association of America, 2008), 123–37; Robert H. Stein, "The Ending of Mark," *BBR* 18 (2008): 79–98; Larry W. Hurtado, "The Women, the Tomb, and the Climax of Mark," in *A Wandering Galilean: Essays in Honour of Seán Freyne* (ed. Zuleika Rodgers; JSJSup 132; Boston: Brill, 2009), 427–50; Daniel A. Smith, *Revisiting the Empty Tomb: The Early History of Easter* (Minneapolis: Fortress, 2010); Antoinette Clark Wire, *The Case for Mark Composed in Performance* (Biblical Performance Criticism 3; Eugene, OR: Cascade, 2011), esp. 163–74; Nicholas P. Lunn, *The Original Ending of Mark: A New Case for the Authenticity of Mark 16:9-20* (Eugene, OR: Pickwick, 2014). Several major commentaries on Mark that address the last twelve verses have been published since Kelhoffer's monograph; these I cite within my survey and exegesis as appropriate.

[15] After navigating the history of LE scholarship, Kelhoffer concludes: "There also remain numerous aspects of this passage that have never been explored. These twelve verses thus give rise to a plethora of questions meriting exploration" (*Miracle and Mission*, 46).

addition, has diverted scholarly attention from many aspects of the narrative content of these verses.[16] With few exceptions over the past two hundred years, scholars have employed the same evidence—manuscript attestation, patristic attestation, and internal lexical and theological coherence (or incoherence) in relation to Mk 1:1–16:8—to argue for or against Mk 16:9-20 as the original ending of the Second Gospel. It seems clear that, without further manuscript discoveries, there is no definitive proof to which both sides can assent. Recent trends in scholarship, however, have opened avenues for inquiry despite the "standstill."[17] There is more to be said about the LE than the unending battle over the polarizing options of "authentic" versus "spurious."

The way the debate over Mark's ending developed historically seems to have excused defenders of the LE from considering how it brings conclusion to the Second Gospel. While some scholars were interested in overturning the incursion of the new discipline of textual criticism, which dared to call into question the long-accepted NT passage, others used text-critical findings to defend the LE's authenticity (as the vast majority of manuscripts conclude Mark at 16:20). In either perspective, for defenders of the LE, seeing 16:20 as the conclusion to Mark was historical fact, not a new proposal in need of defense or explanation. Those who advocated the shortest ending—"they said nothing to anyone, for they were afraid [ἐφοβοῦντο γάρ]" (16:8b)—however, expended considerable effort explaining how the women's fear and silence at the tomb function in light of the whole Gospel. They took up the challenge to show that the earliest and best ending could make sense *as an ending* of Mark. Arguments on this side of the debate seldom remain confined to Mk 16:1-8 or rehash only that ending's manuscript attestation.

The supposition that 16:8 forms an intentional conclusion to the Second Gospel is rarely taken as established fact, without exegetical defense; however, explanations of how the abrupt, shortest ending fits with the Markan author's aims vary widely. Some scholars have argued that a reading of the whole Gospel of Mark indicates that the original conclusion was *lost*.[18] Others have suggested that, although v. 8 appears to be the earliest recoverable ending, it was not the ending with which Mark intended to conclude.[19] Even those interpreters of Mark who doubt that the ending of Mark at 16:8 was the conclusion he intended for his Gospel make their arguments based on thematic trajectories within the whole Gospel. Those who think 16:8 was originally and intentionally Mark's conclusion go to even greater lengths to connect the ending with the narrative and theology of the Second Gospel as a whole.[20]

---

[16] Beyond the quest for origins, the primary exegetical interest has been in showing the dependence of the resurrection narratives on other canonical Gospels. A secondary interest has been to determine the nature of the LE's description of the signs that follow belief (snake-handling and poison-drinking, particularly).

[17] E.g., increasing interest in reception history, currents in text criticism, and the application of insights from oral performance as the communal composition of Gospels have already provided new avenues for discussing Mark and its LE. See section 4 in this chapter.

[18] See Appendix A in Croy, *Mutilation*, 174–7.

[19] On Mark's being prevented from completing his intended Gospel, see Lachmann in section 3 in this chapter.

[20] I will sample several different versions of this opinion in section 3.

When the LE is connected to the rest of Mark, it is usually to enforce the view that Mark expects a resurrection appearance (14:28; 16:7), missing in 16:8, but present in 16:9-20. Whether the LE presents the *kind* of appearance narrative the Gospel prepares readers to expect seldom enters the discussion.[21] That is so, I think, because there exists the perception that the LE merely contains a generic conglomeration of resurrection appearances. By contrast, I shall attempt to demonstrate that the way the LE describes Jesus's appearances to Mary Magdalene, the two on the road, and the Eleven constitutes a deliberate collection of specific interactions. Although they are recounted in sparse prose, these episodes highlight a contrast between faithful and faithless response to the resurrection. The resurrection accounts privilege markers of belief (e.g., *telling* by Mary Magdalene and the two in vv. 10-11, 13; baptism as concomitant with faith in v. 16; signs that indicate belief in vv. 17-18), rather than simply authenticating that Jesus was raised. Peter's witness—which one might expect to be prominent, based on 16:7—is only implied.

My selective exegesis of 16:9-20 and comparison to other Gospel traditions is, in some ways, an attempt to highlight what should be obvious: Mary is the first witness to the resurrection and the Eleven disbelieve. Yet, as the survey of representative treatments of the LE illustrates, the characterization of Mary Magdalene and the male disciples within the spectrum of faith has not been an object of attention in studies of Mk 16:9-20. Few interpreters have explored the way that the LE functions as an early "reading" of Mark, supplying narrative closure to trajectories that were of interest to ancient readers (which both align with and differ from modern readers' concerns).

This chapter's survey of scholarship seeks to illustrate this deficit, while showing how arguments for an ending—even a secondary one—can be enriched by investigating it in light of its relationship to the literary whole. Finally, this survey of scholarship will conclude by summarizing a few recent studies of Mark and its endings that do discuss the implications of the LE, or of each ending, on the reading of the whole Gospel, and vice versa.

1. In Defense of Mark's Ending at 16:20: Burgon as Paradigm

Dean John William Burgon is undoubtedly history's staunchest defender of the authenticity of 16:20 as Mark's rightful ending. His impassioned apology for both the canonicity (against the "inference" of spuriousness) and historical authenticity (contrary to the "premises" of evidence against its originality) appears in the epistolary foreword to his book in 1871:

---

[21] E.g., both 14:28 and 16:7 point to Galilee as the location for Jesus's post-resurrection encounter with his disciples. But Mk 16:9-20 gives no indication of any specific locale. Likewise, 16:7 singles out Peter among the disciples, but the LE does not mention any male disciple by name (cf. the Intermediate Ending; see the Appendix on the Markan endings, section 3). Only Mary Magdalene is named (16:9).

Recent Editors of the New Testament insist that these "last Twelve Verses" are not genuine. The Critics, almost to a man, avow themselves of the same opinion. Popular Prejudice has been for a long time past warmly enlisted on the same side. I am convinced as I am of my life, that the reverse is the truth. It is not even with me as it is with certain learned friends of mine, who, admitting the adversary's premises, content themselves with denying the validity of his inference. However true it may be,—and it *is* true—, that from those premises the proposed conclusion does not follow, I yet venture to deny the correctness of those premises altogether. I insist, on the contrary, that the Evidence relied on is untrustworthy,—untrustworthy in every particular ... If I may be allowed to say so,—S. *Mark's last Twelve Verses shall no longer remain a subject of dispute among men.* I am able to prove that this portion of the Gospel has been declared to be spurious on wholly mistaken grounds: and this ought in fairness to close the discussion. But I claim to have done more. I claim to have shown, from considerations which have been hitherto overlooked, that the genuineness must needs be reckoned among the things that are absolutely certain.[22]

It is certain that Burgon was wrong about at least one thing: Mark's last twelve verses, without question, remain a subject of serious dispute to this day. Twenty-first-century readers of Burgon's claims may be startled by his remarkable degree of certitude in interpreting the evidence.

Burgon's antiquated prose is alternately more bellicose and florid than the evidence warrants.[23] Yet, amid his repeated appeals to absolute truths, Burgon was not unsophisticated in his logic. Unlike his self-proclaimed descendants ("The Dean Burgon Society"),[24] he was clearly *uncertain* about Markan authorship: "We know absolutely nothing whatever about 'the circumstances of S. Mark,' (or of any other Evangelist,) 'when he wrote his Gospel:' neither indeed are we quite sure *who* S. Mark *was*."[25] Burgon, as the previous excerpt indicates, did not equate the book's inspiration to the identity of its author.[26] But he collapsed the questions of originality

---

[22] John W. Burgon, *The Last Twelve Verses of Mark: Vindicated against Recent Critical Objectors & Established* (Oxford: James Parker and Co., 1871), v–vi; italics original.

[23] Hostility: "[So] proceeds the learned veteran,—(unconscious apparently that he has been demanding acceptance for at least half-a-dozen wholly unsupported as well as entirely gratuitous conjectures)" (ibid., 6). Sarcasm: "The alacrity displayed by learned writers in accumulating hostile evidence, is certainly worthy of a better cause. Strange, that their united industry should have been attended with such very unequal success when their object was to exhibit the evidence *in favour of* the present portion of Scripture" (39; italics and punctuation original). Magniloquence: "The precious *warning clause* [16:16b], I say, (miscalled 'damnatory,') which an impertinent officiousness is for glossing with a rubric and weakening with an apology, proceeded from Divine lips,—at least if these concluding verses be genuine" (3; emphasis in the original).

[24] The Dean Burgon Society, named after the erstwhile dean of Oxford's Oriel College, still exists. Burgon was made a hero by his followers because of his defense of what he believed to be the original ending to the Gospel of Mark. The Society's motto is "In Defense of Traditional Bible Texts."

[25] Ibid., 11; italics original. In the context of Burgon's argument, he is accepting some of Tregelles's premises but rejecting his conclusion that this ignorance of Mark's situation also leaves us ignorant of whether or not the Gospel originally had an ending.

[26] I.e., the author of Mark may not have been named "Mark" nor had any relationship to the John Mark of Acts 12:12, 25; 13:13; 15:37-40.

and genuineness: "Have the codices been *mutilated* which do *not* contain these verses? If they have, then must these verses be held to be *genuine*. But on the contrary, Have the codices been *supplemented* which contain them? Then are these verses certainly *spurious*."[27]

Burgon inaugurated the most rigid statement of two possibilities with regard to Mark's LE. These have set the terms of the debate as it has continued ever since, with few exceptions. The adjectives used for *genuine* have varied—authentic, original, Markan—as well as those for *spurious*—inauthentic, later, pseudonymous, forged— but the debate has played out between two sides with otherwise surprising continuity.

Not only have the alternatives remained unchanged, but the sources marshaled to engage the debate have been modified very little. Burgon intends to silence the questions raised regarding Mark's LE. The unintended consequence, however, is that he becomes the author of the subsequent debate. Categorically, the materials remain similar—whether for aspersions on the authenticity of Mk 16:9-20 or for defense of these verses—in Burgon's time and the present: (1) manuscript evidence, (2) early Fathers' testimony, and (3) internal evidence. Few (if any) of those "critics" Burgon attempted to disprove had addressed the question as systematically as he. Of course, new manuscript evidence has been discovered since Burgon's era, most significantly the Freer Codex.[28] Ongoing critical scholarship has also mitigated some of the most elaborate historical reconstructions proposed by those who consider the LE secondary.[29]

Burgon's impetus for writing was not purely scholarly; his primary concern was to guard against the negative impact of dismissing Mk 16:9-20 on "the next generation of English Churchmen."[30] Attention to the ecclesial implications of scholarly opinions is shared by his contemporary scholarly opponents and supporters alike: Should the later supplement to Mark's Gospel (16:9-20) still be read in church? Generations afterward, separated from that decision—*in or out*—by many footnoted comments and inserted brackets in today's versions of Mark, scholars are faced with the question of how to interpret a text that is seldom read in churches. The text remains affixed to 16:8, but with an asterisk, like a baseball player's homerun record after a doping scandal. Thus, present inquiries can remain somewhat "removed" from practical, church concerns.[31]

---

[27] Ibid., 11; italics original.

[28] See the Appendix on the Markan endings, section 5, for information on the Freer Logion.

[29] Consider the elaborate and conjectural proposal from F. F. Bruce: Mark intended to conclude his *first* volume at 16:8, and, although he never completed writing his second one, "it cannot be doubted that Luke availed himself of Mark's knowledge" in writing Acts ("The End of the Second Gospel," *The Evangelical Quarterly* 17 [1945]: 175). Bruce sees evidence of an Aramaic oral source underlying the early chapters of Luke's second volume. Thus, even without an ending to the Second Gospel beyond 16:8, Bruce can provide "evidence" that Mark knew of resurrection appearances.

[30] Burgon, *Last Twelve*, 9. Burgon is discussing the trickle-down effect of a view that started with Griesbach and was gaining contemporary appeal, so that two common textbooks by Tregelles and Alford would "undoubtedly colour" future church leaders' opinions (9).

[31] Of course, there are denominational and localized exceptions to this functional "removal" of Mk 16:9-20 from public reading: notably, the Church of God (Cleveland, TN). It relies on Mk 16:17-20 as the primary textual grounds for its doctrinal commitment to "signs following believers." For most of my college students and fellow church people, editorial brackets in English versions, biblical illiteracy, and functional Gospel harmonization have cooperated in such a way that few can recall having read the endings of Mark—whether the ending be set at 16:8 or at 16:20.

describing the question of Mark's ending as "still open." Farmer addresses the evidence for and against the LE in two major sections: external evidence—which contains subsections treating patristic attestation and manuscript evidence—and internal evidence,[42] followed by his conclusions. Farmer never claims to have settled the question,[43] but he seems to answer Burgon's challenge: to explain how there resulted ancient fourth-century manuscripts *without* Mk 16:9-20.

Farmer does not begin with the manuscript attestation. The oldest two manuscripts with 16:8 as the ending of Mark (B and ℵ) date to only the fourth century, relatively late in comparison with the Second Gospel's presumed composition. He begins with the early Fathers' witnesses for and against (or silence regarding) the last twelve verses of Mark. Farmer opens with Eusebius's *Quaestiones ad Marinum*,[44] an unusual starting point, both logically and chronologically, but it enables him to address Burgon's scenario[45] in a new way.

The *Quaestiones ad Marinum* is the second of the two known parts of *Quaestiones et Responsiones* by Eusebius of Caesarea (ca. 260–340).[46] The work consists of questions and answers on various Gospel details, particularly beginnings (genealogical data) and endings (comparing crucifixion and resurrection accounts).[47] The questions

---

[42] Note that these are the same categories as Burgon employs. Farmer makes reference to Burgon's argument several times throughout, and proceeds with *Quaestiones ad Marinum* ("the Mai Fragment"), in fact, utilizing Burgon's translation of the Eusebian text (Farmer, *Last Twelve Verses*, xii–xvi, 3–5).

[43] E.g., Farmer states,

> This is not an argument for the authenticity of Mk. 16:9-20. Rather it points out that if these verses were known as a part of the received textual tradition in Alexandria at some time in the second century, and if some time later, but still before the end of the second century, under the influence of Alexandrian textual criticism ... they were "expurgated" from some or all copies of Mark made at some important Alexandrian scriptorium, then the fate of this Alexandrian effort to introduce a "cut" is similar to the fate of the Alexandrian efforts in Homeric criticism. (Farmer, *Last Twelve Verses*, 72; italics added)

[44] Ibid., 3. Farmer mistakenly calls the text a "fragment." For two recent treatments of the *ad Marinum*, see Kelhoffer, "The Witness of Eusebius' *ad Marinum*," 99–107; and Claudio Zamagni, *Eusèbe de Césarée, Questions Évangéliques: Introduction, texte critique, traduction et notes* (SC 523; Paris: Cerf, 2008).

[45] Burgon's question asks, in sum, what causes would account for the LE having been removed from NT mss in the early fourth century (Burgon, *Last Twelve Verses of Mark*, 243).

[46] Kelhoffer's study of the *ad Marinum* raises the question of authorship but does not answer it, citing "rather little evidence" for scholars "unquestioningly" accepting its attribution to Eusebius ("Witness of Eusebius," 81). Zamagni's full-length study of the text has been published since Kelhoffer wrote (*Questions Évangéliques*). Zamagni rebuffs the suggestion that the text might be pseudonymous (*Questions Évangéliques*, 11n1). He points to Eusebius's *Demonstratio evangelica* VII.3, which references the *Quaestiones* (cf. PG 22, col. 556; W. J. Ferrar, ed. and trans., Eusebius's *The Proof of the Gospel* [Eugene, OR: Wipf and Stock, 2001; repr. 2 vols. SPCK, 1920], 2:88). In light of the internal reference to the first part of the *Quaestiones* in another, accepted work of Eusebius, attributing the question-and-answer text to him seems far less speculative than Kelhoffer suggests.

[47] At present we have access to much more of the *ad Marinum* text than Burgon, Farmer, or Kelhoffer treated. Scholars note that the full work has been "lost," but we are unsure what percentage of the text survives. So it seems better to speak of the text as we know it presently. I cite J.-P. Migne's edition: (1) Vat. Palat. 220, containing (a) sixteen question-and-answer pairs addressed to Stephanus (PG 22:879–936), and (b) four question-and-answer pairs addressed to Marinus (PG 22:937–958); (2) "Supplements" to the *ad Stephanum* (PG 22:957–982); (3) a lengthy "Supplement" to the *ad Marinum* (PG 22:983–1006); and (4) "Minor Supplements" to the *ad Marinum* (PG 22:1007–1016).

purportedly asked by Stephanus and Marinus are brief and addressed to Eusebius. His lengthy answers follow. Farmer addresses only one question-and-answer pair, relying heavily on Burgon's treatment of the excerpt.[48]

Eusebius responds to Marinus's question about the timing of the women's coming to the tomb, on which Mt 28:1 and Mk 16:9 seem to contradict each other. Eusebius's answer confused subsequent interpreters: "For this one there might be a double solution" (Τούτου διττὴ ἂν εἴη ἡ λύσις; I.1). Continuing in the subjunctive mood, Eusebius suggests what one who rejects the passage (16:9-20) *might* say: One may simply discard Mk 16:9, because it is "not conveyed in all copies" (μὴ ἐν ἅπασιν αὐτὴν φέρεσθαι τοῖς ἀντιγράφοις) of the Gospel. But discarding the less well-attested text does not solve the problem entirely. This is only Eusebius's first possible solution.

Solution two, as Eusebius sees it, is one of careful preservation. He credits this approach to "someone" (τις) who "dares not reject anything whatsoever that is conveyed in any way [οὐδ ὁτιοῦν τολμῶν ἀθετεῖν τῶν ὁπωσοῦν] in the text of the Gospels." An interpreter with this mindset, who accepts anything that wound up in the Gospels by any means (the inference of the term ὁπωσοῦν) as deserving preservation, declared: διπλῆν εἶναι ... τὴν ἀνάγνωσιν (the reading is double). That is, wherever an apparent conflict arises between two texts, both testimonies are to be upheld as true. One is not to be privileged at the expense of the other.

Much more could be said about the implications of Eusebius's twofold solution, but I have provided only enough to illuminate Farmer's arguments. He refers to Eusebius's answers as an "ambidexterous or ambiguous solution."[49] Farmer seeks to prove that the varied manuscript evidence shows that 16:9-20 was *omitted* in the second century, not added. His proposed rationale for the excision is quite speculative.

Farmer begins with Eusebius's claim that verses beyond 16:8 are "met with seldom" in the most "accurate" copies, delving into what constituted accuracy in the ancient world. In Alexandrian treatments of Homeric texts,[50] *accuracy* entailed not the oldest

---

[48] My quotations from the Greek text rely on the most recent critical edition: Zamagni, *Questions Évangéliques* (2008). Portions of the text and partial English translations are available in Burgon, *Last Twelve Verses of Mark*, 44–6, 265–6; Farmer, *Last Twelve Verses*, xiii–xvi, 4; Kelhoffer, "Witness of Eusebius," 83–9. In 2010 Roger Pearse edited the first English translation of the whole work and fragments. Pearse's edition is based not on the Zamagni's critical text but on existing published editions (Eusebius of Caesarea, *Gospel Problems and Solutions: Quaestiones ad Stephanum et Marinum* [trans. David J. D. Miller and Adam C. McCollum; Ipswich, UK: Chieftain, 2011]). The most detailed portion of Kelhoffer's study focuses only on questions I–II.1 (the portion he translates), which explicitly involve the LE of Mark. In this he expands on the percentage of the *ad Marinum* that Burgon and Farmer treated. Furthermore, Kelhoffer discusses the work and the genre more generally, ignoring the additional portion of the *ad Marinum* known from Nicetas's catena (included in Migne's edition). See Zamagni's selective bibliography for further treatments (*Questions Évangéliques*, 65–74).

[48] Cf. Burgon's appendix on the *ad Marinum* (*Last Twelve*, 265–6) and discussion thereof (41–51); Farmer reprints and relies on Burgon's translation of the portion of the *ad Marinum* (*Last Twelve Verses*, 4–5; cf. n1).

[49] Farmer, *Last Twelve Verses*, 30.

[50] Ibid., 13–17. He relies on secondary sources such as B. H. Streeter (*The Four Gospels* [London: Macmillan, 1924]) and J. E. Sandys (*A History of Classical Scholarship* [2d ed.; vol. 1; Cambridge: Cambridge University Press, 1906–8]). Cf. Farmer, *Last Twelve Verses*, 14n1.

textual reading, but the one freest from offense.[51] Farmer presumes that Origen (an Alexandrian) probably applied similar criteria to judging accuracy in biblical texts.[52] Farmer then conjectures that Eusebius's "twofold solution" is "Origenic" in style (as is his preference for harmonizing Gospel diversity).[53] Alexandrian text-critical practice[54] made "improvements" in clarity or honorability, unlike modern text-critical practices, which tend to select the earliest retrievable and most difficult readings.[55]

This leads Farmer to conclude that Mk 16:9-20 was likely "omitted with 'good cause'" by Alexandrian scribes.[56] He argues that *"external evidence from the second century for Mk. 16:9–20 is stronger than for other parts of that Gospel."*[57] Farmer invests considerable time establishing an Alexandrian provenance for texts that omit the LE.[58] He suggests several potential reasons why scribes may have omitted the ending at 16:20 in favor of an "improved" version, for example, details that made harmonization with other Gospel-endings difficult,[59] or increasing misuse of the idea of signs following belief (especially use of poison and snakes) in light of the Montanist movement.[60] Sparing the church from external criticism, Farmer proposes, might have meant the following:

> "Faithful" and "circumspect" teachers like Origen generally speaking would not have argued for the omission of a textual reading that had been received in the church. But insofar as they were trained in the ways of Alexandrian text criticism *and had a concern for what was edifying for the church* they would have tended to respect received exemplars which omitted this kind of doubtful reading, and in

---

[51] Farmer, *Last Twelve Verses*, 17. Citing the principles utilized by Alexandrian editors of classical Greek texts, Farmer notes: "This principle called for the omission of any passage which was regarded as offensive to or unworthy of the gods" (15).

[52] Ibid., 14.

[53] Ibid., 30.

[54] Farmer admits, "We know of no such project for producing a more accurate text for the New Testament writings" comparable to Origen's OT Hexapla project (ibid., 14).

[55] Farmer says,
> To the extent that phrases and passages which might be deemed "improper" or "undignified" were omitted or altered, these "improved" editions were closer to the original only when the said "offensive" phrases and passages actually had been introduced by "impious" men bent on corrupting the morals or beliefs of the readers (to follow the rationalization of the ancient editors). But in every case where the words, expressions, or passages were original, their omission or alteration resulted in the production of an "improved," but *less original* text. It must be borne in mind that in this sense the "improved" texts produced by ancient textual experts were also "censored" texts. (Ibid., 17–18)

[56] Ibid., 18. Later in the same section Farmer cites an example of Origen's preference for a known ms. variant that presents Jesus in a less scandalous light (omitting the description of him as a carpenter) in his argument *Contra Celsum* (cf. ibid., 20).

[57] Ibid., 31; italics original.

[58] Ibid., 22–58, esp. 40–58.

[59] This alone could not have been the reason, Farmer argues, because omitting only v. 9 would have been sufficient to make the text cohere with Matthew (ibid., 63–5). Yet this is one part of the LE's narrative about which we have ancient objections (Eusebius, *Ad Marinum* I).

[60] Farmer, *Last Twelve Verses*, 65–74. Farmer noted also *hermeneutical measures* (i.e., allegorical interpretation) that sought to nullify similar threats of too-literal interpretations of Mk 16:17-18.

some situations could have tolerated and perhaps even approved the production and use of copies of Mark ending with ἐφοβοῦντο γάρ.[61]

While Burgon and Farmer represent the same side of the debate over the LE's authenticity, their arguments for 16:20 as the best ending of the Second Gospel are exact opposites: Burgon considers the omission of Mk 16:9-20 as a modern text-critical decision antithetical to faithful readings of Scripture. Farmer suggests that the LE was excised by ancient critics concerned with upholding faithful readings.

Ultimately, for Farmer, both the external and internal evidence for the LE are inconclusive: The "question of the last twelve verses of Mark [is] 'still open.'"[62] Still, Farmer's arguments oppose the majority opinion.[63] He suspects that the question could be settled only by external evidence yet undiscovered at the time of his study.[64] Farmer spends little time describing the content of 16:9-20,[65] and when he does, it is a diction-study. So, while he examines the language of the LE "with special reference to the question of the relationship of these verses to the rest of Mark,"[66] the focus tightly "zooms in" on vocabulary, rather than comparing "widescreen"-issues such as Mark's themes and theology. Farmer identifies a combination of evidence for Markan authorship and the use of "tradition akin to that preserved in the resurrection stories found in the other Gospels."[67] On this basis, he concludes that the most likely explanation for the origin of the last twelve verses of Mark is that 16:9-20 "represents redactional use of older material by the evangelist and belonged to the autograph."[68]

A more recent scholar to stand contrary to the scholarly majority has moved the question forward, but not with new data. Instead, he proposes several new ways of interpreting the material. Maurice Robinson, a major advocate for Byzantine-priority,[69] writes on the Markan conclusion subsequent to Kelhoffer.[70] His 2008 treatment of the LE[71] argues for the originality of

---

[61] Ibid., 71.
[62] Ibid., 109.
[63] This fight for the scholarly underdog may be an academic disposition of Farmer's, as in his published defense of Matthean priority, i.e., a renewal of the "Griesbach Hypothesis," evidences (William R. Farmer, *The Synoptic Problem: A Critical Analysis* [Dillsboro, NC: Western North Carolina, 1976], 199–202).
[64] Ibid., 109.
[65] Internal considerations comprise only 25 pages of his 109-page study.
[66] The quotation comes from Farmer's section heading, initiating the portion of his study in which he proceeds verse-by-verse and compares individual words and small phrases to usage in Mark and the canonical Gospels (ibid., 83).
[67] Ibid., 108.
[68] Ibid., 107.
[69] I.e., he considered the best text the Majority Text, believing "that the original text is best preserved in the vast majority of the witnesses produced in the Middle Ages" (Metzger and Ehrman, *Text of the New Testament*, 218). Underlying this view is a theological claim that God actively preserves the inspired text and, thus, the text that persisted throughout the Eastern churches for centuries and forms the basis for the King James Version is to be trusted. See Maurice Robinson and William G. Pierpont, *The New Testament in the Original Greek according to the Byzantine/Majority Textform* (Atlanta: Original Word, 1991).
[70] Kelhoffer's *Miracle and Mission* and "Witness of Eusebius' ad Marinum" were published in 2000 and 2001, respectively.
[71] Maurice A. Robinson, "The Long Ending of Mark as Canonical Verity," in *Perspectives on the Ending of Mark: 4 Views* (ed. David Alan Black; Nashville: Broadman and Holman, 2008), 40–79.

16:9-20.[72] He deploys the standard evidence for the ending, mostly unchanged since Burgon,[73] and echoes Samuel Tregelles's insistence that there is nothing doctrinally suspect in the last twelve verses.[74]

Robinson's most novel contribution to the debate is to argue that the ending at 16:8 represents an "intentional shortening," probably by the Evangelist himself.[75] In this way, he moves beyond Farmer's suggestion that there is something inherently questionable in the content of the LE that accounts for its removal.[76] Robinson instead finds an analogous situation in the multiple published renditions of the same work by a modern poet.[77] The modern author's documented modifications suggest to Robinson a different way of looking at the various, ancient endings of Mark.[78] He acknowledges that although "we know the entire transmissional history" of the modern work, "with Mark we have 'only hints followed by guesses.'"[79] This analogy throws a different light on the Markan ending—particularly the idea that 16:9-20 might have been purposely removed—in comparison to other scholars' treatments. In this view the removal is an act of artistic freedom and an author's adapting his or her work to a new situation, rather than accident, loss, or censoring. It is worth noting that the context for understanding the longer versus shortest endings of Mark is *external* to Mark. *How* these changes alter one's interpretation of Mark is another vein of inquiry.

Although Robinson's unconventional approach to the question is refreshing, his analogy sidesteps several major differences between Mark's ancient context and likely authorial purpose and that of a Western, twentieth-century poet: (1) the ease and means of publishing, or republishing, in the twentieth century in contrast to those of the first or second; (2) vast discrepancies in the concept of authorship and intellectual

---

[72] In the same compilation, David Alan Black reasons for the LE as resulting from a later—yet still *Markan*, but not Petrine—phase in the Gospel's development ("Mark 16:9-20 as Markan Supplement," in *Perspectives on the Ending of Mark*, 103-23). Black identifies four chronological/geographical phases of development (Jerusalem, Gentile Mission, Roman, Johannine) and Matthew's as the first Gospel (ibid., 106-8). He assures his audience, "As for the Longer Ending of Mark, we need not doubt that it is part of Holy Scripture, even if it is Mark's supplement to Peter's account of the life of Jesus" (122).
[73] This Robinson readily acknowledged: "In reality, twenty-first-century scholars continue to deal with issues raised during the nineteenth century, albeit in a redirected manner. Yet the presumed complexity regarding the ending of Mark remains an ongoing fascination, driving scholarly imagination for more than 150 years, with little or no end in sight" ("Canonical Verity," 44).
[74] Ibid., 43. Cf. Samuel Prideaux Tregelles, *An Account of the Printed Text of the Greek New Testament* (London: Samuel Bagster and Sons, 1854), 258.
[75] There are fifteen other points to the case that Robinson makes (ibid., 74-8).
[76] While Farmer goes to great pains to make this claim (see *Last Twelve Verses*, 13-22; 59-75), it seems unlikely. No ancient author raises significant objections to the elements—particularly snake-handling and poison-drinking—that strike many modern readers as astonishing. See the discussion of Kelhoffer's work on these two signs in section 4 in this chapter.
[77] He uses the poem "Poetry," written *and* modified by the American poet Marianne Moore, as an example of multiple versions of a text reflecting authorial intention. She published versions of the same poem varying from forty lines in length (1919, 1932), an "intermediate version" of thirteen lines (1925), and one only three lines long (1967). For Robinson's explanation, see ibid., 48-9.
[78] "Not only are the various versions of Moore's 'Poetry' analogous to the Markan ending issue, but commentators upon Moore favor the differing versions of that poem in accord with their interpretative fancy. Some favor the 'longer version;' some favor the 'intermediate version;' and even the 'short version' has its advocates" (ibid., 49).
[79] Ibid.

property; (3) a genre gap (especially the intended use of poetry in a modern context, versus gospel or resurrection report in the early church).

Befitting a defender of the LE's authenticity who must imagine reasons why ancient copyists would have excised the verses,[80] Robinson has suggestions regarding the author's own "rationale for omission."[81] His approach adapts, with modifications, Farmer's suggestion: Robinson examines perceived contradictions in chronology[82] or a shift in context[83] among the plausible rationale for ancient excision of vv. 9–20. Robinson is concerned to highlight the biases at work in scholarly analyses of the LE's supposed non-Markan style and vocabulary.[84] After providing several examples that run contrary to the conventional wisdom about the LE's variation from style of the rest of Mark, he writes: "Appeals to 'Markan style' or 'Markan vocabulary' thus appear problematic, and rest upon data more coincidental and transitory than substantial. Such comparisons do not disprove Markan authorship of the [LE], nor suggest that the [LE] is based upon derivative tradition. The [LE] may best be regarded as a Markan summary of resurrection appearances, provided as a fulfillment *testimonium*."[85] Robinson argues against the LE as a pastiche, citing "new" information that is not derived from other known gospels.[86] Robinson's final sentence restates his position: "With this, the present investigation fittingly concludes, leaving the [LE] of Mark firmly in its traditional location within the Second Gospel, and—most probably—written by St. Mark himself."[87]

Robinson also suggests several thematic ties connecting the LE to the rest of Mark.[88] Although they constitute a small part of his chapter-length study, Robinson notes Elijah/Elisha thematic connections, for which Jesus's ascension in 16:19 forms

---

[80] This strikes me as a strange project: if the modern advocate could have fathomed an objection too damning for the text—one that could have caused its purposeful removal by Christian scribes—it is unlikely that she or he would have taken up the cause.

[81] Ibid., 50.

[82] Like those cited by Eusebius (*ad Marinum*) and echoed by Jerome (*ad Hedybiam*).

[83] Among the historical factors that could have sparked the need for modification, Robinson cites: "sign gift concerns" sparking neo-Montanist red flags (ibid., 54) and liturgical interests, given the Greek Orthodox lectionary's division of the text for various occasions (cf. esp. 58).

[84] Ibid., 59–64. For Robinson, "Style and vocabulary remain ephemeral, particularly when dealing with a limited portion of text and matters involving the Synoptic Problem" (62; cf. his example regarding the uses of ἀκολουθέω, 62). Especially interesting is the correspondence Robinson finds between the "staccato style" of 16:9-20 and the uncontested Markan temptation narrative (when compared to the more fleshed out Synoptic parallels; 64).

[85] Ibid., 66.

[86] Ibid., 72–3. Many of Robinson's examples—e.g., Mary Magdalene's appearance alone and the disciples' "mourning and weeping"—are among the descriptions that I highlight in Chapters 2 and 3 of this study. In my view, these details are not inconsistent with well-known Gospel traditions, but represent a creative rearrangement of and differing emphasis among them.

[87] Ibid., 78. D. A. Black's paper, contributed to the same volume as Robinson's, agrees with many of Robinson's claims ("Markan Supplement," in *Perspectives*, 103–23). They differ in their methods of argumentation. Black relies heavily on historical reconstruction of Synoptic Gospel composition, which involves Matthean priority (106–21). Both Robinson and Black agree that: (1) Mk 16:9-20 was authored later by the author of the rest of the Gospel (104); (2) arguments based on internal vocabulary differences are "highly subjective" (105); and (3) God actively controlled both the authorship and the manuscript realities—their differences and preservation—with the result that both Markan compositions are equally inspired (104, 106).

[88] On the surface, this constitutes counterevidence to my claim that very few defenders of the LE's originality explain what difference its presence as *the Markan conclusion* makes to the narrative of Gospel. Yet, Robinson's "thematic" ties are either keyword driven (micro- versus macro-connections)

the proper conclusion.[89] Likewise, he provides a chart demonstrating what he finds to be purposeful parallels between the opening and closing chapters of Jesus's ministry (chs 1 and 16),[90] as well as several other pericopes.[91] He cites a more conventional way in which the LE properly concludes the expectations established earlier in the Gospel: "total fulfillment" of resurrection predictions, the absence of which would be "destructive of Markan style and purpose."[92]

Both Robinson and David Alan Black renew skepticism about studies that attempt to compare the LE's vocabulary with that of the rest of the Gospel of Mark.[93] They argue that these "internal" criteria are inherently biased by scholars' presuppositions. The project of comparing the diction of the two parts is a gesture toward explaining how the LE brings the Gospel of Mark to a fitting conclusion. But it cannot account for larger narrative patterns, particularly between texts so dissimilar in length (Mk 1:1–16:8 versus 16:9-20).

Travis B. Williams takes up just such a challenge. His aim is to bring methodological clarity—perhaps even objectivity—to the question Robinson cites as most problematic: How may we measure style and vocabulary as "Markan" or "non-Markan"?[94] His article represents a more recent attempt to address in a systematic fashion this divisive element of the puzzle. Stylistic criteria for determining the LE's originality have always relied on interpreters' "gut instincts." After all, passages that *seem* Markan do not incite the same rigorous analysis (detailing the terminology, propensity toward certain verb tenses, or proclivities for a particular preposition) as do those that *seem* questionable to a given interpreter. Subjectivity in assessing whether or not Mk 16:9-20 demonstrates a "fit" with the rest of the Gospel[95] is precisely what Williams seeks to avoid.

Williams is not the first to tally vocabulary usage and grammatical style, but his project is more scrupulous than most. He judges, "One of the major reasons that interpreters have rejected the longer ending is stylistic variance. But in many cases, stylistic assessments have been based on surface-level examinations of the text without any methodological constraint."[96]

Williams acknowledges variations in any author's style. He cites both defenders and detractors of the LE's authenticity. He distinguishes between *intratextual* and

---

or fit under the heading of prophecy-fulfillment, which has long been the reason cited for the insufficiency of 16:8 (cf. the seemingly unfulfilled promise in 14:28).

[89] To support this typological connection, Robinson cites a then-unpublished essay by Warren A. Gage (now part of an e-book: *Essays in Biblical Theology* [St. Andrew's House, 2010]; Robinson, "Canonical Verity," 67–8).

[90] These vary between substantial ties (exorcism; 1:34 and 16:17), less persuasive connections ("having risen early" in 1:35 and 16:9), and nonparallels ("many people" in 1:33 and "one alone" in 16:9; Robinson, "Canonical Verity," 68–9).

[91] Robinson also compares Mk 3:14-15; 6:7-13; and 7:24–8:38 to 16:9-20 (ibid., 70–2).

[92] Ibid., 76.

[93] Robinson, "Canonical Verity," 59–66; Black, "Markan Supplement," 104.

[94] Williams, "Bringing Method to the Madness," 397–418.

[95] The best example and, in my opinion, most well-rounded analysis of the theological and literary fit (or rather disjuncture) of the LE as it relates to Mk 1:1–16:8 appears in C. Clifton Black's commentary titled *Mark* (ANTC; Nashville: Abingdon, 2011), 356–60.

[96] Williams, "Bringing Method to the Madness," 397.

intertextual stylistic changes.[97] The former recognizes shifts in writing style between different works by the same author,[98] while the latter refers to stylistic disjuncture between different parts in one work. Williams grants that absolute certainty is beyond his study's reach; his goal is only "to determine (with a relative degree of probability) whether or not the longer ending is *written in the same syntactic style* as the rest of Mark's Gospel."[99] Taking into consideration both statistics (vocabulary usage, etc.) and usage criteria,[100] Williams's conclusions support the opinion of the scholarly majority:

> We tested for both similarity and dissimilarity, although the latter was our primary concern. When this method was implemented, the results were clearly against an authentically Markan style. Although we did discover a few moderately strong syntactical connections (for example, the partitive use of δυσὶν ἐξ αὐτῶν [v. 12]; the use of σημεῖον [v. 17]), the vast majority of instances pointed toward stylistic divergence.[101]

In light of Robinson's implication that claims of stylistic variation are the result of interpretive bias, Williams's study stands as a counterexample. He attempts to remove subjectivity—and errs on the side of skepticism toward the prevailing opinion—and achieves results that confirm the majority's impulse.

In a 2014 monograph, Nicholas P. Lunn renews defense of the LE as the intended ending of Mark.[102] Given the persistent appeal to manuscripts, patristic attestation, internal style, and vocabulary among defenders of 16:20 as the original Markan ending, many aspects of Lunn's argument hardly constitute a "new case." Nevertheless, Lunn collects together effectively evidence that casts doubt on the presumed conclusiveness of the consensus against the LE's originality. For example, he draws attention to the relative late date of the earliest manuscript attestation of the ending at 16:8.[103] He also brings forward a broader range of evidence within apostolic, noncanonical, and patristic-era writings that indicate familiarity with the content, if not the text, of the LE.[104] Although his work is to be commended for its extensive engagement with

---

[97] Ibid., 400.

[98] Williams argues the aforementioned defenders are more likely to point out these *intratextual* style shifts: Burgon, for instance, cites distinctions between the style of John's Gospel and Revelation, and Charles Wordsworth points to the stylistic differences in Paul's *Hauptbriefe* and the Pastoral Epistles (both cited in ibid., 400).

[99] Ibid., 401; emphasis in the original.

[100] I.e.,

> A better way to assess whether something is un-Markan in its syntactical style is to ask the question "how does the evangelist consistently communicate the same idea elsewhere?" If there is evidence that Mark communicates a certain idea in his Gospel, and if that idea is normally conveyed in a consistent manner, then any variation in the way that idea is communicated could raise suspicion that we are dealing with a different style. (Ibid., 403).

[101] Ibid., 417.

[102] Lunn, *Original Ending*.

[103] Ibid., 27, 357.

[104] Among noncanonical material, Lunn treats *Gos. Mary*, *Gos. Pet.*, and *Ep. Apost.* (ibid., 71–6). The last of these is treated in detail in this present study, although that work was completed prior to the publication of Lunn's work (see Chapter 3 in this volume). He surveys a wide range of early Christian writings. In his summary of the findings of his chapters examining "external evidence,"

ancient sources, Lunn's conclusions seem to presume that ancient authors had the same conceptions of scripture and canon that modern interpreters do, as though alluding to a passage or finding it useful in the midst of an argument were tantamount to canonization. This is anachronistic.[105] Lunn devotes two chapters to detailed linguistic features of the LE and concludes that it belongs "linguistically within the Markan domain."[106] Two more chapters treat literary techniques and themes that Lunn finds deeply interwoven between Mk 1:1–16:8 and 16:9-20. In another chapter, he rejects any dependence on other Gospels or Acts by the author of 16:9-20.[107]

In light of Williams's and Lunn's work, it seems likely that internal criteria and characteristics will remain the battleground of the originality debate, since the external sources (manuscripts and patristic citations) promise little new information when asked the same old question. Further, several aspects of Lunn's work and my own have significant commonalities, particularly in that we expend substantial energy highlighting thematic connections throughout Mark and its longer ending and take seriously the Gospel-canonical resonances. Those affinities notwithstanding, we offer starkly differing interpretations of our findings.

In summary, interpreters have proposed good, even intriguing, arguments for maintaining 16:9-20 as the original ending of Mark's Gospel. The defenses remain primarily prefatory, however. They seem to expend space and energy trying to reclaim or retain the LE as Mark's ending. This has meant that they fail to move on to the actual exegesis of 16:9-20 or to suggest how that ending shapes, or reshapes, a reading of the Gospel as a whole. Except for vocabulary and prophecy-fulfillment (which could align with any canonical Gospel), there is little attempt to show that or how this ending is Markan at all. These defenders argue the implications of retaining (or losing) the LE as canonical or inspired in general terms, but leave unexplored or taken for granted its function as a conclusion to the Second Gospel.[108]

Lunn concludes that in terms of antiquity, ubiquity, diversity, and quantity, "the external evidence weighs in on the side of the originality of the longer Markan ending" (115).

[105] In light of the tendency to project modern assumptions of authorship, scripture, and literary forms onto ancient texts, Matthew D. C. Larsen's recent work, *Gospels before the Book* (New York: Oxford University Press, 2018), offers a helpful corrective.

[106] Lunn, *Original Ending*, 201. Chapters 4 and 5 of Lunn's work are devoted to showing that the LE is not linguistically distinct from other isolated sections of Mark's Gospel and to defending the theory that such a linguistic similarity is not mere imitation by a latter author, respectively.

[107] Ibid., 317.

[108] At least two scholars have suggested that only *part* of Mk 16:9-20 is original to Mark. Although their proposals represent deviation from the norm, they do not connect the reconfigured ending (the "original" portion) with the rest of Mark's Gospel. Their procedures vary widely, but they have in common arguments that are dislocated from the rest of Mark: one is internal to the LE (P. A. Mirecki); the other, based on comparisons to other Gospel closures (Eta Linnemann). Linnemann proposes, based on a stylistic shift ("auffälliger Stilunterschied") in the LE, that the original ending can be reconstructed from Mt. 28:16-17 and Mk 16:15-20 ("Der [wiedergefundene] Markusschluß," *ZTK* 66 [1969], 258). I will not devote more space to her claims in light of the thorough (although too severe) rebuttal from Kurt Aland ("Der wiedergefundene Markusschluß? Eine methodologische Bemerkung zur textkritischen Arbeit," *ZTK* 67 [1970]: 1–13). Mirecki's proposal makes some important structural observations regarding the transitional terms in the first half of the LE, which I discuss in Chapter 2 (Paul Allan Mirecki, "Mark 16:9–20: Composition, Tradition and Redaction" [ThD diss., Harvard, 1986], 125–6). His study receives a thorough assessment by Kelhoffer (*Miracle and Mission*, 42–5), with which I concur. Apparently unaware of Mirecki's findings, a 2004 article by Matthew D. McDill analyzes the structure of the LE along

There is a narrow slice of scholarship on Mark's LE that is neither consumed with text-critical arguments nor vocabulary studies. The portion of the LE that has garnered most interest regarding the text's narrative content are the fantastic signs—speaking in tongues, healing, exorcism, drinking poison unharmed, and handling serpents— which the risen Jesus of the LE says believers will enact ἐν τῷ ὀνόματί μου (in [his] name). Kelhoffer's *Miracle and Mission* provides the most thorough study to date of the historical context for and analogies to the two most unusual signs,[109] snake-handling and poison-consumption. But for some Christian traditions, however, the question has contemporary import: these verses inform their regular practices. Mk 16:17-18 supports their articles of faith.

Several Protestant denominations draw from these verses to form the majority of the biblical support for their distinctive practices and denominational identity.[110] One finds, however, few technical or scholarly articles defending such positions. Some defenders of the LE's authenticity have come from these denominations and argue for the originality of manuscripts containing Mk 16:9-20.[111] More often, however, churches merely cite these verses in support of their particular practices.[112]

John Christopher Thomas and Kimberly Ervin Alexander provide self-reflective explorations of Pentecostal hermeneutics and the use of Mark's LE. Thomas considers Pentecostal biblical interpretation from within the tradition *and* as an NT specialist.

---

these same three temporal indicators: Ἀναστὰς δέ, Μετὰ δὲ ταῦτα, and Ὕστερον δέ ("Textual and Structural Analysis," 38–42).

[109] While Kelhoffer's primary "context" for interpreting the signs is the wider ancient Mediterranean cultural milieu, he relates this extension of the Markan ending to the *literary context* of the Second Gospel itself as well. For this reason, he is treated in section 4 of this chapter.

[110] The most publicized example is the movement localized in the US region of Appalachia—although lacking in structural organization—in which snake-handling sometimes takes center stage in gatherings. The name of the "Church of God with Signs Following" demonstrates the direct correlation between Mk 16:17-18 and the church's *raison d'être*. The disparate groups described in Dennis Covington's *Salvation on Sand Mountain* are representative of this predominantly rural, southern American phenomenon (*Salvation on Sand Mountain: Snake Handling and Redemption in Southern Appalachia* [Cambridge, MA: Da Capo Press, 2009; reprinted from Addison Wesley, 1994]).

[111] Restoration Christians (as those part of the "Stone-Campbell Movement" call themselves; i.e., Churches of Christ and related groups) have traditionally held a vested interest in supporting the authenticity of the LE, particularly in light of the verse directly preceding the enumerated signs (Mk 16:16), in which belief and baptism are connected (Stanley N. Helton, "Churches of Christ and Mark 16:9-20," *Restoration Quarterly* 36 [1994]: 32–52; and Bridges, "The Canonical Status of the Longer Ending of Mark," 231–42). This was also the verse that seems to have inspired Burgon's indignant defense (cf. Burgon, *Last Twelve*, 254). For both Churches of Christ authors surveyed here, Helton and Bridges, the question of authorship and canonical status are separable (Helton, "Churches of Christ," 50).

[112] Numerous nondenominational congregations appeal to selections from Mk 16:17-18 in a similar manner. Three Pentecostal denominations are representative of the practice: (1) The Church of God (Cleveland, TN) lists several one-phrase "Doctrinal Commitments," e.g., "Repentance," "Justification," or "Water Baptism," and the supporting scripture references. Of the twenty-two doctrines listed, the twelfth is "Signs following believers," which lists Mk 16:17-20; Rom. 15:18, 19; and Heb. 2:4 (http://www.churchofgod.org/index.php/pages/doctrinal-commitments [cited August 10, 2012]). (2) The Foursquare Church's statement of faith on "Divine Healing" appeals to Mk 16:17-18 and Jas 5:14-16 (http://www.foursquare.org/about/what_we_believe/spirit_filled_life [cited August 10, 2012]). (3) The Church of God in Christ (COGIC) cites and partially quotes Mk 16:17 in support of their "What We Believe" statement on demons (http://www.cogic.org/our-foundation/what-we-believe/ [cited August 10, 2012]).

Nearly two decades prior, early in his scholarly career, Thomas published on the LE and deemed it inauthentic.[113] Alexander's contribution grows out of her research into the history of testimonial accounts of healing within the early Pentecostal movement, which frequently cited Mk 16:9-20 as the biblical foundation for charismatic experiences.[114]

Thomas and Alexander's interdisciplinary approach highlights not only the passages that were frequently referenced in early Pentecostal publications, but also the manner and rationale for applying these verses to the early charismatic experiences of those within the Pentecostal Movement.[115] The signs described in Mk 16:17-18 became a "litmus test for a movement of God," as Thomas and Alexander explain it.[116] A second portion of the article deals not only with the Pentecostal movement's adoption of these verses as a motto and confirmation of its present experience, but also the movement's response to then-contemporary text critics who challenged the passage's authenticity.[117]

Thomas and Alexander's contribution to the discussion is their suggestion that recognizing Mk 16:9-20 as a later addition to Mark's Gospel should not negate its usefulness for Pentecostals. That is, they resist equating authorship with scriptural relevance. Rather, they state, "owing to this text's unrivaled significance in early

---

[113] Cf. J. C. Thomas, "A Reconsideration of the Ending of Mark," *JETS* 26 (1983): 405–19. More recently, Thomas reflects, "My own methodological journey took me from the somewhat narrow confines of historical criticism to the worlds of narrative readings, reader-response criticism, canonical approaches, as well as a somewhat mysterious approach to the text known as the history of effects or *Wirkungsgeschichte*" (Thomas and Alexander, "Signs Are Following," 148).

[114] "As she scoured the early Pentecostal literature with reference to healing, it began to become clear that the place of Mk 16.9–20 was unrivaled within the early Pentecostal literature in position and significance!" (Thomas and Alexander, "Signs Are Following," 149).

[115] Thomas and Alexander report,

> Often in banner headlines, the earliest Pentecostals declared that "the signs were following"! When an inductive approach is utilized in the study of early Pentecostal periodical literature, "signs following" language emerges from each of the periodicals as one of the dominant beliefs and practices ... These Pentecostals, who understood themselves to be apostolic, restoring the faith of the New Testament church, were experiencing manifestations and phenomena delineated in the Mk 16.9–20 passage. (Ibid., 150)

Numerically, the emphasis on Mk 16:9-20, as compared to other commissioning passages (Thomas and Alexander compare Mt. 28:20 and Acts 1:8), shows the clear focus on Mark's LE: "The Mk 16 text was decidedly favored over the other commissions. A scripture index of *The Church of God Evangel* (1910–1919) lists twenty-six references to Mt. 28.18-20, sixteen references to Acts 1.8, and seventy-five to Mk 16.9–20" (ibid., 150).

[116] Ibid., 151, 155. Thomas and Alexander note the debated interpretation of the snake and poison signs—whether such encounters were to be accidental or purposeful means of testimony (154).

[117] Ibid., 157–61. Throughout the writings of early Pentecostal publications Thomas and Alexander survey (most from the first quarter of the twentieth century), there is an expressed confidence that God maintains control of Scripture, even in the particulars of manuscript discovery, perhaps "saving" the vitally important manuscripts (usually seen as containing the LE) until just the right time (159). One such claim centers on the discovery of the Freer Codex (Washingtonianus; W) in 1906, which contains not only the LE but an additional insertion—the "Freer Logion"—between verses 14 and 15 (Arthur Frodsham, in the *Pentecostal Evangel* publication [1923], as cited by Thomas and Alexander, "Signs Are Following," 158). Frodsham found significant the coincidence of the manuscript's discovery in the same year as the Azusa Street Revival (beginning in April 1906), the meeting that is named as the origin of the modern Pentecostal Movement.

Pentecostalism, perhaps biblical scholars working in the tradition have been too quick to dismiss the role of this text in the canon, owing to its non-Markan origins."[118]

The usage of the LE in certain Pentecostal denominations and their historical forbears is primarily isolated to two verses: 16:17-18. As with the other defenders of the LE's authenticity, the passage of interest is not privileged for its function as a conclusion to Mark's Gospel. The LE finds champions because it "houses" verses that support their distinctive practices.[119] My point is not that this approach is unique (Scripture has long been cited in isolated snippets to undergird a dogmatic claim or ecclesial practice). Instead, I am demonstrating that these discussions of selections from the LE do not relate the verses to the Gospel they conclude.[120] My project aims to do this (re)connective work.

3. Reading Mk 16:8 as the Ending of the Second Gospel

Readers of Mark who argue that the shortest ending at 16:8 was the earliest and best conclusion to the Second Gospel can be quick to dismiss the LE as later and inauthentic. It might seem illogical for a project that addresses the LE to give so much attention to approaches that treat Mk 16:9-20 as at best an appendix—a vestigial organ—and at worst a parasite, detracting from the Gospel's original and intended ending at 16:8. But there are good reasons for examining these approaches. First, such an approach to Mark's endings is the prevailing view at present, sometimes adopted without discussion. Second, some interpreters use the consensus understanding of 16:8 as Mark's original ending as a reason to avoid consideration of the LE entirely, as if it never existed. Third, as I hope to demonstrate, interpretations of 16:8 often hinge on an estimation of the women as either successful or failed followers of Jesus.[121] Fourth, for these interpreters, making sense of the ending at 16:8 requires readers to delve back into the fuller Gospel text to explain why an abrupt ending in fear and silence might fit a Gospel like Mark's.

---

[118] Thomas and Alexander, "Signs Are Following," 170.

[119] As with Burgon and baptism, early Pentecostals and some present-day denominations "protect" scriptural support for distinctive signs.

[120] Bucking my categorization of the tendency to privilege the text's content for reasons of tradition and practice, rather than noting its function to conclude Mark, Robert W. Wall's response to the article by Thomas and Alexander proceeds into broader considerations of canon and the function of Scripture ("A Response to Thomas/Alexander, 'And the Signs Are Following' (Mark 16:9–20)," *Journal of Pentecostal Theology* 11 [2003]: 171–83). His claims resonate with—and likely have been influential in forming—many of my convictions regarding the too-easy equation of originality with authority, as well as the canonical function of this passage. Wall expresses his position boldly in his introductory paragraphs: "I accept Mk 16.9–20 as divinely inspired Scripture and formative of Christian faith and practice. This conclusion results not beause I challenge the critical consensus about its production as a non-Markan text, with which I mostly agree; but because I privilege the ecclesial experiences of this text's performance as a word of God when determining its canonicity" (172).

[121] My interest in the LE is tied closely to its depiction of female disciples.

Explaining the ending in light of the rest of the Gospel is an approach few interpreters of the LE undertake. The present study intends to remedy this shortcoming. My reading of Mark's longest ending will pursue an approach similar to that of scholars who prefer its briefest conclusion.

Whereas the LE's narrative content and its relationship to the Markan literary whole are seldom mentioned, these approaches can model how one might do so (despite apparent difficulties). For, in order to argue for the viability of 16:8 as the right ending, these interpreters have had to explore a variety of ways to explain the sudden conclusion as a fitting resolution to Mark's Gospel.[122] The serious roadblocks to reading v. 8 as Mark's intended ending are (at least):

1. Would an ancient Christian author have seen "And they said nothing to anyone, for they were afraid" as a suitable closure to a story about Jesus, particularly for a Gospel that foreshadows Jesus's being raised (8:31; 9:31; 10:34; 14:28; 16:7)? And is it grammatically possible for ἐφοβοῦντο γάρ to end a sentence?
2. What kind of a conclusion is this, if it is the ending? Is it disappointing? Is it satisfying?
   i How is a reader to understand the women's final reaction? (Do they respond rightly or wrongly?)
   ii How does this conclusion relate to the rest of the Gospel of Mark?

What follows will not be a thoroughgoing treatment of scholarly responses to the above questions; instead, it will highlight paradigmatic and recent approaches to 16:8 as the ending of Mark's Gospel.

Even some advocates for the ending at Mk 16:8 as the earliest and best reading find it difficult to imagine that v. 8 could have been Mark's planned conclusion. Robert H. Stein explains: "Mark 16:8 is clearly the most authentic ending of Mark that we possess; it is the oldest ending we possess for the Gospel of Mark. But is it the *original* and *intended* ending of Mark? ... [These] are two separate issues."[123]

Birch's pioneering claim regarding the ending he found in Vaticanus was simply that 16:8 was the correct reading.[124] Subsequent interpreters wrestle with *how* that came to be. Was it accidental or purposeful? The first popular explanation was that the original ending was lost, which not only accounts for the alternate endings that crop up in the manuscript tradition, but also provides an explanation for the awkward

---

[122] Christine E. Joynes provides intriguing examples of the premodern reception history of Mk 16:1–8 in sermons, poems, Easter plays, hymns, and art ("The Sound of Silence: Interpreting Mark 16:1–8 through the Centuries," *Int* 19 [2011]: 18–29).

[123] Stein, "Ending of Mark," 85; emphases in the original. Stein's article contains one of the most concise categorizations of approaches to Mk 16:8, although I disagree with many of his conclusions.

[124] Birch suggests only that Vaticanus (Codex 1209) should be used as a correction to Latin versions (*Variae Lectiones*, xv–xvi). Further, he mentions that when 16:9-20 appears in the Eusebian Canons, it is not by Eusebius, but rather by a "pious scribe" (*librariis pia*) who inserted it by deceit, wanting to authenticate the reading (*Variae Lectiones*, 226). Griesbach seems to have been the first to suggest that the actual ending was lost (Kelhoffer, *Miracle and Mission*, 7–10).

ἐφοβοῦντο γάρ of 16:8.[125] This solution has never gone away, even as its popularity waned for a time. Rudolf Bultmann and D. Moody Smith entertain the possibility that Mark's missing ending—containing the narration of a resurrection appearance—may have been moved to form the ending of John's Gospel (ch. 21).[126] In fact, the hypothesis that Mark's rightful ending was lost may be regaining adherents.[127]

The most thoroughgoing hypothesis regarding the lost Markan ending is found in N. Clayton Croy's 2003 monograph. He proposes that both the beginning and ending of Mark's Gospel were lost in the earliest stages of its transmission.[128] In *The Mutilation of Mark's Gospel*, Croy argues a threefold thesis, which explains the irregular beginning and ending of the Second Gospel.[129] He postulates that the outer leaves of the codex

---

[125] Clayton Croy's list of the scholarly explanations for the Markan ending (besides those who deem 16:8 the original, intended conclusion) demonstrates that the early and ongoing majority favored a "lost ending" theory (*Mutilation*, 174–7).

[126] Bultmann says, "That this story [the resurrection appearance and miraculous catch of fish from John 21:1–14], or a variant of it, formed the original conclusion of Mk. (and of the Gospel of Peter) has a certain probability" (*The Gospel of John: A Commentary* [trans. G. R. Beasley-Murray, R. W. N. Hoare, and J. K. Riches; Philadelphia: Westminster, 1971], 705n5). D. Moody Smith provides some literary rationale for the Johannine editor's decision to relocate an episode that fits better in Mark than in John. He states, "While this whole episode is unexpected in John's narrative, it answers to the expectation aroused in Mark (16:7; cf. 14:28) that the risen Jesus will appear to the disciples, Peter specifically included, in Galilee" (*John*; ANTC; Nashville: Abingdon, 1999), 390. Further, Smith suggests that this "implies that the Johannine narrator knew it was a resurrection story and added it here, where it leads nicely over into Jesus's conversation with Peter" (391). Joel Marcus mentions Bultmann and Smith's opinions in his own discussion of the lost ending hypothesis (*Mark 8–16* [AYB; New Haven, CT: Yale University Press, 2009], 1,091). Although Marcus entertains the suggestion, he concludes that "the style of John 21:1–14, however, is basically Johannine ... If there is a Markan source here, it has been thoroughly worked over by the Johannine redactor" (ibid.).

[127] This explanation for the ending at 16:8 diminished in popularity in the latter half of the twentieth century, perhaps in tune with larger cultural shifts toward an appreciation of ambiguity. However, in my survey of relevant literature, I noticed that this view might be experiencing a resurgence, an inclination that Stein confirms ("Ending of Mark," 98). Robert H. Gundry thought the earliest ending of Mark is lost but suggested a reconstruction using Mt. 28:9-10, 16-20 and Lk. 24:9b-12 (*Mark: A Commentary on His Apology for the Cross* [Grand Rapids: Eerdmans, 1993], 1020–1). Craig Evans follows Gundry's suggestion, but with considerably less certainty (*Mark 8:27–16:20*, 539). Evans refrains from making a final judgment on the matter, but observes that the "cumulative effect" of the evidence "tips probability in favor of the view that v. 8 was not the intended ending of the Gospel and that either a narrative resurrection appearance was composed, but then later lost, or was planned, but then was not penned" (539). For two more instances of this potential "shift" in opinion, see the discussion of Croy and Metzger and Ehrman in this chapter.

[128] Croy's Appendix A is especially helpful. It contains a chronological list of scholars who reject 16:8 as Mark's "intended ending." He offers a general categorization of each scholar's opinion of the Markan ending: lost, unfinished, or suppressed (*Mutilation*, 174–5).

[129] Croy's interest in the Markan ending derives from the manuscript variety and the narrative disjuncture at 16:8, which is not an unusual starting point for scholars. His more unique contribution, however, is that he reads the beginning of Mark's Gospel as similarly abrupt to its ending—so much so, in fact, that he postulates a mutilation of the autograph or influential copy shortly thereafter that removed both the beginning and ending of the Second Gospel. While there is a less obvious text-critical problem with the beginning of the Gospel (i.e., no copies of Mark contain text preceding v. 1), Croy demonstrates the irregularity and wide variation in initial wording (ibid., 114–17). He details grammatical and interpretive problems as well (117–24). He suggests that Mk 1:1 was added by a scribe in an attempt to introduce the remaining text, which began at what we now know as v. 2. This well-meaning scribe did not intend Ἀρχὴ τοῦ εὐαγγελίου Ἰησοῦ Χριστοῦ (Mk 1:1) to act as a first line, but to indicate "the text of the Gospel begins here" (124).

were lost through "mechanical means."[130] This loss happened either to the first and last leaves of the autograph, or to "an early copy from which all extant manuscripts derive."[131] Croy expresses more certainty regarding the mutilation and probable contents of the ending, but also posits "a lost beginning ... less perceptible than a lost ending."[132] Croy highlights interpretive, theological payoff in acknowledging that the ending of Mark at 16:8 is *not* the author's intended one: "Mark has prepared his readers for an appearance narrative, and the lost ending surely contained one. A resurrection appearance would not undercut Mark's call to cruciform discipleship. A 'theology of glory' or vindication is not utterly incompatible with a 'theology of the cross.'"[133]

In the fourth edition of *The Text of the New Testament* (2005), Bruce M. Metzger and Bart D. Ehrman cite Croy's theory as a possible scenario.[134] The authors do not explicitly support Croy's twofold mutilation proposal. They affirm, however, the impulse of those scholars who postulate a lost Markan ending: "It appears, therefore, that ἐφοβοῦντο γάρ of Mark 16:8 does not represent what Mark intended to stand at the end of his Gospel."[135] Metzger and Ehrman refrain from speculating on the cause of the Second Gospel's truncation, but reinforce the idea that "more than one person in the early Church sensed that the Gospel is a torso and tried in various ways to provide a more or less appropriate conclusion."[136]

Scholars who think the original ending of Mark was "amputated" consider the LE a clunky prosthesis, not the original limb. At the same time, these proponents of the post-composition mutilation of the text reject 16:8 as an appropriate conclusion for the Second Gospel. Text-critical insights press them to conclude that v. 8 forms the earliest extant ending. But, in light of a reading of the whole Gospel, they reject that this was the way Mark completed it.

Despite its initial popularity, many dismiss the "lost ending" theory for lack of evidence. The initial shift away may have been in the *Zeitgeist* after the mid-twentieth century, which began to value indefiniteness over completion. It is plausible that interpreters found increasingly far-fetched the proposed scenarios for the rapid loss of such a valuable a text (a source used by at least two other Evangelists). There are two ways of arguing for the originality of the ending at Mk 16:8, each depending on the *intentionality* of the Evangelist.

An early alternative to the "lost ending" theory seems different, but relies on a similar explanation of the relationship between v. 8 and the rest of the Gospel. Thus: the Second Gospel did, indeed, originally end at 16:8, but the Evangelist *intended* to conclude it beyond that point. He was prevented from doing so by his

---

[130] Croy summarizes his theses and their degree of probability (ibid., 164–7). By "mechanical means" of mutilation, he refers to an inadvertent loss due to materials, not a purposeful excision.
[131] "Given the paleographical practices of the early Christians, it is more likely than not that Mark existed in codex form at a very early stage, perhaps even in the autograph, and that damage to the autograph ... resulted in the simultaneous loss of the first and last leaves" (ibid., 166). For a critical evaluation of Croy's claims, see Marcus, *Mark 8–16*, 1091–3.
[132] Croy, *Mutilation*, 166.
[133] Ibid., 169.
[134] Cf. Metzger and Ehrman, *Text of the New Testament*, 326n44.
[135] Ibid., 326.
[136] Ibid.

death or an act of violence against him. The net effect is similar to the theory of Markan mutilation: Mark's ending is still lacking, halted against his will, midsentence. The benefit of this explanation for the abrupt closure—deemed "incoherent" in light of Mark's narrative tone and trajectory—is that it exonerates Mark's earliest transmitters of carelessness. Furthermore, it reinforces that Mark's text was not so undervalued that its clumsy copyists accidentally lost a leaf. Instead, the unfinished work was left sacred and inviolate. Even when the author was incapacitated, the incompleteness of the Gospel did not prevent its circulation.

Karl Lachmann, an early proponent of the "unfinished" theory, considers the ending of Mark as only one example of its fragmentary state in its early transmission.[137] In this view, the LE and other modifications are evidence of later scribal corrections. Many of the signals of incompleteness to which Lachmann points fall in the beginning and ending of the Gospel.[138] Thus, the evidence cited resembles that which Croy marshals in favor of Markan mutilation. Lachmann, however, postulates incompletion as its first cause. Their major difference is in the assignment of responsibility. The "lost ending" theory blames inept internal, early Christian forces—scribal copyists and transmission; proponents of the "incompletion" theory may shift the blame to intentional, external forces inimical to Christianity to explain the sudden ending.[139]

Literary approaches have popularized the theory that Mark ended originally and intentionally at 16:8. This seems to be the predominant view today.[140] Although both this and the "incompletion" approach affirm 16:8 as the *original* ending of Mark, these approaches represent opposing opinions on the ending itself. The literary view does not postulate that the final form was accidental or caused by external forces; the conclusion at 16:8 conforms to the author's intention. For these interpreters, the women's fear and silence represent a fitting final act for Mark's Gospel. They explain *how* and *why* it does so in a variety of ways: whether because the women illustrate that

---

[137] On the Markan ending, Lachmann wrote: "So wird die Menge von schwankenden Lesarten im Evangelium des Marcus jedem die Ueberzeugung geben, daß es uns wenig sorgfältig überliefert und gewiß in manchen Stellen verdorben seh: dadurch wird dann wieder glaublicher, daß es unvollendet und am Schluß ungebührlich vermehrt sehn möge" (Author's translation: "Thus, the volume of variant readings in the Gospel of Mark will give anyone the conviction that it was delivered to us with little care and is certainly corrupt in some places; thus, it is more believable that it may be seen as incomplete and improperly augmented at the ending"; "Rechenschaft über seine Ausgabe des Neuen Testaments," *TSK* 3 [1830]: 841). Like Croy's theory of Markan mutilation, Lachmann points to irregularities in the opening sentences of Mark as further evidence of alteration (843–5).

[138] Ibid., 844.

[139] For an example of this kind of conjecture, see Andrews Norton, *The Evidences of the Genuineness of the Gospels* (6th ed.; Boston: American Unitarian Association, 1877), 448–9.

[140] Recent significant commentaries on Mark illustrate the prevalence of this view, although articulated without a tone of certainty. Adela Yarbro Collins, in her 2007 commentary, cites the consensus of "most scholars" that v. 8 represents the "earliest recoverable ending" as her view (*Mark*, 797, 801). Joel Marcus's 2009 commentary, the second of two volumes on Mark, treated the Gospel only through 16:8. He acknowledged that "there is not enough evidence to say definitively whether Mark intended his work to end at 16:8" (*Mark 8–16*, 1096). But he judges that "it behooves us … to try to make sense of that ending as it stands" in our earliest manuscripts (ibid.). In his 2011 commentary, C. Clifton Black states: "Though few things in biblical interpretation can be certain, the evidence favoring the shortest of all Markan endings is as solid and coherent as one could expect" (*Mark*, 348).

humans always disappoint,[141] or their silence is *anything but silent* as the final instance of Markan irony,[142] or because the women are rightfully silent in holy reverence.[143] Coupled with their view that Mk 16:8 aligns with the tone and direction of the larger Gospel is often distaste for the verses (16:9-20) that subsequently became attached to that ending in the manuscript tradition. Austin Farrer quips about 16:9-20: "If the mice in the bishop's house at Rome ate the appendix, what highly discriminating mice they must have been!"[144]

Together with the need to explain how v. 8 brings a suitable conclusion to Mark, proponents of the shortest ending as the one intended by Mark seek to explain its unconventional closing phrase, ἐφοβοῦντο γάρ. Samuel P. Tregelles was among the first to suggest this necessity (although he himself remained uncertain of its status as original).[145] Unlike many others, Tregelles rejects the claim that the content of Mk 16:9-20 is foreign to the apostolic age[146] or worthy of censure.[147] And yet he deems the LE discernibly different from the rest of Mark. These "internal considerations" of style, accompanied by external evidence, "possess very great weight."[148] He points out comparably abrupt book endings, scriptural and otherwise,[149] and notes the obvious: Many ancient copies of Mark *did* end at 16:8.[150] Vaticanus stands as evidence: "Such a peculiarity would not have been invented."[151] In conclusion, Tregelles defends two propositions, quoted here:

---

[141] Donald H. Juel says, "There is surely disappointment as the women flee, dashing hopes that at least one group of followers will prove faithful" (*A Master of Surprise: Mark Interpreted* [Minneapolis: Fortress, 1994], 120).

[142] Marie Sabin, "Women Transformed: The Ending of Mark Is the Beginning of Wisdom," *Cross Currents* 48 (1998): 149–68.

[143] David Catchpole, "The Fearful Silence of the Women at the Tomb: A Study in Markan Theology," *JTSA* 18 (1977): 3–10.

[144] Austin Farrer, *A Study in St. Mark* (London: Dacre Press, 1951), 178.

[145] Tregelles, *Printed Text*, 246–61. Tregelles entertains several speculative explanations for Mark's ending at 16:8, before ultimately admitting that we simply do not know: "Perhaps we do not know enough of the circumstances of St. Mark when he wrote his Gospel to say whether he did or did not leave it with a complete termination" (257). His view stems from a wider acquaintance with and greater appreciation for patristic opinion on the Markan endings than his text-critical predecessors. Tregelles considers patristic comments on the LE before turning to the manuscripts (253). On the ancient awareness of manuscripts lacking 16:9-20, he cited most of the Fathers who are a part of surveys today, including Irenaeus and Eusebius (251, 247–9). Tregelles weighs the arguments of his scholarly contemporaries on the LE and finds them wanting. Lachmann is aware of the patristic testimony, noting variation between East and West and textual "vacillation" (*schwanken*), but he ends up taking the opposite view to Tregelles ("Rechenschaft," 843–4). On the earliest citations of 16:9-20, Tregelles names Irenaeus as the first sure attestation (*Printed Text*, 251).

[146] Tregelles rejected the argument that the LE's naming of Mary Magdalene as the "first" witness to the resurrection (16:9) and the high view of baptism (16:16) indicate "inauthenticity." He found its claims perfectly coherent with the apostolic age (ibid., 256).

[147] On the claim that the LE was too difficult to harmonize with other Gospel accounts and was thus removed, Tregelles responded: "We have no reason for entertaining the supposition that such a Marcion-like excision had been here adopted" (*Printed Text*, 255–6).

[148] Tregelles was likewise aware that stylistic arguments are often "very fallacious, and *by themselves* they prove very little" (ibid., 256; emphasis in the original).

[149] Tregelles claimed that the biblical books Ezra and Jonah and the last book of Thucydides all lack "proper termination" (ibid., 257).

[150] Sinaiticus (א) had not yet been discovered, so only Vaticanus (B) and several versions could attest to the ending at 16:8.

[151] Ibid., 257–8.

I. That the *book of Mark himself* extends no farther than ἐφοβοῦντο γάρ, xvi. 8.
II. That the remaining twelve verses, by whomsoever written, have a full claim to be received as an authentic part of the second Gospel, and that the full reception of early testimony on this question does not in the least involve their rejection as not being a part of Canonical Scripture.[152]

Tregelles's willingness to distinguish text and canon, along with affirming the antiquity of the LE, set him apart from many scholars up to today who share his opinions about 16:8.[153] For Tregelles, the LE was just as certainly non-Markan as it was divinely inspired.[154] Among those who found these two positions impossibly contradictory was Tregelles's younger contemporary J. W. Burgon. Recall that Burgon's defense of the originality of Mk 16:9-20 sets the tone and material parameters for most subsequent arguments for, and often against, the LE.[155]

Austin Farrer was among the first to insist that interpreters make sense of 16:8 as the intended Markan conclusion. He advocates taking the conclusion at 16:8 on Markan terms, in light of the full Gospel, not to judge it by an external standard for

---

[152] Ibid., 258; emphasis in the original. Tregelles noted Henry Alford's similar conclusion. Alford judged 16:9-20 "*an authentic fragment, placed as a completion of the Gospel in very early times*: by whom written, must of course remain wholly uncertain; but coming to us with very weighty sanction, and having strong claims on our reception and reverence" (*The Greek Testament* [vol. 1; Boston: Lee and Shepard, 1874], 438; emphasis in the original). Both Alford and Tregelles were able to separate the questions of "authentically Markan" and "canonical." Tregelles assigned a second-century date to the LE. It was not written by Mark, but it was a part of the canonized text of the Second Gospel. Theologically, inspiration belongs to the canonical process, not to original authors:

> There is in some minds a kind of timidity with regard to Holy Scripture, as if all our notions of its authority depended on our knowing who was the writer of each particular portion; instead of simply seeing and owning that it was given forth from God, and that it is as much his as were the commandments of the Law written by his own finger on the tables of stone … I thus look on this section as an authentic anonymous addition to what Mark himself wrote down from the narration of St. Peter … and that it ought as much to be received as part of our second Gospel, as the last chapter of Deuteronomy (unknown as the writer is) is received as the right and proper conclusion of the books of Moses. (259)

[153] The conventional assumption seems to be that text and canon are to be equated. Although scholars are aware of the eclectic, critical text of the Greek NT—which does not replicate any extant manuscript—this awareness is not always reflected in discussions of the relationship of text to canon. The settled canon did not itemize the precise contents or wording of the canonical books. Historically, canonization was of a particular set of books, not a delineation of their constituent parts.

[154] This posture of accepting a textually disputed passage as secondary, yet canonical, may be more common in reference to Jn 7:53–8:11. About that passage, Gail R. O'Day summarizes, "Importantly, although the text's relationship to Johannine tradition is debated, the consensus is that the story does indeed preserve a primitive piece of Jesus tradition" ("John 7:53–8:11: A Study in Misreading," *JBL* 111 [1992]: 639). One of the main reasons this passage is thought to be quite early is due to its patristic attestation—not connected to the Fourth Gospel—by Papias, reported by Eusebius (*Hist. eccl.* 3.39). While there are parallels between the LE and Jn 7:53–8:11 in their text-critical uncertainty and later near-ubiquity, no one makes an analogous argument that the LE is both unoriginal to Mark *and* preserves early (and otherwise unknown) Jesus tradition.

[155] Burgon was incredulous over Tregelles's willingness to doubt the Markan attribution of 16:9-20 while maintaining its status as Scripture. He declared: "The learned writer betrays a misapprehension of the question at issue, which we are least of all prepared to encounter in such a quarter. *We admire his piety but it is at the expense of his critical sagacity*" (Burgon, *Last Twelve*, 11; emphasis added).

The Long Ending as a Conclusion to Mark's Gospel

what a Gospel ending "should" include. Like Tregelles and Alford, Farrer accepts divine inspiration, without insisting (as they do) that 16:9-20 was the completion of that inspiration. He explains *why* Mark ended his Gospel at 16:8:

> The answer we have to give to this question is not a simple one. There can be no final answer. St Mark chose to do what he chose to do, or to speak more Christianly, was inspired to do what he was inspired to do. His inspired choice might have been different, for the inspired choices of the other evangelists were in fact different ... We commonly make St Matthew and St Luke vote together against St Mark about the proper conclusion to a Gospel; but that is an arbitrary representation of the facts, based on the ignoring of St Luke's second volume. St Matthew, certainly, decided to round off and finish St Mark with two rather slightly drawn scenes of Christ returning; I prefer St Mark's poetry, but I allow that St Matthew better meets the need of Christian people for plain instruction.[156]

Farrer's *A Study in St. Mark* anticipates the current trend in Gospel scholarship in his preference for "St Mark's poetry."[157]

Growing appreciation for the Gospels *as literature* has opened contemporary scholars to the inconclusive closing to the Second Gospel. Despite detractors, the shortest ending of Mark (at 16:8) has proven capable of supporting weighty theological reflection. The rise of literary readings of the NT popularized interpretations of the whole Gospel that made sense of the ending at 16:8.[158] Compelling literary readings have persuaded many modern readers to consider the meaningful uncertainty of the ending in fear and silence.[159] Some, however, claim that such readings merely reflect modern sensibilities. Could ancient readers have seen 16:8 as a fitting conclusion to Mark's story? I have already mentioned two technical hurdles for accepting this possibility.

The first obstacle is that the two-word concluding phrase of v. 8, ἐφοβοῦντο γάρ, seems an unlikely way to conclude a Gospel. Not only is it truncated, but it ends with a postpositive conjunction. "For" strikes many as an awkward, if not nonsensical, final word for the Second Gospel. Scholars cite other ancient works that conclude with γάρ,[160] and a passage from the LXX with a similar

---

[156] Farrer, *Study in St Mark*, 178–81.
[157] Farrer's study was published in 1951 and, therefore, ahead of scholarly trends in appreciating the artistry of Mark's narrative.
[158] Donald Juel credits text criticism and a growing consensus of Markan priority as mainly responsible for "the current fascination with" Mark's ending at 16:8. Among "additional factors," he mentions "the willingness to read Mark as a narrative." Earlier critics had been preoccupied with detached verses and speculative explanations arising from hypothetical original settings. "The verses sound rather different as the conclusion of a narrative" (Juel, *Master of Surprise*, 107–8).
[159] Frank Kermode suggests that the ending actually confounded the practice of meaning-making itself and ultimately disappoints one who would seek to understand (*The Genesis of Secrecy: On the Interpretation of Narrative* [Cambridge, MA: Harvard University Press, 1979]). Most interpreters, however, seek to make meaning of an ending, deeming it either satisfying or unsatisfying. In this chapter, I have provided some examples of interpretations of the ending at 16:8 that connect its abruptness to Mark's overall narrative goal, particularly Juel's approach.
[160] Andrew T. Lincoln points to Plato's *Protagoras* and Musonius Rufus's *12th Tractate* ("The Promise and Failure: Mark 16:7, 8," *JBL* 108 [1989]: 284n4). The classic treatment of the question comes

phrase.¹⁶¹ Mark's fondness for the postpositive conjunction and the verb φοβέομαι makes the sentence seem much less of an aberration in the Second Gospel.¹⁶²

Beyond the lexical and grammatical considerations, the second hurdle to seeing Mk 16:8 as the intended ending of Mark is its ability to function coherently as a literary ending. Interpreters have long asked whether Mark's ending in fear and silence—in contrast to its fellow Gospels' endings with resurrection appearances—can possibly be the way an ancient Evangelist would have wanted to conclude a story about Jesus.

On this point, J. Lee Magness argues convincingly for what he calls a "suspended ending" as a tenable, even fitting, ending for Mark's Gospel. Magness's *Sense and Absence* is a study of narrative closure and openness in the NT and parallel literature.¹⁶³ It has been met with broad approval.¹⁶⁴

Magness first surveys Greco-Roman epic, *bioi*, drama, and novels, establishing that foreshadowing and expectation in a larger literary work can make the omission of a conclusion even more poignant. Contrary to accusations that such literary nuance is anachronistic, he finds—as far back as the *Iliad*—that simply because "these events are foreshadowed, that they are expected, that we assume them, that they are crucial to the closure of the whole story, is no guarantee that they were originally narrated in the epic poem."¹⁶⁵ As Magness puts it, "The point is, the absence of these events is felt as keenly, if not more so, than their presence."¹⁶⁶

---

from P. W. van der Horst. He appeals to the final γάρ in Plotinus (*Enn.* 5.5), insisting, "The proof was really not necessary for common sense alone could argue that, if a sentence or paragraph can end with γάρ, a book can too" ("Can a Book End with γάρ? A Note on Mark 16:8," *JTS* 23 [1972]: 123–4). More recently, Croy has renewed the debate over the two-word final sentence of Mark. The appendix to his book charts the comparative frequency of the final γάρ (*Mutilation*, 180–5). He not only notes the simple occurrences of the word, but also considers the *sorts of* literary works that contained final γάρ (48–50). Although he rejects absolute claims based on style, he concludes: "The limited use of 'final *gar*' sentences in narrative prose and their extreme scarcity at the end of narrative works (I am not aware of any such instance) argues *against* the likelihood that Mark concluded his entire Gospel with such a clause" (49). Two articles respond to Croy's claims: Denyer, "Mark 16:8 and Plato, *Protagoras* 328D," 149–50; Iverson, "A Further Word on Final Γάρ (Mark 16:8)," 79–94. Iverson contests Croy's interpretation of his statistical data:

> The argument from genre aids little in the discussion of Mark's ending, as it occurs infrequently at all times and across all kinds of literature. The construction is so infrequent that the evidence can be used to argue both for and against the theory of a mutilated text or an abrupt ending. What the research does affirm is that scholars should use caution in utilizing final γάρ as a basis for postulating a theory of Mark's ending. (94)

¹⁶¹ The parallel is in diction and grammar, not in the phrase's placement in the literary work as a whole: LXX Genesis 18:15: ἐφοβήθη γάρ (Lincoln, "Promise and the Failure," 284).
¹⁶² "The ending can be said to fit Mark's style. He frequently uses the postpositive γάρ in short clauses and five times has employed φοβέομαι absolutely (cf. 5:15, 33, 36; 6:50; 10:32)" (ibid., 284).
¹⁶³ J. Lee Magness, *Sense and Absence: Structure and Suspension in the Ending of Mark's Gospel* (SemeiaSt; Atlanta: Scholar's Press, 1986).
¹⁶⁴ Magness's argument is frequently cited as proof that Mark's "suspended ending" was the Second Gospel's intended conclusion. But his arguments have their detractors as well (see Gundry, *Mark*, 1019). Philip Oakeshott seems unaware of Magness's work, but argues in a 2010 article, directly contrary to Magness, that ancient narrative conclusions lack the subtlety required to understand Mark 16:8 as the intended ending ("The Wrong Conclusion," 106–7, 111).
¹⁶⁵ Ibid., 33–4.
¹⁶⁶ Ibid., 34.

Within OT literature, Magness finds a similar pattern of unmet expectations within shorter narrative sections[167] and full books (2 Kings, 2 Chronicles, Song).[168] He devotes considerable attention to Jonah's ostensibly incomplete conclusion; the "end" of the prophet's story is entirely unspecified.[169]

Within NT literature, Magness observes that parables rely often on the enigmatic absence of conclusions.[170] The Book of Acts is the closest book-length parallel to Mark's inconclusiveness.[171] At the outset of his study, Magness considers whether there is too great a distance between the literary sensibilities of antiquity and modern literary theory to support recent readings of Mark's suggestive but incomplete ending. Would such subtlety have been available to ancient readers or intended by an ancient author like Mark?[172] After surveying many literary analogies he concludes: "A close reading of the Gospel of Mark suggests the kind of openness common to modern literature but characteristic of much great ancient literature as well—a closure achieved in spite of and by means of the suspension of the narrative climax from the text."[173] Magness successfully demonstrates that 16:8 could have been a comprehensible ending to ancient readers of Mark, particularly in light of the Gospel's established expectations in the narrative as a whole.

It remains to consider *how* we are to interpret the ending at 16:8. What *is* the meaning to be made of this ending, if one accepts it as historically prior to the addition of 16:9-20 and as a reading that might have made sense to its audience?[174] Uniformly, interpreters answer this question by pointing back to narrative signals throughout Mark's story of Jesus. Marcus considers the ending at 16:8 to be consonant with "characteristic Markan concerns about faith, fear, and silence."[175] C. Clifton Black connects the ending to Mark's way of telling Jesus's story all along: "Mark is a book about God's shattering of human expectations; Mark *as* a book shatters everything its readers thought [they] understood—even the conventions of how a Gospel should end."[176]

Donald H. Juel is one of the most influential interpreters of the Markan endings at the turn of the twenty-first century. He addresses the ending at 16:8 in several treatments of the Second Gospel.[177] He notes that there is no consensus as to how

---

[167] E.g., Jephthah's daughter's non-narrated but anticipated death (Judg 11:39; Magness, *Sense and Absence*, 52) and the unstated outcome of the widow whose deceased husband was a member of "the sons of the prophets" associated with Elisha (2 Kgs 4:1-7; Magness, *Sense and Absence*, 55).
[168] Ibid., 55-7.
[169] Ibid., 60-3.
[170] Ibid., 74-80.
[171] Ibid., 83-5.
[172] Citing Rabkin's literary theory and Kermode's explanation of Mark's open ending, Magness says, "But the leap from twentieth century literary theory to first century gospel is an abrupt one. Only if these principles are clearly present in the ancient literary context of which Mark was a part can we confidently claim that our assessment of Mark's suspended ending is anything other than a modern imposition on an ancient text" (ibid., 24).
[173] Ibid., 108.
[174] Not all literary critics, who focus on the unified narrative of the Second Gospel, uniformly argue for the ending at 16:8 as "original" in a text-critical sense. They, instead, emphasize the necessity of interpreting the earliest "final form" available. See, e.g., Juel in n. 169.
[175] Marcus, *Mark 8-16*, 1093.
[176] Black, *Mark*, 362; emphasis in the original.
[177] See Juel, *Master of Surprise* and idem, *The Gospel of Mark* (Interpreting Biblical Texts; Nashville: Abingdon, 1999), 167-76. Juel distinguishes between thinking 16:8 is the *probable*

the inconclusive ending affects interpretation, even among the majority of scholars who agree on 1:1–16:8 as boundaries of Mark's Gospel.[178] For Juel, taking the ending of Mark at 16:8 seriously means resisting the impulse to skip over disappointment.[179] Each ending has a vastly different impact on readers and cannot be valued only for the information it includes.[180]

Juel considers 16:7 intrinsically hopeful, recounting Jesus's predictions of his resurrection (in 8:31; 9:31; 10:33). The unexpected and "unsatisfying" surprise comes in 16:8, when "even in the face of an empty tomb and testimony to Jesus's resurrection, the women cannot believe in such a way as to perform the most basic task of disciples: testimony."[181] Holding together both concluding verses, Juel insists: "Mark's Gospel ends with both hope and disappointment. The relationship between the last two verses embodies the critical tension in the story between blindness and insight, concealment and openness, silence and proclamation. The tension is not resolved."[182] This noted tension has been at work all throughout Mark and its impact remains to the very end.

Juel's treatment of the Markan ending as resisting conventional closure is based, in part, on a theological reading of the whole Gospel.[183] He highlights in the Second Gospel an uncomfortable lack of interpretive control. The "good news" is not something humans can control, even as God works within the realm of human speech. God has the last word, not interpreters.[184]

---

earliest ending and "describ[ing] our printed text as the original version of Mark's Gospel" (*Master of Surprise*, 109). He calls for "greater modesty" but firmly places his own interpretation within the scope of "the experience of the ending" (108). After his untimely death, Juel's colleagues and friends undertook a memorial volume that honors his contribution to the question of the Markan ending: Gaventa and Miller, eds., *The Ending of Mark and the Ends of God*. Another posthumous collection is Donald H. Juel, *Shaping the Scriptural Imagination: Truth, Meaning, and the Theological Interpretation of the Bible* (ed. Shane Berg and Matthew L. Skinner; Waco, TX: Baylor University Press, 2011).

[178] Juel, *Master of Surprise*, 108.
[179] Ibid., 112.
[180] This is because particular endings do particular things: "Endings are important more for what they do than for the ideas they include. Verse 8 does something radically different as an ending than does verse 20, something that shapes the whole experience of reading the Gospel" (ibid., 110).
[181] Ibid., 116.
[182] Ibid.
[183] Juel insists:

> Mark's Gospel forbids precisely ... closure. There is no stone at the mouth of the tomb. Jesus is out, on the loose, on the same side of the door as the women and the readers. The story cannot contain the promises ... The doors in Mark's Gospel are emphatically open: The curtain of the Temple is rent asunder (as is the curtain of the heavens at Jesus's baptism) and the stone is rolled back from the tomb. There is surely disappointment as the women flee, dashing hopes that at least one group of followers will prove faithful. But Jesus is out of the tomb; God is no longer safely behind the curtain. To hear in Mark's elusive ending the strains of Handel's "Halleluia Chorus" would require drowning out the music being performed. But to insist that the discordant ending offers no promise of resolution whatever is to do equal violence to the story. Jesus has promised an end. That end is not yet, but the story gives good reasons to remain hopeful even in the face of disappointment. The possibilities of eventual enlightenment for the reader remain in the hands of the divine actor who will not be shut in—or out. (Ibid., 120)

[184] Juel's conclusion is poignant: "There is reason to hope that our defenses will finally prove insufficient and that we will not have the last word" (ibid., 121).

Many scholars addressing the Markan ending wrestle with similar questions and argue for more interpretive certainty about how the ending acts as a conclusion than Juel allows. Brian Blount, for example, takes up Juel's interpretation but pushes for a more active role for readers, who, with God's help and promise, "finish the story."[185] This reader-response makes sense of the conclusion in light of a call to discipleship found in reading the rest of the Gospel. Joel F. Williams sums up a variety of literary approaches to the ending of Mark. These range from irony, to a positive response to the miraculous, to utter failure on the disciples' behalf.[186]

Often the question of the ending's impact is taken as identical to the question of the women's success: Do the women get it right or wrong? Andrew Lincoln, for instance, interprets the women's silence in 16:8 as direct disobedience of what they were commanded. This functions as an inverted parallel to the earlier instances in which Jesus commanded others to remain silent and they disobeyed.[187] Verses 7 and 8 must be taken together, Lincoln insists, as the final set in the sequence of paired divine promise and human failure that represents human existence for Mark.[188] The juxtaposed themes are to have an effect on the reader: Verses "7 and 8 are the final and climactic example of a promise–failure juxtaposition pattern which runs through the second half of the Gospel's narrative, once the theme of discipleship as the way of the cross has been introduced in 8:27ff."[189] In Lincoln's way of reading Mark's ending at 16:8, the confounding finale sends the reader back into the text of the Gospel to find answers.

Recently, Larry Hurtado has weighed in that the women's final actions in 16:8 should be seen positively, not negatively.[190] Hurtado interprets the response of the women in Mk 16:7-8 in a sanguine light.[191] He points to various narrative signals that the women's faithfulness remains unsullied, despite the apparently faithless silence. He demonstrates that, from a broader narrative standpoint, the characterization of the women disciples in 15:40–16:8 makes clear that they are central to the author's literary strategy overall. In Hurtado's view, Mark's interest in the women, demonstrated in the crucifixion and burial accounts, was surely not to be "wasted" on the women's ultimate failure.[192] Hurtado explains the phrase καὶ οὐδενὶ οὐδὲν εἶπαν in 16:8 (usually

---

[185] Brian K. Blount, "Is the Joke on Us? Mark's Irony, Mark's God, and Mark's Ending," in Gaventa and Miller, eds., *The Ending of Mark and the Ends of God*, 15–20, 29–30.
[186] Joel F. Williams, "Literary Approaches to the End of Mark's Gospel," *JETS* 42 (1999): 21–35.
[187] "Now that the resurrection has taken place, the silence can be broken and the women are given the commission to begin the process of telling. Yet, as has now become clear, the narrator's telling of the story has carefully created such an expectation only to shatter it immediately" (Andrew Lincoln, "The Promise and the Failure: Mark 16:7, 8," *JBL* 108 [1989]: 290–1).
[188] Ibid., 293.
[189] Ibid.
[190] Contra those such as Lincoln and Juel who take the women's response to be inadequate and amounting to failure.
[191] Published in a 2009 Festschrift for Seán Freyne, Hurtado's essay, "The Women, the Tomb, and the Climax of Mark," marked a reassessment of some of his previously published opinions (ibid., 427n3) and sought to counteract readings by Juel (and others) that interpreted the Markan ending as "anti-climactic" (427) or as a trap for readers (437; cf. n.44). For a previous interpretation in the same vein, see Catchpole, "Fearful Silence," 8–9.
[192] Hurtado, "Women, the Tomb," 428. I defend a similar centrality in Chapter 2. Thus, I agree with Hurtado that "the narrative dynamics of 15:40–16:8 present the women as crucial to the story-line." He, however, sees this as a "strong reason for rejecting the view that they fail in the end"

translated, "they said nothing to anyone"), as "they did not broadcast their experience beyond those to whom they were sent."[193] He interprets the final scene of Mk 16:1-8 in its larger narrative context, not as one of disappointment or disobedience, but instead as "powerfully triumphant."[194]

Lars Hartman offers an alternative to the two contrasting perspectives on the women's actions in 16:1-8 as either entirely negative or positive. He suggests that the locus of reading (in a worship setting) affects how the ending works. He considers 16:1-8 a fitting ending for Mark's Gospel precisely because of the sociolinguistic function of a "gospel" in a worship-setting,[195] which fuses past and present. The final pericope of Mark acts as "an important pointer to the readers that Mark's whole text is a gospel to them in their present situation."[196] The narrative action of the women need not be deemed "good" or "bad"; it functions to engage the audience and enlivens the applicability of the whole Gospel.

As I have demonstrated, for those who see 16:8 as the best and earliest ending of Mark, the broader Markan literary context is vital for interpreting its significance. At the same time, these interpreters see that something "surgical" has happened on the final pages of the Gospel. One gets the impression that this implanted "limb," 16:9-20, is something unnatural and unfitting, resulting in something like Frankenstein's monster. Its interpretation, then, cannot be connected back to the whole of the Second Gospel, as its origins are perceived as foreign to Mark. The accusation of an "unnatural" conclusion goes both ways, however. Adherents of the Received Text, which concludes

---

(440). Hurtado demonstrates that in preceding pericopes Mark treats women in an entirely positive light. He then locates a *unity* through the ending: women are named (429–31); women feature as observers (431–2); and the women's presence highlights a "Markan emphasis on the dead Jesus" (432). Nevertheless, some points of Hurtado's interpretation require too much special pleading. For instance, he reads Mark's silence about female disciples from the beginning of the Gospel until their appearance on the scene after the crucifixion (in 15:40) as intentionally drawing attention to their presence in the closing scenes of the Gospel. He argues that the lack of prior mention "was probably intended to make their sudden appearance here all the more noticeable to readers" (429). It seems more likely that Mark's silence about women followers throughout the vast portion of the narrative points to a lack of information, ambivalence, secondary-status, or *disinterest*. But, as I will show in Chapter 2, women feature prominently in encounters with Jesus as recipients of miracles or exemplary figures throughout Mark's Gospel. Granted, they are not mentioned as part of the band of *followers* with whom Mark has explicit interest, namely the Twelve. The last remaining members of Jesus's inner circle abandon him in 14:72, just before the women enter the Evangelist's field of vision. Hurtado's argument, nonetheless, underscores the vitality of the women's witness to the crucifixion, burial, and empty tomb. Thus, I applaud Hurtado's general sentiment—but not its application to 16:8—that discrediting the women "would also clearly amount to the author discrediting Jesus" (441).

[193] Ibid., 439. Hurtado sees the καὶ-consecutive in 16:8b as connoting an obedient follow-through, rather than introducing a contrast (disobedience), which typically requires a δὲ or an ἀλλά (ibid.).

[194] Ibid., 442.

[195] Part of Hartman's agenda is to advocate for a more nuanced definition of the "gospel" genre. He expresses hope that this will help elucidate the shortest ending of Mark and its function within Mark's particular genre ("Ending of a Biography-Like Narrative," 31–47). Hartman distinguishes *gospel* from the *bios*. He favors a worship-centered genre that emphasizes greater participation on the part of the hearer. In contrast to *bios*, which can be merely informative or wherein a figure may be exemplary, "the listeners' encounter with the gospel had a more fundamentally existential bearing on their lives" (37).

[196] Ibid., 47. The recent history of Jesus's death and resurrection is made "present" and immediately relevant when the Gospel is read in worship (46–7).

Mark at 16:20, find the ending at 16:8 a gruesome hack job. Yet their defense for 16:9-20 as the authentic ending of Mark has historically emphasized factors either internal to the last twelve verses (inspired content) or external to it (early patristic awareness).

One can concede many things about the LE—for instance, that Mk 16:16 contains a support for the cooperative nature of belief and baptism or that 16:19 expresses Jesus's ascension in a way that confirms the Lukan accounts—without becoming convinced that it concludes all of Mark in a way that enriches or reflects a coherent reading of the Gospel. There are, however, a few interpreters whose variations from this conventional approach deserve attention.

4. Reading through to Mk 16:20 as *an* Ending of the Second Gospel

As the survey in this book reveals, many books and articles on the LE add new insight, perspective, or comparisons to the study of this divisive text. Few, however, ask new questions of the text itself and its relationship to the rest of Mark's Gospel. Its interpretive history has worn deep grooves into the imagination, limiting the scope of inquiry into the text. As the bibliographical annotations throughout this chapter make clear, there has *not* been a dearth of treatments.

The neglect is one of breadth. On the one hand, restriction is understandable: we are referring to twelve verses and their place in the NT canon. On the other hand, scholars have overlooked many mysterious elements of these verses or sidestepped interpreting the text itself in pursuit of *the right* answers to the presumed "big" questions. Perhaps, our lack of progress on the LE is due to the fact that these are not the only questions needing to be asked. The question of originality to Mark seems preliminary to any further study of the LE, but it is not the final question of interest in interpreting the Markan endings.

Several scholars have sought to bypass or supplement the well-trod trails of scholarly research: Mirecki, for instance, disavows questions of the LE's originality almost entirely.[197] Kelhoffer's *Miracle and Mission* is invaluable because he addresses the traditional questions of authenticity and then also proceeds to inquire further regarding the purpose of the signs and how they form a new conclusion to Mark for a new historical context.[198]

Kelhoffer's study is unquestionably historical in orientation. He offers a systematic and thorough historical study of the two most fantastic signs found among Jesus's commission of Mk 16:17b-18.[199] In the second half of the LE, Kelhoffer demonstrates

---

[197] Mirecki, "Mark 16:9–20: Composition," 23–4. Just because Mirecki's positions on the matter of the LE's origins are unstated does not preclude the fact that his presuppositions inform his literary and structural arguments.
[198] Kelhoffer, *Miracle and Mission*, chapters 5–7.
[199] Chapters 5–7 are focused on the signs to follow belief (Kelhoffer, *Miracle and* Mission, 245–472). Chapter 5 compares the LE to other descriptions of miraculous deeds. Chapters 6 and 7 treat, in turn, the individual signs of "picking up serpents" and "drinking a deadly substance with impunity" (340–416 and 417–72, respectively).

its intrinsic connection to the Gospel to which it was attached: "Jesus, the wonder-worker *par excellence*, continues to work through those who carry out the post-Easter mission."[200] He treats the two particular signs of picking up snakes and drinking poison in a way that places the statements within a spectrum of interest in their ancient context.

In seeking literary analogies for the sign of picking up serpents, Kelhoffer identifies a transition in emphasis, comparing the LE to other texts in the NT, apocryphal acts, and second- and third-century apologists.[201] Writings of the first category are interested, almost exclusively, in miraculous deeds performed by the twelve apostles and Paul. With rare exceptions, apocryphal acts focus on the miracles performed by an apostolic figure.[202] Authors in the third category tell, almost exclusively, of contemporary believers' wondrous signs. Kelhoffer concludes:

> Perhaps the most distinctive feature of the LE's statements related to miracles is the expectation that 'those who believe' (16:17a) will perform the miraculous signs listed in Mark 16:17b-18 ... Therefore, the otherwise surprising expectation of Mark 16:17a that believers in general will perform miracles corresponds most closely to one saying in the Fourth Gospel (John 14:12) and numerous writings of these Christian apologists, who maintain that such power has, in fact, been given to ordinary believers.[203]

Literary comparison offers Kelhoffer a glimpse into the historical situation of the LE's author, based upon a trajectory he identifies within the description of miraculous deeds.

An even wider swath of ancient literature, particularly religious texts, supports Kelhoffer's comparison concerning snakes. The numerous Greco-Roman texts he surveys—from Eleusian mysteries to philosophers—offer many intriguing nuances to ancient understandings of snakes. Perhaps most pertinent for Kelhoffer's study of serpent-handling in the LE is his observation that "among authors and artists in antiquity, Mark 16:18a hardly represents a unique formulation."[204] Within the wider milieu, "such an activity would hardly come as a surprise in a promise like that in the LE concerning the deeds to be performed by the emissaries of a god or divine man—in this case, Jesus."[205] Although picking up snakes might sound bizarre to modern

---

[200] Ibid., 246.
[201] Kelhoffer's chapter 5 places the LE in a context of other texts that "touch upon both miracles *and* missionary activity" (*Miracle and Mission*, 246; emphasis in the original) in the NT (245–81), in apocryphal acts (281–310), and finally in apologetic writers of the second- and third-century (310–37).
[202] Kelhoffer summarizes,

> Only certain exceptional passages portray someone other than an apostle performing a miracle (*Acts of John* 24, 46–47, 81–82, *Acts of Peter* 25, *Acts of Thomas* 54). In each of these unusual instances, the role of the apostle is nonetheless prominent in giving instructions to the person who performs the miracle, which in these five passages involves the raising of a dead person. (Ibid., 338)

[203] Ibid., 338–9.
[204] Ibid., 409.
[205] Ibid.

The Long Ending as a Conclusion to Mark's Gospel   41

interpreters, it would have not been unfamiliar to ancient audiences. Although he finds many related traditions, Kelhoffer is left with an interesting result to his search for parallels: "It is possible that Jesus's promise that believers 'will pick up snakes (ὄφεις ἀροῦσιν)' is *both* rooted in some historical practice and, at the same time, completely *without* parallel in early Christian and other literature."[206]

Searching for ancient literary analogies to the poison-drinking sign,[207] Kelhoffer surveys Jewish, Greco-Roman, and Early Christian descriptions of poison in a roughly chronological manner.[208] Both Jewish and Greco-Roman authors evidence an interest in immunity to poison, but there is very little that bears any similarity to Mk 16:18b.[209] Extracanonical Christian sources provide the most striking analogies to the LE's vision of someone drinking poison without ill effect.[210] Kelhoffer affirms that there would have been a constellation of possible interpretations for surviving after drinking

---

[206] Ibid., 416; emphases in the original. According to Exod. 4:1-5, at the Lord's command Moses's staff is turned into a snake and it returns to its original form when he picks it up. Similarly, in 7:8-13, Aaron's staff is likewise transformed. Kelhoffer finds here less analogy to Mk 16:18a than one might expect. On the one hand, all three texts have elements in common: both present picking up snakes "as an authenticating sign for those who believe" (390). Ultimately, Kelhoffer does not find sufficient evidence that the author of the LE wrote in imitation of Moses's act. He notes that in Aaron's case it is never narrated that he picks up the snake/rod again. Exodus shows a lack of interest in picking up serpents. Its concern is to demonstrate the power and calling of Moses and Aaron (391). Some later Jewish writings outside the biblical tradition demonstrate an interest in snakes, particularly human beings' resilience or lack thereof correlating to the effects of sin (410). These writings do not, however, have the expectation of snake-handling as a practice. Again, no exact parallel exists in the NT or extracanonical Christian writings to the practice of snake-handling. The closest comparison Kelhoffer finds is Acts 28:1-10, but "[a] profound difference exists between the Paul of Acts and those depicted in Mark 16:18a, because the former does not intend to have any interaction with a snake while the latter do" (411). For more on the symbolism of serpents, and especially the possible connection between Mk 16:18 and Greek mythology (e.g., Dionysian rites), see James H. Charlesworth, *The Good and Evil Serpent: How a Universal Symbol Became Christianized* (New Haven: Yale University Press, 2010), esp. 360.

[207] Kelhoffer shows that the language used to express the action of this sign is the most complex, grammatically, of all the signs enumerated in the LE: κἂν θανάσιμόν τι πίωσιν οὐ μὴ αὐτοὺς βλάψῃ ("and if they should drink any deadly thing, it would certainly not harm them"; 16:18b). Kelhoffer thinks that this "anomalous grammatical formulation" indicates that the LE's author "chose to deviate from the noun-verb parallelism he consistently employed elsewhere throughout the miracle list, in order to express at somewhat greater length his expectation that the faithful will not be harmed if they should drink anything deadly" (ibid., 418-19). First, he noted that the expression does not make explicit whether the believer willingly drank poison or was forced to do so. Second, Kelhoffer wonders why the author of the LE did not use a typical word for poison, but used instead the adjective "deadly" with the indefinite pronoun τι—"something" (419).

[208] Ibid., 420-67.

[209] Ibid., 432.

[210] Kelhoffer summarizes the sources, which date between the first and sixth centuries (ibid., 433), but longer descriptions follow (433-67). He concludes:

> In retrospect, it should be noted that all of the evidence—whether Jewish, Greco-Roman or Christian—concerning poison drinkers in antiquity before the sixth century is *literary* rather than historical. Although Hippolytus offers the Eucharist as a protection for ordinary believers, there is nothing to indicate that his early third-century community intended to drink anything deadly, much less to demonstrate their faith by performing such an act ... As a result, one must conclude that Mark 16:18b, if indeed it bears witness to a community of poison-bibbers, is not corroborated by any other testimony of antiquity. It is far more likely that the author of the [LE] has adapted this motif from one or more earlier traditions and included it in the repertoire of signs that will follow those who believe. (Ibid., 470; emphasis in the original)

poison—moral uprightness, vindication by God, or vindication *of* one's God—but we have no record that any group in antiquity actually drank deadly substances as a practice.

In his quest for historical analogies for understanding the signs that are part of Jesus's commission in the LE, Kelhoffer leaves behind, quite literally, the text of the rest of Mark's Gospel and the century in which it was likely composed. His findings, however, have impacted the way in which scholars have subsequently discussed the signs. Kelhoffer says:

> Despite the fact that the ultimate origin of the signs involving snakes and poison lies beyond a simple explanation, the perceived magnitude of this quandary may implicitly attest more to the surprise of modern scholars that such expressions came to be a part of the NT, than to the likelihood that an ancient person would find these miracles any more or less amazing than speaking in new languages or the performing of exorcisms and healings ... That is to say, if the [LE] had not been written as an appendix to the Gospel of Mark but appeared instead as an independent composition in volumes like W. Schneemelcher's *New Testament Apocrypha* or J. K. Elliot's *Apocryphal New Testament*, it would hardly be surprising to find such surreal deeds predicated of those who believe.[211]

This text, Kelhoffer emphasizes, should not be disconnected from the Gospel it was written to conclude.[212]

In Kelhoffer's opinion, the author of the LE sought to provide Mark with a conclusion that was, first, applicable to his current situation and missionary endeavors and, second, ensured that the "newly-augmented copies of Mark [would] enjoy a lasting reception among future generations of Christians."[213] Kelhoffer explains this second-century addition to the Second Gospel as an attempt to secure a reading of the whole Gospel and to underscore the ongoing efficacy of the "ascended Christ, who both grants miracles to the itinerant preachers, and in so doing actively participates in the mission and expansion of the Christian movement."[214]

Bridget Gilfillan Upton has applied speech-act theory to Mark's endings in a way that accounts for their aural reception in their earliest contexts.[215] How would each of these endings have been heard? To answer this question, she treats the narrative that comes before each of the endings, and not the concluding texts in isolation. In light of

---

[211] Ibid., 479.
[212] On the debate over whether the LE was written specifically to conclude Mark (Kelhoffer's opinion and mine), or whether it was a fragment that came to be attached to the Second Gospel, see ibid., 158–69.
[213] Ibid., 479.
[214] Ibid.
[215] Bridget Gilfillan Upton analyzes the shortest ending (16:8), the longer ending (16:20), and the intermediate ending (affixed to 16:8 in Codex *k*, but usually sandwiched between the shortest and longer in its other appearances). Explaining her aim, Upton states: "The main point of this study has been to argue that an appropriate method for the interpretation of ancient popular texts should incorporate an element of attention to the aural nature of the material, forging a link between ancient and modern readings by the use of rhetorical insights and aspects of communication theory" (*Hearing Mark's Endings*, 196).

the implied audience's hearing of the story, she conjectures which narrative elements might have caused disjuncture, surprise, or satisfaction.[216] She notes how a hearing of Mk 1:1–16:8 might have required significant "work" of an audience.[217] Likewise, the disjuncture between vv. 8 and 9 might have been jarring—especially when followed up by narrative-details contrary to expectations—but ultimately would have been satisfactorily resolved by 16:20.

Upton's explanation regarding her treatment of the "Longer Ending" in light of how it follows from the preceding narrative shares much in common with my approach. She does not treat vv. 9–20 in isolation, but "as part of the whole resurrection story of 16:1–20, and, indeed, as an inherent part of the whole narrative of the gospel, and a conclusion to the passion and resurrection account."[218] Upton's emphasis on the aural setting, which is the foundation of her monograph, leads her to an even more emphatic conclusion that the conventional separation of what is deemed "original" from that which has been in use is anachronistic: "Whichever ending represents the most 'original' or 'authentic' use, they were all used by at least some communities in the early years of the Christian tradition, and despite modern scholarly opinion, the 'longer ending' has been by far the most commonly received conclusion to the gospel in overall terms, eventually becoming part of the textus receptus." Upton divides the text into small episodes (16:9, 10-11, 12-13, 14, 15-18, 19, 20a, 20b)[219] and investigates how the implied audience hears each portion of text successively as intelligible. She notices

---

[216] Upton's treats the "shorter" (in her terms) or "intermediate" ending (as termed by Parker, *Living Text*, 125–7, 137–8) third. Although the text forms the *ending* of Mark in only one codex (see earlier and the Appendix on the Markan endings), a fact that Upton acknowledges (*Hearing Mark's Endings*, 171), she treats it as an ending equivalent to 16:8 or 16:20. This makes her treatment both intriguing and misleading. She interprets the lone codex in which this reading forms the Gospel's conclusion:

> Unlike an audience listening to the ending at 16:8, they do not have to deal with the disobedience and failure of the women; unlike those who heard the ending at 16:20, the momentum of their story is not muted by extraneous detail. This audience ... is left with the security and excitement of a completed story which is, at the same time, undeniably supernatural and personally demanding. (195)

Her treatment is intriguing because, if she is right, the Intermediate Ending of Mark would have asked least of its audience in terms of suspense or discomfort. Her interpretation is misleading because there is very little manuscript evidence that many ancient audiences would have had the aural experience about which Upton theorizes (if any, given the garbled Latin of Codex *k* that one expects would make an oral presentation difficult). This "comfortable" conclusion was not the one that gained prominence.

[217] "This audience, confronted with a suspended ending ... has much to do. Left without the comfort of the series of repetitions [as in Xenophon's *Ephesian Tale*], they must resort to implicature to make the most of the narrative they have heard, which has begun with an announcement of εὐαγγέλιον for the Markan community" (ibid., 152–3).

[218] Ibid., 156.

[219] The divisions are introduced on p. 157 and treated on pp. 157–70 of *Hearing Mark's Endings*. Perhaps Upton's divisions are too small to be useable by any other methodology than the specific one she lays out in her book (81–107). I find Joseph Hug's divisions by temporal indicators ("indications de temps") to flow more naturally from the text: πρῶτον (vv. 9–11), μετά (v. 12–13), ὕστερον (v. 14), [καί (v. 15–16)], and μετά (vv. 19–20; *La Finale de L'Évangile de Marc: Mc 16,9–20* [Paris: J. Gabalda, 1978], 33).

throughout a cluster of words related to the theme of faith, which "are concentrated in a way which can hardly be accidental."[220]

Alongside insightful observations about the text itself,[221] Upton's greatest contribution is her speculation as to the narrative's impact on the implied audience. She suggests regarding the sudden new appearance report in 16:9:

> The actual perlocutionary effect of such an utterance, following so closely the shock of the women's silence, could only be one of bewilderment; … Suddenly the disarray of the women is replaced by an appearance of the risen Jesus, absent except in the words of the νεανίσκος in the first part of the narrative, to a named one of them, who appears to get a belated second chance to remedy her earlier disobedience. Perhaps the fact of her earlier disability offers some sort of excuse for her behavior.[222]

Upton concludes that the implied audience would have been unprepared for the new cluster of appearance narratives, "clustered generally around the theme of unbelieving response."[223] At the same time, she reasons that the verbal ties between 16:2 and 16:9 might have produced echoes such that an audience of practiced listeners[224] could have reconnected the narrative strands.[225]

Upton's insights are particularly pertinent to the present study when she highlights the intersection between audience expectations based on the foregoing Gospel according to Mark and the LE's thematic emphasis on belief. Because the audience knows that discipleship requires faith,[226] the impact of the Eleven's disbelief is strong: "To have Mary's word doubted is bad enough, given her status as the object of Jesus's healing power; to disbelieve the words of the two disciples makes things even worse."[227] Upton notes that discipleship "has been a problem" throughout the Second Gospel.[228] Although the audience might have expected a change in the post-resurrection environment,[229] this recurring disbelief only further establishes the "hierarchy of authority" in the LE: "Neither Mary Magdalene nor yet two of their own number carry sufficient power; only the crucified and risen one can proclaim his own

---

[220] Upton, *Hearing Mark's Endings*, 157.
[221] Between 16:8 and 16:9 Upton has noticed the uneven transition, made "jerkily" (ibid., 158), and that "Mary is introduced [in v. 9] as though she had not already appeared in 15:40, 47 and 16:1, and somehow requires to be identified as one who had been possessed" (159). These are exegetical details I discuss in Chapter 2.
[222] Ibid., 159.
[223] Ibid., 159–60.
[224] I.e., an audience accustomed to receiving information aurally.
[225] Instead of seeing the two time statements of 16:2 and 9 as redundant, Upton suggested they could be forming auditory links to help an audience make sense of the narrative. Both phrases are setting the stage at a similar time, but their two shared terms are πρωΐ and σάββατον (see ibid., 160).
[226] Upton draws on Christopher D. Marshall's term "kerygmatic faith," which entails the trusting acceptance of Jesus's proclamation (*Faith as a Theme in Mark's Narrative* [SNTSMS 64; New York: Cambridge University Press, 1989], 228).
[227] Upton, *Hearing Mark's Endings*, 162. Upton sees a gender hierarchy at work, so disbelief of the two (perhaps both males) is a greater offense than only disbelieving Mary (ibid.)
[228] Ibid., 161.
[229] Ibid.

authenticity."²³⁰ Jesus's ascension reinforces this authority (16:19),²³¹ which underscores the reliability of Jesus throughout Mark.²³² Upton credits a speech-act reading for emphasizing the nature of the text as communication, "drawing attention to the levels of power and authority within the text in a way which would help the implied audience experience the intention of the implied author and respond appropriately."²³³

Upton successfully connects the driving theme of the LE with the Christological perspective of the Gospel as a whole, illustrating the connections with more minor aspects as well, from wording to the expectations of the implied audience. The LE represents, in Upton's perspective, "a much more satisfactory conclusion than the quirky ending at 16:8," and one that the majority of audiences throughout the centuries have encountered.²³⁴

Another recent treatment of Mark that pays close attention to the oral performance of the text in its earliest settings and applies those insights to the endings of Mark is Antoinette Clark Wire's *The Case for Mark Composed in Performance*. This 2011 book does not include specific treatment of the text of the LE (or any of the endings other than 16:8), but Wire's innovative proposal for understanding Mark's composition carries with it implications for the Gospel's alternate endings. Wire offers a sustained case for "Mark as the story of a community told by several favored oral performers rather than the product of a single writer."²³⁵ She sees her model of Markan communal-authorship as offering a realistic way to understand the growth of the Second Gospel's endings:

> Here we need a new multidimensional format to present this gospel in at least three different stages of its development, the short ending in our earlier text, and each longer ending in separate second century renditions of the gospel. The question remains how the extensions were added. They could be forgeries by scribes, either to harmonize the four gospels when they were being copied together, or to address new issues at that time ... But if the gospels were shaped in performance, storytelling would continue after writing and a difficult ending might well generate various adaptations ... The [LE] suggests oral provenance by the way pieces have been added to the short ending seriatim, first brief reports of some appearances of Jesus told in other gospels, then Jesus's rebuke of the disciples for not believing, his instruction to preach, his promise of miracles, and finally a report of proclamation and ascension.

Not only does Wire think this is plausible, given the growth of storytelling traditions (along with the protection of established traditions), but she recognizes an interpretive

---

230 Ibid., 163.
231 Ibid., 169.
232 Upton referred to Jesus as "the totally reliable and authoritative Jesus" throughout his ministry and proclamation, even though he was not believed then as in the resurrection context (ibid., 162–3).
233 Ibid., 170.
234 Ibid.
235 Antoinette Clark Wire, *The Case for Mark Composed in Performance* (Biblical Performance Criticism 3; Eugene, OR: Cascade, 2011), 5.

benefit: "The oral composition thesis can honor both later endings as evolutions of Mark in different second century contexts." Yet she privileges the ending at 16:8: "This must be done in some format which does not obscure the difficult ending at 16:8 that apparently *preceded* and *provoked* them."[236] In Wire's presentation, there need be no erasure of the later expansions of Mark's Gospel in order to privilege the earliest ending; on the contrary, the accumulation of further storytelling testifies to the degree of interest in and reflection upon the hard closure of 16:8.

One further aspect of Wire's work relevant to my study is the favored place it grants women. She asks one of the recurring questions one sees in studies of Mark's endings: "What are we to make of these women?"[237] She notes their named (not anonymous) reappearances at the cross, burial, and tomb. Wire explains: "Many women's stories have been told in Mark, but these are the first women who are primary actors, upon whose witness depends the climax of the tellers' story. The low status of these women on so many indicators does not lead to any explanations or apologies, suggesting that the early tellers may come from the same social milieu."[238] Wire points out the subordination of the testimonies of women witnesses in other Gospel accounts, but not in Mark. In this telling, "the women are the resurrection witnesses," which Wire says "could be proposed as a covert signature of a female author."[239]

I am unsure how anyone could validate Wire's claims about oral and communal authorship definitively. However, she puts forth a helpful proposal that draws on notions of oral performance, while also taking clues from the text itself (such as the repeated naming of women). Her observations lend credence to my proposal to attend carefully to the portrayals of gender in the LE. The interplay of storytelling and expectation—whether narrative or regarding gender stereotypes—surely shaped the hearing, and possibly the telling, of these endings.

5. Conclusion

Much of the work surveyed in this chapter answers, in multiple ways and with a variety of interests, the same basic question: Is Mk 16:9-20 original to the Gospel? Using the same materials—internal (style and vocabulary; narrative and didactic content) and external criteria (manuscript and patristic attestation)—scholars come to vastly different conclusions. Gathering and analyzing data will never bring agreement on the question of authenticity. Even those who agree that Mk 16:8 was *not* the author's intended conclusion would displace 16:8 for vastly different conclusions: lost endings, nonexistent (interrupted) endings, or even the LE.

My survey highlights the work of those who first proposed particular answers to the "originality question" and contributions since the year 2000, the date of Kelhoffer's thorough literature review. Few major claims or pieces of evidence cited have changed

---

[236] Ibid., 164; italics added. At the same time, Wire argues that the endings representing later evolutions of the text "have no business" being printed in editions that seek the earliest available text (165).
[237] Ibid., 166.
[238] Ibid.
[239] Ibid., 168.

in the arguments during the two-century debate. That is not to say that no progress has been made. Burgon set the terms as an "either/or": either a text is original or it is not canonical. Many have tacitly accepted these two options, thinking that if 16:9-20 is not original to Mark's Gospel, it is of no churchly use. Contemporaries of Burgon, like Tregelles, did not agree with these irreconcilable alternatives. I take it to be progress that recent studies seem to have shied away from both the vitriol and presuppositions about what is original and inspired.[240]

No one has yet presented evidence sufficient to settle the debate over Mark's proper closure. The same evidence some use to support the originality of 16:9-20 is used by others to dispute it. Even those who agree in theory on the earliest retrievable ending of the Gospel According to Mark disagree on the significance of that ending. Well-informed arguments have been made on most sides of this question. Nonetheless, the scores of opinions Mark's readers have voiced have largely addressed a single question. From Burgon to Croy, Aland to Williams, attention to the LE has been *mainly* focused on whether or not it was written by the Evangelist to conclude the Second Gospel.

The standard questions asked of the LE and elaborated in this selective *Forschungsbericht* are preliminary to understanding anything the LE *does* as a conclusion to Mark. It is important to take account of these approaches to the endings. For instance, I understand 16:9-20 to be a later (second-century) addition to Mark's Gospel, written by an author with a penchant for harmonization and with the intention of providing a conclusion fitting for this particular Gospel. It seems likely that he utilized narrative resources of other written traditions that were becoming proto-canonical, even solidifying their authoritative position by including them in Mark's LE.

In the midst of the scholarly fixation on originality, however, the questions of what the LE *does to, for, and with* Mark remain wide open and largely ignored. Typically, these issues have been raised with regard to the Markan ending at 16:8. How does this shortest ending bring conclusion to and reflect the nature of the preceding Gospel? This approach interprets Mark's Gospel and its abrupt conclusion in a mutually illuminating light. There remains much work in assessing how Mk 16:9-20 functions differently to conclude Mark, opening an alternative interpretive window into the Gospel as whole. Kelhoffer, Upton, and Wire have made measurable advances in providing historical context and methodology, encouraging interpreters to ask more theologically and narratively probing questions.

My study of the resurrection encounters found in Mk 16:9-20 cannot encompass all of the work yet to be done on this text. I attempt to highlight previously ignored details of characterization, engagement with gender-stereotype expectations, and thematic ties to the Gospel according to Mark in its entirety. This approach allows me to set aside questions of inspiration and "the ideal text" in favor of examining one of the actual textual configurations that Christians heard and read for centuries. On a theoretical level, the equation of authorial authenticity and canonical function seems

---

[240] Some text critics have reassessed the entire notion of "originality." Epp and Parker, in particular, reframe the goals and possibilities of the discipline in ways that may move the LE-question beyond the "in or out" alternatives. See Epp, "Multivalence," and Parker, *Living Text*, as well as further discussion in Chapter 4 (section 2).

arbitrary. With Tregelles, I find it unnecessarily restrictive to foreswear interpretation of this early Christian appendix simply because it comes from a later hand than that of the larger Gospel According to Mark.[241] It is not inappropriate to ask what the LE *does* as an ending of Mark. And one can do so without rejecting the literary and theological beauty of the ending at 16:8.

Whether or not it should be where it is, we find the LE even in our most up-to-date English translations. But it is usually disguised and disfigured by brackets and annotations, affixed to the ending of an already confounding Gospel. Verse 9 begins with a resurrection appearance, *the first*, the text insists, to a lone woman: Mary Magdalene. And whether it is original or not, drawn from other sources or not, we must pause to ask, "Why should it start with her?"

---

[241] The closest comparable passage (based on length and attestation) is the *Pericope Adulterae* found in John (usually 7:51–8:11). The account of Jesus's interaction with a woman accused of adultery has the added complication of being found in different textual contexts in John within the manuscript tradition. This story has been the object of much interest and interpretive imagination despite its uncertain originality.

2

Mary Magdalene in the Long Ending and Mark

In Mk 16:1-8 Mary Magdalene, Mary the mother of James, and Salome are at the tomb at daybreak on Sunday morning.¹ To this company there is the surprising addition of a young man as messenger at the empty tomb (v. 5). He communicates the news of Jesus's resurrection, to which the women respond in fear, trembling, flight, and silence (v. 8). Although scholars disagree whether this silence was obedient or disobedient²— that is, constitutive of success or failure on the part of the women—ancient readers clearly found it incomplete.³

The Long Ending (hereafter LE) that was added to the earliest ending at 16:8 is at once a Gospel harmony and an innovation. In many aspects, it integrates and confirms resurrection appearances known from other canonical Gospels. In other respects, like the descriptions of signs demonstrating belief (16:17-18), the LE is recognized as innovative among other Gospel endings. One element, comprised of elements new and old, that has been underappreciated by interpreters is Mary Magdalene's believing the proclamation of Jesus's resurrection.

---

[1] Mark 16:1 states the time as διαγενομένου τοῦ σαββάτου, or "after the Sabbath was past." Verse 2 specifies: καὶ λίαν πρωῒ τῇ μιᾷ τῶν σαββάτων ἔρχονται ἐπὶ τὸ μνημεῖον ἀνατείλαντος τοῦ ἡλίου; i.e., "And they came to the tomb early in the morning on the first day of the week, after the sun was risen." The "after" is implicit in the aorist, adverbial participle, taken temporally; it is not explicitly stated.

[2] See Chapter 1 for more evaluations of the women's reported silence in 16:8. Hisako Kinukawa's summary of the traditional debate and feminist approaches to the question is helpful (*Women and Jesus in Mark: A Japanese Feminist Perspective* [Maryknoll, NY: Orbis, 1994], 112–19). Recently, Larry Hurtado has argued anew for a positive reading of the women's silence (Larry W. Hurtado, "The Women, the Tomb, and the Climax of Mark," in *A Wandering Galilean: Essays in Honor of Seán Freyne* [ed. Zuleika Rodgers; JSJSup 132; Boston: Brill, 2009], 438–43). On the other hand, many authors who regard the women's actions as a collective failure understand nonetheless that this failure is an appropriate ending—or, more emphatically, the only right sort of ending—for Mark's Gospel (Donald Harrisville Juel, "A Disquieting Silence: The Matter of the Ending," in *The Ending of Mark and the Ends of God: Essays in Memory of Donald Harrisville Juel* [ed. Beverly Roberts Gaventa and Patrick D. Miller; Louisville: Westminster John Knox, 2005], 1–13).

[3] The multiple conclusions to Mark's Gospel that sprang up, as evidenced by the ms. tradition, illustrate the perceived need for a conclusion beyond 16:8. The preponderance of manuscript attestation to the Long Ending (abbreviated as "LE" throughout), in particular, 16:9-20 (without the Intermediate Ending or the Freer Logion), suggests that this ending was widely perceived as the most satisfactory. The slight possibility that this outnumbering is merely an accident of preservation on a wide scale is unlikely. In this way, while *one* ancient reader of Mark may have penned the ending, *many readers* over many centuries supported the coda by copying Mark with it firmly affixed.

This chapter seeks to focus on what others have overlooked: Mary's role as the first, reliable, and paradigmatic witness in the LE. First, we shall focus on Mary's witness to Jesus within its immediate context in Mk 16:9-20 and in the preceding verses in Mark to which the LE was appended. Second, a comparison with other Gospel endings will demonstrate that Mary's role in Mk 16:9-20 introduces some unique emphases among other resurrection accounts. Finally, we shall see how Mary's discipleship in 16:9-11, read within the context of the Second Gospel, picks up important narrative threads from Mk 1:1-16:8, in which women's actions demonstrate belief in Jesus. Mary Magdalene's presentation in the LE, simple though it be, is perfectly suited to recall and give finality to aspects of women's faithfulness that arise throughout the undisputed remainder of Mark's Gospel.

Mark 16:9-20 progresses with the following narrative sections[4]: First, the risen Christ appears to Mary Magdalene, and she reports the encounter to the disciples, but they do not believe (16:9-11); second, a subsequent resurrection appearance to two unnamed disciples while they are walking is reported to the disciples, who again do not believe (16:12-13); third, Jesus appears to the Eleven, upbraids them for their disbelief (16:14), and commissions them to go and proclaim the good news, describing the signs that accompany belief (16:15-18); fourth, Jesus ascends into heaven, and the believers preach worldwide (16:19-20).

The episode recounted in Mk 16:9-11 is far from elaborate. In fact, the entirety of Mary Magdalene's role in the appendix to Mark's Gospel is contained in just two verses, consisting of only twenty-five words. Verse 11, the final verse that refers to Mary, describes only the disciples' response to her message, rather than any actions or statements on her part. The prose is spare and matter-of-fact. Mary displays nothing of the pathos she exudes in John's account (20:11-18). Perhaps this bare-bones narrative is partly responsible for scholarly inattention. In comparison to the sensational signs (snake-handling, demon-busting, poison-guzzling) that follow, the story of Mary Magdalene's encounter with the risen Jesus in Mark's LE seems derivative and uninteresting.

Yet the fact that Mary Magdalene reappears in the narrative expansion *at all* suggests that her role is more than perfunctory. Her final act in the Gospel could have been that described at the tomb in Mk 16:1-8. Peter and John could have run onto the scene to save the day (reminiscent of Jn 20:3-10). Jesus could have performed a monologue instructing believers on scriptural prophecies concerning him (expanding on Lk. 24:25-27). Yet the text added to "complete" Mark's Gospel starts with Mary Magdalene. She is the initial witness to the risen Jesus, highlighted in her role as first, obedient, and—I will eventually argue—faithful.

---

[4] These sections agree with the paragraph divisions in the NA[28]. I surmise that its editors have, like this author, ascertained the logical breaks in the passage based not only on sense, but also on the instances of transitional particles δὲ and μὲν. The third and longest portion, vv. 14-18, may be subdivided between criticism and commission by the conjunction καί, which marks a slight transition at the start of v. 15. While there is a change in tone, a transition from indirect to direct speech, as well as a divide between assessment of past actions and a command for future actions, vv. 14-18 together contain the risen Jesus's communication to the Eleven and, therefore, are best viewed together. See Appendix on the Markan endings.

1. Mary Magdalene's Role in Mk 16:9-14

This exegetical section aims to take note of Mary Magdalene's positive characterization within a narrow textual context, with only occasional comparisons to the broader Markan narrative. From its beginning the LE's placement in time is completely without reference to the preceding episode.[5] Instead, the timing is oriented to the participle relating Jesus's resurrection (ἀναστάς), the first word in 16:9. It is "after he arose," early on the first day of the week, that he appeared to Mary Magdalene. Verse 9 provides no apologies or explanation for the fearfulness of Mary and her companions just one verse earlier. Instead, it highlights the singular position of Mary as the witness to Jesus's *first* (πρῶτον) appearance after he rose. The entrance of the resurrected Jesus (v. 9) confirms the young man's statement of 16:6; Jesus's later appearance to the Eleven fulfills the expectation set up in 16:7. But between the resurrection and Jesus's appearance to the Eleven, there are two other encounters with the risen Christ. The LE narrative lists Jesus's appearance to Mary first among three total encounters with the risen Jesus. The supplemental description πρῶτος, however, indicates that the order is more than mere happenstance: Jesus appears to her *first*. It is as if the women's flight and silence of 16:8 must be set right before anything else can be.

More of Mary's personal history with Jesus becomes clear in the further description of her: "from whom [Jesus] had cast out seven demons" (v. 9). It is not unheard of within the Gospels for recipients of Jesus's healings or exorcisms to seek to follow Jesus (e.g., the man who had been possessed by the "Legion" of demons in Mk 5:18). In Mark's account the recipients of healing or exorcism are commonly silenced or rebuffed (the exception being formerly blind Bartimaeus: 10:52). Within Mark, however, there is no identifying information regarding the larger band of followers who accompanied Jesus, beyond the Twelve whom he "made" (ἐποίησεν δώδεκα) and named apostles (3:13-19). There are clear signals that Jesus's companions included more than twelve (e.g., 4:10; 10:32). Nevertheless, after Jesus's crucifixion, Mk 15:40 constitutes the first indication that there were women among the disciples' number. At that point, we read three female followers' names—Mary Magdalene, Mary the mother of James the small and Joses, and Salome—but no descriptions of their previous lives. These three are among a larger company of women who have come all the way from Galilee, where they followed Jesus and ministered to him (15:41), yet readers are left ignorant of their identities beyond accompanying Jesus. It is in the LE that the reader gains a backstory that makes sense of why Mary Magdalene might have been the most tenacious of the disciples: seven demons had formerly plagued her but were cast out by Jesus. The reader can assume that her discipleship resulted from the exorcism, taking her from Galilee to Judea, to the cross, and finally to the tomb, keeping close to the one who had freed her from diabolical forces.

The details of Mary's encounter with the resurrected Jesus are not narrated. We read that "he appeared" (ἐφάνη) to her. There is no specification of what Jesus says, no record of their conversation, or whether she is directed to do what follows. This is a

---

[5] See section 2.1 for more discussion of the timing of the resurrection appearance to Mary Magdalene.

significant omission, as the risen Jesus commissions verbally the reluctant Eleven (vv. 14-15) before they spread the news. Yet Mary Magdalene goes and tells without narrated prompting. These two verbs, πορεύομαι (as an aorist participle, πορευθεῖσα) and ἀπαγγέλλω, comprise Mary's active participation as a witness to Jesus's resurrection. The command she heard from the young man at the tomb in 16:7 was to go (ὑπάγετε) and tell (εἴπατε) Jesus's disciples. Whereas in 16:8 she fled and remained silent along with her two companions, in 16:10 Mary goes and announces the news to "those who had been with him" (τοῖς μετ' αὐτοῦ γενομένοις).[6] The verb pairs are parallels between v. 7 and v. 10: the first verb in each pair denotes travel (ὑπάγω and πορεύομαι), while the second verb pertains to expression (λέγω and ἀπαγγέλω). In the LE, Mary does what she and her companions could not in 16:8.

"And those did not believe" (κἀκεῖνοι ... ἠπίστησαν) is the primary subject-verb pair in v. 11. Those "who had been with him," the recipients of Mary's message in v. 10, reject its validity. This verse, however, contains a summary of the content of Mary's message: ὅτι ζῇ καὶ ἐθεάθη ὑπ' αὐτῆς (that he is living and he was seen by her). Of course, this is not new information. On a literary level, Mark's earliest ending has already informed readers that Jesus is alive, for *he was raised* (ἠγέρθη; 16:6). The LE has already reasserted that reality in v. 9 (ἀναστάς). The narrative reaffirms Mary's status as an eyewitness with the passive verb "he was seen," modified with the prepositional phrase "by her" (ὑπ' αὐτῆς).

In its most immediate context, within the twelve verses of the Markan appendix, Mary's role is not expansive. Yet it is arguably central. She occupies a primary position as the first to whom the risen Jesus appears (cf. 1 Cor. 15:5). Mary's willing proclamation of Jesus's resurrection stands in contrast to the male disciples' disbelief. Moreover, as the LE continues, her role as a faithful witness is reinforced by Jesus's reproof of the Eleven, who are blamed for disbelieving those who had seen Jesus alive (16:14). Jesus's accusation does not target a general spirit of skepticism toward the theoretical possibility of resurrection, nor the fact of his own resurrection (a conundrum which would have been solved by his appearance). Instead, Jesus blames the disciples for disbelieving the human witnesses to that resurrection (τοῖς θεασαμένοις αὐτὸν ἐγηγερμένον). In other words, Jesus defends Mary's reliability at the expense of his closest remaining associates, the Eleven (ἕνδεκα).

2. Mary Magdalene's Place in Resurrection Narratives: The Long Ending's Derivation and Innovation

Thematically and in terms of plot movement, the constituent portions of the LE's story exhibit similarities to the endings of Matthew, Luke, and John. Several elements, especially the resurrected Jesus's appearance "in a different form" to the two disciples

---

[6] This phrase may echo their calling *that they might be with him* (ἵνα ὦσιν μετ' αὐτοῦ) in Mk 3:14. This group of Jesus's companions is further described as "mourning and weeping" (πενθοῦσι καὶ κλαίουσιν). These and other details that may point to the Eleven's failure to fulfill their call as disciples will not escape notice in Chapters 3 and 4 of this study.

as they were walking into the countryside (Mk 16:12-13) and the ascension (16:19), seem to be vague summaries of material we know from Luke (24:13-33a, 51). Mary Magdalene's position as the only woman—and first person—to whom Jesus appears after his resurrection resembles her singular role in John's account (20:1-2, 11-18), albeit brief by comparison. The commission functions similarly to Matthew's Great Commission (28:19-20), although the content of the commands differs (Mk 16:15-18). In the midst of this apparent incorporation of widespread gospel traditions, several of the signs the LE expects to demonstrate belief—snake-handling and poison-drinking—are fantastic enough to divert attention paid to the account away from the more familiar elements.

Despite the apparent similarities to existing Gospels, ascertaining the dependence of the LE's words or phrases on known traditions has notoriously stymied scholars.[7] The diction of the ending demonstrates degrees of independence from Matthew, Luke, and John; that ending also alters familiar plot lines. Exorcism, speaking in new languages, holding snakes, and imbibing deadly liquids are certainly the chief examples of novel additions.[8] Nonetheless, throughout the twelve-verse addition to Mark's Gospel, the story is told with new twists and unique elements that cannot be attributed in full to any extant Gospel ending (see Table 2.1).[9]

This section will proceed through the LE's brief narrative about Jesus's resurrection appearance to Mary Magdalene, making *redaction-critical* observations regarding the passage's relation to other extant accounts. This approach is most suited to this exegetical endeavor, as it is apparent that the author of the LE wrote with an eye to existing canonical traditions, likely already gathered into a proto-canonical, Four Gospel collection.[10] I will seek out the similarities and differences between the LE's depiction of Mary Magdalene's role after Jesus was raised with other existing resurrection narratives. Because the LE was almost certainly written later than the four canonical

---

[7] See Chapter 1 of this study and Kelhoffer, *Miracle and Mission*, 48–156.

[8] This list of signs is novel in the sense of its collection as commissioned activities for followers and, moreover, as demonstrations of faith. Several of the signs listed in Mk 16:17-18 have extensive precedents in the NT: e.g., exorcism (cf. Mk 6:7, 13); speaking in tongues (only here in the Gospels, but cf. Acts 2:4-13; 1 Cor. 12:10, 30); and healing the sick (by laying on of hands: cf. Mk 1:41; 6:5; 8:25). Snake-handling is far less common but not entirely unique (cf. treading on snakes and scorpions in Lk. 10:19; cf. also Acts 28:3-6). There is no analogy to drinking deadly liquids in the NT; Kelhoffer finds the closest OT parallel in Num. 5:11-31 (the "water of testing"). Kelhoffer's chapter on "Drinking a Deadly Substance with Impunity (Mark 16:18b)" examines Greco-Roman, Jewish, and Early Christian depictions of poison, the latter of which highlights some of the *Wirkungsgeschichte* of Mk 16:18b in the circulated story of Justus Barsabbas (*Miracle and Mission*, 417–63, esp. 441–2). While most of these signs are not "new," their collection is unique. Further, as David Alan Black notes, the expectation that signs will confirm belief is quite novel in the Second Gospel: "Previously in Mark 'signs from heaven' have been regarded askance (8:11-12), as characteristic of false prophets who would deceive God's elect (13:22)" (David Alan Black, ed., *Perspectives on the Ending of Mark* [Nashville: Broadman and Holman, 2008], 352).

[9] Discussing the goals of his own project, Kelhoffer observes that "there also remain numerous aspects of this passage that have never been explored" (*Miracle and Mission*, 46).

[10] See ibid., 123. Douglas R. A. Hare suggests that just such a Four-Gospel Canon was the occasion for the LE's authorship, not as a conclusion tailored to Mark, but to wrap up the whole Four-Gospel corpus (*Mark* [Westminster Bible Companion; Louisville: Westminster John Knox, 1996], 227–8). Although I am not persuaded by his proposal, the fact that such can be argued illustrates well the even distribution of Gospel tradition the LE reflects.

Table 2.1 The dependence of the LE on the canonical Gospels and Acts

Verses	Text of Mk 16:9-20		Dependence*	
9	Ἀναστὰς δὲ <u>πρωῒ</u> πρώτῃ <u>σαββάτου</u>	(Mk 16:2)	(πρωῒ τῇ μιᾷ τῶν σαββάτων)	
	ἐφάνη πρῶτον <u>Μαρίᾳ τῇ Μαγδαληνῇ</u>,	Jn 20:1, 11, 14	John's story in which Mary Magdalene is the first to arrive at the tomb and see the Lord.	
	παρ᾽ ἧς ἐκβεβλήκει <u>ἑπτὰ δαιμόνια</u>.	Lk. 8:2b	Μαρία ἡ καλουμένη Μαγδαληνή, ἀφ᾽ ἧς δαιμόνια ἑπτὰ ἐξεληλύθει ...	
10	ἐκείνη πορευθεῖσα <u>ἀπήγγειλεν τοῖς μετ᾽ αὐτοῦ γενομένοις</u>	Mt. 28:8;	... ἔδραμον ἀπαγγεῖλαι τοῖς μαθηταῖς αὐτοῦ.	
		Lk. 24:9;	... ἀπήγγειλαν ταῦτα πάντα τοῖς ἕνδεκα καὶ πᾶσιν τοῖς λοιποῖς	
		Jn 20:18	ἔρχεται Μαριὰμ ἡ Μαγδαληνὴ ἀγγέλλουσα τοῖς μαθηταῖς ὅτι ἑώρακα τὸν κύριον, καὶ ταῦτα εἶπεν αὐτῇ.	
	πενθοῦσι καὶ κλαίουσιν·	–	[Mary's crying is mentioned thrice in Jn 20:11 and 13, but the disciples are not so described other than in the LE.]	
11	κἀκεῖνοι ἀκούσαντες ὅτι ζῇ καὶ ἐθεάθη ὑπ᾽ αὐτῆς <u>ἠπίστησαν</u>.	Lk. 24:11	καὶ ἐφάνησαν ἐνώπιον αὐτῶν ὡσεὶ λῆρος τὰ ῥήματα ταῦτα, καὶ ἠπίστουν αὐταῖς.	
12	Μετὰ δὲ ταῦτα <u>δυσὶν</u> ἐξ αὐτῶν περιπατοῦσιν ἐφανερώθη <u>ἐν ἑτέρᾳ μορφῇ πορευομένοις</u> εἰς ἀγρόν·	Lk. 24:13-32	Καὶ ἰδοὺ δύο ἐξ αὐτῶν ἐν αὐτῇ τῇ ἡμέρᾳ ἦσαν πορευόμενοι εἰς κώμην ἀπέχουσαν σταδίους ἑξήκοντα ἀπὸ Ἰερουσαλήμ, ᾗ ὄνομα Ἐμμαοῦς ...	
13	κἀκεῖνοι ἀπελθόντες ἀπήγγειλαν τοῖς λοιποῖς·	Lk. 24:33-35	Καὶ ἀναστάντες αὐτῇ τῇ ὥρᾳ ὑπέστρεψαν εἰς Ἰερουσαλὴμ καὶ εὗρον ἠθροισμένους τοὺς ἕνδεκα καὶ τοὺς σὺν αὐτοῖς ...	
	οὐδὲ ἐκείνοις ἐπίστευσαν.	–		
14	Ὕστερον δὲ ἀνακειμένοις αὐτοῖς <u>τοῖς ἕνδεκα</u> ἐφανερώθη	Mt. 28:16-17;	Οἱ δὲ ἕνδεκα μαθηταὶ [in Galilee]	
		Lk. 24:9, 24:33	τοῖς ἕνδεκα [and others, hear women's news] τοὺς ἕνδεκα [and others, in Jerusalem]	
		Acts 1:26, 2:14	τῶν ἕνδεκα ἀποστόλων [appt. of Matthias] ὁ Πέτρος σὺν τοῖς ἕνδεκα ...	
	καὶ ὠνείδισεν τὴν ἀπιστίαν αὐτῶν καὶ σκληροκαρδίαν ὅτι τοῖς θεασαμένοις αὐτὸν ἐγηγερμένον οὐκ ἐπίστευσαν.	–	Even of "doubting" Thomas in Jn 20:24-29 there is no rebuke from Jesus, much less to the scale as it is here against the Eleven.	
15	καὶ εἶπεν αὐτοῖς· πορευθέντες εἰς <u>τὸν κόσμον ἅπαντα κηρύξατε</u> τὸ εὐαγγέλιον <u>πάσῃ τῇ κτίσει</u>.	Mt. 28:19	πορευθέντες οὖν μαθητεύσατε πάντα τὰ ἔθνη	
		Lk. 24:47	καὶ κηρυχθῆναι ἐπὶ τῷ ὀνόματι αὐτοῦ μετάνοιαν εἰς ἄφεσιν ἁμαρτιῶν εἰς πάντα τὰ ἔθνη.	
16	ὁ πιστεύσας καὶ βαπτισθεὶς σωθήσεται,	–	Matthew 28:19 contains the baptismal formula as part of the commission, still this pronouncement is unique.	

	ὁ δὲ <u>ἀπιστήσας</u> <u>κατακριθήσεται</u>.	Jn 3:18b	… ὁ δὲ μὴ πιστεύων ἤδη κέκριται …
17	σημεῖα δὲ τοῖς πιστεύσασιν ταῦτα παρακολουθήσει·	–	Potential connection to Jn 14:12.
	ἐν τῷ ὀνόματί μου δαιμόνια ἐκβαλοῦσιν,	(Mk 6:13)	(καὶ δαιμόνια πολλὰ ἐξέβαλλον)
		(9:38)	(διδάσκαλε, εἴδομέν τινα ἐν τῷ ὀνόματί σου ἐκβάλλοντα δαιμόνια …)
	γλώσσαις λαλήσουσιν καιναῖς,	Acts 2:4, 11	ἤρξαντο λαλεῖν ἑτέραις γλώσσαις …
18	καὶ ἐν ταῖς χερσὶν ὄφεις ἀροῦσιν κἂν θανάσιμόν τι πίωσιν οὐ μὴ αὐτοὺς βλάψῃ,	–	
	ἐπὶ ἀρρώστους χεῖρας ἐπιθήσουσιν καὶ καλῶς ἕξουσιν.	(Mk 6:5)	(εἰ μὴ ὀλίγοις ἀρρώστοις ἐπιθεὶς τὰς χεῖρας ἐθεράπευσεν) [of Jesus]
19	Ὁ μὲν οὖν κύριος Ἰησοῦς μετὰ τὸ λαλῆσαι αὐτοῖς <u>ἀνελήμφθη εἰς τὸν οὐρανὸν</u>	Lk. 24:51	… ἀνεφέρετο εἰς τὸν οὐρανόν …
		Acts 1:2, 11, 22	ἀνελήμφθη …; οὗτος ὁ Ἰησοῦς ὁ ἀναλημφθεὶς ἀφ' ὑμῶν εἰς τὸν οὐρανὸν …; ἀνελήμφθη ἀφ' ἡμῶν
	καὶ <u>ἐκάθισεν ἐκ δεξιῶν τοῦ θεοῦ</u>.	(Mk 14:62)	(καὶ ὄψεσθε τὸν υἱὸν τοῦ ἀνθρώπου ἐκ δεξιῶν καθήμενον τῆς δυνάμεως …)
		Lk. 22:69	… καθήμενος ἐκ δεξιῶν τῆς δυνάμεως τοῦ θεοῦ.
		Acts 7:55-56	…Ἰησοῦν ἑστῶτα ἐκ δεξιῶν τοῦ θεοῦ [Stephen's speech]
20	ἐκεῖνοι δὲ ἐξελθόντες ἐκήρυξαν πανταχοῦ, τοῦ κυρίου συνεργοῦντος καὶ τὸν λόγον βεβαιοῦντος διὰ τῶν ἐπακολουθούντων σημείων.	–	

* In determining the dependence of Mk 16:9-20 on the other canonical gospels and Acts, I was helped by James A. Kelhoffer's discussion (*Miracle and Mission: The Authentication of Missionaries and Their Message in the Longer Ending of Mark* [Tübingen: Mohr Siebeck, 2000], 121–2). I did not rely on his decisions in many instances, as he is concerned with determining (or speculating upon) vocabulary dependence by the LE's author down to specific words (sometimes as simple as ἐκείνη [71–2] or μετὰ δὲ ταῦτα [84–5]). I preferred identifying *content* with a resemblance, rather than isolated terms. Comments and negative parallels (i.e., lack of comparison, connoting uniqueness) are my own.

Gospels, its use of related traditions is likely derivative of them.[11] Investigating the mode of derivation will not concern us; instead, I will seek out the observable themes

---

[11] For the debate between oral and literary dependence, see Kelhoffer, *Miracle and Mission*, 48–122. Minority positions that argue for a second-century date for both John and Luke complicate this assumption. On John (and the use of P[52] in dating), see Brent Nongbri, "The Use and Abuse of P[52]: Papyrological Pitfalls in the Dating of the Fourth Gospel," *HTR* 98 (2005): 23–48; on Luke, see Richard I. Pervo, *Dating Acts: Between the Evangelists and the Apologists* (Santa Rosa, CA: Polebridge Press, 2006), 340–1. Dating ancient manuscripts has indeed been a subjective "science," as Nongbri's most recent work illustrates: *God's Library: The Archaeology of the Earliest Christian Manuscripts* (New Haven: Yale University Press, 2018), 247–68.

and emphases in the ways the LE author has described Mary Magdalene as a witness to the resurrection. The aim is to understand the significance of those new and repeated details as a contribution to an already existing body of resurrection testimonies.

2.1 Mary Magdalene Is Alone

While the LE apparently seeks to repair the abrupt Markan ending at 16:8, it does so in a way that does not disguise the uneven seam. Only one verse separates the three women's apparent failure to tell of Jesus's resurrection and the conveyance of that news by one of those women, Mary Magdalene, to "those who had been with him" (16:10). In manuscripts that conclude Mark with the LE—that is, the majority of extant manuscripts[12]—the previous ending at 16:8 is left entirely unmodified.[13]

Further, instead of making clear that 16:9 begins a new episode, subsequent to 16:1-8, vv. 9-11 point to a time simultaneous with that of the previous episode. Within the narrative flow there is a restatement of the timing of the story: "After he was raised in the morning on the first day of the week." Oriented to the participle ἀναστάς, the time hinges on Jesus's resurrection.[14]

Another disorienting result of the scene-change is a character shift. Suddenly, where there were three women, there is now only one. Mary Magdalene is at center stage. And instead of being addressed by an unnamed young man, she is met by the risen Lord. Timing and characters pose problems for coordinating verses 8 and 9. The statement of the place in time is ostensibly the same in 16:1 and 16:9, yet v. 9 demonstrates progression on Mary's part. The surprise and fear of the women must logically precede the epiphany of Jesus to Mary Magdalene. Both the discovery of the empty tomb and the appearance of the resurrected Jesus must be "after he was raised," although

---

[12] The LE is not found in the important, early codices Vaticanus (B) and Sinaiticus (ℵ), but in 99 percent of the surviving Greek manuscripts and the rest of the tradition (Kurt and Barbara Aland, *The Text of the New Testament* [2d ed.; Erroll F. Rhodes, trans.; Grand Rapids: Eerdmans, 1989], 292). See Adela Yarbro Collins, *Mark* (Hermeneia; Minneapolis: Fortress, 2007), 802–7; D. C. Parker, *The Living Text of the Gospels* (New York: Cambridge University Press, 1997), 124–47.

[13] In the vast majority of extant manuscripts, v. 9 continues immediately from v. 8 with only a slight interruption by the mild adversative particle δὲ (in postpositive position).

[14] The wording is somewhat repetitive, using the πρωΐ of v. 2. The day of the week is again mentioned but modified in vocabulary and grammar to πρώτῃ σαββάτου, which is unlike the usual form, attested across the Four-Gospel Canon, in which the day is denoted by the number, μία, and the term for *week* is declined in the plural: τῇ μιᾷ τῶν σαββάτων (Mk 16:2; Lk. 24:1; Jn 20:1), or slightly abbreviated, μίαν σαββάτων (Mt. 28:1). The description of the early hour of morning varies across the four evangelists' accounts: from Mark's "very early in the morning" (λίαν πρωΐ; 16:2), to "as it began to dawn" in Matthew (τῇ ἐπιφωσκούσῃ; 28:1) or the classical phrase for "early in the morning" used by Luke (ὄρθρου βαθέως; 24:1), to John's "in the morning while it was still dark" (πρωΐ σκοτίας ἔτι οὔσης; 20:1). With the noteworthy exception of 16:9, the mode of expression for the day of the week remains unchanged, allowing for Matthew's exclusion of the article and use of μία in the accusative. Kelhoffer argues that the LE's expression is an improvement on the tradition: "The LE's formulation ... is best understood as a deliberate attempt to achieve agreement with Mark's timing while improving his wording" (*Miracle and Mission*, 68). If it is an improvement, it is unexpected that among the many modifications of the expression of the resurrection traditions (e.g., the analysis of Mt. 27:55-56 in Ulrich Luz, *Matthew 21–28* [Hermeneia; Minneapolis: Fortress, 2005], 572) none of the other Gospel authors had found such a change necessary. It seems more likely that the expression—πρωΐ πρώτῃ σαββάτου—is modified in the LE precisely because it is meant to add to, but not repeat word-for-word, the already existing Markan ending.

the adverbial participle is used only in v. 9. While it is clear that the women receive news of Jesus's resurrection as they are standing at his tomb, the LE does not specify where Mary Magdalene meets Jesus. Readers trying to make sequential sense of the two conflicting narratives may surmise that Mary's solo encounter took place after or during her flight from the tomb (cf. Mt. 28:8-9). Yet the author of the LE does not take any pains to clarify when, how, or where her two female counterparts abandoned her.[15]

The appearance to Mary by herself finds an analogy in John's account, the only Gospel in which Mary is alone when she encounters her risen Lord (20:11-18). Like the earliest ending of Mark, its Synoptic counterparts depict a group of women coming to the tomb on Easter morning (Mk 16:1; Mt. 28:1; Lk. 24:1, 10).[16] Yet, if John 20 is the source for the LE account, it has been whittled down so starkly as to be barely recognizable. Even the one-verse summary that concludes the Johannine episode, in which Mary conveys Jesus's words to the disciples, contains more explicit narrative detail (e.g., direct quotation) than does Mk 16:9-11. Within the canonical Gospels, however, Mark's LE corroborates an otherwise unique detail in John, a one-on-one encounter between Mary Magdalene and the resurrected Jesus.

2.2 Mary Magdalene Is First

As discussed in the preceding exegetical section, the LE recapitulates for Mary Magdalene the opportunity to proclaim Jesus's resurrection. Not only is she listed alone, but her singularity and significance are also underscored by the added detail that Jesus appeared to her *first* (πρῶτον) after he was raised. Linguistically, the term πρῶτος does not carry an inherent significance and can simply refer to ordinal position.[17] Frequently in the NT (as in English usage), however, the item or person

---

[15] On the other hand, the Intermediate Ending (often called the "Short Ending"), which functioned in the manuscript tradition as a connector between 16:8 and 16:9, ostensibly corrects the seeming failure of the women from 16:8 by saying, "But they [the women] proclaimed briefly all that they were commanded to those around Peter." This makes clear that the summary conclusion takes place subsequent to the women's fear and silence. Their "failure" was merely "step one" in their eventual success as messengers. This summary closing is more properly called the "Intermediate Ending," because it connects 16:8 to 16:9-20 whenever it is attested (including four uncial Greek manuscripts of the seventh, eighth, and ninth centuries, L Ψ 099 0112). There is one exception: the Intermediate Ending is found on its own in the Old Latin Codex Bobbiensis (k) of the fourth/fifth century. Bruce M. Metzger translates the brief summary (with "trifling variations"): "But they reported briefly to Peter and those with him all that they had been told. And after these things Jesus himself sent out through them, from east to west, the sacred and imperishable proclamation of eternal salvation" (*A Textual Commentary on the Greek New Testament* [2d ed.; Stuttgart: Deutsche Bibelgesellschaft, 1994], 103). See the Appendix on the Markan endings.

[16] It is, thus, that in Matthew's account of Jesus's resurrection appearances that Jesus greets a small group of women, who worship him (28:9-10). In Luke's account, the women do not see Jesus but receive and successfully convey the message from the angels (24:8-9), which is not well received (24:11).

[17] E.g., Paul Allen Mirecki sees the term πρῶτον in 16:9 as a chronological indicator of time, functioning similarly to μετὰ δὲ ταῦτα and ὕστερον δὲ (16:12, 14) in the next two narrative movements ("Mark 16:9–20: Composition, Tradition and Redaction" [ThD diss., Harvard 1986], 26, 109). It is at least that but may be explained alternatively. Joseph Hug sees the chronological terms πρῶτον, μετὰ δὲ ταῦτα, and ὕστερον as redactional markers, helping to organize narrative material: "En résumé, les indications de temps dans la Mc ne sont pas des données établissant une chronologie des apparitions

that is ordinally *first* denotes a special priority.[18] For example, when the Twelve are listed in Matthew's Gospel, Peter is not merely placed first (10:2-4). Instead, Matthew designates as explicitly *first* Simon who is called Peter (πρῶτος Σίμων ὁ λεγόμενος Πέτρος), the disciple who undoubtedly holds a special place in the First Evangelist's outlook.[19]

Not only do John 20 and Mark's LE agree that Mary has a solitary encounter with the risen Lord,[20] significantly, both texts tell the story in a way that presents Mary Magdalene as the first witness to Jesus's resurrection.[21] Despite that, John never uses πρῶτος to refer to Mary, even though in the flow of the narrative of Jn 20:1-18 it seems that Mary arrives first at the tomb (20:1)[22] and is certainly the first to see Jesus (20:14-17). Instead, when πρῶτος *is* used in John (20:4, 8), it is to distinguish between the two male disciples, Simon Peter and "the other disciple" (ὁ ἄλλος μαθητὴς). The latter is "first" (πρῶτος) to reach the tomb in their race (20:4) and, although he enters after Peter,[23] he is remembered as the disciple who arrived "first" (πρῶτος) when he ducks into the empty tomb, sees, and believes (20:8).

In John's account Mary Magdalene stands in stark contrast to the "other" or "first" disciple, who, seeing an empty tomb and separated linens, believes (20:8). Mary Magdalene does not demonstrate anything like immediate faith when she sees Jesus himself. In fact, according to John, she does not even recognize Jesus and confuses him

---

et du départ de Jésus. Elles servent avant tout de supports à la composition du texte" (*La Finale de l'Evangile de Marc* [Paris: J. Gabalda, 1978], 53).

[18] Although πρῶτον clearly functions as a transition, its significance may be more than merely moving the story along. Order, or priority, is not a value-neutral concept in the Gospels. The frequently recurring phrase, "The first shall be last and the last first" (Mk 10:31; Mt. 19:30; 20:16; Lk. 13:30), imputes eschatological significance to such a sequence. In commands, the most vital action is to be done *first*/πρῶτος (e.g., Mt. 5:24; 6:33; 7:5; Mk 7:27; Lk. 14:28, 31; 15:22). Another use of the term πρῶτος by Paul in 1 Corinthians may demonstrate both ordinal significance as well as priority: Καὶ οὓς μὲν ἔθετο ὁ θεὸς ἐν τῇ ἐκκλησίᾳ πρῶτον ἀποστόλους, δεύτερον προφήτας, τρίτον διδασκάλους ... (1 Cor. 12:28). Yet the *first* is not universally a preferable position: e.g., in the Parable of the Wheat and the Tares, the weeds are to be gathered first (συλλέξατε πρῶτον τὰ ζιζάνια; Mt. 13:30) and thrown into the fire to be burned. Nevertheless, the expectation is that those in the *first* position are privileged (such is the scandal of the Parable of the Laborers in the vineyard, when the first are treated identically to the last; cf. Mt. 20:10).

[19] Although Peter is the most commonly named disciple in each of the four Gospels, he receives additional attention in Matthew, especially in the episodes of Jesus walking on water (14:22-33) and the confession at Caesarea Philippi (16:13-23; esp. vv. 17-19). It is noteworthy that in the resurrection tradition from which Paul cites in 1 Cor. 15:3-7, Jesus's appearance to Cephas—although before the appearance to the twelve (denoted by the εἶτα)—the term πρῶτον does not occur (καὶ ὅτι ὤφθη Κηφᾷ εἶτα τοῖς δώδεκα; 1 Cor. 15:5).

[20] With Kelhoffer, *Miracle and Mission*, 69.

[21] Scholars have often designated Mary Magdalene as the "first" witness, despite lack of reference to Mark's LE. Thus, Claudia Setzer states: "In two of the Gospels (Matthew and John) Mary Magdalene is the first to see the risen Jesus" ("Excellent Women: Female Witness to the Resurrection," *JBL* 116 [1997]: 260). Matthew's relevance for Setzer's claim is unclear: Mt. 28:9 refers to a general appearance to both women ("[Jesus] met them" [αὐταῖς]), not to Mary "first."

[22] In Jn 20:1 Mary is the only disciple who is named as coming to the tomb. But when she speaks to Peter and the "other disciple," she leaves room for the possibility that others accompanied her by using the first-person plural: "we do not know where they put him" (οὐκ οἴδαμεν ποῦ ἔθηκαν αὐτόν; 20:2).

[23] Even though Peter enters the tomb first, he is described as "Simon Peter, the one who followed after him [the other, 'first' disciple]" (Σίμων Πέτρος ἀκολουθῶν αὐτῷ; 20:6).

for the gardener (20:14-15). In contrast, in Mark's LE, Mary's status as *first* is not due to outrunning another or to any explicit belief,[24] but to being the *first* person to whom the resurrected Jesus appears. The attribution of "first" to Mary is a position bestowed, rather than merited.

2.3 Mary Magdalene Is Named

Mary Magdalene's name appears for the fourth time in the Gospel of Mark once the LE is affixed (16:9; cf. 15:40, 47; 16:1). There are four mentions of her two-part name, Μαρία ἡ Μαγδαληνή, within seventeen verses, which indicates that the LE sustains an interest in this particular woman as an individual after she has been already mentioned three times in the earliest edition of the Gospel.[25] Often when arguing for the significance of what a particular text *does*, interpreters try to imagine what the author *might have done* instead. While conceivable options in narration and omission seem innumerable, textual realities are finite. In the case of the LE, however, there exist two immediate examples of how else the Second Gospel might have ended, rather than how the LE does. Obviously, Mary Magdalene's third appearance in the Markan text (16:1) along with the two other women, which ends in fear and silence (16:8), might have been her last (as in Mark's earliest recoverable ending). Alternatively, the Intermediate Ending[26] demonstrates the possibility of resolving the perceived failure by the women in 16:8 without reference to Mary Magdalene or any other women by name. There, a simple third-person plural verb indicates that "*they* reported [ἐξήγγειλαν] briefly to those with Peter."[27] The "sacred and imperishable message" (τὸ ἱερὸν καὶ ἄφθαρτον κήρυγμα)[28] goes forth with no express mention of the women who first conveyed the news.

Luke's Gospel, however, affords another possibility. Luke differs from the other Synoptics in that he includes names of several of Jesus's female followers within the Galilean narrative (8:2-3).[29] In the crucifixion and empty tomb stories, however, the women's names are only cited once they have completed their task, conveying the news from the two men in shimmering clothes (ἄνδρες δύο ... ἐν ἐσθῆτι ἀστραπτούσῃ; 24:4) at the tomb to the disciples (24:10). An anonymous group of women enters the

---

[24] That Mary believes and is faithful—both being aspects of πιστεύω—is implicit in the LE, which will be discussed in Chapter 3.

[25] It is noteworthy that, although Mary Magdalene occupies more narrative space in Jn 20:1-2, 11-18 than in Mk 16:9-11, she is only named twice in John and present in two episodes (the aforementioned and 19:25). It is impossible to quantify whether the narrative space in which Mary Magdalene is included in Mark (15:40-41, 47; 16:1-8, 9-11) makes her more or less significant to Mark's Gospel than she is to John's. In both she is an individual of significant interest, but this interest is expressed in different ways. In Mark 15–16, the presence of other Marys in the same stories may account for the repetition of her full name in the interest of clarifying her presence (rather than or in addition to another Mary's presence).

[26] See the "Intermediate Ending" section in the Appendix on the Markan endings (and n. 16 in this chapter).

[27] It is important to note that this alternative ending stands as a solitary conclusion in only one extant manuscript, *k* (Old Latin Gospel Codex Bobbiensis), from the fourth to fifth century. More often, it is found between 16:8 and the LE. See Appendix.

[28] This quotation comes from the grandiose concluding line to the Intermediate Ending (see Appendix).

[29] See section 2.4 for more discussion of these women from Luke 8.

scene in several key locations of crucifixion (23:27-31, 49), burial (23:55-56), and the empty tomb (24:1-11). Until 24:10, Luke refers to the group of women in various yet unspecific ways: as women who follow and lament (γυναικῶν αἳ ἐκόπτοντο καὶ ἐθρήνουν αὐτόν) Jesus as he goes to the cross (23:27); as "Daughters of Jerusalem" (θυγατέρες Ἰερουσαλήμ) in Jesus's direct address (23:28); as female members of his acquaintance who had followed from Galilee (γυναῖκες αἱ συνακολουθοῦσαι αὐτῷ ἀπὸ τῆς Γαλιλαίας), observing Jesus's crucifixion from a distance (23:49); as female followers from Galilee (αἱ γυναῖκες, αἵτινες ἦσαν συνεληλυθυῖαι ἐκ τῆς Γαλιλαίας αὐτῷ) who observe Jesus's entombment (23:55); finally, by feminine plural participles (φέρουσαι, 24:1; εἰσελθοῦσαι, 24:3; ἐμφόβων, γενομένων, and κλινουσῶν, 24:5; and ὑποστρέψασαι, 24:9) and feminine plural pronouns (αὐτὰς, 24:4, 5; αὐταῖς, 24:4). As this long list of examples indicates, Luke uses many ways to point out the involvement of female disciples without referring to them by name.[30] In fact, once Luke lists three names among those who brought the news to the disciples—Mary Magdalene, Joanna, and Mary of James—these are only *some* among the women to whom Luke refers. To conclude that list, he references "and the rest of the women with them" (καὶ αἱ λοιπαὶ σὺν αὐταῖς, 24:10).

Mark's LE does something different: by referring to Mary Magdalene again by name in 16:9, she is selected out of the three women already highlighted in Mark's concluding verses. This prominence afforded to Mary Magdalene is, however, at the same time a canonical move. In each of the four canonical Gospels, Mary Magdalene is counted among the group of women at the cross and/or tomb (Mk 15:40, 47; 16:1; Mt. 27:56; 28:1; Lk. 24:10; Jn 19:25; 20:1). In all but John, she is consistently listed first in every list's configuration of female disciples' names.

What Table 2.2 demonstrates—among items of tangential interest, such as the oddly varying references to the second Mary in Mark's lists[31] and the prevalence of the name

---

[30] Luke Timothy Johnson suggests the reason for the late inclusion of the women's names: "It is only at this point that Luke provides the names of the women, because it is not in their mute witness of the empty tomb but in their having become 'ministers of the word' (Luke 1:2) that their real significance lies" ("The Not-So-Empty Tomb [Luke 24:1–11]," in *The Living Gospel* [New York: Continuum, 2004], 144).

[31] The shifting designations for Mary the mother of James and/or Joses have led some interpreters to argue that there are four women present in Mark's shifting lists. Rudolf Pesch is often cited as the major proponent of this view: "Von den zuschauenden Frauen werden zunächst *vier* namentlich vorgestellt: Maria von Magdala, Maria, die Mutter oder Frau des Jakobus des Kleinen, (Maria) die Mutter des Joses und Salome" (*Das Markusevangelium* [2 vols; Freiburg: Herder, 1984], 2:505). In agreement are Luise Schotfroff ("Maria Magdalena und die Frauen am Grabe Jesu," *EvT* 42 [1982]: 8n16) and Esther de Boer (*Mary Magdalene: Beyond the Myth* [trans. John Bowden; London: SCM Press, 1997], 105, esp. n. 21). Vincent Taylor concedes that if the ἡ before Ἰωσῆτος in Vaticanus (B) is original, there are four women present; but finds three probable otherwise (*The Gospel According to St. Mark* [London: Macmillan, 1959], 598). E. Elizabeth Johnson sees only three women (total) in Mark's lists but argues that the second Mary is a reference to Jesus's mother. Both James and Joses are named as brothers of Jesus in 6:3 (along with Jude and Simon). Johnson, in "Who Is My Mother? Family Values in the Gospel of Mark" (in *Blessed One: Protestant Perspectives on Mary* [ed. Beverly Roberts Gaventa and Cynthia Rigby; Louisville: Westminster John Knox, 2002]), reasons that

> the reader or listener who has attended to Mark's narrative from its beginning cannot help remembering that these characters have appeared in it before ... The coincidence is too great that [the three names—Mary, James, and Joses—although they are common] should

Table 2.2 Named/identified women in the canonical Gospel crucifixion and resurrection narratives*

	Mark	Matthew	Luke	John
Mary Magdalene	15:40 Μαρία ἡ Μαγδαληνή (1 of 3) 15:47 ἡ Μαρία ἡ Μαγδαληνή (1 of 2) 16:1 Μαρία ἡ Μαγδαληνή (1 of 3) [16:9] Μαριὰ τῇ Μαγδαληνῇ	27:56 Μαρία ἡ Μαγδαληνή (1 of 3) 27:61 Μαριὰμ ἡ Μαγδαληνή (1 of 2) 28:1 Μαριὰμ ἡ Μαγδαληνή (1 of 2)	24:10 ἡ Μαγδαληνή Μαρία (1 of 3)	19:25 Μαρία ἡ Μαγδαληνή (3 of 3) 20:1 Μαρία ἡ Μαγδαληνή 20:11 Μαρία 20:16 Μαριάμ 20:18 Μαριὰμ ἡ Μαγδαληνή
Mary the mother of James and Joses	15:40 Μαρία ἡ Ἰακώβου τοῦ μικροῦ καὶ Ἰωσῆτος μήτηρ (2 of 3)			
Mary of Joses	15:47 Μαρία ἡ Ἰωσῆτος (2 of 2)			
Mary of James	16:1 Μαρία ἡ [τοῦ] Ἰακώβου (2 of 3)		24:10 Μαρία ἡ Ἰακώβου (3 of 3)	
Mary the mother of James and Joseph		27:56 Μαρία ἡ τοῦ Ἰακώβου καὶ Ἰωσὴφ μήτηρ (2 of 3)		
The Other Mary		27:61 ἡ ἄλλη Μαρία (2 of 2) 28:1 ἡ ἄλλη Μαρία (2 of 2)		
Salome	15:40 Σαλώμη (3 of 3) 16:1 Σαλώμη (3 of 3)			
The mother of the sons of Zebedee		27:56 ἡ μήτηρ τῶν υἱῶν Ζεβεδαίου (3 of 3)		
Joanna			24:10 Ἰωάννα (2 of 3)	
The mother of Jesus				19:25 ἡ μήτηρ αὐτοῦ (1 of 3) 19:26 τὴν μητέρα
The sister of Jesus's mother, Mary of Clopas				19:25 ἡ ἀδελφὴ τῆς μητρὸς αὐτοῦ, Μαρία ἡ τοῦ Κλωπᾶ (2 of 3)

* Each entry includes: (1) the verse of each instance of the name or identification; (2) the Greek of the name (demonstrating minor differences); and (3) in the case of the Evangelist listing a group of women, the woman's position in the list.

Mary in general[32]—is that, among the women associated with the final episodes of Jesus's life in Gospel traditions, Mary Magdalene was foremost. Her persistent naming in the Second Gospel and eventual spotlight in its supplement are not unique. What we find in Mark confirms and elaborates an already obvious trend: Mary Magdalene is *the* prominent female witness to Jesus's crucifixion and resurrection.[33]

2.4 Mary Magdalene Is Formerly Demon-Possessed

In 16:9 Mary is not only named, she is also characterized as the woman from whom Jesus had cast seven demons. This description, however, is a detail that does not arise from extant Gospel endings. Mary Magdalene's identification as a former demoniac has its only parallel in Luke 8, where Luke describes numerous women who, having benefited from Jesus's healing or exorcism,[34] became Jesus's benefactors (Lk. 8:2-3). Mary, "called Magdalene" (Μαρία ἡ καλουμένη Μαγδαληνή), is the only woman whose particular ailment is described. Joanna (Ἰωάννα), one of the other two named women, is described by a relationship, as the wife of Chuza who was Herod's steward (γυνὴ

---

all three occur in two different households in the same small circle of people without any mention of the similarities. (41)

While Johnson's reading is appealing, one wonders whether the first reference to James as Ἰακώβου τοῦ μικροῦ (James "the small" or "Little James") is not just that: an explanation that, although similar names are present, this is a different James of a different family. On "the small" as a better representation of τοῦ μικροῦ than "the younger," see Richard Bauckham, *Gospel Women: Studies of the Named Women in the Gospels* (New York: T&T Clark, 2002), 210n35. Cf. Collins, *Mark*, 772, for the alternative view.

[32] The initial impression of a modern reader upon studying the list of women's names in any of the Gospels might rightly be, "How many Marys could there possibly have been?" In a study of Jewish names in Palestine between 330 BCE and 200 CE, Tal Ilan surveyed 317 women's names—a much smaller pool of evidence than for men's names represented in the collection of all the recorded names used by Jews in Palestine during that time period—to determine the popularity of names (*Lexicon of Jewish Names in Late Antiquity: Part I, Palestine 330 BCE-200 CE* [Tübingen: Mohr Siebeck, 2002]). Among those 317 female names, 80 were *Mariam* and 63 were Salome (25 percent and 20 percent, respectively), both of which appear in Mk 15:40, 47, and 16:1 (57; Table 8). Ilan does not require orthographical uniformity for each name; among possible spellings for *Mariam*, she includes, e.g., Μαριάμη, Μαρία, Μαριάδος, and several more Greek and Hebrew renditions of the name (242-4).

[33] That she represents even more than this sentence claims will be developed later. On the present subject, scholars vary on how to interpret the significance of named persons in the Gospels, from Bauckham's more recent thesis that naming connotes eyewitness status (*Gospel Women*, 297-8) to form critics' frequent dismissals of named persons, often women, as superfluous (cf. Martin Dibelius, *From Tradition to Gospel* [trans. Bertram Lee Woolf; rev. ed.; Cambridge: James Clarke, 1971], 190; and Rudolf Bultmann, *Die Geschichte der synoptischen Tradition* [10th ed.; Göttingen: Vandenhoeck & Ruprecht, 1995], 296). My view lies closer to Bauckham's than to that of the form critics, who tend to see the women's names as superfluous detail, perhaps due to a historicizing tendency (Dibelius) or added simply to fill in the absence of the male disciples (Bultmann). The repeated naming of Mary Magdalene—not merely the presence of her name—in the last chapters of Mark and in the LE points to the significance of her status as witness.

[34] The initial description of the women is "certain women who were healed from evil spirits and ailments" (γυναῖκές τινες αἳ ἦσαν τεθεραπευμέναι ἀπὸ πνευμάτων πονηρῶν καὶ ἀσθενειῶν; Lk. 8:2). The use of the periphrastic participle means, as François Bovon notes, that the person who performed the healing is unexpressed (*Luke 1* [Hermeneia; trans. Christine M. Thomas; Minneapolis: Fortress, 2002], 301). Nonetheless, Bovon holds that the healings were "doubtless by Jesus" (301).

Χουζᾶ ἐπιτρόπου Ἡρῴδου).[35] Susanna is described neither by her former malady nor her marriage, which might mean that she would have been recognizable by name alone to Luke's audience. Luke further reinforces that "certain women" (γυναῖκές τινες) who had been aided by Jesus (v. 2) were not merely these three named; there were "many other women" (καὶ ἕτεραι πολλαί) who also reciprocated by serving him "out of their possessions" (v. 3).[36]

It is impossible to know for sure why Luke specifies Mary's former state of possession, while leaving in general terms the conditions under which the other women suffered. Perhaps the severity of being possessed by *seven demons* (δαιμόνια ἑπτά) calls for extra attention.[37] As in the LE, the possession is already past in Luke's account, which uses the pluperfect to state that Mary is the one "out of whom *had gone* [ἐξεληλύθει] seven demons." Nonetheless, Luke recalls the extent of Mary's wretchedness, which perhaps accounts for her devoted service to Jesus. She is listed first among his female benefactors. Along with Mary the mother of James and other women who reported on Jesus's empty tomb, Luke names for the second time Jesus's benefactors, Mary Magdalene and Joanna (ἡ Μαγδαληνὴ Μαρία καὶ Ἰωάννα; 24:10).

Although Mary Magdalene's name appears thrice previously in Mark (15:40, 47, and 16:1), the first mention of any former demon possession comes in the LE. Her state as a former demoniac and the particularity of the number seven (ἑπτὰ δαιμόνια; 16:9) are shared between Luke 8 and the LE. The description clearly refers to Luke's account or to a related tradition, but the phrasing does not necessarily imply literary dependence.[38]

Even among the few scholars who weigh in on this parenthetical description, there is interpretive variety: neutral, negative, or positive. In the "neutral" camp, Mirecki deems this description of Mary Magdalene a secondary addition, because of its apparent relationship to Lk. 8:2b and because it disrupts the neat, tripartite form he ascribes to the "core narrative" of the LE.[39] He perceives the description as an exception to the tight, original formula: "the only description of the essential nature of an actor in the story, whereas the other actors' activities are described."[40] He deems it *not* unusual that Mary is the only actor referred to by name, but finds it unlikely that she would be *both* named and described, while other characters function with a degree of anonymity. This rationale

---

[35] Both "Joanna" and "Chuza" are, according to Bovon, rare enough that the names themselves would have made this reference quite identifiable (ibid.).

[36] Bovon comments, "For contemporary sensibilities, Jesus's willingness to accept female disciples was unheard-of, as was the freedom of these women, who left their homes to enter Jesus's band of disciples" (ibid., 300).

[37] So Dibelius on Legion: "The magnitude of the miracle is seen in the number of the demons, just as with Mary Magdalene (Mark xvi, 9)" (*From Tradition to Gospel*, 89).

[38] The vocabulary for the exorcism is different (Luke, ἐξέρχομαι; Mark, ἐκβάλλω), as well as the preposition used to express the demons' exit *from* Mary Magdalene (Luke, παρά; Mark, ἀπό). In Lk. 8:2, the demons are the subject of the phrase "*seven demons* had gone out" (δαιμόνια ἑπτὰ ἐξεληλύθει), whereas in Mk 16:9 Jesus is the implied subject and the demons are the object: "*he* had cast out seven demons" (ἐκβεβλήκει ἑπτὰ δαιμόνια). Even the order of δαιμόνια and ἑπτά are reversed from Luke's in the LE's parenthetical comment.

[39] Mirecki, "Mark 16:9–20," 145. One of Mirecki's arguments in his ThD dissertation is that the core structure of the LE was original to Mark's Gospel (147–51). The description of Mary as a former demoniac, however, is part of the LE that was added secondarily.

[40] Ibid., 145–6.

reveals Mirecki's underlying perception that Mary Magdalene is not an individual of particular interest but merely fulfills a narrative function. For Mirecki, the two disciples (16:12-13) might as well have been first and Mary second, as there is simply a threefold pattern to uphold, a pattern that a later editor renders uneven by inserting the description of Mary as a former demoniac. In my view, however, the particulars attributed to Mary—to be elaborated presently—show that the author's interest in her involves more than a commitment to maintaining threefold structure. Mirecki is surely right to notice a repetitive pattern that gives shape to the simple narrative of the LE, but that is no reason to minimize her individual characteristics.[41]

Thomas Shepherd, however, considers "out of whom he cast seven demons" an important, but negative, component that connects the LE with the ending at 16:8.[42] He sees Mary Magdalene as part of a reflexive pattern that starts with the characterization of the women in 16:1-8. Initially, the women are portrayed positively, due to their devotion to Jesus. When they fail to obey the command in 16:7, they end up depicted negatively. Shepherd summarizes, "Thus the roles of the women reverse: vv. 1-8, an initially positive role turning to negative; vv. 9-10, an initially negative role turning to positive."[43] As part of this pattern, Shepherd sees the identifying detail about Mary's past as a critique: "Mary Magdalene is first presented in a negative light in which she was formerly possessed by no less than seven demons."[44] Beyond its fit within his perceived pattern, Shepherd offers little explanation for how he arrives at his negative interpretation of past possessions. Clearly, demon possession is not a desirable condition, but Shepherd's interpretation implies that Mary is the one to blame for her possession. He acknowledges that Jesus had already performed the exorcism, thereby rectifying her plight.[45] The negative implication is that even a demon possession in the past is, in Shepherd's view, detrimental to her character.

---

[41] See Kelhoffer's critique of Mirecki's approach (*Miracle and Mission*, 42–5), with which I agree. Another reason that Mirecki's easy dismissal of Mary Magdalene's importance needs to be resisted is that it conforms to a deleterious trend in biblical scholarship. Historically, it has been easier and more automatic to dismiss women characters' roles in the Gospels than their male counterparts' (for varying reasons: form, structure, history, etc.). This was truer of scholarship of a previous generation, before the awareness that feminist interpreters have generated. Yet some of the greats of NT scholarship, from whom there is still much to learn, have interspersed in their arguments a casual disregard for women in the biblical text. The sorts of dismissal applied to female figures in the Gospels are more frequent, more automatic, and less defensible than when male characters are disregarded. E.g., Bultmann asserts the superfluity of the women in 15:40-41 and its Synoptic parallels: "Wie bei der Auferstehung werden hier Frauen als Zeugen aufgeboten. Sie sind hier so wenig geschichtlich wie dort; man brauchte sie, weil man die geflohenen Jünger nicht auftreten lassen konnte" (*Geschichte der synoptischen Tradition*, 296). The German original of Bultmann's statement conveys better his perception that the mention of the women was merely perfunctory: that they are named (inexplicably) and function simply as stand-ins, necessitated by the flight of the twelve, male disciples. My translation: "As at the Resurrection, women are established here as witnesses. They are just as unhistorical here as there; they are needed because one cannot bring back the disciples who fled."

[42] Thomas R. Shepherd, "Narrative Analysis as a Text Critical Tool: Mark 16 in Codex W as a Test Case," *JSNT* 32 (2009): 77–98.

[43] Ibid., 80.

[44] Ibid.

[45] Shepherd acknowledges that "Jesus had already resolved that problem," but he still judges the description as reflecting negatively on Mary (ibid., 80).

In my view, Shepherd's schema for understanding the women in the Markan endings—positive to negative (16:1-8), negative to positive (16:9-10)—oversimplifies the relationship between the two episodes and does not account for several imbalances in the comparison. First, Mary Magdalene is present in both passages and her status as an exorcised woman applies, retrospectively, in the earlier episodes as well (15:40, 47). Second, the description of Mary's demon possession relates only a past condition, whereas the failure of the group of women is in the narrative present (16:8). Third, we never find in the whole NT witness any indication that a person's moral failure has led to demonic possession; there is no reason to find it in the LE of Mark. Demon possession is a condition from which one needs to be freed; until emancipation, one is powerless to act on his or her own behalf.[46] Fourth, the LE returns to the act of

---

[46] There is no question that being possessed is an undesirable state. But the implication that being or having been possessed reflects negatively on the possessed person is indefensible. As seen in Jesus's first miraculous act, an exorcism, in Mk 1:23-27, Jesus's harsh command is directed to the spirit, not to the possessed person himself. Onlookers marvel that *he commands unclean spirits and they obey him* (καὶ τοῖς πνεύμασι τοῖς ἀκαθάρτοις ἐπιτάσσει, καὶ ὑπακούουσιν αὐτῷ; 1:27). Again in 1:34 and 3:11-12 the demons are restricted from speaking, as they are the ones that recognize Jesus's identity. The scribes who come from Jerusalem seem to associate exorcism with allegiance to evil powers, but it is *the exorcist* who is implicated in their view: Βεελζεβοὺλ ἔχει καὶ ὅτι ἐν τῷ ἄρχοντι τῶν δαιμονίων ἐκβάλλει τὰ δαιμόνια (3:22). Jesus flatly refutes this association with Satan in a series of parables (3:23-27). The Markan Jesus performs numerous exorcisms (specific: 1:21-27; 5:1-13; 7:24-30; 9:17-29; generalized: 1:34, 39; 3:10-12) but never attributes to the possessed person the wickedness of the controlling power. For the most part, demonic possession is treated similarly to infection and disease: as a condition under which the possessed or ill person is afflicted unwillingly. In miracle summaries, healings and exorcisms are sometimes paired (Mk 1:34; 3:10-12; and performed by the disciples in 6:12-13). It is interesting that the exceptions to this rule—in which guilt or sin is ascribed to the sufferer—are always in the case of bodily illness, not possession. When he heals the paralytic in Capernaum, Jesus equates saying "Your sins are forgiven" with saying "Pick up your mat and walk," much to the chagrin of onlooking scribes (and Pharisees, in Luke's version; Mk 2:5-9; Mt. 9:2-5; Lk. 5:20-23). In John the question is raised most poignantly when the disciples ask Jesus to assign blame for the condition of a man born blind: "Who sinned, this man or his parents?" (Jn 9:2). In this instance, Jesus rejects the connection of sin to infirmity. It is even more striking, then, that the question of responsibility—τίς ἥμαρτεν—is never raised of a victim of demonic oppression. A similar pattern is discernable in ancient literature outside of Mark. In Tobit, Sarah, the daughter of Raguel, is plagued, if not possessed, by the "wicked demon" (τὸ πονηρὸν δαιμόνιον) Asmodeus, who kills each of her seven husbands, each before the marriage is consummated (Tob. 3:7-8). Although she is reproached by a family maid for killing her husbands (3:7-9), the text demonstrates that such an accusation is patently false. In fact, Sarah's righteousness and piety are highlighted in her prayer (σὺ γινώσκεις κύριε ὅτι καθαρά εἰμι ἀπὸ πάσης ἁμαρτίας ἀνδρὸς καὶ οὐκ ἐμόλυνα τὸ ὄνομά μου οὐδὲ τὸ ὄνομα τοῦ πατρός μου; 3:14-15a), which is heard and answered by sending the angel Raphael (3:16-17). Beverly Bow goes so far as to suggest that, by comparing the similar prayers of Tobit and Sarah, Sarah is subtly preferred as an "unselfish, besieged woman" ("Sarah 2," in *Women in Scripture: A Dictionary of Named and Unnamed Women in the Hebrew Bible, the Apocryphal/Deutero-canonical Books, and the New Testament* [ed. Carol Meyers; Boston: Houghton Mifflin, 2000], 153). Whether or not there is a preference, both Tobit and Sarah are ultimately healed, confirming their status as righteous in the narrative. Josephus makes a passing reference to demons as the spirits of evil people, who can possess other humans and kill them (*J.W.* 7.185). In this brief assertion, there are wicked humans in Josephus's purview (ταῦτα δὲ πονηρῶν ἐστιν ἀνθρώπων), but, again, this wickedness is not attributed to the possessed individuals, who are merely described as *living* (ζῶσιν). For further study of this subject, see Loren T. Stuckenbruck, "The Human Being and Demonic Invasion: Therapeutic Models in Ancient Jewish and Christian Texts," in *Spirituality, Theology, and Mental Health: Multidisciplinary Perspectives* (ed. Christopher C. H. Cook; London: SCM Press, 2013), 94–123; idem, "Jesus' Apocalyptic Worldview and His Exorcistic Ministry," in *The Pseudepigrapha and Christian Origins: Essays from the Studiorum Novi Testamenti Societas* (ed. Gerbern S. Oegema and James H. Charlesworth; New York: T&T Clark, 2008), 68–84;

exorcism later in the passage, treating the performance of exorcism as a positive sign of belief (16:17).

Finally, Graham Twelftree reads Mary Magdalene's former demoniac status as a positive attribute. In his study of exorcism among early Christians,[47] he suggests that the presentation of Mary as the beneficiary of an early exorcism by Jesus "draws attention to the power of Jesus to deal with a person who was so demonized that there could be no worse state imagined."[48] Unlike Shepherd's assumption that Mary Magdalene is guilty by virtue of possession, Twelftree argues that the emphasis of the description is on Jesus's power to reverse her dire situation completely. Twelftree connects the description of Mary to the other reference to exorcism in the LE, which is found in v. 17.[49] As Jesus forecasts the signs that will evidence belief, he begins with ἐν τῷ ὀνόματί μου δαιμόνια ἐκβαλοῦσιν ("in my name they will cast out demons"). Twelftree's perspective on Mary Magdalene's characterization as a former demoniac is positive, associated with Jesus's power to heal and the future potential of his followers to exorcise demons.

While Mary was the recipient of exorcism, rather than the exorcist, as far as the LE tells us, the activity of both exorcist and the one exorcised are nonetheless inscribed into the pattern of believers' commissioned ministry.[50] She is presented, then, as a beneficiary of Jesus's power, whose life did not merely return to normal after her encounter with him but instead resulted in her becoming a follower.[51] Apparently, Mary's response to Jesus's exorcism was one of highest devotion, as she reappears in

---

idem, "Prayers of Deliverance from the Demonic in the Dead Sea Scrolls and Related Early Jewish Literature," in *The Changing Face of Judaism, Christianity, and Other Greco-Roman Religions in Antiquity* (ed. Ian H. Henderson and Gerbern S. Oegema; JSHRZ 2; Munich: Gütersloher, 2006), 146–65.

[47] Graham H. Twelftree's study of exorcism in the NT and in early Christian documents covers a lot of literary ground. He demonstrates that in the early second century there was little or no interest in exorcism (see *In the Name of Jesus: Exorcism among Early Christians* [Grand Rapids: Baker Academic, 2007], 285–6, for his summary). For the LE, however, he postulates as a backdrop a mid-second-century community in Rome with a renewed interest in exorcism. The interest is not only in exorcisms Jesus performed, but in those performed by later followers: "The miracles are proofs of belief and are evidence of a unity between Jesus and his followers so that it is as if Jesus (perhaps understood to be his Spirit) were performing the miracles. Thus the exorcisms could be said to be regarded as the result of, or even inherent in, the message" (286).

[48] See ibid., 235n29.

[49] So Hug: "Cette référence à la guérison de Marie, qu'on ne retrouve pas dans les autres récits de l'apparition, anticipe en quelque sorte la promesse de chaser les démons (v. 17)" (*La Finale*, 164). [Translation: This reference to the healing of Mary, which is not found in the other accounts of the appearance, anticipates somewhat the promise of exorcising demons (v. 17).]

[50] Jesus's encounter with disbelief in his hometown (6:1-6) is pertinent to the question of the cooperative nature of healings and exorcisms. Jesus's inability (οὐκ ἐδύνατο) to do any acts of power, apart from a few healings, seems tied to an astonishing lack of faith among the townspeople (in light of a limited number of healings, Jesus "marvels" [ἐθαύμαζεν] on account of their disbelief [διὰ τὴν ἀπιστίαν αὐτῶν]; 6:6).

[51] In this way, she is much like blind Bartimaeus in Mk 10:46-52, who, after being healed by Jesus, follows him along the way (καὶ εὐθὺς ἀνέβλεψεν καὶ ἠκολούθει αὐτῷ ἐν τῇ ὁδῷ; v. 52). By contrast, after most healings or exorcisms in Mark, the person healed is forbidden from following, or commanded to do something else (i.e., Legion; 5:19-20). The Bartimaeus episode is different in this respect. Joel Marcus points to Bartimaeus, for instance, as "paradigmatic" and "a symbol of the new disciple of Jesus," citing narrative features similar to the early Christian baptismal rite (*Mark 8–16* [AYB 27A; New Haven, CT: Yale University Press, 2009], 765).

every scene where his closest male compatriots do not (15:40, 47; 16:1). The repeated mentions of Mary Magdalene and the other women by name draw attention to their faith and durable adherence, unlike the male disciples who flee and are absent from all of the final episodes of Jesus's life.[52] And now in the LE it is Mary, formerly possessed by seven demons, who inaugurates the post-resurrection life of discipleship, by declaring to the wayward Eleven that Jesus is alive and was seen *by her*.

2.5 Mary Magdalene Is a Proclaimer

When Mary goes and shares the news of Jesus's resurrection, what she says is based on direct experience: Jesus is living and he was seen by her (ὑπ' αὐτῆς; v. 11). As mentioned earlier, there is incongruity between the message the women were charged to—and initially failed to—convey and the proclamation Mary is reported to have made in 16:11. Earlier the young man told them, "Go and say to his disciples and to Peter, 'He is going before you to Galilee. There you will see him, just as he told you'" (16:7). As far as readers of the LE can tell, Mary's proclamation, after seeing the risen Jesus, relates none of this information. Instead, the message is that Jesus is alive and that she herself has seen him.

It is clear to the reader that Mary's proclamation—that Jesus is alive and that she has seen as much—is accurate. The narrative content of 16:9 relates that "after [Jesus] was raised, he appeared first to Mary Magdalene," which contains the same two component parts as Mary's witness in 16:11: that is, Jesus is raised/alive and has appeared to/was seen by Mary. From a reader's standpoint, there is no further need to establish the authenticity of Mary's witness to the Eleven. She has spoken truly, conveyed the good news. Mary says what she knows to be true and, noticeably, not what the young man's commission of 16:7 instructed her and her companions to communicate. The LE narrates Mary Magdalene's seized opportunity to bear the news of a living Lord, no longer caught in a fearful silence but a bold *evangelist* herself.

Mary Magdalene's primary roles in this brief narrative are that of proclaimer and witness (16:9-10); she reinforces testimony by the content of her proclamation (v. 11). Mary's successful completion of these roles reverses the fearful silence and failure of 16:8. Her proclamation in Mk 16:9-11 retains a strong connection to her portrait in each of the Gospels' resurrection narratives: all depict Mary as similarly commissioned, but not every Gospel relates her successful completion of that task.

In Matthew, Mary Magdalene is among the group of women who run from the tomb in fear and "great joy" (φόβου καὶ χαρᾶς μεγάλης; 28:8), rather than seized by "trembling and amazement" (τρόμος καὶ ἔκστασις; Mk 16:8). Matthew 28:8b informs us that their object was to proclaim the message to Jesus's disciples (ἀπαγγεῖλαι τοῖς μαθηταῖς αὐτοῦ). And yet their fulfillment of this command is never narrated. First, Jesus meets them on the way, at which point they grab his feet and worship him (28:9). Then Jesus re-instructs them to go and tell his disciples (ὑπάγετε ἀπαγγείλατε

---

[52] The last appearance of the Twelve (presumably based on the reference in 14:17) is in 14:50, when at Jesus's arrest, they all leave him and flee (Καὶ ἀφέντες αὐτὸν ἔφυγον πάντες). Peter's final appearance consists of his threefold denial (14:66-72), concluding with his weeping (v. 72).

τοῖς ἀδελφοῖς μου), the task in which he had delayed them (28:10). The goal of their proclamation is *in order that* (ἵνα) the disciples should meet Jesus in Galilee.[53] Subsequently, the women start back on their mission,[54] but their narrative path is intersected by an ἰδού that functions more as a "meanwhile." The scene shifts suddenly to the activities of some men from the guard who relate what has happened to the chief priests. After explanations about bribes and false stories circulating "up to today" (28:15), the story never returns to the women. We presume that they completed their task, for the Eleven make their way to Galilee in v. 16. But the would-be proclaimers, twice-commissioned and twice-interrupted, never fulfill their task on the pages of the First Gospel.

In John's account, Mary Magdalene's announcement to the disciples is narrated in first-person quotation and in summary. We have the first recorded direct quotation of a witness to the resurrection: "I have seen the Lord" (ἑώρακα τὸν κύριον; Jn 20:18a). Then Mary tells the disciples what Jesus said to her (20:18b). This one verse contains more information about Mary's proclamation than what we find in the LE. And yet, in the context of John's longer episode recounting Mary's interaction with Jesus, her role as "proclaimer" is not the characteristic most emphasized. In eight verses, Mary is most frequently described as weeping. In v. 11 she is twice described in reference to her crying (κλαίουσα; ὡς ... ἔκλαιεν). The two angels' first question to Mary is, "Woman, why are you weeping?" (γύναι, τί κλαίεις), a question that comprises the risen Jesus's first words to her as well (20:13, 15). Crying is not a trait toward which the Fourth Gospel, on the whole, takes a negative tone; famously, Jesus himself weeps (ἐδάκρυσεν ὁ Ἰησοῦς) at Lazarus's death (11:35).[55] Yet, in the context of John 20, Mary's crying corresponds to an ignorant[56] blindness (or misperception, as with the "gardener" in 20:15b) that may carry with it negative connotations.

I highlight Mary's weeping in Jn 20:11-18 not to set it against Mk 16:9-11, as though to ascertain which depiction of Mary constitutes the "better" disciple or "braver" woman. Such vastly different narratives—one exceedingly sparse, the other replete with direct speech (and with additional narrative aims: the dialogue relating to Jesus's impending ascension and Mary's restriction from "holding on" to him; v. 17)—cannot be quantified in such a way. The recurring reference to Mary's weeping in the Fourth Evangelist's account, however, stands in sharp contrast to the LE's narrative, which

---

[53] Matthew makes sure to confirm this Galilean meeting (28:10, 16); the LE does not corroborate that expectation from 16:7. There is no geographical location identifiable in the extension of Mark's ending.

[54] At least, it seems that the implication of Mt. 28:11, a genitive absolute construction—Πορευομένων δὲ αὐτῶν—refers to the women's travel. Because the genitive plural pronoun is the same across the genders, as is the middle/passive present participle, the gender in reference (female disciples or male members of the guard [τινες τῆς κουστωδίας]) is ambiguous.

[55] For more detailed studies on Jesus's emotion in the Fourth Gospel, particularly in light of ancient Stoicism, see Gitte Buch-Hansen, "The Emotional Jesus: Anti-Stoicism in the Fourth Gospel?" in *Stoicism in Early Christianity* (ed. Tuomas Rasimus et al.; Grand Rapids: Baker, 2010), 93–114; and Harold W. Attridge, "An 'Emotional' Jesus and the Stoic Tradition," *Stoicism in Early Christianity*, 77–92. See also Chapter 3 of this study.

[56] Mary Magdalene *does not know* almost as often as she weeps in John 20: "we do not know [οὐκ οἴδαμεν] where they have laid him" (20:2); "I do not know [οὐκ οἶδα] where they have laid [my Lord]" (20:13). Finally, she sees Jesus but does not know (οὐκ ᾔδει) it is him (20:14).

does not express Mary's emotional state yet *does* relate that the male disciples to whom she proclaimed the message were at that time "mourning and weeping" (πενθοῦσι καὶ κλαίουσιν; Mk 16:10; cf. 14:72). What their doubly depicted despair might imply about the disciples is a matter for discussion in the next chapter. For the time being, it is sufficient to show that the LE does not merely repeat John 20 in its characterization of Mary. Unlike John, Mark's LE dramatizes Mary's forthright proclamation—not her personal grief, misapprehensions, or ignorance.

Finally, the women's proclamation of the news that Jesus was raised from the dead in the Gospel According to Luke is quite different from that in Mk 16:9-11. Most significantly, Luke's is an empty tomb tradition: the (initially unnamed) women do not see Jesus himself but receive a message from two men (Lk. 24:4). Furthermore, readers are privy to the women's "aha" moment, connecting the words of the messengers to words of Jesus himself. After the two men recall Jesus's passion and resurrection predictions (9:22; 18:31-33),[57] the women are said to "remember his words" (καὶ ἐμνήσθησαν τῶν ῥημάτων αὐτοῦ; 24:8).[58] Readers learn nothing of Mary's thought-processes in the LE; her actions and proclamation provide the only hints at what she might have experienced or remembered in seeing Jesus alive after knowing him to have died.

Yet, in another respect, Luke's account includes what is perhaps the closest comparison to Mk 16:9-11 in its canonical context. In Luke's account the women's proclamation receives a negative reception by the disciples.

2.6 Mary Magdalene Is Rejected

When Mary reports to the remaining disciples that Jesus is alive and "was seen by her" (ἐθεάθη ὑπ' αὐτῆς), her credibility is tied up with Jesus's circumstance as raised. That is, the news that the disciples receive is not that the resurrected Jesus was spotted by just anybody. Instead, he was seen *by her*. Mary's report is linked to her own integrity as a witness. When the Eleven do not believe her, what initially seems like a defamation of Mary turns into judgment on their own characters (v. 14).

Because the disbelief of the disciples is the subject of the next chapter, their response will not concern us at present. Mary's status as a rejected witness, however, requires some comparison. The response to her as a witness to Jesus's resurrection is experientially like the response Jesus himself received during his ministry. In his own words, Jesus's predictions of his death and resurrection include rejection by the Jewish leadership (καὶ ἀποδοκιμασθῆναι ὑπὸ τῶν πρεσβυτέρων καὶ τῶν ἀρχιερέων καὶ τῶν γραμματέων; Mk 8:31; par. Lk. 9:22). In Mark, Matthew, and Luke, Jesus is the stone

---

[57] The closest verbal connections are in the resurrection predictions: καὶ τῇ τρίτῃ ἡμέρᾳ ἐγερθῆναι (9:22b); καὶ τῇ ἡμέρᾳ τῇ τρίτῃ ἀναστήσεται (18:33b); and καὶ τῇ τρίτῃ ἡμέρᾳ ἀναστῆναι (24:7).

[58] The women respond to a report of Jesus's resurrection by remembering (and thereby understanding, one presumes) his words: καὶ ἐμνήσθησαν τῶν ῥημάτων αὐτοῦ (Lk. 24:8). This correlates inversely to what the disciples did when they heard Jesus's prediction of his own death and resurrection (18:31-33): καὶ αὐτοὶ οὐδὲν τούτων συνῆκαν καὶ ἦν τὸ ῥῆμα τοῦτο κεκρυμμένον ἀπ' αὐτῶν καὶ οὐκ ἐγίνωσκον τὰ λεγόμενα. Luke may imply that these women had also been present to hear the words ahead of time.

the builders rejected (λίθον ὃν ἀπεδοκίμασαν οἱ οἰκοδομοῦντες), applying Ps. 118:22[59] christologically (Mk 12:10; Mt. 21:42; Lk. 20:17).

Mark 11:31 and 15:32 draw the closest ties between rejection and disbelief.[60] In 11:27-33 the high priests, scribes, and the elders (οἱ ἀρχιερεῖς καὶ οἱ γραμματεῖς καὶ οἱ πρεσβύτεροι; 11:27—a simple reordering of the list from 8:31) question Jesus in the temple regarding his own authority to do unspecified things (*these things*/ταῦτα ποιεῖς; v. 28—likely referring at least in part to his act of audacity of 11:15-19). When Jesus retorts with his own question about John's baptism, the authorities reason among themselves that, if they admit to the heavenly origins of John's baptism, they will be held accountable for not having believed him. Their disbelief—expecting the question from Jesus: διὰ τί οὖν οὐκ ἐπιστεύσατε αὐτῷ; (v. 31)—implies a rejection of John and his baptism.

Disbelief is also directed at Jesus as he hangs on the cross (15:29-32). Jesus's detractors seize on a disconnect between his purported promises and his dire situation: *If* you can destroy and rebuild the temple, *then* save yourself and come down from the cross (vv. 29-30). As one who promised salvation to others, Jesus should be (but apparently is not) able to save himself (v. 31). Verse 32 extends the chief priests' derision, calling Jesus "the Christ" and "the King of Israel," while challenging him to get down off the cross *so that* they might see and believe (ἵνα ἴδωμεν καὶ πιστεύσωμεν). As Jesus does not comply, it is clear that they do not believe, just as they do not accept that Jesus is the Messiah, nor that he is king. The implied rejection of these appellations (in the tone of sarcasm) comports with their stated disbelief in Jesus.

In Mk 16:11 the disciples' disbelief of Mary is a rejection of her witness to Jesus's resurrection. In Luke the disciples dismiss the rationality of the women's witness: "these words appeared before them as nonsense" (καὶ ἐφάνησαν ἐνώπιον αὐτῶν ὡσεὶ λῆρος τὰ ῥήματα ταῦτα, καὶ ἠπίστουν αὐταῖς). The result, however, is the same: "they did not believe them [the women]" (καὶ ἠπίστουν αὐταῖς). Readings of the disciples' rejection of the women's message often highlight the implication of a gender bias: women's witness was unreliable and thus deemed an "idle tale."[61] This implication is absent from the LE's narration. Nevertheless, in both Mk 16:11 and Lk. 24:11, the male disciples' disbelief cannot change the readers' awareness that their rejection of the women's witness is unfounded.[62]

---

[59] λίθον, ὃν ἀπεδοκίμασαν οἱ οἰκοδομοῦντες (Ps. 117:22a, LXX).

[60] Although terminology of *disbelief* is present in the LE (ἀπιστέω, v. 11; ἀπιστία and σκληροκαρδία, v. 14; terms of negation with the verb πιστεύω, οὐδέ, and οὐ, in vv. 13 and 14 respectively), no terms specifically pointing to rejection are found therein. Nevertheless, disbelief implies rejection of some kind, as Mk 11:31 and 15:32 indicate.

[61] This interpretation is not necessitated by the term λῆρος itself, which seems to be used as frequently of men as of women (e.g., of Eleazar in 4 Macc. 5:11), although it might connote excesses or silliness that could have been negatively stereotyped as feminine. Still, the reading of the disciples' disregard of the women as being *due* to their sex is widespread: cf. Thomas Long, "Empty Tomb, Empty Talk," *ChrCent* 118 (2001): 11. Setzer judges that "Luke outwardly denigrates the significance and effect of the women's witness, while his narrative affirms it" ("Excellent Women," 265). I.e., the narrative relies on the truth of the women's witness, but Luke is not supportive of the women as witnesses. Setzer characterizes this as "embarrassment of the women's witness" (264). If Setzer's assessment is accurate of the women in Luke's resurrection context, it cannot be applied to the narrative in reverse: Luke upholds Elizabeth and Mary as testifying truly to the divine purposes at work in them (Lk. 1:39-56).

[62] On the significance of this rejection (and that in v. 13) as a climactic failure on the part of the Eleven, see Chapter 3.

2.7 Mary Magdalene Is the Pattern

Mary is the *first* person to whom the resurrected Jesus appears, the first witness to that fact, and the first to have her witness to the resurrection rejected. But she is *not the only* one to see, tell, and face rejection. The instance of Jesus's appearance to two disciples in transit appears to be either dependent on or related to Luke's Gospel or a similar tradition, where there is an appearance of the risen Christ to "two of them" (δύο ἐξ αὐτῶν, 24:13; compare to the same terms, except with δύο in the dative, δυσὶν ἐξ αὐτῶν in Mk 16:12). In Luke, one of the disciples is named Cleopas (εἷς ὀνόματι Κλεοπᾶς), and the second is never identified (24:18). Because the two disciples in the LE are unnamed, the only indicator of gender is the use of masculine participles (περιπατοῦσιν, πορευομένοις, and ἀπελθόντες) in vv. 13-14 and two demonstrative pronouns (κἀκεῖνοι and ἐκείνοις) in v. 14. This means that at least one of the two disciples in reference is male. The language of Luke's Emmaus road account is no clearer: at times, interpreters have speculated that the companion of Cleopas could be his wife,[63] but that must remain speculation. In that there is at least one male disciple, but possibly two, the LE's cast of characters on the road is consonant with Luke's telling.

Several other connections to the Lukan account of the Emmaus Road are recognizable in the greatly abbreviated episode in the LE. Not only are the two disciples part of a larger group; they are also walking when they encounter Jesus.[64] In Luke, the two are leaving Jerusalem, the location of the crucifixion, and heading to the village of Emmaus, which Luke explains was sixty *stade*, or nearly seven miles, from Jerusalem (εἰς κώμην ἀπέχουσαν σταδίους ἑξήκοντα ἀπὸ Ἰερουσαλήμ, ᾗ ὄνομα Ἐμμαοῦς; Lk 24:13). The LE describes their journey as into the country (εἰς ἀγρόν) more generally (16:12). Luke's account portrays Jesus as unrecognized by the two disciples, because their eyes "were being seized" (οἱ δὲ ὀφθαλμοὶ αὐτῶν ἐκρατοῦντο τοῦ μὴ ἐπιγνῶναι αὐτόν; 24:16). One may interpret this as a divine passive; God is the unstated cause of the blindness. It is only moments before Jesus departs from them that their eyes are "opened," with the result that they can recognize him (αὐτῶν δὲ διηνοίχθησαν οἱ ὀφθαλμοὶ καὶ ἐπέγνωσαν αὐτόν; v. 31). None of the nuance of Luke's account of supernatural and temporary blindness, nor the intervening explication of the scriptures by the mysterious traveler (Jesus), can be found in Mk 16:12. Nonetheless, something like the difficulty of recognition must be in view when Jesus is said to appear "in a different form" (ἐφανερώθη ἐν ἑτέρᾳ μορφῇ; Mk 16:12). In both Luke and the LE, the

---

[63] Ross Shepard Kraemer notes recent interpretations have suggested the possibility that the unnamed person with Cleopas is a woman. Further, she says, "masking the female identity of the second person might be seen as consistent with Luke's representation of the resurrection appearances" ("Unnamed Companion of Cleopas," in *Women in Scripture: A Dictionary of Named and Unnamed Women in the Hebrew Bible, the Apocryphal/Deuterocanonical, and the New Testament* (ed. Carole Meyers et al.; Grand Rapids: Eerdmans, 2001), 453. See also Carolyn Osiek, "Mary 5," in *Women in Scripture*, 123.

[64] Luke 24:13 uses the periphrastic participial construction ἦσαν πορευόμενοι for the disciples on their own. When Jesus joins them, it is as they continue traveling: συνεπορεύετο αὐτοῖς (v. 15). In Luke's account the disciples are talking about recent happenings, and after Jesus joins them he participates in their discussions as well. The LE's account leaves out the discursive element but makes clear that the disciples are walking (περιπατοῦσιν and πορευομένοις in Mk 16:12).

encounter with Jesus spurs the two disciples to return to their comrades and report what they have seen (Lk. 24:33-36a; Mk 16:13).

Besides the noticeable difference in scale of detail, the reception of the two disciples' witness diverges in these two accounts. In Luke, when the two disciples report to the remainder, they are greeted by an affirmation of the Lord's resurrection ("The Lord is truly raised and appeared to Simon"; ὄντως ἠγέρθη ὁ κύριος καὶ ὤφθη Σίμωνι; 24:34). While the two disciples are recounting their own encounter with the Lord,[65] Jesus himself appears and stands in the midst of them (v. 36). Although they react in terror at the sudden sight of him, the immediacy of a visible, standing, speaking Jesus obviates the other disciples' ability—at least as presented within narrative time—to respond to the witness of the two disciples.

The author of the LE does something rather different. Whereas Luke presents many details of the encounter between the two and Jesus, the details in the LE's version are either greatly abbreviated or omitted entirely. Inversely, in Mk 16:13 (in contrast to Luke), the remaining disciples have ample time to hear and have an opportunity to respond to the testimony of their two brethren. The reaction is similar to v. 11: "Neither did they believe them" (οὐδὲ ἐκείνοις ἐπίστευσαν; 16:13). The use of οὐδέ indicates that a previous instance of unbelief is in view. In fact, there are far more similarities between Mary's witness (16:9-11) and the two disciples' (vv. 12-13) than between the two versions of the account in which two disciples meet Jesus in transit (Mk 16:12-13 and Lk. 24:13-35). Unlike Luke's Road to Emmaus story, the LE's two disciples walking are met with *a negative response* from the other disciples when they tell them about seeing Jesus. That matches the pattern initiated by the response to Mary Magdalene's witness in Mk 16:9-11.

Table 2.3 illustrates the parallels in structure between the second resurrection appearance (to the two disciples, Mk 16:12-13) and the first (to Mary Magdalene, 16:9-11).[66] While the stories are not perfectly mirrored, there are striking similarities.

Mirecki strongly asserts the interconnection between vv. 9-11 and 12-13. He states, "The narrative functions of both Mary Magdalene and 'two of them' are identical, appear to be different characterizations of the same actor, and can thus be considered a single actor. Only at the level of characterization do they acquire identity as separate characters. As actors they play the same part."[67] Mirecki's search for narrative patterns leads him to overlook the small but telling differences between the first two episodes in the LE. I resist equating the position of Mary with that of the two disciples, having demonstrated Mary's pride of place in several respects (i.e., she is "first," named,

---

[65] The present participle (λαλούντων) should be taken, with its whole genitive absolute phrase, duratively: "*While* they were saying these things" (v. 36).
[66] Mirecki ("Mark 16:9-20," 26-8) and Kelhoffer (*Miracle and Mission*, 85) present similar comparative charts. Mirecki labels the disciples "antagonists" due to their response ("Mark 16:9-20," 26; cf. 28-9). More broadly, Hug (*La Finale*, 33) includes a chart that presents structural similarities within five sections of the LE, each introduced by "indications de temps": πρῶτον (vv. 9-11), μετά (vv. 12-13), ὕστερον (v. 14), [καί (vv. 15-16)], and μετά (vv. 19-20)—and followed, in most cases, by verbs that provide the initiative for the action of each section (ἐφάνη, ἐφανερώθη, ἐφανερώθη, εἶπεν, ἀνελήμφθη + ἐκάθισεν, respectively), verbs for the action of the messenger (either πορεύομαι or prefixed-ἔρχομαι, with the exception of v. 14), and terms for belief/faith (πιστεύω or ἀπιστέω, excepting the final section).
[67] Mirecki, "Mark 16:9-20," 129-30.

Table 2.3 Appearance, report, and rejection in 16:9-11 and 16:12-13

16:9-11	
Temporal phrase	Ἀναστὰς δὲ πρωῒ πρώτῃ σαββάτου
he appeared	ἐφάνη
Manner	πρῶτον
Witness	Μαρίᾳ τῇ Μαγδαληνῇ,
Description of witness	παρ᾽ ἧς ἐκβεβλήκει ἑπτὰ δαιμόνια.
she went and proclaimed	ἐκείνη <u>πορευθεῖσα</u> ἀπήγγειλεν
Recipients of report	τοῖς <u>μετ᾽ αὐτοῦ γενομένοις</u>
Description of recipients	πενθοῦσι καὶ κλαίουσιν·
Content of report	κἀκεῖνοι ἀκούσαντες ὅτι ζῇ καὶ ἐθεάθη ὑπ᾽ αὐτῆς
Unbelief	ἠπίστησαν.
16:12-13	
Temporal phrase	Μετὰ δὲ ταῦτα
Witnesses	δυσὶν ἐξ αὐτῶν περιπατοῦσιν
he was revealed	ἐφανερώθη
Manner	ἐν ἑτέρᾳ μορφῇ
Description of witnesses	πορευομένοις εἰς ἀγρόν·
they went and proclaimed	κἀκεῖνοι <u>ἀπελθόντες</u> **ἀπήγγειλαν**
Recipients of report	**τοῖς** <u>λοιποῖς</u>·
Unbelief	<u>οὐδὲ ἐκείνοις</u> **ἐπίστευσαν**.

and described). The fact that Mirecki can argue that Mary Magdalene and the two, unnamed, walking disciples serve *identical* functions in the narrative demonstrates that the parallels between the two episodes are very close. But it is Mary who establishes the pattern in which the other two follow.[68]

The similarities between Mary Magdalene, first, and the two disciples in transit, second, rather than demonstrating a conflation of their characters' roles, demonstrate a unity of orientation: Mary Magdalene's character acts at every stage in a manner oriented *to Jesus*, whether as recipient of his epiphany, proclaimer of his resurrection, or rejected witness on his behalf. Insofar as the "two of them" experience similar phenomena, they reenact Mary's witness, which points to the risen Jesus. The gender of the two disciples (or at least one of the two), who are present for the second appearance of the resurrected Jesus, is not emphasized in 16:12-13. The reason to pay any attention to the gender element is precisely due to the second story's resemblance to Mary Magdalene's encounter with her Lord (16:9-11). A man, if not two men, follow(s) the pattern of reception and proclamation that a woman inaugurates. The male response to Jesus mirrors hers in basic form; it neither surpasses nor outshines her witness.

2.8 Mary Magdalene Is Approved by Jesus

For what is, perhaps, the most unique element of the treatment of Mary in the LE, one must skip ahead a few verses to Jesus's encounter with the Eleven. The majority of that

---

[68] This interpretation is preferable, in my view, rather than collapsing all three into an abstract pattern that obscures salient differences among them.

encounter is the focus of the next chapter, but one aspect belongs in our treatment of Mary. When Jesus upbraids the disciples for their disbelief, they are admonished for not believing *the witnesses* of his resurrection (τοῖς θεασαμένοις αὐτὸν ἐγηγερμένον; v. 14). The resurrected Jesus endorses Mary, implicitly along with the other two disciples, as she was the first "one who saw him having been raised." By suggesting that the Eleven should have believed the proclamation made by Mary and the other two witnesses, Jesus gives their testimonies a stamp of approval.

The only other post-resurrection passage in which any disciples are rebuked for disbelief is the Road to Emmaus pericope (Lk 24:13-35).[69] There, the two disciples—who have so far failed to recognize Jesus—are chided as fools (ἀνόητοι) and slow in heart (βραδεῖς τῇ καρδίᾳ). Even though Cleopas and his companion have already acknowledged receiving the women's testimony (24:24), which they must have rejected along with the other disciples (24:11), they are criticized for failing to see that *the prophets* spoke about the Christ (24:25-26). In the LE's account, by contrast, it is not an accumulation of prophetic pointers (πᾶσιν οἷς ἐλάλησαν οἱ προφῆται, as in Lk. 24:25) that the Eleven have missed. The Eleven are chastised for rejecting the witness of fellow disciples—a female and two others—all of whom proclaimed to them that they had seen the Lord (Mk 16:14).

To this point, I have examined the story of Jesus's resurrection appearance to Mary Magdalene and her resulting proclamation to those who had been with him. This study has looked at the narrative in the light of two contexts. First, in the immediate textual context of Mark's earliest ending and the LE affixed to it (15:40–16:20, roughly), we observed the disjunction between Mary's shared failure in 16:8 and her individual, successful proclamation in 16:10. Also noteworthy were her paired actions of *going* and *telling*, which fulfilled her commission in 16:7.

Second, I have studied Mk 16:9-11 in light of the canonical Gospel contexts wherein related narrative elements of resurrection appearances are found. By highlighting elements that are shared between the LE and one or more of the other canonical Gospels, I have focused on Mary's priority, name, former demon-possession, proclamation, rejection, pattern, and approval by Jesus. Several of these elements either arise out of or are related closely to attributes of Mary known from other Gospels: she is a consistently named witness to the empty tomb (Mk 16:1;[70] Mt. 28:1; Lk. 24:10; Jn 20:1-2) and/or Jesus's resurrection (Mt. 28:9; Jn 20:18); Mary has a history as a healed demoniac (Lk. 8:2); she encounters Jesus alone (Jn 20:11-18). Of course, even though these elements are found elsewhere, no other evangelist presents them all together. Further, although sparse in detail, the LE's description of Mary manages to present her in novel ways; its presentation cannot simply be attributed to any extant resurrection narrative. Particularly pronounced, in light of parallel canonical passages, is the LE's presentation of Mary Magdalene as *first* (πρῶτον) in status among the disciples, her solitary witness absent any explanation of her thoughts or feelings, and her rejection, despite having seen Jesus firsthand and declaring

---

[69] Jesus's statement to Thomas in Jn 20:27b encourages him to move from unbelieving to believing (μὴ γίνου ἄπιστος ἀλλὰ πιστός) but does not include any negative estimation of Thomas (although tradition has applied a negative tone to the appellation "Doubting Thomas").

[70] She sees but does not tell in Mk 16:8.

him alive.[71] Her pattern of witness—going and telling—is repeated in the actions of two other disciples (16:12-13), as is her experience of rejection. Her pattern of proclamation does not end when these two emulate her proclamation, as we will discuss later.[72]

Although Mary Magdalene is the first in Mark 16 to see Jesus and to announce his resurrection,[73] she is not the first to move from encounter with Jesus to proclamation in the Gospel as a whole.[74] Further, the LE's tacit approval of Mary's witness (in that its reliability is confirmed within the narrative itself) and Jesus's indicated support for her and her testimony (in 16:14) are worthy of note as a conclusion to a Gospel in which humans scarcely receive approbation from Jesus. This approval by Jesus is one of the connections between Mary Magdalene in the LE and a few anonymous women in Mk 1:1–16:8.

3. Mary Magdalene's Anonymous Female Predecessors in Mark's Gospel

Mary Magdalene is an integral person in the four Gospels' way of telling about the empty tomb and Jesus's resurrection. As a "canonical" ending to Mark, the LE may have contained her proclamation as a witness to Jesus's resurrection in partial confirmation of Matthew's and John's accounts (Mt. 28:9-10; Jn 20:18). In my opinion, however, another reason that the second-century extension of Mark's Gospel brought Mary Magdalene back into the picture is to align the appended ending with the preceding narrative. The LE is not merely a "canonical" ending; it is also a "Markan" ending.

A faithful few female followers had accompanied Jesus further than did the male disciples in his inner-circle (14:50, 72), even to the cross and tomb (15:40-41, 47).

---

[71] Luke's account is both similar and different: he includes Mary Magdalene among those who hear and convey the angelic messengers' report of Jesus's resurrection—rather than a firsthand encounter with Jesus (as in 16:9-11)—but the disciples disbelieve the women's words nevertheless (24:10-11).

[72] See Chapter 4.

[73] It is noteworthy that the initial statement of Jesus's resurrection is placed in the mouth of the young man seated in the tomb, who is generally considered angelic or supernatural, and is found in the undisputed ending (16:6). He states the relevant information both to the women and to the reader: "[Jesus the Nazarene who was crucified] was raised, he is not here" (ἠγέρθη, οὐκ ἔστιν ὧδε). The women are invited to behold for themselves where he had lain. Yet, the LE's statement of Mary's priority (πρῶτον) indicates that, no matter how the messenger at the tomb knows of Jesus's resurrection, he is not counted among the witnesses to the risen Jesus.

[74] In fact, because of the sometimes latent and sometimes overt messianic secret in Mark, witnesses to Jesus are deserving of attention. Joan Mitchell, e.g., finds a common thread between the nameless characters in Mark's narrative who, despite Jesus's prohibition, proclaim the messianic secret (Joan L. Mitchell, *Beyond Fear and Silence: A Feminist-Literary Approach to the Gospel of Mark* [New York: Continuum, 2001], 94–5). In this defiant, faithful group she includes the leper (1:44), the Gerasene demoniac (5:19-20), the hemorrhaging woman (5:25-34), and the deaf mute (7:32-37), all beneficiaries of Jesus's miraculous power to heal and exorcise. Although the designation for these individuals of "Anonymous Preachers" (94) seems a stretch, Mitchell weaves together their audible responses to Jesus's healing convincingly as witnesses to the gospel. For instance, Mitchell interprets the narrative summary that the woman "told him the whole truth" (εἶπεν αὐτῷ πᾶσαν τὴν ἀλήθειαν; 5:33) as an instance of proclamation in the presence of a community (97). It is important for Mitchell's argument that the women's fear and silence in 16:8 be interpreted in a way that calls for audience response. She states,

But the last verse of Mark's earliest ending relates an ostensible failure of the women's followership.[75] The proliferation and popularity of later endings demonstrate that the ending at 16:8 was seen by some as inadequate.[76] The most widespread of the resulting endings attempts to correct the "inadequacy" by introducing Mary Magdalene back onto the scene. Redeeming the women's apparent failure in 16:8 was not the only interest of the LE's author: others included supporting baptism (v. 16), commissioning (v. 15), signs confirming belief (vv. 17-18, 20), and reporting Christ's ascension (v. 19). But restoring the women's discipleship comes first.

This "repair" cannot be attributed merely to a desire to reassure readers that the word of Jesus's resurrection got out eventually. If that were the primary concern, a brief, conciliatory summary statement like that of the Intermediate Ending would surely suffice. Instead, the LE ensures that the women disciples get it right, at least in the person of Mary Magdalene. In the end, Mary did not fail. Jesus's defense of the witnesses, which includes Mary and her testimony, finally, provides the primary connection to a thread that runs through the Gospel.

Throughout Jesus's ministry, as told in Mark, the nameless female recipients of Jesus's healing or recognition have represented most of the (few) bright spots among people whom Jesus encountered. Casual readers of Mark and scholars alike notice the dearth of faithful followers in Mark. Jesus frequently bemoans the disciples' failure to understand his identity and mission.[77] Mark did not by any means present women in a uniformly positive manner.[78] There are numerous counterexamples in which women perform negatively, dismissively, or even villainously: Jesus's own mother (3:31-35),[79]

> The rhetoric of Mark's suspended ending plays to an audience experiencing a transition between the eyewitness generation of Jesus's followers, who are growing old or have already been martyred, and themselves—a potential new generation of Christians ... Markan rhetoric pictures Jesus's earliest women and men disciples in the numinous fear and liminal silence where their faith and commitment began as persuasive encouragement for its hearers to take up their mission. (96)

> In light of the Gospel's ending in the (named) women's fear and silence, as well as the lack of restoration of the (named) deserting disciples (16:7-8), she asserts that it is the anonymous, social outcasts who have the narrated opportunity to declare the good news, which includes the Markan community. In the LE, Mary Magdalene as a named woman does not fit with the neat pattern Mitchell observes in Mk 1:1–16:8. Yet her witness to the resurrected Jesus is utilized in the LE (16:10) as an example and impetus for the ongoing Christian proclamation (as will be argued later), to the same end that Mitchell argues for the anonymous witnesses to Jesus during his life.

[75] Several scholars take the women's silence as a positive, as a silence to all *except* those they were directed to tell (Hurtado, "The Women, the Tomb," 438-43) or as an appropriate, even reverent, response to an epiphany (David Catchpole, "The Fearful Silence of the Women at the Tomb: A Study in Markan Theology," *JTSA* 18 [1977], 9; Elizabeth Struthers Malbon, *In the Company of Jesus: Characters in Mark's Gospel* [Louisville: Westminster John Knox, 2000], 64). See note 2 for more information.

[76] Many combinations of alterations constitute the endings of Mark in the manuscript tradition, even though the LE outnumbers the rest in frequency as the conclusion to the Second Gospel. The reader is directed to the Appendix on the Markan endings for a presentation of the variety of conclusions with which Mark has been known to end.

[77] This is a subject for the next chapter, but see, e.g.: Mk 4:40-41; 8:16-21; 9:18-19.

[78] Malbon's chapter on "Fallible Followers" makes this point effectively (*In the Company*, esp. 46–50).

[79] See Johnson ("Who Is My Mother?" 32–46) for a view on Jesus's mother's redemption in the Second Gospel.

Herodias and her daughter (6:19, 22, 25-26, 28),[80] and the high priest's slave girl, who questions Peter (14:66-69). Neither do men act merely as foils; they are sometimes presented in positive terms,[81] even as Jesus's notoriously obdurate disciples do not *always* disappoint.[82] Although Mark's gender divide cannot be neatly parsed—as if women understand Jesus and men do not—there is a prevalent tendency in Mark for insiders (often men) to miss Jesus, while outsiders (often women) seem to be in tune to him.

Mark has proved to be a fertile ground for investigations into the role of women in the NT and early Christianity. In the past thirty-five years, many studies on women in the Gospels have been published,[83] several on Mark in particular.[84] Other studies

---

[80] F. Scott Spencer offers a "rehabilitative" reading of this text, along with a selective survey of scholarly interpretations of the pair (*Dancing Girls, Loose Ladies, and Women of the Cloth: The Women in Jesus's Life* [New York: Continuum, 2004], 47-75). Spencer acknowledges that "in comparison with the other women in Mark, most of whom are disadvantaged, anonymous examples of 'Christian' faith and service, Herodias stands out like a sore thumb as a powerful, named female representative of treachery and violence, the only 'bad guy', ... in the bunch" (50). Sharon Betsworth provides a survey of varying scholarly opinion on Herodias (and Herod) and her daughter (*The Reign of God is Such as These: A Socio-literary Analysis of Daughters in the Gospel of Mark* [LNTS 422; New York: T&T Clark, 2010], 9-11, 115-26). Her own opinion is that "this evil mother and daughter are juxtaposed in the Gospel with the stories of faithful parents and daughters" (126).

[81] John the Baptist represents a positive male character from the Evangelist's perspective (1:7-8), although a statement of affirmation never comes from Jesus himself (an authority-subverting *hint* of approval comes in 11:30). Two fathers are portrayed positively as seeking Jesus for the healing of their children (Jairus in 5:22-24a; the father of a possessed boy in 9:17-27). The formerly possessed man, "Legion," wants to follow Jesus after he is healed (5:18), but is commissioned as a messenger who goes and tells (ἀπῆλθεν καὶ ἤρξατο κηρύσσειν) his friends (τοὺς σούς) in the Decapolis (5:19-20). After healing Bartimaeus of his blindness, Jesus tells him to go, but instead Bartimaeus follows Jesus (10:52) without any narrated refusal from Jesus. Even among the typically adversarial scribes, there is one who is "not far from the kingdom of God" (12:34). Finally, Joseph of Arimathea is the only man who acts "boldly" (τολμήσας) after Jesus's crucifixion and asks for Jesus's body for burial (15:42-46).

[82] Chapter 3 treats the male disciples in the Gospel According to Mark and the LE.

[83] E.g., Bauckham, *Gospel Women*; Josef Blank, "Frauen in den Jesusüberlieferungen," in *Die Frau im Urchristentum* (ed. Karl Rahner and Heinrich Schlier; Quaestiones disputatae 95; Freiburg: Herder, 1983), 9-91; Holly Hearon, *The Magdalene Tradition: Witness and Counter-Witness in Early Christian Communities* (Collegeville, MN: Liturgical Press, 2004); Spencer, *Dancing Girls, Loose Ladies, and Women of the Cloth*; Ben Witherington, III, *Women in the Ministry of Jesus: A Study of Jesus' Attitudes to Women and their Roles as Reflected in His Earthly Life* (SNTSMS 51; Cambridge University Press, 1984). Even earlier, see Lynn Bode, *First Easter Morning: The Gospel Accounts of the Women's Visit to the Tomb of Jesus* (Rome: Biblical Institute Press, 1970).

[84] On women in Mark: Mary Ann Beavis, "Women as Models of Faith in Mark," *BTB* 18 (1988): 3-9; Betsworth, *Reign of God*; Irene Dannemann, *Aus dem Rahmen fallen: Frauen im Markusevangelium: eine feministische Re-vision* (Berlin: Alektor-Verlag, 1996); Joanna Dewey, "Women in the Gospel of Mark," *WW* 26 (2006): 22-9; Monika Fander, "Frauen in der Nachfolge Jesu: Die Rolle der Frau im Markusevangelium," *EvT* 52 (1992): 413-32; idem, *Die Stellung der Frau im Markusevangelium: Unter besonderer Berücksichtigung kultur- und religionsgeschichtlicher Hintergründe* (Altenberge, Germany: Telos-Verlag, 1989); Hisako Kinukawa, *Women and Jesus in Mark*; Susan Miller, *Women in Mark's Gospel* (JSNTSup 259; New York: T&T Clark, 2004); Mitchell, *Beyond Fear and Silence*; Willard M. Swartley, "The Role of Women in Mark's Gospel: A Narrative Analysis," *BTB* 27 (1997): 16-22. On a woman or women in particular Markan pericopes: Richard Bauckham, "Salome the Sister of Jesus, Salome the Disciple of Jesus, and the Secret Gospel of Mark," *NovT* 33 (1991): 245-75; Mark DiCicco, "What Can One Give in Exchange for One's Life? A Narrative-Critical Study of the Widow and Her Offering, Mark 12:41-44," *CurTM* 25 (1998): 441-9; James A. Kelhoffer, "A Tale of Two Markan Characterizations: The Exemplary Woman Who Anointed Jesus's Body for Burial (14:3-9) and the Silent Trio Who Fled the Empty Tomb (16:1-8),"

happen upon significant insights regarding women characters in Mark via another interest, such as Markan intercalation.[85] Although not without nuance and varying emphases, the studies on women in Mark invariably refer to their positive portrayal.[86]

There is neither space nor cause for a thorough treatment of women in Mark here. Instead, I will focus solely on the women who are the subjects of praise from the mouth of Jesus. It is this positive affirmation, otherwise scarce,[87] and the faithful women who provoke it that offer the most compelling rationale for *why* the LE begins with Mary Magdalene. What follows, though by no means exhaustive, is intended to be a representative consideration of the women and their actions that inspire Jesus's rare praise in the Second Gospel. In Mk 1:1–16:8 there are three women[88] in particular who receive Jesus's scarcely bestowed affirmation: the hemorrhaging woman (5:24b-34), the widow with an offering (12:41-44), and the woman who anoints Jesus (14:3-9).[89]

---

in *Women and Gender in Ancient Religions: Interdisciplinary Approaches* (ed. Stephen P. Ahearne-Kroll et al; WUNT; Tübingen: Mohr Siebeck, 2010), 85–98; Elizabeth Struthers Malbon, "The Poor Widow in Mark and Her Poor Rich Readers," *CBQ* 53 (1991): 589–604; Susan Miller, "The Woman Who Anoints Jesus (14:3–9): A Prophetic Sign of the New Creation," *Feminist Theology* 14 (2006): 221–36; idem, "'They Said Nothing to Anyone': The Fear and Silence of the Women at the Empty Tomb (Mk 16.1–8)," *Feminist Theology* 13 (2004): 77–90; Luise Schottroff, "Maria Magdalena und die Frauen am Grabe Jesu," *EvT* 42 (1982): 3–25; Marla J. Selvidge, *Woman, Cult, and Miracle Recital: A Redaction Critical Investigation on Mark 5:24–34* (Lewisburg, PA: Bucknell University Press, 1990); R. S. Sugirtharajah, "The Widow's Mites Revalued," *ExpTim* 103 (1991): 42–3; Addison G. Wright, "The Widow's Mites: Praise or Lament?—A Matter of Context," *CBQ* 44 (1982): 256–65.

[85] E.g., James R. Edwards's thorough treatment of the interwoven stories of Jairus's daughter and the hemorrhaging woman in Mk 5:21–43 ("Markan Sandwiches: The Significance of Interpolations in Markan Narratives," *NovT* 31 [1989]: esp. 203–5). Narrative observations, as well as descriptive contrasts, lead Edwards to the following Christological and soteriological interpretation: "The woman's faith forms the center of the sandwich and is the key to its interpretation. Through her Mark shows how faith in Jesus can transform fear and despair into hope and salvation. It is a powerful lesson for Jairus, as well as for Mark's readers" (205).

[86] My analysis is oversimplified; a cursory glance through "recent research" section of the most recent book-length treatment of women in the Second Gospel lists variations in approaches and perspectives on the subject. Yet women are usually seen as positive figures in Mark, read as models of discipleship, examples of faithfulness or piety, and compared favorably to the male disciples (Miller, *Women in Mark's Gospel*, 1–4).

[87] It is difficult to designate what constitutes approval in Mark's Gospel. On the one hand, it is surely a positive situation when Jesus assents to heal someone. E.g., he says to the leper, "I am willing, be made clean!" (1:41). Seeing the faith of the paralytic and his friends, Jesus also says to the paralytic, "Child, your sins are forgiven" (2:5). In this latter instance, the reader can infer that the faith of the healed person and his friends was related to Jesus's decision to heal him (connected by the participle ἰδών), but *faith* is not named as the cause of restoration, as it is in the case of the hemorrhaging woman (5:34). On the other hand, a lack of miracles is indicative of a lack of faith (6:5-6). In matters unrelated to healing or exorcism, Jesus's suggestion that those sitting around him (περιβλεψάμενος τοὺς περὶ αὐτὸν κύκλῳ καθημένου, 3:34) are his family is a tacit affirmation.

[88] There are instances in which women are the passive recipients of Jesus's miraculous healing, sought by their family members. In these instances, the worthiness of the women themselves is simply unavailable to the reader (Mk 1:30-31; 5:38-43).

[89] The fourth woman whom Jesus *might* affirm is the Syrophoenician woman (7:24–30). After an initially negative (and insulting) response to her request on her daughter's behalf (v. 27), the woman's humble yet persistent reply seems to be what ultimately prompts Jesus to heal her daughter. His statement regarding the woman, however, cannot be categorized as affirmation, as it is ambiguous on its own. He says, "Because of this saying, go!" (διὰ τοῦτον τὸν λόγον ὕπαγε). Only when he completes his sentence regarding the daughter's status and the woman returns home and finds her daughter restored to health is it finally clear that Jesus regarded her reply as satisfactory. His words alone do not make explicit his approval. On the significance of the exchange, however, Monika Fander notes, "In

In the context of a Gospel in which humans—followers and otherwise—so roundly disappoint, it is likely that Mark's ancient readers noticed that the few who Jesus said "got it right" were women.

3.1 "Daughter, your faith has saved you": The Woman with a Hemorrhage (5:34)

The hemorrhaging woman in Mk 5:25-34 is anonymous, identifiable only by association with her malady.[90] Yet she stands out because Jesus eventually points to her actions as saving faith, which affirms her conduct and belief at once. Outwardly, the woman's attempt to reach Jesus is far less audacious than was the paralytic's and those who assist him in 2:3-12. In fact, after she touches Jesus's hem, he is not sure who among the surrounding throng did so (5:30). Mark's placement of this story, a classic example of the "Markan sandwich" (i.e., narrative intercalation), is more disruptive than the woman herself intends to be. In the midst of telling the story of Jesus's healing of the "little daughter" (τὸ θυγάτριον) of a ruler of the synagogue named Jairus (5:22-23), another "daughter" (θυγάτηρ) interrupts and steals the scene (5:25-34, esp. v. 34).

The woman wishes to remain unknown, yet the narrator will not let her be. Thrust into the spotlight by Mark's narrative cunning, the woman emerges from the mob crowding around Jesus (v. 24) and becomes the focus of Mark's attention (v. 25) long before she receives Jesus's notice (v. 30). The first indicative verb that denotes the woman's activity in the story is in v. 27b, ἥψατο: she *touches* Jesus's garment. Initially, the narration introduces her simply and factually: "And a woman, having a flow of blood for twelve years" (v. 25). After this initial participle (οὖσα), the woman with hemorrhage is the subject of a series of descriptive, participial clauses that progressively fill in the portrait of her character (Table 2.4).

In contrast to the twelve years spent suffering from her unceasing menstrual flow, compounded by her suffering many things under the "care" of many physicians—with the result that she had expended everything she had, had benefitted nothing, and had gotten worse—after she heard about Jesus, her expenditure was almost nil (merely following in the crowd behind him and touching his clothing). Her healing was immediate (εὐθύς; v. 29).

Mark grants his readers greater access to the biography and internal life of this anonymous woman than to many, arguably any, of his named characters,[91] Mary

---

no other controversy story is Jesus the one who loses or the one who changes his point of view. Here, through her quick-witted reply, the Syrophoenician woman changes Jesus's perspective" ("Gospel of Mark: Women as True Disciples of Jesus," in *Feminist Biblical Interpretation: A Compendium of Critical Commentary on the Books of the Bible and Related Literature* [ed. Luise Schottroff and Marie-Theres Wacker; trans. Lisa E. Dahill et al.; Grand Rapids: Eerdmans, 2012 (translated from the German: *Kompendium Feministische Bibelauslegung* [2d ed.; Gütersloh: Chr. Kaiser Gütersloher Verlagshaus, 1999])], 626-44).

[90] This will constitute my most thorough exegetical treatment of one of these women, because it is the story with most detail about the woman and the encounter with Jesus. Additionally, it is exemplary of Jesus's positive encounters with female believers in Mark.

[91] Perhaps most vague is Simon of Cyrene, the father of Alexander and Rufus, who plays a key role in Jesus's road to crucifixion, but is only known by his and his sons' names (15:21). Joseph of Arimathea, although we first hear of him *after* Jesus's crucifixion, is described as a "respected counselor" (εὐσχήμων βουλευτής) and as one who awaited the kingdom of God (15:43). We

Table 2.4 Successive descriptions of the hemorrhaging woman in Mark

Καί γυνὴ	
	οὖσα ἐν ῥύσει αἵματος δώδεκα ἔτη
καὶ	πολλὰ παθοῦσα ὑπὸ πολλῶν ἰατρῶν
καὶ	δαπανήσασα τὰ παρ᾽ αὐτῆς πάντα
καὶ	μηδὲν ὠφεληθεῖσα
ἀλλὰ μᾶλλον εἰς τὸ χεῖρον ἐλθοῦσα,	
	ἀκούσασα περὶ τοῦ Ἰησοῦ
ἥψατο τοῦ ἱματίου αὐτοῦ·	ἐλθοῦσα ἐν τῷ ὄχλῳ ὄπισθεν (5:25-27)

Magdalene among them. Significantly, Mark takes the woman seriously as a full character; the narrator explains the woman's medical history (5:25-26), including her previous suffering physically and economically (v. 26), her inner thoughts (v. 28), the bodily effect of touching Jesus including her sensation of healing (v. 29), and emotional state of extreme fear in addressing Jesus (5:33). This background gives greater weight to her seemingly minor investment in her healing. Her expectation of healing is explicit: "If I only touch his garment, I will be healed [σωθήσομαι]" (v. 28). Her statement expresses an internal *belief* that Jesus can reverse her situation, in contrast to the many physicians in whom she had entrusted her care for twelve years.

There is an intriguing parallel between Jesus's immediate awareness "in himself" (ἐπιγνοὺς ἐν ἑαυτῷ) that power had gone out from him and the woman's twice repeated knowledge that a healing change had occurred *in her body* (v. 29, 33).[92] This is the only time in Mark that *both* the healer and the healed are reported as experiencing a bodily sensation in the process. Jesus asks, "Who touched me?" (5:30-33a). But, unlike the disciples who protest that, with a crowd pressing in, Jesus's question is an inappropriate one,[93] Jesus looks around for a specific person, "the woman who had done this thing."[94] The woman's extreme fear (φοβηθεῖσα καὶ τρέμουσα) does not counteract her conviction about "that which has happened in her" (ὃ γέγονεν αὐτῇ; v. 33). We cannot ignore the woman's gender and her gender-specific illness in light of her fearfulness at

---

know even less about several among Jesus's chosen Twelve, whose names do not recur in Mark's narrative: Philip, Bartholomew, Matthew, Thomas, James (son of Alphaeus), Thaddeus, and Simon the Cananaean/zealot (3:18). These men are never mentioned again after Jesus "makes" Twelve to be with him (ἐποίησεν δώδεκα … ἵνα ὦσιν μετ᾽ αὐτοῦ; 3:14).

[92] Verse 29 is explicit: ἔγνω τῷ σώματι ὅτι ἴαται ἀπὸ τῆς μάστιγος ("she knew in [her] body that she was healed from her ailment"). In light of that, the dative in v. 33 can be read similarly "in her" (versus the potential "to her"): εἰδυῖα ὃ γέγονεν αὐτῇ ("knowing what had happened in her"). The internal nature of her infirmity also lends support to the reading of her awareness as *internal* to her body.

[93] The disciples' incredulous protest to Jesus in 5:31 indicates that they cannot imagine what would distinguish one particular touch from another: βλέπεις τὸν ὄχλον συνθλίβοντά σε καὶ λέγεις· τίς μου ἥψατο; ("You see the crowd jostling you and you say, 'Who touched me?'").

[94] It is not clear whether Jesus knew the one who touched him was a woman, as the feminine participle indicates (τὴν … ποιήσασαν), or whether the participle is feminine because the omniscient narrator knows what Jesus does not yet know within the timing of the story.

the prospect of approaching Jesus. She does so, nonetheless, assuming the posture of supplicant (προσέπεσεν αὐτῷ). But instead of asking for something, the woman *tells* (εἶπεν) Jesus "the whole truth" (πᾶσαν τὴν ἀλήθειαν).[95]

The woman's posture certainly reflects her attitude toward Jesus as the agent of her healing, but it does not reflect her situation; instead of making a request, she reaches out for what she needs and takes it. The deed, the healing, is done and can only be spoken about. Jesus's response says as much: "Daughter, your faith has saved you" (θυγάτηρ, ἡ πίστις σου σέσωκέν σε; v. 34a).[96] It is astonishing that Jesus credits *her* faith as responsible for her healing/salvation, rather than as the cause for his decision to heal her.[97]

Wider literary contexts enrich the emphasis on this woman's active faith. Jesus addresses her as "Daughter." Just two chapters earlier, Jesus had reoriented family to those who do the will of God (ὃς ... ἂν ποιήσῃ τὸ θέλημα τοῦ θεου): "This one is my brother, sister, and mother" (3:35). By implication, then, this restored "daughter"[98] is part of the family by the same definition. Besides the meaningful bracketing of this miracle account with Jesus's healing of Jairus's daughter (5:21-24a, 35-43),[99] the faith and reverent fear of the hemorrhaging woman stand in contrast to the immediately

---

[95] Mitchell interprets this "whole truth" as more than a mere confession of being the person who touched Jesus, but as a "word of faith in the community" and, later, sees the whole of the story, including the woman's speech, as "the woman's testimony to healing from long physical suffering, social isolation, and religious uncleanness" (*Beyond Fear and Silence*, 95-6).

[96] The term σῴζω has two strands of interpretation in English translation: one represents a rescue from a bodily ailment or threat, roughly equivalent to *healing*; and the second is perceived more spiritually as *salvation*, with a less corporeal scope. The TDNT entry on σῴζω highlights especially the phrase "your faith has saved you," as in Mk 5:34 (and par.; also, Mk 10:52 and par.; Lk. 7:50; 17:19) among the Synoptic Gospels' usage. Werner Foerster explains: "In the healings of Jesus σῴζω never refers to a single member of the body but also to the whole man ... The choice of the word leaves room for the view that the healing power of Jesus and the saving power of faith go beyond physical life" ("σῴζω," TDNT 7: 990-2). The entry in the NIDB goes further to explain that distinguishing between the physical and spiritual aspects of the terms σῴζω and σωτηρία is difficult if not impossible in most instances:

> While Jesus's deeds do of course make people well, and while these events are sometimes also described with the verb "to heal," failure to translate these texts with forms of the English verb "save" perpetuates the theological error that Jesus's restoration of people to physical wholeness is something other than salvation ... Salvation by Jesus is restoration to physical, spiritual, and social wholeness, as illustrated especially by the salvation of the woman with a hemorrhage (Mark 5:25-34). (J. Richard Middleton and Michael J. Gorman, "Salvation," NIDB 5:56)

[97] In the story of the paralytic who is carried by others and lowered to Jesus, a participle (likely temporal) connects Jesus's seeing their faith (ἰδὼν ὅ Ἰησοῦς τὴν πίστιν αὐτῶν) and his declaration of the forgiveness of the paralytic's sins (τέκνον, ἀφίενταί σου αἱ ἁμαρτίαι; 2:5). This, Jesus says, is the equivalent of healing him (2:9-11).

[98] Although Jesus's statement does not include "daughters," surely the familial terms were representative in 3:35 (N.B. ἀδελφή). Additionally, it is possible that Jesus is naming her as a daughter of God (or of Abraham [cf. Lk. 13:16]) and, perhaps, a sister of Jesus.

[99] Both are *daughters*: the healed woman is called θυγάτηρ (v. 34) and Jairus's daughter is called θυγάτριον ("little daughter," v. 23) and θυγάτηρ (v. 35). The connection between the years—twelve years of suffering on the woman's part, twelve years of age on Jairus's daughter's part—ties the two together and may signify a place in God's family for women whether young or old, under their father's care or (seemingly) alone (vv. 25 and 42).

subsequent account of Jesus's reception in his hometown. There, familiarity (6:2b-4) and lack of faith (6:6) hamper Jesus's ability to perform miracles (6:5).

Mark's account of Jesus's encounter with the woman who has suffered bleeding for twelve years is far more detailed than found in its Synoptic counterparts (Mt. 9:20-22; Lk. 8:42b-48). It diverges even more in elaborations, for that matter, from the sparsely detailed account of Jesus's resurrection appearance to Mary Magdalene in the LE (16:9-11). Storytelling style is, unquestionably, *not* the connection we should draw between the two pericopes. Instead, in both, a woman acts boldly in confidence in regard to Jesus. For the former, it is confidence that Jesus will be the source of her healing. For the latter, life-altering restorations have already taken place: first, Jesus freed Mary from sevenfold demonic possession; and, second, Jesus's own death has been transformed into life. She conveys the truth that Jesus is risen.

There is one further connection between these two accounts: Just as the two disciples in transit fit the pattern of their female predecessor (16:12-13), later in Mark's Gospel a male beneficiary of Jesus's healing receives the same affirmation from Jesus as did the woman with hemorrhage. After blind Bartimaeus asks Jesus to restore his sight (10:51), Jesus's response is at once a statement of healing and an affirmation of faith. Jesus says to him the same phrase, word-for-word, that he spoke to the woman with the hemorrhage (5:34): "Your faith has saved you" (ἡ πίστις σου σέσωκέν σε; 10:52). In both instances, boldness seems to characterize those actions that Jesus labels as "faith." The woman lays claim on her healing by grabbing Jesus's cloak (5:27-29), while Bartimaeus shouts his request despite rebuke from others (10:47-48). This word of affirmation from Jesus, sufficient praise for a faithful man, is bestowed first on a woman.

3.2 "This poor widow has put in more than all": The Generous Widow (12:44)

Some commentators have noted that, unlike his encounters with the hemorrhaging woman (Mk 5:25-34) and the Syrophoenician woman (7:25-30), Jesus never speaks to the widow in this story.[100] Such comments often hint that Mark dehumanizes the widow in her destitution. Others deem the story an inferior witness to Jesus's view of women.[101] There are good reasons to dispute both such analyses.

Mark not only narrates the widow's small donation to the temple; he also includes Jesus's commentary on the event.[102] The praise Jesus offers the widow, although

---

[100] Miller, *Women in Mark's Gospel*, 115. Kinukawa adds that the widow's complete lack of relationship to Jesus is shared only by the servant-girl of the high priest (14:68-69; *Women and Jesus*, 66).

[101] Against this trend within some feminist interpreters, Kinukawa suggests that, although Jesus can presently do nothing for the widow, his encounter with her changes him and his outlook on his impending future (*Women and Jesus*, 75–6).

[102] Form critics have historically labeled this story a "paradigm" (Dibelius) or an "apothegm" (Bultmann). But the recent consensus has identified it as a "pronouncement story" (following Vincent Taylor, *St. Mark*, 78–9). Robert Tannehill explains the basic form as "a *pronouncement* which is the climactic element in a brief *story*" ("Introduction: The Pronouncement Story and Its Types," *Semeia* 20 [1981]: 1; emphases in the original). Of the varieties of pronouncement stories Tannehill categorizes, the pericope of the widow's offering is one of commendation (the other varieties are largely negative). In this chapter, I compare Jesus's "pronouncement" regarding the widow to other similarly structured instances in Mark.

apparently unknown by her, does not explicitly make her selfless generosity an example to his disciples (12:43-44). The anonymous widow functions as an exemplar, although the narrative never calls her a ὑπόδειγμα and Jesus never enjoins the disciples to imitate (μιμεῖσθαι) her.[103] Instead, by a lesson in contrasts—that is, the presentation of her activity in stark dissimilarity to the behavior of the crowds (12:41a) and in even sharper distinction from the "many wealthy people who cast in much" (πολλοὶ πλούσιοι ἔβαλλον πολλά; 12:41b)—Jesus's endorsement of her extreme giving as an example to his disciples is implicit.[104]

The narrative context for Jesus's comment provides sharp contrasts between the widow and the others contributing to the treasury. The widow is different in every way: she is female, contrary to the representative masculine plural terms; she is singular (μία χήρα), in contrast to the many (πολλοί); she is poor (πτωχή), not rich (πλοῦτος); she gives a specified amount, two of the tiniest coins (λεπτὰ δύο),[105] as opposed to the generalized larger sums (described as χαλκός/"copper coin" and the even more generic πολλά/"much").

As Jesus sits and watches the treasury, he notices the widow's exceptional conduct and calls the disciples to him (προσκαλεσάμενος; 12:43). The verb προσκαλέω is by no means unusual,[106] but its use in this scene marks it as significant. Indeed, προσκαλέω ("to call" or "summon") is used by Mark in settings of commission and instruction.[107]

---

[103] These terms do not appear in Mark, but terms for an example or pattern of behavior were readily available (e.g., Jn 13:15). Paul, e.g., uses τύπος in such a way for himself (Phil. 3:17) and his churches (1 Thess. 1:17). Verbal forms of μίμησις appear in the NT (2 Thess. 3:7, 9; Heb. 3:17; and 3 John 11). Mark's lack of this precise terminology does not preclude his appreciation of the concept's function.

[104] A number of scholars find the woman to be exemplary in some sense (e.g., Taylor, *St. Mark*, 496; Witherington, *Women in the Ministry of Jesus*, 18; Swartley, "The Role of Women in Mark's Gospel," 20; DiCicco, "What Can One Give," 441–9). Others specifically deny her this status. Miller cites a tension between the generosity of the woman and Markan discomfort with the Temple (*Women in Mark's Gospel*, 113). Others find reason to reject the woman's exemplary status, suggesting that Jesus expresses "downright disapproval" (Wright, "Widow's Mites," 261–3) or interprets the widow's act as misguided (Sugirtharajah, "The Widow's Mites Revalued," 42–3).

[105] Λεπτός is an adjective meaning *small, thin,* or *light.* In a telling instance of its usage, Josephus describes the Essenes' understanding of the imperishable soul as ἐκ τοῦ λεπτοτάτου φοιτώσας αἰθέρος (emanating from the lightest, rarified air), using the superlative form of λεπτός to denote the ethereal imagery for the soul in contrast to the weighty chains of the body (*J.W.* 2.155). Thus, when the adjective is used substantively in its nominal, articular form, τὸ λεπτόν, it conveys its sense of smallness or lightness to the monetary amount. Valued at a fraction of a cent, τὸ λεπτόν is a small, copper coin. Collins notes that λεπτόν would denote whatever was the smallest denomination of coins in a given area (*Mark*, 589). Its one other occurrence in the NT outside this story is in Lk. 12:59, in the context of Jesus's instruction to settle with one's adversary on the way to court. This shrewd escape from official legal channels by a plea-bargain (so to speak) is better than the alternative of having to pay ἕως καὶ τὸ ἔσχατον λεπτόν, which carries the sense of the modern idiom "every last cent."

[106] Of the verb's twenty-nine occurrences in the NT, twenty-eight are in the Synoptics and Acts (the other is found in Jas 5:14). Mark accounts for nine of those occurrences (Matthew, six; Luke, four; and Acts, nine). The term means, simply, "to call" or "to summon," and functions in a straightforward sense.

[107] Mark first uses the term in 3:13, when Jesus *summons* those he wants with him. Other scenes in which Jesus's *calling* initiates miracle and mission include his sending of the twelve out in pairs (6:7) and their role in the multiplication of the loaves (8:1). In several instances, Jesus responds to accusation, false teaching, and misconception by *calling* to him opponents (3:23), crowds (7:14; 8:34) and disciples (10:42) in order to teach truly. Collins finds similarity between the summons

In the present pericope, Jesus calls his disciples to witness an ideal act of giving. Seeing the widow's gift as the exemplary gift among many gifts is not obvious; this interpretation requires Jesus's explanation.[108]

Jesus's purpose in summoning his disciples to observe the widow's generosity hinges on his interpretation of the widow's apparently negligible gift as actually *more* (πλεῖον) than all the others', not numerically but in comparative value (12:44). This makes all the difference in Jesus's estimation: while all the others gave from their excess (ἐκ τοῦ περισσεύοντος αὐτοῖς), the widow gave from extreme lack (ἐκ τῆς ὑστερήσεως αὐτῆς). The content of her offering is all she had, her whole means for living (ὅλον τὸν βίον αὐτῆς). Thus, the woman offers her entire life to God.[109] Jesus's interpretation of the widow's gift is presented to the disciples as a teaching of importance. Jesus introduces his explication of her selfless gift with the phrase ἀμὴν λέγω ὑμῖν ("Truly I say to you").[110] Both the narrator and Jesus draw attention to the contrasts between the woman and all the other contributors at the treasury, which heightens the widow's exemplary status.[111]

---

in 10:43-44 and those in 8:34 and 10:42. She rightly suggests that this similarity indicates that "the action of the widow is relevant to the question of discipleship" (*Mark*, 589). Commission and instruction are appropriate contexts for the narrator's use of the verb or participle with Jesus as agent; its use in Pilate's calling for a centurion after Jesus's crucifixion (15:44) is not theologically significant.

[108] A contrast between the widow's extravagance (πάντα ὅσα εἶχεν) with little in 12:44 and the rich man's withholding of much (ἔχων κτήματα πολλά; 10:22), when Jesus asked for as much as he had (ὅσα ἔχεις; 10:21), may be intended. The function of the widow as an exemplary figure, demonstrating the generous abandonment to which Jesus points his followers (in his own life-giving), is something I have tried to establish on a narrative, contextual level. Scholarship is far from a consensus on this issue. Stephen Moore sets up the two polarized readings of the widow's gift: (1) "an exemplary action enthusiastically lauded by Jesus," which Moore calls a "hallowed typological interpretation"; and (2) "epitomizing instead the oppressed peasantry mercilessly bled dry by the indigenous, Rome-allied elites" ("Mark and Empire: 'Zealot' and 'Postcolonial' Readings," in *The Postcolonial Biblical Reader* [ed. R. S. Sugirtharajah; Oxford: Blackwell, 2005], 202).

[109] The wording is different, but one may note the similarity in substance between the woman's generosity and Jesus's promise in Mk 8:35 that the one who loses her life for Jesus's sake and for the gospel's will save it. In 8:35, ψυχή denotes human life, one's very being. Collins finds a parallel in Jesus's quotation of Deut. 6:5 to the scribe as the greatest commandment in 12:30, in which a person is commanded to love God with his whole life (ἐξ ὅλης τῆς ψυχῆς σου). As Collins suggests, ὅλος forms a link between the two passages (*Mark*, 590).

[110] As Collins notes, this phrase functions to introduce emphatic statements by Jesus, either proclamations about discipleship or prophetic sayings (*Mark*, 589-90). Already in Mark by this point, Ἀμὴν λέγω ὑμῖν has preceded sayings about blaspheming the Spirit (3:28); signs refused this generation (8:12); prediction that those present will see the coming of the kingdom (9:1); sharing a cup of cold water (9:41); receiving the kingdom of God like a child (10:15); blessings for followers (10:29); and faith to move a mountain (11:23). It will recur again, significantly, in the next passage under discussion (14:9) and three more times within that chapter (14:18, 25, and 30). Kinukawa observes that these statements are, excepting this instance, always directed to future events (*Women and Jesus*, 76). She suggests that, although Jesus looks to the widow's act of generosity in the immediate narrative past, he is also looking forward to his future in which he, too, will give his whole life. One must "take up his cross and follow": Jesus must deny himself (ἀπαρνησάσθω ἑαυτόν; 8:34) and submit to the pattern of selfless giving that this woman embodies. Jesus's interpretation of the widow's activity is more than mere observation; it evinces her act of extravagant generosity as the type of self-sacrifice that is vital to the life of his followers.

[111] This is one of only two times in which a human other than Jesus within the Markan narrative (rather than in a parable) is used as the positive substance of a lesson. The other instance is the woman

The widow's example of selfless generosity is set up as paradigmatic for the disciples. If their flight at Jesus's arrest (14:50) and absence at Jesus's crucifixion (ch. 15) are any indication, they had not yet absorbed Jesus's lesson in selfless giving.[112] As with Mary Magdalene in the LE, sometimes affirmation from Jesus comes in contrast to others. The widow's generosity is seen most clearly when compared in proportion to her possessions, in contrast with wealthy others giving to the treasury. On its own, the widow's gift was small; it is in Jesus's provision of perspective that it became an example of extravagant generosity. Likewise, Mary's simple witness to Jesus's resurrection gains the most profundity when contrasted to the behavior of other disciples.

3.3 "She has done a good work for me": The Anointing Woman (14:6)

In the house of Simon the Leper (14:3-9), a woman enters, apparently uninvited, and breaks social conventions by her behavior.[113] Again, Mark's penchant for detailed descriptions paints a vivid scene.[114] Mark describes the woman as "having an alabaster jar of expensive ointment of pure nard" (14:3). Instead of simply pouring the ointment on Jesus's head (so Mt. 26:7), in Mark, the woman breaks the alabaster jar[115] before pouring its contents on Jesus's head. The extravagant gesture of breaking the jar illustrates that the contents are entirely spent on their recipient, sparing not one drop.

As the ensuing complaints illustrate, this was an expensive gift. Unlike the widow who gave from her lack (ἐκ τῆς ὑστερήσεως αὐτῆς), the woman anoints Jesus with a highly valuable aromatic ointment. Both women give all they have (πάντα ὅσα εἶχεν ἔβαλεν; 12:44). While Jesus explicitly attests this of the widow, it may be inferred of the woman who anoints Jesus. She expends completely the costly ointment, destroying even the container.[116] Both gifts from these exemplary women are "wasteful": the widow illogically contributes every last cent of her living; the woman pours out costly ointment that might have been invested more wisely.

---

who anoints Jesus (14:2-9). It is possible that the children to be welcomed by Jesus's followers may function as examples (Mk 9:36 and 10:14).

[112] Peter, e.g., goes to great and devastating lengths to preserve himself after Jesus's arrest. In his repeated denials of any association with Jesus in Mk 14:66-72, Peter moves further away from Jesus (both literally [cf. 14:68b] and figuratively). Peter had tied his very identity to Jesus: "Even if *all* are caused to stumble, *I myself* [will not be]" (14:29; represented by the emphatic contrast [ἀλλ᾽ οὐκ] and personal pronoun [ἐγώ]). In v. 31, Peter's promise of fidelity is tied to his very life: "Even if [ἐάν] it is necessary for me [δέῃ με] to co-die with you [συναποθανεῖν σοι], I will never deny you." The awkward *co-die* attempts to represent the συν-prefix and the dative σοι, which intricately tie Peter's fate to Jesus's in a doubled way that English translations cannot duplicate without being cumbersome. In his threefold denial, thus, Peter loses his identity even as he is scrambling desperately to save himself (cf. 8:35-37).

[113] Kinukawa states that the woman "does not mind at all breaking with traditional customs and the propriety required of women" (*Women and Jesus*, 83). It is true that, unlike Luke's account, the woman does not weep while anointing Jesus (Lk. 7:38, 44). But Jesus defends her against her detractors (τί αὐτῇ κόπους παρέχετε; 14:6), which at least opens the possibility that she was troubled by their objections.

[114] Luke and John diverge from Matthew's and Mark's setting details. Matthew's narrative bears the closest resemblance to the narrative content of Mark.

[115] The term ἀλάβαστρον is repeated in again as the direct object of the participle συντρίψασα.

[116] It is, of course, possible that the woman had many such jars of ointment. Yet in 14:8a Jesus indicates that what the woman did was "what she could" (ὃ ἔσχεν [αὐτη] ἐποίησεν). The feminine, singular

The complaint from the unnamed onlookers—emphasized by the estimated value of the "wasted" ointment, three-hundred denarii (14:5)[117]—is not that the woman should not give away something so valuable. Instead, the objectors' offense is at the recipient of the donation, which should have been sold and given to the poor. They are concerned with realizing the item's full worth and appropriately distributing the funds from its sale. It is clear from the objectors' response that Jesus was not, in their estimation, a worthy recipient of such an outpouring.

Jesus defends both the woman ("Leave her be!"; ἄφετε αὐτήν) and her action against her detractors' rebuke. He judges her generous anointing[118] to be a *good*, even *beautiful*, work (v. 6), not wasteful or misdirected. Next, Jesus addresses more fully the concern for the poor that caused the onlookers to take offense initially. The difference between what is *typically* wise and generous, giving to the poor, and what the woman has done *now*, giving to Jesus, is a matter of time (v. 7).[119] *Now* Jesus is with them, but that will not always be the case (οὐ πάντοτε), as it will be for the poor (πάντοτε). At another time, such an expenditure might be rightly deemed a waste, but at this time Jesus cites in the woman's anointing an act done in advance, appropriate to his burial.[120] While allowing that there are times during which caring for the poor is the primary priority, Jesus defends the woman's actions as right for *this* time.[121]

The woman who anoints Jesus clearly stands out as positive in comparison to her fellow characters in Mk 14:1-11. But Jesus goes further to assure that her extravagant giving will live on in the memory of his followers (14:9). As in his teaching about the widow, Jesus begins his pronouncement with ἀμὴν ... λέγω ὑμῖν ("Truly, I say to you"). He announces that wherever the good news is preached throughout the whole world,

---

pronoun is attested in some mss (e.g., A, C, D, 892, and the majority text), but its inclusion in the preceding parentheses is merely for clarity.

[117] An expense of the accumulated pay for 300 days of labor in one act of breaking and pouring is shocking. The description amounts not merely to an extraneous, precise detail, but to one that lends gravity to the woman's sacrifice. As in the widow's case, the wasteful gift is expended on someone or something about to be obsolete: the temple will fall (ch. 13) and Jesus will die (14:18). The money from the ointment might have brought life to many, but was poured out on a body soon to be laid in a tomb.

[118] Jesus describes her action quite unspecifically at first, referring to it not as anointing, but with the cognate accusative, literally, "she worked a good work in me" (καλὸν ἔργον ἠργάσατο ἐν ἐμοί, v. 6).

[119] The indefinite time (ὅταν) and subjunctive θέλω seem, on the surface, to confer an air of flippancy to the translation of Jesus's parenthetical allowance (i.e., "You can do good to the poor whenever"). Rather, the indefinite time structure reinforces that the key to what the woman got right depends on the perception of the *time*. Now, it is unclear that *she* perceives the time thusly: as Mark tells it, the woman who anoints Jesus may not be any more aware of the full significance of her action than was the widow. Both actions depend on *Jesus's* interpretation. Still, she is praised for having done καλὸν ἔργον.

[120] In another point of connection to the story of the generous widow who donated "her whole life" (ὅλον τὸν βίον αὐτῆς; 12:44), Jesus is about to give his life. The woman who anoints him honors this extravagant expenditure with her own.

[121] Shortly after the story of the woman's anointing concludes, Judas exchanges something of great value—the life of his teacher—for the promise of money in an indefinite amount (14:10-11). The woman considers no price, even 300 denarii, too much to exhaust on Jesus. Unlike the woman in another way, Judas does not realize the significance of the present time. Instead he awaits the time when he can conveniently (εὐκαίρως) betray Jesus (14:11b). The woman's conception of time is oriented christologically, but Judas's is determined by selfish convenience.

her good work will be reported in her memory (εἰς μνημόσυνον αὐτῆς).[122] The aptness of her example of generosity and reverence for Jesus is generously extended beyond *this* particular time to all those who receive the gospel.

As with the widow, this woman who anoints Jesus achieves notoriety even as she remains nameless. This narrative element diverges markedly from Mary Magdalene. At the same time, Mary's named status represents mere days—crucial, difficult days— in her long discipleship. For we are told that she, among others, followed Jesus from Galilee (15:41), but was anonymous "on the way" until Golgotha and the tomb. After Mary Magdalene's proclamation in 16:12, she slips back into the anonymous backdrop. Yet, like the woman with a hemorrhage, the poor widow, and the woman who anoints Jesus, Mary leaves an imprint on the meaning of discipleship in the LE and the Gospel. At least within the larger Gospel of Mark, anonymity is not a bad thing: "nobodies" do remarkably beautiful (καλὸν; 14:6) and bold things.

In 14:3-9, this anonymous woman forecasts Jesus's impending death by her anointing, as made explicit by Jesus himself (v. 8). Were it not for Jesus's explanation, however, the reader would not know that the woman did a good thing, much less that her actions were a prophetic and honorific preparation for his death. The woman is available to the audience as worthy of timeless, worldwide memorial. She is enshrined as a result of Jesus's own positive interpretation and stamp of approval on her conduct, not in the form of an explanation from the narrator. Jesus acts as the interpretive advocate for this woman as he did for the widow, rescuing them both—even, or especially, in their anonymity—as models of discipleship.

Jesus's words of approbation constitute the interpretation that wins out in Mark. His words of approval for this woman's anointing, along with the other women surveyed, demonstrate their faithfulness. In the LE, it is easy for readers to skim past Mary Magdalene and the other two disciples who testify to Jesus's resurrection. Like the disciples, readers are eager to see Jesus himself and the fantastic signs that demonstrate belief in him. But Jesus's own words support the decision to pause and ruminate over Mary Magdalene and her testimony. Jesus defends Mary's reliable witness over against the Eleven for whom, apparently, it took seeing in order to believe.

4. Conclusion

I have sought to demonstrate how Mary Magdalene's role as a witness to Jesus's resurrection in the LE not only confirms the canonical resurrection accounts but also presents her also in significant, novel combinations as a reliable proclaimer of Jesus's resurrection. The "repair" of the resurrection account with an extended ending begins with none other than Mary. She has the singular distinction of being the *first* witness to the resurrected Jesus. Her renaming ensures that the reader cannot mistake her identity: she is the same Mary Magdalene who viewed the crucifixion and burial of her Lord. The new detail attributed to her person (new to the Second Gospel, but not to

---

[122] See Elisabeth Schüssler Fiorenza, *In Memory of Her: A Feminist Theological Reconstruction of Christian Origins* (New York: Crossroad, 1985), xii–xiv.

the Third [cf. Lk. 8:2])—that is, her previous demon-possession—entangles her history even more closely to Jesus as a beneficiary of his ministry.

Mary's response to this encounter bears no resemblance to the close-mouthed and terrified flight of 16:8; instead, she proclaims what she has seen (16:10-11) and faces rejection by the remainder of the disciples. This pattern of *seeing Jesus, going, and telling* (and meeting disbelief) is repeated a second time by two other disciples (16:12-13). When Jesus meets his eleven closest followers in 16:14, his first matter of business is not to declare "Peace!" (cf. Lk. 24:36; Jn 20:19, 26), but to blame the Eleven for rejecting the reliable testimony of those who had seen him (16:14). In doing so, the narrator summarizes, in the midst of Jesus's accusation, the reliability of Mary's witness and that of the two who repeated her faithful response. The Eleven are faithless (τὴν ἀπιστίαν αὐτῶν) *because* (ὅτι) they did not believe (οὐκ ἐπίστευσαν) those who had seen Jesus (τοῖς θεασαμένοις αὐτόν; v. 14).

This longer ending to Mark does not forget the narrative that has preceded it; the LE highlights Mary's witness in a way that serves, retroactively, to highlight the faithful women who have come before. Primarily, the connection is Jesus's affirmation of their faith, words, generosity, and actions, just as he is reported to uphold Mary's testimony (16:14). In Mk 1:1–16:8, the faithfulness and praise of the women is most obvious when placed in contrast with Jesus's male opponents and wayward disciples. Likewise, in the LE, the positive treatment of Mary and her pattern of obedient witness is most sharply visible when placed beside the repeated failures of the Eleven.

3

Unfaithful Disciples in the Long Ending and Mark

It does not take long for the twelve disciples[1] to become a punch line in the Gospel according to Mark.[2] At times dense (4:10, 13; 6:51b-52; 8:4, 14-21; 9:32), blundering (9:18-19, 28; 9:38; 10:13; 14:37-41), defiant (6:37; 8:32; 9:33-34; 10:35-40), and fearful (4:38-41; 6:49-50; 9:6; 14:50),[3] the Twelve have been called failures,[4] blind,[5] inept,[6] fallible,[7] and other uncomplimentary things.[8] It is not surprising that ancient readers should have noticed the same faithlessness—or, at minimum, inconstancy—that modern readers of Mark are quick to notice. If we look to Matthew and Luke as some of the earliest "recorded" readers of Mark, their partial[9] attempts to repair the

---

[1] See C. Clifton Black, *The Disciples according to Mark: Markan Redaction in Current Debate* (2d ed.; Grand Rapids: Eerdmans, 2012), 291.
[2] Black's most recent survey (ibid.) of major positive, negative, and "mediate" interpretations of the disciples in Mark (in the past twenty-five years) prevents me from exaggerating the universality of negative treatments (319–28). His summary of representatives of each "Type" and resulting observation of "patterns" helps to sketch out the shape of the debate and to explain why mediating (balancing positive and negative) interpretations have outnumbered the more polarizing types (328–30).
[3] Such a string of quotations does not take into account the times when the disciples are chosen (3:13-14), privileged (4:11), accurate (8:29), sacrificing (10:28), and obedient (14:16).
[4] Mary R. Thompson, *The Role of Disbelief in Mark: A New Approach to the Second Gospel* (New York: Paulist, 1989). This failure is, for Thompson, particularly in the realm of belief: "On the level of human failure, Jesus's family and friends and neighbors, disciples (the twelve and the special three or four), the crowds, Jewish officialdom, see, hear, sometimes perceive, rarely understand and never believe" (29).
[5] Joseph B. Tyson, "The Blindness of the Disciples in Mark," *JBL* 80 (1961): 261–8.
[6] This is the summary of scholarly attitudes that Ira Brent Driggers cites in *Following God through Mark: Theological Tension in the Second Gospel* (Louisville: Westminster John Knox, 2007), 37n2.
[7] Elizabeth Struthers Malbon, "Fallible Followers: Women and Men in the Gospel of Mark," in *In the Company of Jesus: Characters in Mark's Gospel* (Louisville: Westminster John Knox, 2000), 41–69.
[8] For the purposes of this chapter, there is no need for further bibliographic enumeration on this subject. See Black's treatment (note 1 in this chapter) for a nearly comprehensive list of approaches to Mark's disciples.
[9] Significantly, Matthew follows Mark in making clear that the disciples desert Jesus after his arrest (Mk 14:50-52; Mt. 26:56). Both Matthew and Luke recount Peter's threefold denial of Jesus much like Mark's telling of the story, without apologies or much in the way of modification (Mk 14:66-72; Mt. 26:69-75; Lk. 22:54-62; cf. Jn 18:16-27). There are even a few times in which the Matthean or Lukan accounts include a mention of the disciples' failure to understand or another negative characterization where it is not present in Mark: Lk. 18:34 (cf. Mt. 20:17-19 and Mk 10:32-34); and in Mt. 26:8 *the disciples* take offense (cf. Mk 14:4, "some there"; Lk. 7:39, the Pharisee who invited him; and Jn 12:4, Judas Iscariot).

Twelve's depiction when they utilize Markan material demonstrate that they noticed the negative trend, even as they evidence discomfort with it.[10]

The Long Ending (hereafter LE), as a second-century "coda" to Mark, not only continues the trajectory of the Twelve's failure, but also compounds it in the post-resurrection context. A report of a witness or witnesses to Jesus's resurrection does not require recording a response to it (cf. Mt. 28:8-10; Lk. 24:35; Jn 20:18). The LE of Mark includes not only each instance of disbelief (Mk 16:11, 13), but also Jesus's firm reprimand of the eleven remaining disciples (16:14).

In the previous chapter I argued that Mary Magdalene's character and actions were similarly composed of a new configuration of mostly established descriptions, drawn from the other canonical Gospels' endings and adapted to fit existing trends in Mark's Gospel. It is possible to call Mary a witness to the risen Christ, a former recipient of Jesus's work of power (exorcism: v. 9), and a reliable proclaimer of good news. Those descriptions are evident on a surface reading of the text. What remains to be demonstrated is whether the reader has textual warrant to regard her actions as indicative of faith. That is, is her witness a model of faithful response to Jesus's resurrection? A characterization of Mary as a faithful witness on the basis of 16:9-11 is possible but open to debate. She is never described in those terms. It is the Eleven's response, one that is straightforwardly and repeatedly categorized as *unfaithful*, however, that reveals the opposite categorization of Mary as, not merely possible,

---

[10] One may note several examples of tendencies by Matthew and Luke to soften, repair, or omit Mark's reports of Jesus's harsh or negative statements toward the disciples. (Matthew more often repairs; Luke more often omits [e.g., Mk 8:31-33, par. Mt. 16:21-23; cf. Lk. 9:22]).

1. After expressing his "parable theory" (alluding to Isa. 6:9-10, or quoting it in Mt. 13:14-15), Jesus provides an interpretation for the sower parable. In Mark, he prefaces the explanation with a critical question: "Do you not know this parable? How will you understand all the parables?" This challenge, which sets up the possibility of the disciples' ignorance, is missing in the Synoptic parallels (Mt. 13:18 and Lk. 8:11).

2. In the pericope in which Jesus walks on water, which Luke does not include at all, Mk 6:51b-52 records that the disciples were exceedingly amazed (or confused, ἐξίστημι) and explains that "they did not understand about the loaves, but their hearts were hardened." The statement is at the same time contextually enigmatic and negative. Matthew, however, while willing to show Peter doubting (14:30-31), depicts the disciples' response to the event as worship and confession of Jesus as the Son of God (ἀληθῶς θεοῦ υἱὸς εἶ; v. 33). Although Matthew includes an additional episode, Peter's walking on water (vv. 28-31), most of the episode has so many word-for-word parallels that it seems that Matthew must have drawn from Mark (cf. Mk 6:45-52 and Mt. 14:22-33).

3. The Synoptics include Jesus's warning against the "leaven of Pharisees" (Mk 8:15, par. Mt. 16:6 and Lk. 12:1). Luke does not include any of the subsequent conversation between Jesus and the disciples. In both Mark and Matthew, the disciples take Jesus's metaphor literally and begin to discuss bread. Jesus asks a series of accusatory questions in Mk 8:17-21 (reminiscent of Isa. 6:9-10), which culminate in "Do you not yet understand?" (οὔπω συνίετε; Mk 8:21). Matthew softens Mark's questions by removing a central question about whether the disciples' hearts are hardened (Mk 8:17b; cf. Mt. 16:9). Instead of concluding with a question that reinforces the disciples' lack of understanding, as Mark does, Matthew narrates a transition in understanding: "*Then* they understood [τότε συνῆκαν]" (16:12). The impact is that Matthew's resulting portrayal of the disciples has nearly the opposite outcome from that in Mark.

4. In response to Jesus's second prediction of his passion and resurrection, Mk 9:32 says that the disciples did not understand and were afraid to ask Jesus his meaning. Luke 9:45 follows Mark but provides an explanation for the disciples' ignorance (likely, a divine passive): "it was hidden from them" (ἦν παρακεκαλυμμένον ἀπ' αὐτῶν). Matthew 17:23, however, only states that the disciples were "extremely grieved" (ἐλυπήθησαν σφόδρα).

Table 3.1 References to recipients of news of Jesus's resurrection (i.e., disciples)

v. 10	τοῖς μετ' αὐτοῦ γενομένοις	to those who were with him
v. 11	κἀκεῖνοι	and those
v. 12	ἐξ αὐτῶν	from among/of them
v. 13	τοῖς λοιποῖς	to the rest
v. 14	τοῖς ἕνδεκα	to the Eleven

but unambiguous. The Eleven's protracted failure highlights Mary Magdalene's redemption: a step that seems necessary before the good news can progress.

1. The Eleven Disciples' Role in Mk 16:9-14

This exegetical section attends to the repeated, negative characterization of the Eleven[11] in the first half of the LE to Mark's Gospel. It is noteworthy from the outset that, no matter how negatively the disciples are characterized, once v. 14 concludes "they did not believe" (οὐκ ἐπίστευσαν) and the next sentence begins, there remains no residue of Jesus's disapproval. In fact, in the verse after harshly rebuking the disciples, Jesus commissions the same disciples to preach the gospel to the whole creation without any explanation or apology (v. 15).[12] In light of the disciples' global proclamation and fantastic demonstrations of belief—the grandiose conclusions toward the LE is heading—it is remarkable that the earliest references to that group in the LE center on their disbelief.

A preliminary comment is necessary. The groups who disbelieve and receive Jesus's admonition are variously designated. The most specific definition of those who disbelieve is the final one in v. 14: the Eleven. Table 3.1 illustrates the terms in use.

First mentioned in v. 10, the group of followers referred to (at least in their encounters with Mary Magdalene and two other disciples) could be larger than the inner-circle of the Eleven (the Twelve minus Judas). The next two references (vv. 11, 12) are not specific; the terms used to designate the disciples differ in adjacent episodes. By the

---

[11] A word on terminology: In this chapter I will typically refer to the group of (mostly) male disciples either as the "Eleven" or as "male disciples." Neither of these terms is accurate for the whole passage in question, as the terms for those who are "disbelieving" varies. Table 3.1 makes the terminology, ranging from unspecific to specific, clear. The disciples concerned here include *at least* the Eleven, but perhaps a larger group. At the same time, there may be women among that group, just as Mary Magdalene is a female disciple. It is difficult to determine to whom the less precise terminology refers. Sometimes the general term "disciples" covers the group, including the male disciples closest to Jesus, but not limited to them.

The narrow designation "Eleven" may not rightly apply to the earliest encounters, which include but are not limited to the Eleven remaining apostles. The next paragraph details the terms referring to the varying groups of followers.

[12] This may parallel 16:1-8, in which the women are instructed to "Go and tell his disciples and Peter" (v. 7), despite those same disciples' flight (14:50, 52) and Peter's denial (14:72) in their previous narrative appearances. In both endings, the disciples' inconstancy—even when compounded in 16:11, 13—does not negate their calling.

Table 3.2 References to disbelief in the LE

v. 11	κἀκεῖνοι ... ἠπίστησαν	And those ones ... disbelieved
v. 13	οὐδὲ ἐκείνοις ἐπίστευσαν	neither did those believe
v. 14	τὴν ἀπιστίαν αὐτῶν	their unbeliefv
	καὶ σκληροκαρδίαν	and hard-heartedness
v. 14	οὐκ ἐπίστευσαν	they did not believe

fifth reference (v. 14) Jesus finally appears to "the Eleven" (τοῖς ἕνδεκα) while they recline (ἀνακειμένοις αὐτοῖς). It is the Eleven whom Jesus censures for their unbelief and hardheartedness, from which one may infer that they made up part or the majority of the groups that responded to Mary and the other two with disbelief. When Mary goes and tells, it is "to those who were with him" (τοῖς μετ' αὐτοῦ γενομένοις[13]; 16:10). In v. 12, however, it is "two from [among] them" (δυσὶν ἐξ αὐτῶν) who are walking as they encounter the risen Jesus in "a different form" (ἐν ἑτέρᾳ μορφῇ).[14] Thus, when the two return to inform "the rest" (τοῖς λοιποῖς; v. 13), a larger group of disciples is implied.[15]

It is worth noting that all of the terms used for the disciples are masculine. Insofar as the group is unspecified and extends beyond the Eleven, it is not clear that all those included are males.[16] The Eleven remaining from among those Jesus called are males; so are others in Jesus's wider circle of disciples males (cf. 16:12). Yet all need not be male.[17]

Disbelief is the consistent response from the Eleven surrounded by other followers. The author reiterates their lack of faith in several ways, as Table 3.2 indicates.

Verses 11 and 13 narrate the disciples' twofold response of disbelief, whereas v. 14 contains a report of that for which Jesus found fault (ὀνειδίζω) in the disciples' behavior. He identifies a state of unbelief (ἀπιστία) and a hardness of heart (σκληροκαρδία) as the internal causes for external expressions of faithlessness.

Without Jesus's accusation in v. 14, the reader would not have a clear idea of *what* it is that the disciples do not believe. In Mary Magdalene's proclamation, for instance, she tells them that Jesus is living (ζῇ) and that "he was seen by her" (ἐθεάθη ὑπ' αὐτῆς). Do the disciples disbelieve that Jesus is living? Do they disbelieve that he was seen? Is it impossible that Mary would have seen Jesus (when the other disciples have not)? None of these objects of disbelief is specified. The two disciples in transit, who meet Jesus "in another form," proclaim to the rest, but *what* they communicate is unstated

---

[13] It is possible that this characterization alludes to the stated purpose of Jesus's calling the Twelve, *that they might be with him* (ἵνα ὦσιν μετ' αὐτοῦ) in Mk 3:14.

[14] If only the remaining Eleven were in reference in v. 10, and two of them saw Jesus in v. 12, simple subtraction would lead one to expect only nine to remain unconvinced in v. 14. Such is not the case.

[15] This is in keeping with other descriptions in Mark in which the Twelve are present, attended by a wider group of disciples (e.g., 4:10; 10:32).

[16] When referring to groups, or a "class," Greek defaults to the masculine: see Herbert Weir Smyth, *A Greek Grammar for Colleges* (New York: American, 1920), 45 §197a.

[17] The gender make-up of the "disciples" will have pertinence in the discussion that follows of gender-specific stereotypes regarding expressed emotions.

by the narrator. Still, the remaining disciples do not believe. It turns out, when Jesus pronounces judgment on the Eleven, that their disbelief is not directed to a particular message. Instead, their disbelief characterizes a condition of the heart and is directed at the messengers but not limited to their proclamation. Their ἀπιστία and σκληροκαρδία are diagnosable because they did not believe those who saw him after he was raised (ὅτι τοῖς θεασαμένοις αὐτὸν ἐγηγερμένον οὐκ ἐπίστευσαν).

With respect to Jesus's assessment of the condition of the Eleven's hearts, the narrator is generous with information. But, more broadly, the portrait of the Eleven and others is sparse where one might expect detail. For instance, no disciples' names are mentioned, although the young man's commission to the women in 16:7 had named Peter along with the disciples as the intended recipients of the message.[18] The LE mentions no particular locations in which disciples can be found: Is it Judea or Galilee?[19] Only the vaguest suggestion is made; wherever it is, there are two who go from there "into the country" (πορευομένοις εἰς ἀγρόν; v. 12). Given that the place in which Jesus speaks to the disciples during their meal becomes the locale from which he ascends into heaven (v. 19), one might expect the location to have some significance, but the text is silent.

Although sparse in most details, the LE provides several descriptions of the disciples that highlight the continuation of Jesus's followers as a group. First, Mary is apparently able to locate them mourning together (πενθοῦσι καὶ κλαίουσιν; v. 10). Later, the Eleven are reclining for a meal together (ἀνακειμένοις αὐτοῖς τοῖς ἕνδεκα; v. 14) when Jesus appears to them. At last report in Mark's Gospel, the Twelve had fled (ἀφέντες αὐτὸν ἔφυγον πάντες; 14:50) and scattered: Peter appears alone outside of Jesus's trial (14:66-72). Yet, while mourning and weeping after Jesus has been raised, the disciples appear to be back together (16:12). They share a meal that provides the opportunity for Jesus's rebuke (v. 14) and commission (vv. 15-18). Their lack of faith is not individualized (as the telling of Peter's denial, for instance, makes it); that ἀπιστία is a shared response to those few who proclaim Jesus's resurrection.

A second detail suggests the Eleven's continued coalescence. Although things have certainly changed in the LE—Jesus, risen from the dead, has appeared to Mary (v. 9)—the disciples' outlook of sorrow has not. The last of the original Twelve to be featured in the pages of Mark was Peter. In his last "on-stage" appearance in Mk 1:1-16:8, Peter, realizing (ἐπιβαλὼν) that he has denied Jesus, wept (ἔκλαιεν [> κλαίω]). In the collective reference of 16:10, Peter and his fellow disciples have not stopped weeping: κλαίω is the second verb in the pair describing their *mourning and weeping* (πενθοῦσι καὶ κλαίουσιν).

The third detail worthy of attention is based on what the LE *does not say*, rather than what it does. Although the disciples are upbraided for their refusal to believe the witnesses to Jesus's resurrection, their eventual belief (and subsequent proclamation [v. 20]) is initiated by an appearance of the risen Jesus, just as Mary and the other

---

[18] Compare to *Epistula Apostolorum* ch. 11, discussed in section 2 of this chapter.
[19] The post-resurrection traditions scatter geographically: Galilee for Mark (16:7), Matt (28:7, 10, 16), and John 21 (vv. 1-2); and Judea for Luke (24:33, 49) and John 20 (implied vv. 19, 26). The LE neither tries to remedy the disparity nor to tip the scale in either direction.

two seem to have required.[20] While this matter is not addressed in 16:9-20 and no transition into faith is described (neither for the witnesses [vv. 9, 12], nor for the Eleven [vv. 10-11, 14]), only its antithesis, proclamation (both for the witnesses and the Eleven), indicates belief. Jesus's particular critique of the Eleven is not, however, inappropriate, as the Eleven had the opportunity to respond faithfully to the multiple reports that Jesus was alive (vv. 11, 13). Still, in the LE what seems to spark faith for all of the individuals and groups is an encounter with the risen Christ.

2. The Disciples' Place in Canonical and Noncanonical Resurrection Narratives: The Long Ending's Derivation and Innovation

The most basic summary of the disciples' role in the first half of Mark's LE is that they disbelieve. Jesus's initial response to them is one of rebuke (v. 14), which turns to commission (vv. 15-18). For this presentation the strongest traces of dependence upon any canonical Gospel are Lukan.[21] There, the disciples disregard the women's testimony as an "idle tale" (Lk. 24:11). On the road to Emmaus, Jesus criticizes two disciples' failure to believe (24:25-27). Thus, in Luke we have precedents both for the rejection of the women's witness and Jesus's words of judgment in a post-resurrection setting.[22]

2.1 The Disciples Disbelieve Repeatedly

Interestingly, for narratives that are often considered to be statements of early Christian faith, *doubt* figures in Matthew's, Luke's, and John's resurrection narratives to varying degrees. Although commonly cited as evidence of a failure of faith,[23] Mark's ending at 16:8, in which women at the tomb tremble in fear and silently disobey their received command to tell the disciples of Jesus's resurrection, is the only Gospel that ends *without* an explicit description of doubt. In John's account the so-called Doubting Thomas (Jn 20:24-25) has famously embodied in one character the generalized aside of Matthew that "some doubted" (οἱ δὲ ἐδίστασαν; Mt. 28:17).

---

[20] In his *Adversus Marcionem* Tertullian expresses gratitude that the "unbelief of the disciples was so persistent," as it required appearances of the risen Jesus to repair (*Marc.* 4.43). Although the initial statement may reflect a reference to the LE, in his next phrase he explains his particular appreciation of the appearance to the two disciples on the road to Emmaus, because it allowed Jesus to explain himself to be Christ in accordance with OT prophecy (clearly a pointer to Lk. 24:13-35).
[21] Cf. Daniel A. Smith, *Revisiting the Empty Tomb: The Early History of Easter* (Minneapolis: Fortress, 2010), 156, and the discussion in section 2.1.
[22] These elements are our focus, but they should not override the other similarities: first, to John (Mary Magdalene's solo appearance, which we have discussed, and the strong emphasis on faith, which remains for consideration); second, to Matthew (particularly the commission). The LE is truly a canonical composition; yet I shall argue that its primary inspiration in Markan.
[23] Larry W. Hurtado has written recently against viewing 16:8 as depicting the women as failing or disobedient, a reading he regards as a popular, if not the majority, opinion ("The Women, the Tomb, and the Climax of Mark," in *A Wandering Galilean: Essays in Honour of Seán Freyne* [ed. Zuleika Rodgers; JSJSup 132; Boston: Brill, 2009], 437–8).

In Luke's account, the instance of doubt intersects with the role of women in the resurrection appearances.[24] In fact, aside from the LE, Luke's resurrection account returns to the disciples' doubt more frequently than do the other gospels. In Lk. 24:8-10 Mary Magdalene, Joanna, Mary the mother of James, and "the other women with them" remember and report the words the two men in dazzling clothing had told them at the tomb. To the Eleven and "all the rest" (v. 9) the women's words seem an idle tale (λῆρος) and they do not believe (ἠπίστουν; v. 11) them. Next, Peter goes to inspect the tomb for himself, finds the linens without Jesus's body, and leaves wondering at what had happened (v. 12)—which may somewhat lessen Peter's instance of disbelief but still does not indicate belief.[25]

In his study analyzing Easter traditions, which he renames "disappearance" (i.e., empty tomb) and "appearance" (i.e., resurrection appearance) traditions,[26] Daniel Smith takes the LE as an instance of later Christian modifications to Mark's earliest empty tomb account. Smith suggests that the LE epitomized "the 'authentic' resurrection appearances found in the other three Gospels."[27] About the repeated lack of faith on the disciples' parts, he says:

> The idea of disbelief comes from Luke 24:11 and is found elsewhere in early Christian texts about Jesus's resurrection, *but it is not entirely clear why the longer ending stresses this theme through repetition.* One possibility is that the author had understood the idea that we have seen to this point in our study of the empty tomb and appearance narratives: namely, neither the empty tomb nor a report of the resurrection leads to Easter faith, but only a direct encounter with the risen Jesus (as in John 20:14–16).[28]

Smith's suggestion is plausible and, indeed, it was likely the author of the LE's expectation that the earliest disciples' resurrection faith resulted only through seeing Jesus.[29] But this does not fully explain the clear interest in emphasizing the male disciples' disbelief.

For example, if the matter is simply one of derivation or establishing an ending consistent with other Gospel endings, several other subjects might have been considered more pertinent.[30] The LE's author has an eye to complementing other

---

[24] In Jn 20:18 the disciples' reception of Mary Magdalene's claim to have seen the risen Jesus is unstated.
[25] Something—apparently an unnarrated resurrection appearance—evidently happens to Peter in the meantime, for when the Cleopas and the other disciple return to Jerusalem and find the Eleven (Lk. 24:33), they are met with the news: "The Lord was truly raised and appeared to Simon" (λέγοντας ὅτι ὄντως ἠγέρθη ὁ κύριος καὶ ὤφθη Σίμωνι; v. 34).
[26] E.g., Smith, *Revisiting the Empty Tomb*, 184.
[27] Ibid., 156.
[28] Ibid.; italics added.
[29] This was universally the case in the canonical Easter accounts, although the Fourth Evangelist may suggest that the Beloved Disciple's unspecified belief (ἐπίστευσεν) at Jesus's tomb (20:8) was the sort of faith without sight that Jesus later praises (οἱ μὴ ἰδόντες καὶ πιστεύσαντες; 20:29). See discussion of *Epistula Apostolorum* 11–12 for a noncanonical account that blurs the lines of sight and belief in the post-resurrection context.
[30] This is mere conjecture, proceeding from what *might have been, but was not*. In the two paragraphs that follow, I provide examples of Gospel precedence, as well as noncanonical Gospels that are roughly contemporaneous with the hypothesized date of the LE and yet take a quite different approach.

canonical Gospel endings; thus, geographical information about the appearances and ascension (cf. Mt. 28:16; Lk. 24:13, 33, 50; Jn 21:1) could have been fitting foci. The ever-prominent Christian concern regarding the fulfillment of prophecy might have been highlighted with explanations from Jesus about scriptures pointing to his messianic role (cf. Lk. 24:25-27). If the Eleven disciples are a major interest of the LE's author, or *the* main interest (which is Daniel Smith's claim[31]), the focus might rather have been on redeeming them after their desertion of Jesus (cf. Jn 21:15-19). The disciples' future prominence might have been foreshadowed, especially Jesus's foreknowledge thereof (cf. Jn 21:18-23).[32]

So far, I have suggested several possible emphases that might have been mined from the resurrection accounts in Gospel texts to which it seems the author of the LE had access.[33] Other second-century, noncanonical gospels provide clues for other items of particular interest, apologetic or otherwise, which might have held appeal. First, the *Gospel of Peter* contributes additional support to Matthew's account of the Jewish conspiracy to cover up the supernatural cause of the empty tomb (Mt. 28:11-15; cf. Gos. Pet. 11.43-49).[34] Canonical Luke and John emphasize the physicality of Jesus's resurrection (Lk. 24:37-43; Jn 20:27-29), which the *Epistula Apostolorum* makes even more emphatic.[35] The gnostic *Sophia of Jesus Christ* and the (likely anti-gnostic) *Epistula Apostolorum* provide good examples of post-resurrection discourses from Jesus on heavenly or spiritual matters (*Soph. Jes. Chr.*; *Ep. Apost.* chs 12–14, 16–18).[36]

---

[31] Despite the reprimand to the Eleven, Smith says, "It is the appearance to the Eleven that is given the most narrative weight and the most content ... The focus is entirely on the Eleven, their commissioning to proclaim the gospel and to baptize, and the signs that were to accompany the belief of their hearers" (*Revisiting the Empty Tomb*, 157).

[32] *Epistula Apostolorum* 15 includes discourses in which Jesus predicts a disciple's imprisonment and angelic release over Passover (presumably Peter, based on Acts 12:1-19), even foretelling the conversion of Saul/Paul and his mission to the gentiles (Acts 9; 12:25–28:31).

[33] See James A. Kelhoffer, *Miracle and Mission: The Authentication of Missionaries and Their Message in the Longer Ending of Mark* (Tübingen: Mohr Siebeck, 2000), 155.

[34] See Paul Foster, "The *Gospel of Peter*," in *The Non-canonical Gospels* (ed. Paul Foster; London: T&T Clark, 2008), 38, for this document's one-two punch of absolving Pilate and implicating the Jews.

[35] Likely antidocetic, *Epistula Apostolorum* is concerned with Jesus's bodily existence both before and after the resurrection: Jesus explains his own "self"-conception when he "became flesh" (ch. 14). *Ep. Apost.* even increases the physical contact in the story of the woman with a hemorrhage (ch. 5). See Julian Hills, *Tradition and Composition in the* Epistula Apostolorum (HDR; Minneapolis: Fortress, 1990), 55. The *Ep. Apost.*, thought to have been written in the second century, contains post-resurrection discourses of Jesus. In it, Jesus offers three of his disciples the opportunity to authenticate his bodily resurrection: he provides Peter his hand to touch the nailprint, Thomas is shown Jesus's side, and Jesus challenges Andrew to inspect his footprints ("Andrew, see whether my foot steps on the ground and leaves a footprint. For it is written in the prophet, 'But a ghost, a demon, leaves no print on the ground'" [*Ep. Apost.* 11 (Ethiopic column); Hennecke and Schneemelcher, eds., *New Testament Apocrypha* [vol. 1; trans. R. McL. Wilson; Philadelphia: Westminster, 1963], 197). This is the English translation of the *Epistula Apostolorum* that will be in use throughout. *Epistula Apostolorum* 12 provides the disciples assurances that they touched (Coptic version) or felt (Ethiopic) Jesus and were convinced that he was risen in the flesh, which prompts them to fall down and repent. In light of the expanded emphasis on Jesus's physical body post-resurrection, Bart D. Ehrman suggests some likely opponents the *Epistula Apostolorum* seeks to counter (*Forgery and Counterforgery: The Use of Literary Deceit in Early Christian Polemics* [New York: Oxford, 2012], 438; the term "forgery" is used too sensationally, however). See the opposite aim in the gnostic gospel the *Soph. Jes. Chr.* (NHC III.91, 10–19).

[36] The *Sophia of Jesus Christ* is found in two versions (Nag Hammadi Codex III and the Berlin Codex [P. Berolinensis 8502]), along with a related text, *Eugnostos*. *Soph. Jes. Chr.* is dated to the late first or

The Freer Logion, inserted between Mk 16:14 and 15, modifies the LE so that it provides an explanation for the disciples' previous disbelief—basically, "the devil made us do it"—making a smoother transition into the commission.[37] Most of these examples, representing interests active in second-century Christian communities, do nothing to reinforce the disciples' faithlessness, or, in the case of the Freer Logion, attempt its repair. The one exception—which contains many different elements, but also an emphasized recurrence of the disciples' disbelief—is the *Epistula Apostolorum*.[38]

The *Epistula Apostolorum* makes for an intriguing comparison to the LE, as demonstrated in Table 3.3. A cursory comparison demonstrates a few striking similarities. In general terms, the *Epistula* is both traditional and innovative. For example, chapter 3 combines preexistence traditions (like John 1) with birth stories (esp. Luke 2). Then in chapter 14, the *Epistula* places a reinterpretation of the Lukan annunciation account in the mouth of Jesus in which Mary's response to the news is like Sarah's response to Isaac (traditional; Gen. 18:12), but Jesus says that it was actually *he* who appeared "in the form of the archangel Gabriel."[39] The retained traditions relevant to our topic include the following: the women are the first—and rejected—messengers of Jesus's resurrection; the male disciples are as dubious, perhaps more so, than in the LE. These correspondences are eclipsed by vast differences in composition,[40] intention,[41] and emphasis.[42]

The relationship of the *Epistula Apostolorum* to the canonical Gospels has been established,[43] but the dependence that is least clear is on the Gospel of Mark.[44] Darrell Hannah, in his study of the evidence for canonical Gospel traditions in *Epistula*

early second century; *Eug.* to the first century BCE (see Douglas M. Parrot, ed., *Nag Hammadi Codices III, 3–4 and V, 1: Eugnostos and the Sophia of Jesus Christ* [Leiden: Brill, 1991], 6). On the possibility of a likely Greek original of the *Sophia*, see Parrot, *NHC III*, 6–7. An interesting element is that the initial verses of the *Sophia of Jesus Christ*, set after Jesus's resurrection, describe Jesus's addressing his *twelve* disciples—not eleven—and seven women followers (*Soph. Jes. Chr.* [NHC III.90, 14-18]). On the post-resurrection *twelve*, see 1 Cor. 15:5.

[37] The Freer Logion is found in only one extant NT ms. (W, late fourth or early fifth century) but was also known in part in Latin translation from Jerome (*Pelag.*, II.15.5–8). See Appendix on the Markan endings. For more on the theological perspective of the Freer Logion, see William L. Lane, *The Gospel of Mark* (NICNT; Grand Rapids: Eerdmans, 1974), 606–11; C. Clifton Black, *Mark* (ANTC; Nashville: Abingdon, 2011), 356–8.

[38] *Epistula Apostolorum* 10–11 includes a narration of the apostles' disbelief, of one woman's testimony, then another, then of Jesus himself.

[39] More correspondences will be clarified in Table 3.3.

[40] The LE is a mere twelve verses; *Epistula Apostolorum* survives in fifty-one chapters (which, however, are far briefer than typical biblical chapters).

[41] The LE serves to briefly conclude an established Gospel; *Epistula Apostolorum* is a freestanding and lengthy work, which includes pre-crucifixion details (chs 1–6 [Ethiopic]).

[42] The LE spends equal time recounting resurrection appearances and Jesus's commission; *Ep. Apost.* devotes much of its space to the post-resurrection discourses of Jesus.

[43] According to Manfred Hornschuh, *Studien zur Epistula Apostolorum* (PTS 5; Berlin: de Gruyter, 1965), 20, that dependence seems to be derived from oral tradition as well as the written Gospels.

[44] Darrell D. Hannah judges, "Nonetheless, there is good reason—meager though it is—to believe that our author knew the earliest gospel" ("The Four-Gospel Canon in the *Epistula Apostolorum*," *JTS* 59 [2008], 616). The evidence is sparse (as compared to the strong influence obvious from John), but carefully demonstrated by Hannah (615–25). One clue that he explains is the appearance of the name "Sarah" among the three women who come to Jesus's tomb in the Ethiopic version (chs 9–10). This name is not attested in any other Gospel tradition, but likely results from the Markan "Salome" (see 616–22).

Table 3.3 The *Epistula Apostolorum*: outline and relevant excerpts*

Inclusive chapters	Topic, *Excerpt* (if pertinent)	Pertinent[†] NT corre-spondence
1–2	Introduction of trustworthy revelation vouchsafed by Jesus's apostles	
3–4	Preexistence, virgin birth, and infancy of Jesus Christ	
5	Miraculous acts of Jesus and theological reflection thereupon	
6–8	Urging faithfulness to the Lord, based on the disciples' true testimony; warnings about Cerinthus and Simon	
9	Jesus's crucifixion; three women go to his tomb to anoint the body ETH.: *... three women came, Sarah, Martha, and Mary Magdalene* [COPT: *Mary, she who belonged to Martha, and Mary <Magd>alene*]. *They carried ointment to pour out upon his body, weeping and mourning over what had happened*	Mk 16:1-4; three named among others, Lk. 24:10; [two women, Mt. 28:1; one woman, Jn 20:1]
10–12	Resurrection appearances to the women, then to "their brothers" CH. 10 (ETH): *And as they were mourning and weeping, the Lord appeared to them and said to them, "Do not weep; I am he whom you seek. But let one of you go to your brothers and say to them, 'Come, our Master has risen from the dead.'"*	Jn 20:11, 13, 15 20:17
	And Mary came and told us. And we said to her, "What have we to do with you, O woman? He that is dead and buried, can he then live?" And we did not believe her, that our Saviour had risen from the dead.	Lk. 24:11
	Then she went back to our Lord and said to him, "None of them believed me concerning your resurrection." And he said to her, "Let another one of you go saying this again to them."	[Lk. 24:11]
	And Sarah came and gave us the same news, and we accused her of lying. And she returned to our Lord and spoke to him as Mary had. Ch. 11 (ETH.): *And then the Lord said to Mary and to her sisters, "Let us go to them." And he came and found us inside, veiled.*	[Thomas, Jn 20:25]
	And we doubted and did not believe. He came before us like a ghost and we did not believe that it was he. But it was he. And thus he said to us, "Come, and do not be afraid. I am your teacher who you, Peter, denied three times before the cock crowed; and now do you deny again?"	Mt. 28:10
	And we went to him, thinking and doubting whether it was he. And he said to us, "Why do you doubt and why are you not believing that I am he who spoke to you concerning my flesh, my death, and my resurrection?"	[To Thomas, Jn 20:27]
	"And that you may know that it is I, lay your hand, Peter, (and your finger) in the nailprint of my hands; and you, Thomas, in my side; and also you, Andrew, see whether my foot steps on the ground and leaves a footprint.	Lk. 24:39-40

"For it is written in the prophet, 'But a ghost, a demon, leaves no print on the ground.'"

CH. 12 (ETH.): *But now we felt him, that he had truly risen in the flesh. And then we fell on our faces before him, asked him for pardon and entreated him because we had not believed him. Then our Lord and Saviour said to us, "Stand up and I will reveal to you what is on earth, and what is above heaven, and your resurrection that is in the kingdom of heaven, concerning which my Father has sent me, that I may take up you and those who believe in me."*

13–14	Jesus relates his heavenly journey; reflection on angels, particularly the annunciation to Mary by archangel Gabriel (actually Jesus in disguise)
15	Foretells near future: imprisonment of one during Passover
16–18	Questions and answers about Jesus's parousia; Jesus's omnipresence with the Father and with his followers
19	Commission to teach (and what to teach) with Jesus's empowerment, so as to become joint heirs with the Lord
20–26	Dialogue on the resurrection of the flesh with the soul
27–29	Dual necessity of believing in Jesus and keeping his commandment
30	Commission to preach to the twelve tribes of Israel
31–33	Jesus foretells Saul/Paul's ministry
34–39	Eschatological dialogue, prophecies, and signs
40–45	The role and reward of the apostles as fathers and teachers; analogy of the wise and foolish virgins
46–50	Commission to preach and teach, concerning wealth, sin, and admonition, avoiding slander; expectation of conflict
51	Conclusion: Jesus is taken away in the midst of thunder, lightning, and earthquake

---

* All the material quoted from the *Epistula Apostolorum* comes from Hennecke and Schneelecher, eds., *New Testament Apocrypha* (1:191–227). Chapters 1–6 are extant only in the Ethiopic. When quoting from Wilson's translations, the text's origination from either Ethiopic or Coptic will be noted. Often, the differences between the two languages in translation are so minor that the choice between the two is arbitrary.

† As the footnotes in Hennecke and Schneelecher's edition of the *Epistula Apostolorum* illustrate, the text contains an intricate conglomeration of traditions. Most are from the canonical Gospels, but editors identify resonances with noncanonical Gospels as well. E.g., a line on Jesus's childhood includes an interaction over "Alpha" and "Beta" (*Ep. Apost.* 4), reminiscent of the *Infancy Gospel of Thomas*, wherein Jesus "schools" his tutors (*Inf. Gos. Thom.* 6:3; 14:2). Because of the complicated interweaving of traditions, I will highlight the related NT Gospel texts *only* for the selected excerpts. The reader is referred to the textual notes in C. Schmidt, *Gespräche Jesu mit seinen Jüngern nach der Auferstehung: Ein katholisches-apostolisches Sendschreiben des 2. Jahrhunderts* (Leipzig: Hinrichs, 1919; repr. Hildesheim: G. Olms, 1967).

Apostolorum, mentions briefly the Markan LE. Hannah favors dating the composition of the *Epistula* to the first half of the second century, approximately 140.[45] Though I cannot adjudicate this dating, I support his suggestion, contra Kelhoffer,[46] that the

[45] Internal to the document, the dating of the Parousia points to either 140 or 170 (ch. 17, given a time frame that differs between the Coptic and Ethiopic versions, respectively), but Hannah argues for the superiority of the Coptic at this point ("Four-Gospel Canon," 630–1). He also cites several external factors that seem to be reflected in the text that supports his rough dating (632).

[46] Kelhoffer finds the parallels "insufficient to demonstrate a literary connection" (*Miracle and Mission*, 171n49). His caution is a helpful guard against "parallelomania": "Although Jesus's command that only one of the three women tell of the resurrection (*Epistula*, c. 10) could be an expansion of Mk 16:9–11, this passage in the *Epistula* could just as easily represent a conflation of Matthew 28

Epistula Apostolorum reflects knowledge of the LE.[47] One of the inexact parallels is the "weeping and mourning" that appears twice (*Ep. Apost.* 9, 10): instead of describing the disciples to whom Mary brings her news (Mk 16:10), the terms of grief are applied to the three female disciples at Jesus's tomb. If the author were aware of both John and Mark (the latter in a form including the LE), which seems likely, this altered application of the grief descriptors represents a purposeful correction of the LE's unmanly depiction of the Eleven,[48] in favor of John's depiction of weeping Mary, which might conform more closely to ancient expectation.

In addition to the evidence Hannah provides for such dependence,[49] the repeated disbelief of the disciples in the *Epistula Apostolorum* is astonishingly similar to the LE in its exaggeration. In the LE, the disciples disbelieve in response to the testimony of Mary Magdalene and two unnamed disciples (Mk 16:11, 13). The *Epistula Apostolorum* depicts Jesus's sending two women: first, Mary Magdalene (Coptic, Martha) and, second, Sarah (Coptic, Mary[50]). When both women return to Jesus to report their rejection—"None of them believed me concerning your resurrection," Mary Magdalene says (ch. 10 [Ethiopic])—Jesus brings along his posse of women followers to confront the disciples directly.[51] The disciples' lack of faith may be even heightened in *Epistula Apostolorum* in comparison to the LE: of Mary, "we did not believe her"; of Sarah, "we accused her of lying" (ch. 10); and, in response to Jesus, "we doubted and did not believe," "we did not believe that it was he," and "we went to him, thinking and doubting whether it was he" (ch. 11). The disciples relate their own disbelief in the first-person plural ("we"). The very telling is an admission of their own failure to believe. In the end, it takes more than an eyewitness appearance for the disciples to believe; it takes physical touch (*Ep. Apost.* 11).

In the LE of Mark, the gathered disciples "did not believe" (ἠπίστησαν) Mary Magdalene, "nor did they believe" (οὐδὲ ... ἐπίστευσαν) the two others who testify to having seen the risen Jesus. Their disbelief is conveyed simply and briefly; as such, there is no room for speculation as to whether only *some* of them distrust (as in Mt. 28:17 or Jn 20:24-29). Instead, their rejection of the witnesses to Jesus's resurrection continues until Jesus himself appears and again calls attention to their failure of faith. The portrait of the

---

and Luke 24, on the one hand, and John 20, on the other" (ibid.). Yet, as the following discussion illustrates, the *Ep. Apost.*'s retention and development of the Eleven's repeated disbelief tips the scale toward dependence, perhaps apologetic in intention.

[47] "It should perhaps be added that it is possible, but to my mind far from certain, that *Epistula Apostolorum* 9-11 reflects knowledge of the long ending of Mark" (Hannah, "Four-Gospel Canon," 625).

[48] See sections 2.2 and 2.2.1 on crying and gender.

[49] Hannah remains uncertain of the dependence, but includes the following possible connections:

> The detail that the three women went to the tomb "weeping and mourning over what had happened" (ch. 9; cf. also 10) could be an allusion to Mark 16:10, although in the latter it is the disciples who mourn and weep. More persuasively, the risen Christ's initial remarks to his disciples when he found them hiding (ch. 11) could be construed as a fleshing out and dramatization of 16:14. (Ibid., 625)

[50] Given that at least two of the Coptic version's three women are named Mary, it is not clear whether this is Mary of Bethany or Mary Magdalene (see *Ep. Apost.* 9 [Coptic]).

[51] "Then the Lord said to Mary and to her sisters, 'Let us go to them'" (*Ep. Apost.* 11).

male disciples is entirely unsympathetic, an estimation which the description from Mk 16:10b only reinforces.

2.2 The Disciples Are Mourning and Weeping

Two unnamed disciples follow Mary's model of obedient witness almost exactly, but the remainder fail to do so. As previously discussed, we cannot know whether all of the disciples referred to are male, or whether only a substantial contingent of each grouping was men: the terms used are all masculine.[52] It is important to note that on a grammatical level, the two disciples (vv. 12-13) and the remainder (vv. 10-11, 13) *are* masculine. Although the response of disbelief by the majority of the male disciples is presented as a simple statement, and no doubt the most important in its repetition (16:11, 13, 14), there is a further description of particular interest: πενθοῦσι καὶ κλαίουσιν (16:10). Mary Magdalene delivers her resurrection witness to "those who had been with him" (τοῖς μετ' αὐτοῦ γενομένοις), or the disciples, while they *mourned and wept*. This description stands in stark contrast to Mary Magdalene's comportment in the LE,[53] whose narration informs readers that she takes the initiative of proclamation but does not characterize her emotional state in so doing. This fits with much of Mark's undisputed ending: in the three appearances of named women in the crucifixion, burial, and empty tomb narratives, they are *never* described as mourning and crying. Although the women's fear and trembling at the empty tomb (16:8) surely connote extreme agitation,[54] any trace of this is left behind by the author of the LE.

In this respect, the women in Mark's closing pericopes (15:40-41, 46-47; 16:1-8) and Mary Magdalene in the LE (16:9-10) are quite unlike Mary in John's account, in which she weeps (κλαίουσα), disconsolate, outside the empty tomb in 20:11. In John 20, the two angels (v. 13) and Jesus (v. 15) ask her, "Woman, why are you weeping?" (γύναι, τί κλαίεις), redoubling the emphasis on her tears. Luke singles out the women of the group who accompany Jesus to his crucifixion as mourning and lamenting (αἳ ἐκόπτοντο καὶ ἐθρήνουν αὐτόν; Lk. 23:27).[55] Jesus addresses them directly, "Daughters of Jerusalem (θυγατέρες Ἰερουσαλήμ), do not weep [μὴ κλαίετε] for me. Weep [κλαίετε] instead for yourselves and for your children" (23:28).

---

[52] Of the disciples to whom Mary Magdalene conveyed her message in 16:10: τοῖς μετ' αὐτοῦ γενομένοις πενθοῦσι καὶ κλαίουσιν. Four of those terms convey gender-information about the group in reference, all masculine plurals. Verse 11 records their response, which contains two more terms that point to the masculine-identity of the group: κἀκεῖνοι ἀκούσαντες (masculine plurals). See section 2.7 in Chapter 2 (esp. n. 16).

[53] See section 2.5 in Chapter 2. Kelhoffer also takes note of this absence of authorial commentary on Mary's emotions (*Miracle and Mission*, 171n48).

[54] Josephus, writing of the final defeat of the rebels before the end of the Jewish War, demonstrates that fearful trembling was seen unmanly: "Those men, erstwhile so haughty and proud of their impious crimes, might then be seen abject and trembling [ταπεινοὺς καὶ τρέμοντας]—a transformation which, even in such villains, was pitiable" (*J.W.* 6.395 [Thackeray, LCL]).

[55] In 23:27, Luke reports that a "great crowd of people and women" were following Jesus's procession to the cross (Ἠκολούθει δὲ αὐτῷ πολὺ πλῆθος τοῦ λαοῦ καὶ γυναικῶν), but limits verbs of mourning and wailing to the women, using feminine relative pronoun (αἵ).

It seems fitting to point to the ancient trope of crying as "unmanly,"[56] parallel to the modern English aphorism: "Boys don't cry." Interestingly, however, the references to crying in the Second Gospel do not fall on the women's side of the gender divide.[57] The most prominent example is Peter's weeping (ἔκλαιεν) after he denies Jesus thrice (14:72), which is included in the other Synoptic accounts (Mt. 26:75 and Lk. 22:62).

Indeed, while weeping may not indicate gender-delimiting weakness, it might indeed represent a failure of faith (cf. also the crowd at the death of Jairus's daughter, Mk 5:38-9).[58] Jesus's sorrow in Gethsemane, which he himself describes in terms of extreme sorrow, περίλυπος (14:34), tiptoes between willingness and hesitancy, although he remains faithful to the Father's will (v. 36b). Likewise, his cry of dereliction on the cross, however, must be kept in mind in comparison (15:34; par. Mt. 27:46). It could be that this outcry at God's ostensible abandonment was perceived as just that—evidence of (unmasculine) weakness or a lack of faith, or both—which might account for the detail's exclusion in Luke's parallel account.

Given the ambiguity of crying in Mark's Gospel, it is unwise to rush to judgment regarding how these terms characterize the disciples in 16:10. A study of these terms' usage in scriptural context throws light on the possible connotations of "mourning and weeping." The terms related to πενθέω[59] and κλαίω[60] appear sixty-four times in the NT (words from these roots are used three hundred and one times in the Septuagint, although three are translations of Hebrew place names).

Beyond Mk 16:10, the two terms are paired in close proximity five times in the NT. In Luke's Sermon on the Plain, "you will mourn and weep" (πενθήσετε καὶ κλαύσετε) is the threat facing those who laugh now (6:25). In Jas 4:9, in the context of a call to repentance, this set of terms again represents the woeful side of a change of fortune: "Be sorrowful and mourn [πενθήσατε] and weep [κλαύσατε]; let your laughter be changed into mourning [πένθος] and your joy into gloom." The three remaining uses are found

---

[56] Thus, e.g., a consolation from Seneca, in which he cites excessive mourning and grief as "womanish" (Seneca, *Ep.* 99.2). Further, Josephus imagines, within the speech of Eleazar at Masada, that tears have the persuasive potential to "un-man" others (*J.W.* 7.339).

[57] The persons/groups crying and terms used in Mark: of the crowd weeping over Jairus's daughter, κλαίω (5:38-39) and ἀλαλάζω (v. 38); Peter, when he thinks about his denial of Jesus, cries (κλαίω; 14:72). "Crying out" (ἀνακράζω) likely connotes a different response (distress rather than sorrow), but is also used of males: a man with an unclean spirit in the synagogue (ἀνακράζω; 1:23); the disciples who see Jesus walking on the sea (6:49); and Jesus's crying out in a loud voice (ἐβόησεν ... φωνῇ μεγάλῃ) on the cross (15:34). The term used of Jesus's cry of dereliction (βοάω) is also used of the voice crying out (βοῶντος) in the wilderness (1:3), prophetically pointing to John the Baptist, but the verb seems to convey loud expression, but without an undertone of agony.

[58] Noteworthy, regarding this divergence among the Gospels' portrayals of crying, is the story of the woman who anoints Jesus with oil (Mk 14:3-9 and Lk. 7:36-50). In Luke's account, the woman's tears are, in some way, representative of her faith (esp. vv. 44 and 50). In Mark's version, the woman is not recorded as crying. Although her anointing of Jesus is never explicitly equated with faith, Jesus deems it a "good work" (καλὸν ἔργον; 14:6) and pronounces her act worthy of perpetual remembrance (v. 9). Context, then, must guide the reader in interpreting tears. Tears tempered with faith do not engender criticism. As we will see, despite their tears the Eleven lack belief in Jesus's resurrection, for which they receive a haranguing (16:14).

[59] The verb πενθέω itself appears ten times and the noun πένθος, *mourning*, occurs five times (of those, four are in Revelation alone).

[60] The verb κλαίω is used forty times, while its nominal form κλαυθμός, *weeping*, appears nine times. The latter term is nearly always used by Matthew (seven of the nine NT occurrences), six of which

in Revelation 18, which recounts the downfall of Babylon the great city, with cries of "Fallen, fallen!" (ἔπεσεν ἔπεσεν; v. 2) and "Woe, woe!" (οὐαὶ οὐαί; vv. 10, 16, 19). This chapter turns on the irony that a city of such great wealth and prestige should be so dramatically laid waste (cf. v. 17). Again, mourning and weeping express the emotions of those whose situations are drastically changed for the worse. First, the merchants weep and mourn (κλαίουσιν καὶ πενθοῦσιν) over the city because there is no one to purchase their fine wares (18:11). The second occurrence of this pair of terms repeats the scenario of the merchants, this time standing far off weeping and mourning (κλαίοντες καὶ πενθοῦντες), emphasizing that this group had formerly been made rich by Babylon (v. 15). In v. 19 it is the shipmasters who bemoan the city's destruction, for they also were made rich there. They take on the markers of lament, even casting dust on their heads while weeping and wailing (κλαίοντες καὶ πενθοῦντες).

Words from πενθ- and κλαι/κλαυ- roots appear so frequently in the LXX as to prevent a thorough comparison, but they appear as a pair only six times.[61] Whenever terms like πενθέω and κλαίω are conjoined, the expression is one of extreme sorrow. As the following examples show—both those that fit the neat formula (πενθ- και κλαι/κλαυ-) and those that do not—the situation is either mourning the recent death of an intimate acquaintance or significant person, or a comparison that plays on the expectations of such desperate mourning.

In Gen. 37:34-35 both terms appear in proximity (πενθέω twice) describing Jacob's sorrow at Joseph's supposed death. Deuteronomy 34:8 recalls the thirty days of "mourning of weeping" (πένθους κλαυθμοῦ) for Moses's death. At the death of his son Absalom, David mourns and weeps (κλαίει καὶ πενθεῖ; LXX 2 Sam. 19:2), which turns the victory of triumph against threats to the king into a time of mourning for Israel.[62] Nehemiah's weeping and mourning (ἔκλαυσα καὶ ἐπένθησα) follows news of Jerusalem's fallen state (Neh. 1:4). After the work to restore Jerusalem, the situation reverses: when the high priest reads the law in the hearing of the people, they weep, but Nehemiah and the other leaders instruct them neither to mourn nor to weep (μὴ πενθεῖτε μηδὲ κλαίετε), for this day is holy to the Lord (8:9).

---

are found in the characteristic and repeated phrase, "There shall be weeping and gnashing of teeth" (ἐκεῖ ἔσται ὁ κλαυθμὸς καὶ ὁ βρυγμὸς τῶν ὀδόντων, 8:12; 13:42, 50; 22:13; 24:51; and 25:30). One of the two non-Matthean uses in Lk. 13:28 is a repetition of the "weeping and gnashing" phrase, which is not parallel to any of the pericopes in Matthew in which the sentence is used.

[61] For this count, I considered only those occasions when the terms are connected by a conjunction, as in Mk 16:10; 2 Sam. 19:2; Neh. 1:4; 8:9; Sir. 7:34; Bar. 4:11, 23. In the following study, however, I also consider the verses in which the terms are used in a parallel or proximate construction. Further, it is not as if combining these terms is the only way to indicate extreme, sorrowful emotion. In fact, there are several occasions in which the verb and cognate accusative (or dative, or with a participle) of κλαίω connote extreme sadness (LXX Gen. 46:29; Judg. 21:2; 1 Sam. 1:10; 2 Sam. 13:36; 2 Kgs 20:3; Ezra 10:1; Isa. 30:19; 38:3; Jer. 22:10; Lam. 1:2). 1 Macc. 12:52 uses a similar construction using πενθ- words: literally, "And all Israel mourned a great mourning" (καὶ ἐπένθησεν πᾶς Ισραηλ πένθος μέγα). Likewise, other terms express sadness and mourning (e.g., ἀναστενάζω in Lam. 1:4; κόπτω and στεναγμός in Ezek. 24:17; λυπέω in Tob. 7:6).

[62] LXX 2 Sam. 19:3 connects the king's weeping and mourning to a change of fortune for all the people: καὶ ἐγένετο ἡ σωτηρία ἐν τῇ ἡμέρᾳ ἐκείνῃ εἰς πένθος παντὶ τῷ λαῷ ("And the salvation became mourning in that day for all the people"). This is precisely the king's devaluing of his people's sacrifice for his well-being, for which Joab criticizes David (19:5-7).

Elsewhere in the Septuagint these coupled terms remain consistent, except for several instances in which they are used in settings of real weeping over a figurative or idealized death.[63] Relating the actual death of a "savior," 1 Macc. 9:20 conjoins both words but does not pair them as closely as in previous examples. However, the similar circumstances—the loss of a great leader—makes a useful comparison to Mk 16:10: all of Israel is said to weep (ἔκλαυσαν) for Judas Maccabeus and mourn (ἐπένθουν) for many days after his death. The people's lament for Judas, the mighty one who fell, also refers to him as "savior of Israel" (σῴζων τὸν Ἰσραηλ; 1 Macc. 9:21). Baruch 4:11 fits within the "change-of-fortune" motif in which the terms appear frequently. In v. 11 the city of Jerusalem is speaking as a mother, who fed (likely, "nursed," in line with v. 8) her children in joy, but sent them away with weeping and mourning (κλαυθμοῦ καὶ πένθους). Verse 12 reveals that Jerusalem, deserted because of her children's sins, considers herself a widow (χήρα; cf. v. 16). Another reversal of fortune comes into the picture, the substance of Jerusalem's hopes, in v. 21. Although the widow Jerusalem sent her children away with weeping and mourning (πένθους καὶ κλαυθμοῦ), she trusts in God to return them (v. 23).

Most biblical authors[64] do not hold tight the reins controlling honorable mourning, as did the Stoics.[65] Instead, tears and mourning are noted—even commanded—in situations of loss of life, individual or collective. There are things worse than death, which are also deserving of lamentation.

In the Markan LE, however, the remaining disciples are described as sorrowfully mourning as if their Savior were dead, when Jesus is no longer in the grave, but alive (Mk 16:9). This irony is only highlighted by Mary's truthful proclamation without crying (vv. 9-11). The recipients of the good news are unmoved from their posture of mourning; the news of Jesus's resurrection cannot penetrate their sorrow. Therefore, however crying is to be viewed in Mark as a whole, in the LE the disciples' tears are accompanied by a total failure of faith. As such, a tearless Mary Magdalene stands as a sharp counterpoint to their misplaced mourning.

2.2.1 Gender Stereotypes vis-à-vis Crying

In light of the pejorative implications of faithlessness implied in the disciples' mourning and weeping in the LE, it is fruitful to attend to such negative associations accompanying

---

[63] The first instance of the terms in Sirach is straightforward but generalized: Sir. 7:34 instructs, "Do not be late to those who weep [κλαιόντων], and mourn [πενθησον] with those who mourn [πενθούντων]." Further, Sir. 22:11-12 plays upon the expectation that mourning is appropriate for those who have died:

> Weep [κλαῦσον] for the dead one, for he left the light; and weep [κλαῦσον] for the foolish one, for he left intelligence; Weep [κλαῦσον] gladly over the dead, for he is at rest; but for the fool, life is more evil than death. Mourning [πένθος] of the dead is seven days, but for the fool and the ungodly [mourning] is all the days of his life.

Treating sin like a grave illness, Sir. 28:17 commands weeping (κλαυθμόν) and mourning (πένθος) over misdeeds, using the nominal forms in parallel lines.

[64] The exception is the author of 4 Maccabees, whose generalized Stoic perspective results in a narrower range of acceptable emotional expression.

[65] See Seneca, *Lucil.* 63.1-2, 11, 14.

men's crying in the ancient world. Like the modern stereotype that associates a man who cries with immaturity ("crybaby") or femininity ("sissy"), the notion of crying as "unmanly" is widespread in ancient literature. By limiting our selective comparisons to Hellenistic Jewish writings and material roughly contemporaneous with Mk 16:9-20, we may notice the potential for unflattering implications across the gender divide in the LE's pairing of bold Mary Magdalene and the weeping male disciples.

In 4 Maccabees, a discourse arguing that pious reason is superior to emotions (πάθος),[66] the author demonstrates his thesis by eulogizing Eleazar, seven brothers, and their mother (4 Macc. 1:7-8). The subjects of the author's reflection endure extreme suffering and are able to retain their commitment to God and demonstrate a brave face to their oppressors. What is celebrated is not an unfeeling numbness but a bold endurance despite horrific pain.[67] The author employs a mixed simile that illustrates the ideal: Eleazar is like a ship's pilot, who skillfully navigates his craft over raging seas (7:1-5). His piety (steering the ship) is like a cliff that does not nullify the stormy swell (emotions) but disrupts its power.[68] Conversely, those who succumb to their emotions do so on account of their *weak* reason (διὰ τὸν ἀσθενῆ λογισμόν; 7:20). Godliness is equated with a bravery that allows triumph over the passions: "For only the wise and courageous are masters of their emotions [μόνος γὰρ ὁ σοφὸς καὶ ἀνδρεῖός ἐστιν τῶν παθῶν κύριος]" (7:23).

---

[66] Hans-Josef Klauck classifies it as "epideictic speech" (*4 Makkabaërbuch* [JSHRZ 3.6; Gütersloh: Mohn, 1989], 659). In an active debate over dating the work, E. J. Bickerman's thesis is that it was composed sometime between 18 and 54 CE ("The Date of Fourth Maccabees," in *Studies in Jewish and Christian History* [2 vols; AGJU 9; Leiden: Brill, 1976], 275–81 [rev. version of a 1945 original]). See Stephen D. Moore and Janice Capel Anderson for more bibliographic commentary ("Taking It Like a Man: Masculinity in 4 Maccabees," *JBL* 117 [1998]: 251n4).

[67] Describing the elderly priest Eleazar, the author does not hide the physical hardship's toll on the man:

> But the courageous and noble man, like a true Eleazar, was unmoved [κατ' οὐδένα τρόπον μετετρέπετο = lit., "he was changing according to *no* manner"] as though being tortured in a dream; ... Although he fell to the ground because his body could not endure the agonies, he kept his reason upright and unswerving [ὀρθὸν εἶχεν καὶ ἀκλινῆ τὸν λογισμόν = "he *kept having* upright and unswerving reasoning"] ... Like a noble athlete the old man, while being beaten, was victorious [ἐνίκα] over his torturers; in fact, with his face bathed in sweat, and gasping heavily for breath, he amazed even his torturers by his courageous spirit [εὐψυχίᾳ]. (4 Macc. 6:5-11; unbracketed translation, NRSV)

As Harold W. Attridge ("An 'Emotional' Jesus and Stoic Tradition," in *Stoicism in Early Christianity* [ed. Tuomas Rasimus et al.; Grand Rapids: Baker, 2010]) summarizes Stoicism's approach to emotions:

> The ways in which the emotions are treated in the cases of grief, anger, and fear merit attention. The critical point is that even for the sage, the ideal limiting condition of rational humanity, it is not impossible to have what we might call feelings, stirrings of the soul, occasioned by sensory impressions. What made these psychic motions emotions was the judgmental assent to their propositional content by the ἡγεμονικόν, the controlling element of the soul ... The ideal embodiment of ἀπάθεια will not be devoid of external impressions and stirrings of the soul but will shape them and subject them to rational control. (84)

Eleazar fits this model. It is not that he is made superhuman or deadens his senses; instead, in the midst of bodily weakness, his reason trumps his emotions.

[68] "For in setting his mind [τὴν ἑαυτοῦ διάνοιαν] firm like a jutting cliff, our father Eleazar broke the maddening waves of the emotions [περιέκλασεν τοὺς ἐπιμαινομένους τῶν παθῶν κλύδωνας = 'he bent the furious waters of the emotions/passions']" (7:5; unbracketed translation, NRSV).

The term for *courageous* or *brave* (ἀνδρεῖος) may be literally translated as *manly* (cf. ἀνήρ); this term is used frequently in 4 Maccabees to describe the ideal response to pain and fear.[69] Lack of control over the emotions can be equated with unmanliness in Stoic thought; failure to meet expected masculine norms are equated with effeminacy.[70] After recounting the grisly deaths of the seven brothers, the author rehearses their "holy chorus" of mutual fortification: "Let us not be cowardly [δειλανδρήσωμεν] in the demonstration of godliness" (13:10).[71] But it would be misleading to give the impression that the strength to push down the emotions was ascribed only to men; in special cases women as well could be praised for reason (or religion, εὐσέβεια, as in the following example) triumphing over the passions. 4 Maccabees never hesitates to employ melodramatics or repetition to drive home a point; yet the martyrdom accounts of the priest Eleazar and then of seven sons are outshone by the grand finale: the eulogized death of the fearless mother.[72]

After watching her sons die, the mother goes unflinching to the same fate. After devoting some space to explain that women have greater internal sympathy for their children than do fathers (15:4),[73] and expressing a lower, initial expectation for a woman (as the "weaker sex" [NRSV]; lit., "weak-minded," ἀσθενόψυχοι; 15:5), the author commends the mother in this way:

> When the firstborn breathed his last, it did not turn you aside, nor when the second in torments looked at you piteously nor when the third expired; *nor did you weep* [οὐκ ἔκλαυσας] when you looked at the eyes of each one in his tortures gazing boldly at the same agonies and saw in their nostrils the approach of death ... *you did not shed tears* [οὐκ ἐδάκρυσας]. (4 Macc. 15:18-19, 20b, NRSV; italics added)

Three verses later the mother of the Maccabean martyrs is paid another compliment for her Stoic piety. Pious reason (ὁ εὐσεβὴς λογισμός) strengthened her heart "by making her brave"—that is, *manly* (ἀνδρειώσας)—and allowed her to temporarily overlook her parental love (v. 23). This Jewish mother is remembered as comparable in fortitude to

---

[69] Cf. verses in 4 Maccabees containing terms that share this stem: 1:4, 6, 11, 18; 2:23; 5:23, 31; 6:21; 7:23; 8:16; 10:14; 13:10; 15:10, 23, 30; 17:23-24.

[70] Discussing the impact of a king on his populace, Seneca makes this association: "But an uncontrolled, passionate, and effeminate [*inpotens, cupidus, delicatus*] soul changes kingship into that most dread and detestable quality—tyranny; then it becomes a prey to the uncontrolled emotions [*adfectus inpotentes*]" (*Ep.* CXIV.24, "On Style as a Mirror of Character"; Gummere, LCL). A lack of control over one's emotions is associated with effeminacy.

[71] The previous verse, a summary "quotation" from the brothers, exhorts imitation of the three young men who went bravely into the fiery furnace in Assyria (13:9; cf. Daniel 3). Although LXX Daniel does not use any terms sharing a root with ἀνδρεῖος ("manly") to describe the three young men (although ἀνδρίζομαι is used to describe Daniel in 10:19), that story demonstrates the young men's boldness in the face of mortal danger. The LXX addition the Prayer of Azariah especially presents the men in the furnace not fearful or despairing, but glorifying and blessing God (1:28-68).

[72] Moore and Anderson put it well: "Paradoxically, as we shall see, the prime exemplar of masculinity in 4 Maccabees is a woman" ("Taking It Like a Man," 252).

[73] I.e., μάλιστα διὰ τὸ τῶν παθῶν τοῖς γεννηθεῖσιν τὰς μητέρας τῶν πατέρων καθεστάναι συμπαθεστέρας (v. 4b). This συμπαθής (sympathy) is related to φιλότεκνος (love of children) in vv. 5 and 6.

the father of her nation, Abraham (v. 28). The highest compliment paid her, however, is a citation of her bravery as not only manly but even exceeding men in the triumph of reason: "O more noble than males [ἀρρένων] in steadfastness, and more courageous [ἀνδρειοτέρα] than men [ἀνδρῶν] in endurance!" (v. 30, NRSV). The second comparative may be literally rendered, "more manly than men in endurance"; this gendered irony—that a woman should be manlier than men—was surely intentional, judging by the word-choice.[74] The mother's superior "manliness" is both ironic and the lynchpin example in an ongoing argument that "devout reason [ὁ εὐσεβὴς λογισμός] is sovereign over the emotions" (16:1).[75] This lack of tears stands as an example of exceptional strength, given the circumstances, and particularly for a woman. Even the androcentric terms used to denote bravery (verb, ἀνδρειόω; adjective, ἀνδρεῖος) demonstrate cultural suppositions about those to whom the term is likely to pertain.[76]

Without a doubt, 4 Maccabees is a different text from Mark or its LE in nearly every way, being a discourse elaborating one aspect of a widely known narrative (4 Maccabees), rather than a brief story itself (Mark and the LE). But 4 Maccabees states outright some assumptions that may underlie the LE: men are more likely to be brave than women, and crying is a unmanly act. Many ancient readers may have held such assumptions. If the perspective of 4 Maccabees were applied to the LE, the male disciples would come off as doubly weak: they face no immediate suffering nor bodily harm themselves, yet they continue to cry for their Lord three days after his death. Moreover, their tears manifest their failure to believe that he was raised.

In Josephus's account of the Jewish War against Rome, he comes eventually to a different Eleazar, who leads the last forces of the Jewish rebellion ensconced at Masada (J.W. 7.8–9). This charismatic leader suggests a mass suicide—a noble death rather than survival in enslavement—which is not received with uniform eagerness. Josephus narrates:

> Thus spoke Eleazar; but his words did not touch the hearts of all hearers alike. Some, indeed, were eager to respond and all but filled with delight at the thought of a death so noble; but others, softer-hearted [μαλακωτέρους], were moved with compassion for their wives and families, and doubtless also by the vivid prospect of their own end, and *their tears* as they looked upon one another [εἴς τε ἀλλήλους ἀποβλέποντες τοῖς δακρύοις] revealed [ἐσήμαινον] their unwillingness of heart.[77]

The term μαλακωτέρος literally means "softer," The comparative of μαλακός, it is a word that carries connotations of "effeminacy,"[78] covering a range of meaning from weak to

---

[74] The prior comparative phrase uses a different term for men (ἄρρην); the proximate pair in the second phrase, ἀνδρειοτέρα (braver/manlier) and ἀνδρῶν (than men), demonstrate the shared root.

[75] There is a repeated inference to this effect: If *even* a woman could withstand this level of suffering, then devout reason must be responsible for it (cf. 4 Macc. 16:1-2, 5-13).

[76] In their thorough investigation Moore and Anderson examined the gender ideals on display in 4 Maccabees. They summarize, "Mastery—of others and/or of oneself—is the definitive masculine trait in most of the Greek and Latin literary and philosophical texts that survive from antiquity" ("Taking It Like a Man," 250).

[77] Josephus, J.W. 7.337-8 (Thackeray, LCL); italics added.

[78] Craig A. Williams summarizes a wide swath of mostly Roman literary sources: "Implied throughout the ancient sources: *softness* is the antithesis of *masculinity*. So it is that the language of softness appears

morally lax.⁷⁹ The "softer" men are those with compassionate feelings for their family members and who cry together.⁸⁰ While this cluster of associations—crying, familial affection, and unmanliness—is clearly negative in Josephus's portrait of Eleazar and his principled comrades, crying is not a uniformly negative act. Even in Eleazar's speech, weeping is not always a sign of weakness; the thought behind the tears matters.⁸¹

Although this survey has not been exhaustive, it allows a glimpse into the sort of values that weeping or a display of emotion could evoke. Emotional displays are not automatically neutral in ancient literature; they could have negative connotations like impaired reason or piety. Even if a particular author does not adhere to Stoic thought, or subverts it, the readers' sphere of interpretive possibility retains that potential lens through which to view the text. After all, utter subversion of a trope cannot work without an existing expectation.⁸² Finally, expressed emotions are not ambiguously gendered. A depiction of an emotional male may trigger the same level of surprise that the unemotional and "manly" mother does. In the case of the males, however, there is the additionally negative potential to fail to conform to masculine ideals that are considered honorable.⁸³ Using gender as a lens through which to view this narrative element can highlight not only a narrative's divergence from ancient gender stereotypes, but also conformity to such stereotypes as a "corrective" measure.⁸⁴ The LE does not correct; it compounds the disciples' dishonor, if only temporarily.⁸⁵

in allusions to the most extreme type of unmanly men: eunuchs" (*Roman Homosexuality: Ideologies of Masculinity in Classical Antiquity* [New York: Oxford, 1999], 128; emphases in the original). Because Williams is drawing primarily from Latin texts, the term in reference here is *mollio*, which means to "make soft." See also Dale Martin, "*Arsenokoitēs* and *Malakos*: Meanings and Consequences," in *Sex and the Single Savior: Gender and Sexuality in Biblical Interpretation* (Louisville: Westminster John Knox, 2006), 37–50.

⁷⁹ The most straightforward definition of the term is "textural softness."
⁸⁰ The familial affection referred to here suggests a link to the sentimentality 4 Maccabees expects of women to a far greater degree than men (cf. 4 Macc. 15:4; see earlier).
⁸¹ Later in Eleazar's speech, he uses the example of "the Indians" who celebrate death (Josephus, *J.W.* 7.351-57). Referring to "their dearest ones" (family of the deceased), he commends them favorably: "For themselves they weep [δακρύουσιν], but them they count as happy as now regaining immortal rank" (7.356).
⁸² Moore and Anderson explain this clearly:

> The irony of 4 Maccabees is that a feeble, flabby old man, a gaggle of boys, and an elderly widow—all persons who should rate low on the hierarchical continuum of (masterful) masculinity and (mastered) femininity—triumph over someone who should be at the privileged end of the continuum. The continuum must still exist or the irony could not exist. And the continuum still has masculinity at its superior end and femininity at its inferior end. That the continuum is employed rather than destroyed in this text is especially apparent in the treatment of the martyr-mother. ("Take It Like a Man," 273)

⁸³ A cursory treatment of such deeply entrenched and varying experiences of gender runs the risk of oversimplifying and taking tropes as historical fact. For more nuanced approaches (most with an eye to NT contexts), see ibid., esp. 250; Williams, *Roman Homosexuality* (esp. chapter 4, "Effeminacy and Masculinity," 125-59); Todd Penner and Caroline Vander Stichele, *Contextualizing Gender in Early Christian Discourse: Thinking beyond Thecla* (London: T&T Clark, 1999); Stephen D. Moore and Janice Capel Anderson, eds., *New Testament Masculinities* (SemeiaSt 45; Atlanta: Society of Biblical Literature, 2003); Jennifer Larson, "Paul's Masculinity," *JBL* 123 (2004): 85–97; Colleen Conway, *Behold the Man: Jesus and Greco-Roman Masculinity* (New York: Oxford University Press, 2008).
⁸⁴ The *Epistula Apostolorum* (chs 9–10) returns the activities of mourning and weeping to the female disciples at the tomb.
⁸⁵ The bravery to hold snakes, ingest poison (Mk 16:18), and proclaim the gospel to the whole world (vv. 15, 20) surely reverses any view of the Eleven as "weak." The LE is simply willing to extend description of the disciples' disfavor.

2.3 The Eleven's Lack of Faith Highlights the Faithfulness of Others

As in chiaroscuro painting, in which the subject is highlighted by virtue of the dimness and obscurity of the scene around it, the significance of Mary Magdalene's faithful response to Jesus's appearance to her in the LE can be fully appreciated only in comparison to the failure of those around her in the passage. Her obedience shines brighter against the dark portrayal of the male disciples' collective and repetitive disbelief. Multiple terms illustrating the Eleven's lack of faith are applied within a few short verses: they reject the witnesses (ἠπίστησαν, v. 11; οὐδὲ ἐκείνοις ἐπίστευσαν, v. 13); Jesus reproaches them for their faithlessness (τὴν ἀπιστίαν αὐτῶν) and hardheartedness (σκληροκαρδίαν), because they did not believe (οὐκ ἐπίστευσαν) the witnesses (v. 14).

If a stagnant faithlessness is represented by misplaced sorrow and stubborn refusal of good news, then Mary's active witness is its opposite: faithfulness. Mary's *going* and *telling* (16:10) exemplifies the basic commission of 16:15, into which the Eleven are drawn. My focus on Mary Magdalene diminishes neither the faithfulness of the other two witnesses (16:12-13) nor the Eleven's eventual participation (16:20). Yet Mary enjoys a particular privilege: she seizes the chance to be the *first* to exercise Jesus's commission.

2.4 The Eleven Are Rebuked

The author of the LE not only repeats the disciples' instances of disbelief, but also depicts Jesus's judgment against them as quite severe. Kelhoffer points out that the combination of *reproach* (ὠνείδισεν), *unbelief* (ἀπιστίαν), and *hardness of heart* (σκληροκαρδίαν) in v. 14 is distinctive among other terms used for judgment in Mark and the NT.[86] He points to J. K. Elliott's judgment: "This is the only place in the New Testament where these faults are leveled at the disciples."[87] Jesus has had harsh words for his closest companions (cf. Mk 8:17) and calling Peter "Satan" (Mk 8:33; par. Mt. 16:23) may exceed in virulence even the LE's combination of terms. Although Mk 16:14 is harsh, it is not alone in ascribing forceful reprimands to Jesus.

In Luke, as Cleopas and his companion walk to Emmaus (24:13-27), their failure to recognize Jesus when he joins them is attributed by the narrator not to disbelief, but to their eyes being "seized" (ἐκρατοῦντο; v. 16). This imperfect construction may be a divine passive, perhaps better rendered, "their eyes were hindered [*by God*] with the result that they did not recognize him." Interestingly, when the two disciples recount their reaction to the women's report to their fellow traveler (the risen Jesus), they describe the disciples as *astonished* (ἐξέστησαν; v. 22), perhaps reflecting the later reevaluation of the women's report after the fact of the empty tomb is substantiated by others (v. 24). Jesus shifts the blame for the disciples' ignorance from divine obfuscation to human idiocy and disbelief: "Oh, you fools and slow of heart to believe all that the prophets said!" (v. 25). The question—"Is it not necessary that the Christ

---

[86] Kelhoffer, *Miracle and Mission*, 95.
[87] J. K. Elliott, "Text and Language of the Endings to Mark's Gospel," *TZ* 27 (1971): 260.

should suffer in order to enter his glory?" (v. 26)—expects a "yes" (indicated by οὐχί), as if the conclusion were self-evident. Luke draws further attention to the disciples' failure to understand and believe apparently available evidence about Jesus, for as the unrecognized Jesus leads the two disciples through Israel's scriptures, he explains "the things concerning himself" (τὰ περὶ ἑαυτοῦ; v. 27). Yet Jesus contributes to the pair's (divinely?) impaired skills of observation and seems to have somewhere farther to go (προσεποιήσατο πορρώτερον πορεύεσθαι; v. 28). Whatever part the two disciples played in their blindness to Jesus's true identity, when their eyes are opened (presumably, *by God*: διηνοίχθησαν), they can recognize Jesus. In Luke, the disbelief of the disciples can only be abrogated by Jesus, who "opens" their faculties for understanding.[88]

Some scholars have attributed Jesus's rebuke (Lk. 24:25) to an implicit critique of the men's failing to believe women's testimony.[89] Such a reading, in which Jesus supports the witness of women, is surely open to interpreters but is left unspecified in Luke's text. When Jesus calls Cleopas and his companion "fools" and decries their slowness of heart to believe, it is "all that the prophets have said" and not the women's testimony that is the explicit referent of their disbelief. The prophecies or the divine necessity of Jesus's death are inferred as the weight of what should have convinced them: "Was it not necessary for Christ to suffer these things and to enter his glory?" (v. 26). When he appears to the larger group of disciples, Jesus expresses incredulity at their fear and speculation, all the while reassuring them of his fleshly presence (vv. 38-39). As earlier, however, the veracity or worthiness of the women's rejected report is never mentioned or reaffirmed.

In Mark's LE, it is not as though the Eleven failed to perceive the object of prophetic foretelling (πᾶσιν οἷς ἐλάλησαν οἱ προφῆται) as Luke 24:25 reports. Likewise, they are not charged with having expressed a direct disbelief that Jesus could be, would be, or had been raised bodily.[90] He upbraided them (ὠνείδισεν) for their unbelief and hardness

---

[88] As Luke tells it, despite the growing belief that Jesus has been raised, after the disciples are back together in Jerusalem and Jesus appears, their first response is terror (πτοηθέντες δὲ καὶ ἔμφοβοι) and they suppose him to be a spirit (v. 37). That Jesus perceives in their fear some sort of doubt is revealed in his second question to them: "Why do speculations arise in your hearts?" (διὰ τί διαλογισμοὶ ἀναβαίνουσιν ἐν τῇ καρδίᾳ ὑμῶν; v. 38). In its most basic sense, διαλογισμος means "ruminative thought." Here, the *thoughts* arising in their hearts might be better classified *speculations* or *doubts*. Even after Jesus explains that he is not a spirit, but has "flesh and bones" (σάρκα καὶ ὀστέα) that can be touched and displayed (vv. 39-40), the disciples still "disbelieve and marvel for joy" (ἔτι δὲ ἀπιστούντων αὐτῶν ἀπὸ τῆς χαρᾶς καὶ θαυμαζόντων; v. 41). This comment about "disbelieving" does not seem to refer to lack of faith primarily, but instead to the sort of astonishment conveyed by the English idiom, "They could not believe their eyes!" The final resolution of their disbelief, whether fearful or joyful, comes with a supernatural corrective: Jesus opens the disciples' minds to understand the scriptures (v. 45).

[89] As Richard Bauckham (*Gospel Women: Studies of the Named Women in the Gospels* [New York: T&T Clark, 2002]) says:

> As far as Luke's account of the empty tomb goes, we have already noticed that by means of his statement that the apostles did not believe the women, he makes explicit the rebuke to assumptions of male priority that the revelation given first to the women entails. The point is rubbed in when the two travelers to Emmaus repeat the story of the women (Luke 24:22-23) to the stranger, who consequently rebukes them for their unbelief (24:25). (279)

[90] Jesus's corporeal presence is affirmed in Luke's resurrection appearances (i.e., as a touchable body [24:39-40] rather than a spirit [vv. 37, 39]), including his ability to eat food (vv. 41-43).

of heart (Mk 16:14). The term σκληροκαρδίαν (hardheartedness) is reminiscent of the rebuke to Cleopas and his companion for their slowness of heart, βραδεῖς τῇ καρδίᾳ (Lk. 24:25). The critique of hardheartedness (σκληροκαρδίαν), or slowness of heart in Lukan terms, is freighted with a sense of failure to grasp the meaning of a scripture in its other Synoptic uses (cf. Mt. 19:8 and Mk 10:5).[91] In the case of the LE, however, the Eleven earn the label hardhearted (σκληροκαρδίαν) "because they did not believe [οὐκ ἐπίστευσαν] those who saw him after he had been raised [τοῖς θεασαμένοις αὐτὸν ἐγηγερμένον]" (Mk 16:14). These disciples' blameworthy disobedience is directly dependent on their rejection of the witness by those having seen the risen Jesus.

The witnesses' testimonies are twofold in the LE: first, Mary Magdalene's encounter with the risen Christ and her proclamation to the Eleven; second, the abbreviated and similar account of the two disciples who meet Jesus while walking and report to the disciples. Paul Allan Mirecki summarizes the disciples' response to both instances of witness to the resurrection as antagonistic.[92] Whereas the primary actors are protagonists, the conflicting response by the disciples can only be described in opposite terms.[93] Mary Magdalene and the two unnamed disciples were recipients of a resurrection appearance and responded faithfully by spreading the news. Antithetically, the rest of the disciples were recipients of eyewitness testimony to the resurrection and responded faithlessly.

Finally, Jesus vindicates Mary Magdalene's testimony as true in response to those who disbelieve it. Whether or not her identity as a woman plays a part in the disciples' dismissal of her witness in the LE (as Lk. 24:11 suggests), Jesus's rebuke makes clear that the messenger's gender does not excuse any disbelief of the message. Mary's role as worthy proclaimer is upheld in Jesus's words to those who would reject the proclamation. It is not my claim that the LE author is exclusively vindicating Mary over against the two unnamed disciples, Jesus defends the message of all three. What I would emphasize, rather, is that this effort on the part of the ancient author is particularly noteworthy on behalf of a woman whose testimony might have been culturally suspect or expendable.[94]

---

[91] The term σκληροκαρδίαν is used in the passage in which Jesus answers the Pharisees' test about the legality of divorce in Mk 10:2-12 and its Matthean parallel (19:13-21). While the Pharisees seem to perceive the debate to be over Mosaic legal interpretation (Mk 10:4; Mt. 19:7), Jesus cuts to the hardness of human hearts and points to God's intention for marriage, which originates at creation (Mk 10:6; Mt. 19:4, 8b). Human misuse or misunderstanding of sacred scripture connects the σκληροκαρδίαν of Mt. 19:4 and Mk 10:6 to the accusation, in Luke's resurrection narrative, that the disciples are βραδεῖς τῇ καρδίᾳ (slow of heart; 24:25). A similar concept is represented in the phrase ἡ πώρωσις τῆς καρδίας (stubbornness of heart), used to denote the Pharisees' refusal to acknowledge that doing good is in keeping with the law's vision for the Sabbath (Mk 3:5). In Mk 6:52 and 8:17 the passive participle of πωρόω describes the disciples' hearts, in both instances due to a lack of understanding of Jesus's miracles or speech. In these two contexts, while disbelief or misuse of scripture is not explicitly in view, the disciples' lack of understanding should be considered scripturally scripted (Mk 8:18; Isa. 6:9-10; 44:18; Jer. 5:21; Ezek. 12:2; cf. Mk 4:12).

[92] Paul Allen Mirecki, "Mark 16:9-20: Composition, Tradition and Redaction" (ThD diss., Harvard, 1986), 29.

[93] Ibid., 26, 29.

[94] I will discuss women's witness more fully in Chapter 4, but Claudia Setzer gives a basic introduction to the possibility of "embarrassment" in regard to women's testimony ("Excellent Women: Female Witness to the Resurrection," *JBL* 116 [1997]: 264–8).

2.5 The Eleven Are Commissioned

Matthew's account of Jesus's commission to the disciples is, as the common shorthand title indicates, the "greatest" among the Gospel parallels.[95] Its emphasis is heavily on instruction. Without resolving the briefly mentioned doubt (28:17), Jesus takes the authority (v. 18) to command his disciples to *make disciples* (μαθητεύσατε; v. 19) of all the nations (or "gentiles"; πάντα τὰ ἔθνη). Participles further contextualize this teaching mission as "going" (πορευθέντες) and entailing baptism (βαπτίζοντες) and more teaching (διδάσκοντες; v. 20).

In Luke, Jesus utilizes several proofs of his bodily resurrection (24:39-43) before forecasting the disciples' future mission. These provide a transition between their past unbelieving reception of the women disciples' report (v. 11) and their future commission (24:46-69). Both Luke and Acts describe Jesus's commission to his disciples as the charge to be witnesses. In Luke, Jesus states that the disciples are witnesses of "these things" (ὑμεῖς μάρτυρες τούτων; 24:48). In Acts, Jesus foretells their future status as witnesses (ἔσεσθέ μου μάρτυρες; 1:8). In both, the direction of the witness is pointed to people groups in progressively larger geographical scope. In Lk. 24:47, Jesus says that the message of repentance and forgiveness of sins will be preached "to all nations" (εἰς πάντα τὰ ἔθνη), beginning in Jerusalem (ἀρξάμενοι ἀπὸ Ἰερουσαλήμ). In Acts 1:8, the advancement of the message is more precisely enumerated: Jerusalem, all Judea, Samaria, and until the end of the earth (ἔν τε Ἰερουσαλὴμ καὶ ἐν πάσῃ τῇ Ἰουδαίᾳ καὶ Σαμαρίᾳ καὶ ἕως ἐσχάτου τῆς γῆς). In Luke-Acts, the disciples' ability to be witnesses is contingent on the Holy Spirit's arrival and enabling (Lk. 24:49; Acts 1:8), which is the empowering "transition" between faithlessness and effective witness.

John collapses the disciples' first encounter with their risen Lord with their receipt of the Holy Spirit (20:22). In doing so, the disciples (minus Thomas, who was absent at the time; v. 24) are invested with great authority over the forgiveness or retention of sins (v. 23). In addition, John recounts Jesus's commands to individuals to share news (Mary Magdalene in 20:17) or fulfill a pastoral task (Peter in 21:15-17, 20). Peter's reassurance that he loves Jesus paves the way for his reinstatement as one worthy of the task of following Jesus.

The LE descends deepest—among the canonical Gospel endings—into the Eleven's failure of faith, but does not go to great lengths to reinstate them. Returning momentarily to the *Epistula Apostolorum*, the male disciples' grave lack of faith is followed by both commission and revelation. Even as there is an amplification of the disciples' disbelief, there is also development in the direction of a repair of their relationship with their risen Lord. Between the failure and commission, there is a transition. The *Epistula Apostolorum* details the disciples' repentance and tells of them falling on their faces. This prostration is followed immediately by Jesus's implicit forgiveness ("Stand up": ch. 12). The *Epistula Apostolorum* is concerned with the restoration of the disciples' faith in an overt way in the section in which Jesus addresses individual disciples and provides his hand, side, and feet as evidence for his bodily resurrection (ch. 11). In line with the

---

[95] Its scope, however, may be more human-centric (aimed at all the nations; v. 19) in comparison to the LE's cosmic sweep: "Going into the whole world, preach the good news to every creature!" (Πορευθέντες εἰς τὸν κόσμον ἅπαντα κηρύξατε τὸ εὐαγγέλιον πάσῃ τῇ κτίσει; Mk 16:15).

Freer Logion—which provides an explanatory defense of the disciples' disbelief[96]—*Epistula Apostolorum* demonstrates an interest in rehabilitating the disciples, even while it does not delete sections that recount their failure of faith.[97]

The LE, on the other hand, leaves the disciples' faithlessness and Jesus's unparalleled words of rebuke unresolved. Jesus moves directly to commissioning the Eleven he has just reprimanded. A transition might have helped; at least the scribal editor responsible for the Freer Logion thought so.[98] The narrative time span is practically nonexistent between Jesus's sharp reproach (ὠνείδισεν) of the Eleven in v. 14 and his expansive commission that they go into the whole world and preach the gospel to all creation in v. 15.[99] The only possible indicator of time elapsing is the transition between indirect speech (v. 14) and direct address (v. 15), indicated by καὶ εἶπεν αὐτοῖς ("and he said to them").[100] Perhaps all the resolution that was needed, moving from faithlessness to faithfulness, from the LE author's perspective, was Jesus's words entrusting the gospel proclamation to the Eleven.

It is, of course, possible that some readers would have found laudable the Eleven's skepticism about the news of Jesus's resurrection. That is, unwilling to be beguiled by a false messenger, the disciples wait for irrefutable proof (the risen Jesus), rather than believing the seemingly impossible. While this interpretation is possible, it does not align with the tone of the LE. Faith and disbelief are important and become mutually exclusive categories for the author of the LE: belief is a good thing, and its antithesis is a bad, even damnable, thing. The rough transition between the rebuke for faithlessness and the commission to preach the gospel is accentuated by the verse that follows: "The one who believes [ὁ πιστεύσας] and is baptized will be saved, but the one who does not believe [ὁ ... ἀπιστήσας] will be condemned" (v. 16). The future stakes for each response, belief or disbelief, could not be more dissimilar or more irreparable. The visible indicators, signs (σημεῖα), that should follow those who believe are notorious[101]

---

[96] See the Appendix on the Markan endings for the full text and translation of the Freer Logion.

[97] This is far from "proof of literary dependence" of the *Epistula Apostolorum* on the LE. Kelhoffer is likely correct to keep any judgments about literary dependence on this noncanonical text at the level of speculation (cf. *Miracle and Mission*, 171). Yet, if the *Epistula* draws on the LE as the inspiration for its reinforcement of the Eleven's disbelief, the repair is logically subsequent and depends upon other theological resources and gospel themes in order to form a transition between lack of faith and an honored position as recipients of Jesus's revelatory discourses and commission.

[98] The insertion in the Freer Codex (W) begins with this defense from the disciples: "And they [the Eleven] defended themselves saying, 'This age of lawlessness and unbelief is under Satan, who does not permit the truth [and] power of God to overtake the unclean things of the spirits.'" Jesus responds that the time in which Satan's authority has reigned is drawing to a close. See the Appendix on the Markan endings for more information.

[99] There are no text-critical grounds for the abrupt change in Jesus's tone. See Kelhoffer for a summary and rebuttal of the argument that vv. 14 and 15 represent the seam between two different documents (*Miracle and Mission*, 164–9).

[100] The phrase καὶ εἶπεν αὐτοῖς is replaced simply with ἀλλά in Codex W. This is explained by W's unique insertion of the "Freer Logion": i,e., an extended dialogue between Jesus and the disciples inserted between vv. 14 and 15. This Logion begins with the disciples' defending their faithlessness because of the overpowering satanic age. Jesus's direct speech in response is indicated with καὶ ὁ χριστὸς ἐκείνοις προσέλεγεν ὅτι ... ("And the Christ replied to them that ..."). When v. 15 resumes, it is midstream in Jesus's speech, connected by a simple "but" (ἀλλά).

[101] The simple meaning of the term "notorious" as "famous" and "well-known" surely applies; the charismatic acts featured in this expansion to Mark's Gospel are among its best-known attributes. But the negative connotation of "notorious" sometimes accompanies this awareness of the signs.

in the LE: casting out demons, speaking in new tongues, handling snakes, drinking deadly substances, and laying hands on the sick for healing (vv. 17-18). Neither the comprehensive scope of the gospel's proclamation (v. 15) nor the fantastic signs demonstrating faith (vv. 17-18) remain a distant dream within the LE. On the contrary, after Jesus's ascension and enthronement at God's hand (v. 19), the disciples go out and preach everywhere (πανταχοῦ)—with the assistance, or coworking (συνεργοῦντος), of the Lord—and their message is confirmed (βεβαιοῦντος) by the signs that follow (v. 20). The reception of the good news of Jesus's resurrection that began as mostly unfaithful, with scanty bright spots of faithful witness by Mary Magdalene and the two others, quickly shifts into a story of the vast success of the gospel.

3. The Eleven when They Were Twelve: Disciples in Mark's Gospel

The repeated disbelief of the disciples in Mark does not appear to be either mandatory or accidental, in light of the many alternative presentations in canonical and noncanonical gospels. The LE's derivation from other Gospel endings cannot account for its unique emphases or surprising omissions. For instance, of all things possible to include,[102] why would the disciples' failures be a subject of such great interest? It does, however, fit as a continuation of a trend that one finds early on in the full Gospel according to Mark. Mark highlights the disciples' waywardness, which the author of the LE seems to reinforce—even worsen, though only temporarily—in his "completion" of the Second Gospel.

In Mk 1:1–16:8 the disciples' shortcomings fall more explicitly in the realms of obduracy and inconstancy rather than in expressed disbelief (or acknowledged faith, for that matter). The disciples are given unparalleled access to Jesus's teaching

---

Thus, Douglas R. A. Hare (*Mark* [WBC; Louisville: Westminster John Knox, 1996]) is most emphatic:

> It must be emphasized that these lines about handling poison snakes and drinking poisonous liquids are not scriptural. They do not belong to the authentic Gospel of Mark, and therefore are not part of the biblical canon. They should not be taken as authorization of aberrant practices that disregard the clear biblical injunction: "Do not put the Lord your God to the test." (227)

Other commentators treat the signs dismissively (e.g., Larry W. Hurtado, *Mark* [NIBC; Peabody, MA: Hendrickson, 1989], 289) or ignore them entirely (e.g., Kent Brower, *Mark: A Commentary in the Wesleyan Tradition* [New Beacon Bible Commentary; Kansas City: Beacon Hill, 2012]). Of course, notoriety has a flipside: for some narrow circles of Christian practice, it is precisely the statement that these visible out-workings accompany faith that makes the LE attractive. Indeed, for "snake-handling" churches, Mk 16:18 is foundational for those groups' definitive practices (see Dennis Covington, *Salvation on Sand Mountain: Snake Handling and Redemption in Southern Appalachia* [Cambridge, MA: Da Capo Press, 2009; repr. Addison Wesley, 1994]).

[102] Of course, any list of possibilities *not* taken (as in section 3.1) remains theoretical. Such a list cannot take into account different audiences and intended functions for the texts. This is the point toward which I am driving: the LE is no haphazard regurgitation of traditional resurrection materials. It might have included multiple conglomerations of traditions. Therefore, the content and emphases that it expresses are evidence for the kind of conclusion with which the author was most interested in finishing the Second Gospel.

and miracles and are set up as the quintessential "insiders" (4:11-12). Yet this status collapses as soon as it is established: Jesus informs the disciples that the "mystery of the Kingdom of God" has been given to them (ὑμῖν τὸ μυστήριον δέδοται τῆς βασιλείας τοῦ θεοῦ, v. 11)—whether or not they grasp this gift—and almost immediately asks how they will understand *all* the parables, if they do not understand this first one (v. 13).

A failure to understand Jesus and his mission persists through much of Mark's narrative (e.g., 6:52; 7:18; 8:17-21; 9:6, 32; 10:13-16, 38). When Peter shows a glimmer of comprehension about Jesus, he follows it up by earning the harshest rebuke in the Gospel (8:29, 32-33). The Twelve's abandonment of Jesus starts with one (14:10-11) but soon claims the whole group (14:27, 50)—even Peter, the most tenacious among them (14:66-72)—despite adamant claims to the contrary (10:39; 14:29-31). These few examples suffice; as has been established, this is well-trodden scholarly ground.[103]

Although Matthew often equates the mistaken impressions and partial knowledge of the disciples with low levels of faith, when Jesus speaks his common refrain, "O ye of little faith [ὀλιγόπιστοι],"[104] Mark seldom relates the disciples' obduracy to disbelief. The exception may be Mk 9:19, in which Jesus's exasperation with the *faithless generation* (γενεὰ ἄπιστος) seems to be directed at the disciples who could not cast out the boy's mute spirit (πνεῦμα ἄλαλον; vv. 17-18).[105] Most often, the terminology for the disciples' shortcomings gravitates toward a lack of understanding.[106] This failure to comprehend occasionally leans toward the realm of disbelief in several references to their hearts' hardening or callousing (ἡ καρδία πεπωρωμένη; 6:52; 8:17). Mark certainly allows for the reality of partial faith, as with the father of the boy with an unclean spirit (that the disciples are unable to cast out), who he says, "I believe, help my unbelief" (Mk 9:24). Two chapters later, Jesus can describe faith as excluding doubt (11:22-23).[107] Jesus is not hesitant to show frustration with the disciples: "Do you *not yet* understand?" (8:17).

Although terms related to the πιστ- root are scarce in the passion narrative, the disciples ultimately prove utterly faithless according to Mark's Gospel, at least in the sense of failure to keep following Jesus. Jesus's death occurs, therefore, in the midst of abandonment by his closest Twelve and by God (15:34; cf. vv. 40-41). It is no wonder ancient readers, along with many modern readers, could attribute their behavior to a lack of faith. The disciples' infidelity to Jesus is punctuated by their scattering at

---

[103] See notes 1, 4-7, in this chapter for bibliographic information for thorough studies of scholarly approaches to the disciples.

[104] This term seems to be part of Matthew's special vocabulary, spoken by Jesus five times: Mt. 6:30; 8:26; 14:31; 16:8; and 17:20. (It appears in Luke once [12:28], which parallels Mt. 6:30.) Of Matthew's uses, the latter four are explicitly directed to the Twelve. The first instance occurs in the Sermon on the Mount and, therefore, is addressed to the Twelve, but also to the crowds (5:1).

[105] This is the same pericope in which the father expresses simultaneous faith and unbelief (v. 24).

[106] E.g., *Not understanding* (οὐ συνίημι; 6:52; 8:17, 21); *lacking understanding* (ἀσύνετος), *not/not yet perceiving* (οὐ/οὔπω νοέω; 7:18; 8:17); *not remembering* (οὐ μνημονεύω; 8:18); *not knowing* (οὐκ οἶδα; 9:6; 10:38); *being ignorant* (ἀγνοέω; 9:32).

[107] Jesus instructs Peter and the disciples simply to have faith in God (11:22), which he explains as the ability to move a mountain into the sea by simply commanding it *and* not doubting in one's heart (μὴ διακριθῇ ἐν τῇ καρδίᾳ αὐτοῦ), but instead believing that what one says will come to be (ἀλλὰ πιστεύῃ ὅτι ὃ λαλεῖ γίνεται; v. 23).

Gethsemane, but that is certainly not the first symptom of their lack of faith in the Second Gospel. While the terms for hard-heartedness (τῇ πωρώσει τῆς καρδίας or σκληροκαρδία) and the term "disputing" (διαλογίζομαι)[108] are used first to characterize Jesus's self-selected opponents (2:6, 8; 3:5; 10:5), soon they are applied to the disciples' own stubborn failure to recognize Jesus (cf. 8:16; 9:33).

There is a tendency in the LE to move matters from a "gray area" into the realm of "black and white," in which faith versus disbelief is the one issue that matters.[109] The Gospel of Mark proper tells the story of Jesus's disciples in a way that maintains tension to the very end: are they faithful or faithless?[110] Much of the time, one cannot tell whether they are faithful in their adherence to Jesus (e.g., 10:28-31) or completely lack loyalty (e.g., 14:50). The LE makes matters plainer.[111] Particularly as it pertains to belief, the LE states the alternatives as dramatic opposites: those who have faith and are baptized will be saved, whereas those who do not will be damned (16:16).[112] This claim is unparalleled in Mk 1:1–16:8. In some ways, the signs that will follow belief are similarly automatic. The statement is as simple as this: if people believe, these signs will follow and no further explanation is provided.

In the context of an expansion that expresses life in polarities, it is no wonder that the disciples can be said simply to disbelieve. Perhaps they were mourning, or confused, or fearful. For the author of the LE, there is neither space nor time nor necessity to explain any of these things. Instead, because the disciples do not respond in faith to the reliable witnesses, they are unbelievers. Before one rushes too quickly to caricature the author of the LE as simple or naïve, one must take into account the fact that the disciples are just as quickly reinscribed into Jesus's mission for the world. Their failure is impermanent, as the presence of Jesus clears away any doubt. His continued attendance enables the confirmatory signs (16:20).[113] Jesus's followers are on the ground floor of the worldwide proclamation of good news and all of the fantastical validating signs that come along with it.

For this second-century author and others following him (*Ep. Apost.*), the Christians who undertook a grand, global mission did not need their history whitewashed and

---

[108] This term almost always refers to something Jesus cannot hear, either because it is internal (ἐν ταῖς καρδίαις αὐτῶν; 2:6, 8) or, perhaps, because of distance (i.e., the disciples "to one another" [πρὸς ἀλλήλους] in 8:16). In both cases Jesus perceives the conditions anyway.

[109] See Lane, *Gospel of Mark*, 604. There seems to be a shift in perspectives from tracing Jesus's steps (in the undisputed Gospel) to prescribing right and wrong actions for followers (LE). Instead of belief being ineffable and identified by Jesus alone (i.e., 2:5; 5:30-34), the LE's description of belief is visibly associated with baptism (16:16) and miraculous proofs (16:17-18).

[110] This question is pertinent for the female disciples as well, not only for the Twelve, because even the women who hold on longer than any (15:40-41; 16:1-8) leave the reader with just this conundrum at the book's breathless conclusion (16:8).

[111] This simplicity is coupled with a lack of specificity. Although the signs that result from believers' faith are elaborated upon in vv. 18-19, nothing is said about those who receive the disciples' proclamation or witness the signs.

[112] For similarities between 16:16 and other second-century Christian writings, see Joseph Hug, *La Finale de L'Évangile de Marc: Mc 16,9-20* (Paris: J. Gabalda, 1978), 94–102; and Kelhoffer, *Miracle and Mission*, 62-3.

[113] In both the whole of Mark and in the LE, faith and its wonders appear to be products of grace, given by God or by the risen Lord.

embellished, nor did the women whose faith led the way need to be swept under the rug of history. This is clear in the LE, though it is not the perspective one gains from reading biblical scholarship about the earliest generations of Christian writers. The suggestion that a woman might function as a model of the faith to which *all* of Jesus's followers were commissioned stands as striking counterevidence to common scholarly assumptions about early Christian interpretation and the impulse that compelled second-century authors to write. In the next chapter, I seek to retrieve the LE's depiction of Mary Magdalene as exemplar for Christian discipleship, which both complicates and enlivens the too-often-monotonic reports about early Christianity.

4

Being Disciples Like Mary Magdalene: Implications of the Long Ending's Reading of Mark

In the foregoing chapters I demonstrated that scholarship on the Long Ending (hereafter LE) has evidenced an isolation of focus, being predominantly concerned with the question of textual origins. While there are exceptions to this narrow concentration, studies of the ending at 16:8 ask questions about the characterization of the women at the tomb, and how the theological emphases and structure of the sudden ending function as a conclusion relative to the whole of the Second Gospel. The endings that represent later attempts to conclude the same Gospel, particularly the most popular and widely accepted ending, historically—Mk 16:9-20—have seldom been examined in a similar way.

Foremost in my examination of the resurrection appearances in the LE is a study of the characterization of Mary Magdalene in 16:9-11 in the light of two important literary contexts. Mark and the other canonical Gospels. While most of the information related about her person can be located elsewhere in the four Gospels, their descriptions illuminate a positive depiction of her as the *first* witness to the resurrected Jesus and her response of *going* and *telling*. The remaining disciples—certainly the Eleven, likely others—disbelieve her message and are found in a state of collective and profound mourning, despite hearing her good news about Jesus. When two other disciples encounter Jesus in another form on their way into the country, their response of active proclamation and their rejection by other disciples mirror Mary's own experience.

I have highlighted what is almost certainly a purposeful extension of the eleven disciples' faithlessness far beyond Gethsemane and into the period after Jesus's resurrection. The author of the LE states the fact of their disbelief repeatedly and in stark terms. Additionally, the presentation of the male disciples' unbelief, coupled with a description of their emotional state in terms of weeping—particularly when Mary's emotions are not mentioned—may function to further disparage the Eleven by casting them as weak or unmanly, in accordance with that culture's aspersion of excessive passion.

While vindicating Mary Magdalene after her and her companions' ostensible failure in 16:8 was not the sole aim in the LE's appended conclusion to Mark, it was clearly a necessary first step. Jesus defends all the witnesses to his resurrection—of whom Mary was first—as reliable, wielding their faithful testimony as cudgels for harsh accusations against the Eleven. This chapter will take the final exegetical step by demonstrating that Mary's active discipleship—going and telling—becomes the basic pattern of discipleship commissioned by Jesus (16:15) and fulfilled by the disciples (16:20). Mary's gender neither makes her discipleship a model only for women, nor does it disqualify her from being the first of several—mostly male—examples of the same active faithfulness.

1. The Commission and Success of Jesus's Followers

The LE proffers a vision of discipleship in which disciples cooperate with their Lord in universal proclamation, resulting in remarkable signs of confirmation. Their accomplishment, predicted and realized, is nearly enough to make readers forget how the disciples arrived at such success. Yet, the author of the LE encodes their achievement in a way that unravels the failure of 16:8. In order to get there, Mary Magdalene receives sustained treatment in the LE, in a manner not solely dependent on other Gospel traditions, setting her apart as the first and formative[1] witness to Jesus's resurrection. Additionally, the negative portrayal of the Eleven as unbelieving extends their failure and, meanwhile, serves to bolster Mary's faithfulness in contrast to their failure. Indeed, it is precisely for their rejection of Mary's and the two disciples' testimony to the resurrected Jesus that the eleven male disciples are upbraided when they finally reunite with their Lord.

All of this paints Mary positively and as a subject worthy of honor,[2] but her characterization as a trustworthy witness does not necessarily make her role exemplary for ongoing discipleship.[3] After all, it is the Eleven who, despite their disparaged disbelief, apparently receive the commission from Jesus (16:14-20). The references to Mary Magdalene by name discontinue as soon as her proclamation falls on the deaf ears of those followers of Jesus who "had been with him" (τοῖς μετ' αὐτοῦ γενομένοις; v. 10).[4] The formerly unbelieving disciples are the auditors and, apparently, the addressees of Jesus's commission, rather than the faithful woman who saw him through cross, tomb, and resurrection. It seems painfully ironic that the once faithless

---

[1] The assessment of Mary Magdalene's witness as "formative" is based on the demonstrable parallel between her experience and response to Jesus and that of the two disciples who meet Jesus as they leave Jerusalem (16:12-13). Her activity of faithful reception and proclamation initiates the pattern with which the LE also narrates the second faithful response to the risen Jesus.

[2] Gospel readers may have noted her honored position in other Gospel traditions (esp. Jn 20:1, 11-18).

[3] That women should be exemplary in Mark's Gospel is not unheard of, for even minor female characters at times receive (otherwise scarce) approbation from Jesus (cf. 5:34; 7:29; 12:43-44; 14:6-9). See also Mary Ann Beavis, "Women as Models of Faith in Mark," *BTB* 18 (1988): 8.

[4] Mary Magdalene's obedient service as proclaimer of the good news of Jesus's resurrection was spurned, a situation that only the risen Jesus himself could reverse. In that sense, the LE's Mary Magdalene and two traveling disciples are in good company, for not even Israel's sacred texts had reached the insensate apostles in Luke's telling (24:25-27). There is a parallel irony in the disciples' ongoing ministry: they experience resistance as they proclaim the crucified and risen Messiah using the very scriptures to whose proper understanding they had been impervious (cf. Acts 3:12–4:3).

Table 4.1 *Going* and *telling* in the LE

	Person/s doing the actions	Participle denoting movement	Declaratory verb
v. 10	[v. 9: Μαρία ἡ Μαγδαληνή]	πορευθεῖσα	ἀπήγγειλεν
	[v. 9: *Mary Magdalene*]	*going*	*she proclaimed*
v. 13	[v. 12: δυσὶν ἐξ αὐτῶν]	ἀπελθόντες	ἀπήγγειλαν
	[v. 12: *Two of them*]	*going away*	*they proclaimed*
v. 15	Imperative Mood	πορευθέντες	κηρύξατε
	(Jesus's command)	*going*	*preach!*
v. 20	ἐκεῖνοι [v. 14: οἱ ἕνδεκα]	ἐξελθόντες	ἐκήρυξαν
	Those ones [v. 14: *the Eleven*]	*going out*	*they preached*

male disciples should be entrusted with a salvation-bringing mission—one in which *belief* (with concomitant baptism) and *unbelief* are the respective conditions for future salvation or condemnation (16:16).

However, just as the two disciples follow Mary's lead in receiving and proclaiming the resurrection of Jesus, her influence extends even into the perpetual Christian mission throughout the earth. In Jesus's commission (16:15) and the LE's report of its successful fulfillment (v. 20), the response of the earliest witnesses to Jesus's resurrection—that is, the response to *go* and to *proclaim*—becomes ratified as the mission for all the disciples who will follow.

In v. 9, when Mary encounters Jesus, alive after the tomb, she goes (πορευθεῖσα) and brings the news (ἀπήγγειλεν); likewise, the two disciples after her go (ἀπελθόντες) and proclaim (ἀπήγγειλαν; v. 13). The verbs describing the simple actions of obedient witnesses constitute the basic formulation for the remaining disciples' propulsion into mission (v. 15): "Go [πορευθέντες] and preach the gospel [κηρύξατε τὸ εὐαγγέλιον]." Mary's first response to the good news of Jesus's resurrection is magnified in this commission; her response is the impetus to spread the good news on the grandest scale, into the whole *cosmos* (εἰς τὸν κόσμον ἅπαντα), and to every possible recipient, to all creation (πάσῃ τῇ κτίσει; v. 15). The LE closes in v. 20 with a report of the fulfillment of just this commission; the disciples go out (ἐξελθόντες) and preach everywhere (ἐκήρυξαν πανταχοῦ), following Jesus's command and Mary Magdalene's lead.

The successful *going* and *telling* reported in the LE—first, by Mary Magdalene; then, by two unnamed disciples; finally, by the Eleven—corrects the failure and flight of Jesus's followers previously in Mark (14:50-51, 66-72; 16:1-8; Table 4.1). In those contexts, the Twelve and the women, most tenacious among all, had no problem "going"; they *went* quickly—they *fled*. But as 16:8 makes emphatic, Mary Magdalene, Mary the mother of James, and Salome said nothing to anyone (lit., "they said *nothing* [οὐδὲν] to *nobody* [οὐδενὶ]").

Table 4.2 illustrates the phenomena that the episodes in the LE reverse. One after another of Jesus's followers departs in haste. In some ways, Jesus is bereft of followers in the first statement of their hasty exit: *all* (πάντες) go, fleeing the site of Jesus's arrest (14:50). Nevertheless, there are two more recorded instances of his followers fleeing

Table 4.2 *Flight* and *silence* in the Gethsemane and empty tomb narratives

	Person/s doing the actions	Participle and/or verb denoting movement	Report of speech
14:50	πάντες [v. 32: οἱ μαθηταὶ αὐτοῦ] *everyone* [v. 32: *his disciples*]	ἀφέντες ... ἔφυγον *abandoning ... [they] fled*	– –
14:52	[v. 51: νεανίσκος τις] [v. 51: *a certain young man*]	ἔφυγεν *he fled*	– –
16:8	[v. 1: Μαρία ἡ Μαγδαληνὴ καὶ Μαρία ἡ τοῦ Ἰακώβου καὶ Σαλώμη] [v. 1: Mary Magdalene, Mary of James, and Salome]	ἐξελθοῦσαι ἔφυγον *going out, they fled*	οὐδενὶ οὐδὲν εἶπαν *they said nothing to anyone*

before the end. This grim abandonment and silence (shown in Table 4.2) is, as Table 4.1 shows, emphatically undone in the LE.

Viewed in the context of the LE's statement of the disciples' success in partnership with the Lord (τοῦ κυρίου συνεργοῦντος), clearly the author of the supplement regarded the women's actions in 16:8 as a failure.[5] That failure, however, was not so deeply entrenched as to be irreversible; the followers' flight and silence are repeatedly overturned by the subsequent faithfulness of Mary Magdalene and other disciples (16:10, 13). The participles of movement are cognates of the same term in 16:8 and 16:20 (ἐξέρχομαι)—absent the "fleeing"—but v. 20 replaces the utter silence of v. 8 with worldwide proclamation. At the culmination of the LE, the act of *going and telling* is the basic mode of discipleship to which all believers are commissioned: "And he said to them, 'Go into the whole world and proclaim the gospel to all creation!'" (16:15; cf. 13:10). A threefold sequence characterizes the pattern: *first*, Mary goes and proclaims Jesus to be raised (16:10); second, two disciples go and proclaim (v. 13); finally, the Eleven overcome their disbelief to go and preach (v. 20).

2. A Woman as the Primary Example of Faithful, Post-Resurrection Discipleship

Reading the LE with an eye to gender highlights new dimensions of its play with expectations and common tropes. These do not subvert the plain content of the brief narration of three resurrection appearances (16:9, 12, 14): Mary Magdalene remains a reliable witness, as are the two on the way, while the Eleven remain stubbornly unbelieving until Jesus confronts them. Rather, the contours of gender underscore the extreme, alternative responses: faithful or faithless. Mary Magdalene is shown to be reliable, when a woman might have been pilloried as fickle and discounted as untrustworthy (an open interpretation, in light of 16:8).[6] In 16:14 the male disciples are

---

[5] Modern authors' debate over the matter of the women's silence as success or failure has already been discussed. See section 2 in Chapter 1 and note 2 in Chapter 2.
[6] More examples of this stereotype are examined later.

shown to be emphatically faithless without the intervention of Jesus, when they might have been defended immediately and overtly redeemed, posthaste, as model pillars of the faith. Neither of these possibilities comes to pass.

It is not that the Eleven fail to be rehabilitated (although it comes in a flash at Jesus's commission [v. 15] and not through a process of repentance[7]); they do, ultimately, become integral missionaries to every place (v. 20). Nevertheless, it seems that, from the author's perspective, the frightened silence of the women in 16:8 must be undone by Mary Magdalene's faithful proclamation before Jesus's encounter with the Eleven (anticipated in 16:7) can take place. Were that not so, the author of the LE would have had no reason to narrate 16:9-11 at all. Colloquially put, the impression created by those verses is something like, "If Mary ain't fixed, ain't nobody fixed."

It is unlikely that this ancient author's attempt to correct the depiction of the women in 16:8 arose from a latent feminist impulse,[8] reclaiming the historical pride of place for the unjustly maligned female followers of 16:8. (Modern interpreters are welcome to interpret the text in this manner, though ascribing it to the second-century author is anachronistic.) Neither did the author's repeated restatement of the male disciples' disbelief endanger their reputations, which were likely fixed by the time this supplement to the Second Gospel was written and circulated. If church tradition is reliable, most of the Eleven had died (some of them martyrs' deaths) decades beforehand.[9] But more is at stake in the LE than a simple need to confirm Jesus's resurrection by a collection of postmortem appearances, a motive to which some have attributed the rise of Mark's manifold endings.[10] If such were the case, the Intermediate Ending or an abbreviated version of any one of the other Gospels' endings would have sufficed. This may indeed be *among* the concerns the LE serves to mend, but there was another predicament, preliminary and pronounced, in need of a fix.

The integrity of the women *was* at stake; not their worth as women per se, but as capable witnesses to the resurrection message. Time and again, in varying instantiations, the women at the empty tomb and Mary Magdalene resurface in the early traditions of Christianity and its opponents.[11] How are they to be characterized?

---

[7] Cf. Jn 21:15-19; *Ep. Apost.* 11–12.

[8] Or remarkably "protofeminist," to adopt a term that has been used by Heather Weir and Nancy Calvert-Koyzis in their edited volume, *Strangely Familiar: Protofeminist Interpretations of Patriarchal Biblical Texts* (Atlanta: SBL, 2009).

[9] See Acts 12:1-2 on James (son of Zebedee); on Peter, see Eusebius, *Hist. eccl.* III.1.2; Eusebius puts John's death during the reign of Trajan (III.23.3-4), but does not indicate that he or Philip died of unnatural causes (III.31.2-4).

[10] D. C. Parker (*The Living Text of the Gospels* [New York: Cambridge University Press, 1997]) assesses,

> The existence of the rival endings makes clear that the issue here is of a Gospel without a resurrection appearance. For if the story ends at verse 8 with [Sinaiticus and Vaticanus], there is no triumphal conclusion to the Gospel ... It cannot be believed that the evangelist knew no accounts of resurrection appearances. But, remarkably, he decided that a Gospel did not need them. The Intermediate and Long Endings are in marked contrast. A Gospel without resurrection appearances is incomplete, for the Gospel is about the resurrection and salvation. (143–4)

This is an oversimplification in my view; if proof that Jesus was raised were perceived to be the sole missing component, an account like that in the *Gospel of Peter* would provide more details of the mechanics of Jesus's resurrection (*Gos. Pet.* 39–41).

[11] Some of Celsus's criticisms will be treated in sections 1 and 2 of this chapter.

Are they fearful? Tearful? Indignant? Is Mary Magdalene defensive? Especially chosen? How is the timing of Jesus's resurrection, in which the women are entangled, to be understood?[12] Do the Gospels conflict, implicating the women's account of events? Or is there a harmony among the Gospel accounts in which the women's involvement fits seamlessly? Are the women trustworthy? Are the men more trustworthy, or perhaps equally flawed?

Into this swirling debate and range of opinions, the LE secures the Gospel of Mark's position on the question of faithful discipleship. Rather than ambiguity—on several matters, salvation and condemnation among them—the LE seeks certainty. Mary Magdalene accurately proclaimed the good message of Jesus's resurrection, contrary indicators (i.e., the overcome silence of 16:8) and subsequent negative responses notwithstanding.

2.1 The Trouble with Women and Belief

The impression that women are more prone to trust—resulting in greater religiosity—persists in popular culture to the present day.[13] This stereotype dates from antiquity. Several examples help in documenting the widespread ancient perception that women were more trusting than men and, thus, more gullible.[14] This proclivity toward easy trust meant, conversely, that women were untrustworthy.[15] Because both women and men were participants and leaders in Roman religious rites, the overlap of religious

---

[12] Christian writers, particularly in the Question-and-Answer genre that arose in the third century, addressed (in what amounts to internal dialogue among believers) points of ostensibly "apologetic" concern. Arguably the most famous, in Eusebius's *ad Marinum*, concerns the timing of the women's visit to the tomb on Easter. On the "Question-and-Answer" genre—which is also called *erotapokriseis* (from ἐρωτᾶν, "to ask," and ἀποκρίνεσθαι, "to answer") or ζητήματα (issues), among other things, by the authors themselves—see Annelie Volgers, "Preface," in *Erotapokriseis: Early Christian Question-and-Answer Literature in Context* (ed. Annelie Volgers and Claudio Zamagni; CBET 37; Dudley, MA: Peeters, 2004), 3–4.

[13] A Google search for the terms "women" and "gullible" or "religious" yields an overwhelming number of hits. For evidence for (and engagement with) the persistence of this perception, see Marta Trzebiatowska and Steve Bruce, *Why Are Women More Religious Than Men?* (Oxford: Oxford University Press, 2012).

[14] Cicero's offhand comment in *De divinatione* illustrates the general sentiment: "Upon my word, no old woman is credulous enough now to believe such stuff!" (*Div.* II.xv.36). The implication is clear: if an old woman is not gullible enough to buy an assumption (in this case, "divine will" as acting upon entrails in the practice of divination), then *nobody* would.

[15] The *Letter of Aristeas*, dated between the third century BCE and the first century CE, purports to be a private letter recounting the invitation, courtly conversation, and sponsored translation of the Jewish Scriptures into Greek under the benefaction of Ptolemy Philadelphus (see Translation and Introduction by R. J. H. Shutt; OTP II: 7–11). During the seven-day banquet, the king puts one question after another to the Jewish translators present. (They invariably answer wisely in a way that impresses.) In the *Letter of Aristeas* 250, the king asks, "How can one reach agreement with a woman?" The translator's answer, which is wise enough to please Ptolemy (cf. *Let. Aris.* 252), is as follows: "By recognizing … that the female sex is bold, positively active for something which it desires, easily liable to change its mind because of poor reasoning powers, and of naturally weak constitution. It is necessary to have dealings with them in a sound way, avoiding provocation which may lead to a quarrel" (*Let. Aris.* 250-251a [Shutt; OTP II]). The underlying stereotype reflects an interrelation between an excess of emotions (passion), as discussed in section 2.2.1 of Chapter 3, and a deficient ability to reason, which results in an estimation of essential weakness.

practice and gender was not always the cause for such grave suspicion.[16] Yet when, in the second century, Celsus decries Christianity as a religion of women, slaves, and children, the implication is that only the weak-minded would fall prey to that sort of superstition:

> Their injunctions are like this. "Let no one educated, no one wise, no one sensible draw near. For these abilities are thought by us to be evils. But as for anyone ignorant, anyone stupid, anyone uneducated, anyone who is a child, let him come boldly." By the fact that they themselves admit that these people are worthy of their God, they show that they want and are able to convince only the foolish, dishonorable and stupid, and only slaves, women, and little children.[17]

For Celsus, as cited by Origen, only inferior persons—uneducated slaves, naïve children, and too-trusting women—were susceptible to the Christian proclamation. It is clear that Celsus sees these classes of people as self-evidently gullible; in this way, his association of these persons with the Christian movement is meant to cast all Christians under suspicion.

One might expect this sort of denigration of female belief from an opponent of Christianity in its earliest days. Antagonism need not be the authorial intent, however, in order for literature to trade on the trope of women's overabundant belief. In Apuleius's story-within-a-story of Cupid and Psyche (related by an old woman in *The Golden Ass*[18]), Psyche is admired for her beauty[19] and her innocence, but both attributes move quickly from blessing to curse. Her beauty incites the ire of Venus (4.34); the girl's credulity prevents her from protecting herself from her own scheming sisters (5.9–11), let alone the vindictive goddess (5.28–6.22).

Easily persuaded from any side, as soon as Psyche makes a promise, whether in her best interest or against it, she can be turned away from it easily.[20] Although the story is

---

[16] Ross Shepard Kraemer's work on "women's religions" in the Greco-Roman world has become a modern classic. Her chapter on "Women's Religious Offices in Greco-Roman Paganism" provides an overview of female deities and priests (*Her Share of the Blessings: Women's Religions among Pagans, Jews, and Christians in the Greco-Roman World* [New York: Oxford University Press, 1992], 80–92). Likewise, her caution against relating religious acknowledgment of female deities and roles for women in priestly functions to an overall positive view of women is fitting to the present discussion:

> Surely women's service as priestesses to goddesses and even gods cannot by itself be taken as any sort of status indicator for women, given the vast evidence from classical Greece, for example, for pervasive misogyny and narrow delimitation of the roles available to women of any social class. We should not be too quick to equate service to ancient deities with power and authority. The evidence we have considered suggests that, under some circumstances, priesthoods and other religious offices are related to the power, prestige, and authority of those who held office. (90)

[17] Celsus, *True Doctrine*, cited in Origen, *Contra Celsum* 3.44 (trans. Henry Chadwick; New York: Cambridge University Press, 1953).

[18] The book may be dated around or after 160 CE (P. G. Walsh, "Introduction" to Apuleius, *The Golden Ass* [ed. and trans. P. G. Walsh; Oxford World's Classics; New York: Oxford University Press, 2008], xix–xx).

[19] "Peerless" beauty, revered as Venus herself (Apuleius, *Metam.* 4.28).

[20] E.g.: Cupid, Venus's son and Psyche's secret husband, warns her to "show greater circumspection" and to refrain from telling her sisters too much information (5.5). Cupid cannot trust that Psyche will act in her own best interest: "So if those depraved witches turn up later, ready with their

intended to entertain and takes a mythological form, the lesson is clear: even Psyche's acquired grit is insufficient to undo the trouble her gullibility causes (cf. 6.1, 17); in the end it takes a double rescue, first by Cupid (6.21), then by Jupiter (6.22–24), to bring her happy ending. Women seem to fit one of two models in the story: either too ready to believe (like Psyche) or vindictive and treacherous (like Psyche's sisters and Venus).[21]

The extracanonical extension of the Adam and Eve story, *Life of Adam and Eve*,[22] proceeds from a point after the couple's exclusion from Eden. The author summarily shifts the blame for God's curse on humanity's progenitors firmly onto Eve's shoulders.[23] When Adam devises a regimen of fasting, silence, and river-standing[24] that he hopes will spark the Lord's pity, he acknowledges Eve's weakness and lower capabilities.[25] Eve undertakes this same regimen of penance for *eighteen days* (*LAE* 9:1) before Satan disguises himself as an angel and shows up to commiserate with her (9:2). By all appearances, the devil is a messenger for the Lord and tells Eve that the end for which she and Adam had hoped—God's forgiveness—has taken place: "The LORD God has heard your sighs and accepted your repentance; and all we angels have entreated for you and interceded with the LORD, and he sent me to bring you up from the water and give you food which you had in Paradise, and for which you have been lamenting."[26] The result is that Eve believes what she sees and hears, leaves the water, and is led to Adam (10:1-2). The fault of her trust is immediately evident to Adam, who cries out in sorrow and asks, "How have you *again* been seduced by our enemy?"[27] Later, Eve again removes all guilt from Adam for the redoubled fall from grace: "You have done neither the first nor the second error, but I have been cheated and deceived, for I have not kept the command of God."[28]

---

destructive designs, and I am sure they will, you must not exchange a single word with them, or at any rate *if your native innocence and soft-heartedness cannot bear that*, you are not to listen to or utter a single word about your husband" (*Metam.* 5.11 [trans. Walsh]; emphasis added). After further warnings, Psyche protests, with tears, in defense of her own trustworthiness and discretion (5.13). These qualities lure her into a sense of security, and—due to her "excessive" naïveté—she mixes up her explanations aimed to keep her divine spouse incognito (5.15). With a few ominous words from her sisters, Psyche can be persuaded that her beloved husband and father of her child is, instead, a dragon fattening her up for a future meal (5.17–18). Inconstant due to her all-too-eagerness to believe, the storyteller says: "Poor Psyche, simple and innocent as she was, at once felt apprehension at these grim tidings" (5.19).

[21] This is a simplistic interpretation of a more complex and allusive character, Psyche, not to mention the whole myth's relationship to the story of Lucius in which it is imbedded. For a more nuanced introduction, see P. G. Walsh, "Introduction," *The Golden Ass*, esp. xlii–xliii.

[22] The text, which survives in Greek, Latin, and Slavonic, likely dates from the end of the first century CE. See M. D. Johnson's introduction in *OTP* II: 250–2.

[23] "And Eve said to Adam, 'My lord, would you kill me? O that I would die! Then perhaps the LORD God will bring you again into Paradise, for *it is because of me* that the LORD God is angry with you'" (*LAE* 3:1 [Johnson; *OTP* II]; emphasis added).

[24] This is an unusual act of penitence. Gary A. Anderson thinks the narrative about the "river ordeal" has a loose biblical basis in Josh 3–5 ("The Penitence Narrative in the *Life of Adam and Eve*," *HUCA* 63 [1992]: 4).

[25] Adam to Eve: "You are not able to do so much as I; but do as much as you have strength for" (*LAE* 6:1 [Johnson; *OTP* II]). The penitence Adam prescribes for Eve involves fasting (6:1), silence (6:2), and standing in the Tigris River upon a stone, with water up to her neck, for thirty-seven days (6:1–2), while Adam does something similar in the Jordan for forty days (6:3).

[26] *LAE* 9:3–4 (Johnson; *OTP* II).

[27] *LAE* 10:3–4 (Johnson; *OTP* II; emphasis added).

[28] *LAE* 18:1 (Johnson; *OTP* II).

The scarcely veiled undercurrent of this narrative is that Eve *should not have believed* her eyes and *should not have trusted* that God had accepted her prayers and repentance. She lacks the ability—because of her femininity—to judge between fact and fiction, truth and deception. Ultimately, Eve garners a blessing from the angel Michael, but only by virtue of her association with the pious Adam (*LAE* 21:2). Further, Adam's demotion into mortality comes *not* from sin, but, as God tells him, "since you have listened rather to the voice of your wife, whom I gave into your power, that you might keep her in your will. But you listened to her and disregarded my words."²⁹ Adam dies, quite literally, because he listened to and believed a woman.

I could provide a wider array of examples illustrating the motif of women's dangerous gullibility in ancient sources,³⁰ but this sampling provides sufficient evidence for how female belief *could have been* construed as ignorance (so Celsus), mistaken or unfortunate (with Apuleius), and even treacherous and sinful (as with *Life of Adam and Eve*). On the contrary, in the LE of Mark it is not Mary's belief but the lack thereof among Jesus's associates that is foolish, mistaken, and symptomatic of a disordered heart (σκληροκαρδία; 16:14). The woman's actions of *going and telling* of Jesus's resurrection make clear her belief (v. 10, reversing v. 8); this is presented, not as a cautionary tale, but as the first of many to model the correct response to Jesus: belief (v. 16).³¹ Trusting is not a flaw of the female. It is the essential form of a follower, whether a man or a woman.

2.2 The Trouble with Women's Testimony

Presenting Mary Magdalene as the first to believe and proclaim in Jesus's resurrection might have opened Christians up to external attack. Indeed, if protecting the church against outsiders' accusations had been the preoccupation of the LE's author, placing the proclamation of Jesus's resurrection in the hands of a woman would have been ill advised. We know that entrusting the first witness of the risen Jesus to women drew the ire of Celsus.³² This famous, early opponent of Christianity mocks the unreliability of witnesses to Jesus's resurrection. Celsus asks (as Origen quotes): "Who saw this? A frenzied woman [γυνὴ πάροιστρος], as you tell it, and perhaps another [τις ἄλλος] of those under the same spell" (*Cels.* ii.55).³³ The term "woman" is wielded

---

²⁹ *LAE* 26:2 (Johnson; *OTP* II).
³⁰ E.g., Gaius, *Inst.* 190–1; Juvenal, *Sat.* 6.511–91; Apuleius, *Metam.* 5.15; Strabo, *Geogr.* 7.3.4. See also Emily A. Hemelrijk, *Matrona Docta: Educated Women in the Roman Elite from Cornelia to Julia Domna* (New York: Routledge, 1999), 63, 261n22; Lynn Cohick, *Women in the World of the Earliest Christians: Illuminating Ancient Ways of Life* (Grand Rapids: Baker, 2009), 22, 184, 192; Claudia Setzer, "Excellent Women: Female Witness to the Resurrection," *JBL* 116 (1997): 271.
³¹ As I have noted in Chapter 3, the importance of belief (versus unbelief) is heightened in the LE. One of James A. Kelhoffer's concluding observations about the author of the LE is as follows: "Seven uses of πιστεύω and its cognates in the LE (vv. 11b, 13b, 14b [two occurrences], 16a, 16b, 17a) indicate that, as for the author of the Fourth Gospel, the issue of faith or belief was of great importance to this individual" (*Miracle and Mission: The Authentication of Missionaries and Their Message in the Longer Ending of Mark* [Tübingen: Mohr Siebeck, 2000], 479).
³² According to Origen, *Cels.* 2.55.
³³ Although some have suggested it, it is unlikely that Mk 16:9-11 is the primary object of Celsus's complaint. At least the portion of Celsus's accusation that we know from Origen's rebuttal in *Contra*

as an insult equal to hysteria (which, by definition, was assigned to the realm of women[34]).

Women were often seen as unfit witnesses in courts of the day,[35] which proceeded from a general view that they were less reliable than men.[36] In ancient Rome, the convention was to minimize women's capacity for judicious thought or reliability. This deprecation was closely tied to the understanding that women were basically credulous.[37] Lack of suspicion is cause not only for the invalidity of women's testimony, but also for a perceived inability to make judgments on matters of importance. For this reason, in Roman society, women were under the *potestas* of a male[38]—whether husband, father, or tutor—except in rare cases.[39] The prevalence of such a stereotype has led many scholars to suggest that the Gospel stories in which women were the

Celsum bears no direct allusion to Mk 16:9-20. Instead, Celsus seems privy to a view "in the air" at the time in which the reliability of a "hysterical female" at the empty tomb was in question (2.55). On the other hand, Samuel Prideaux Tregelles (*An Account of the Printed Text of the Greek New Testament* [London: Samuel Bagster and Sons, 1854]), in his 1854 text-critical treatment of the Greek NT, counts Celsus among the witnesses to the LE in the second century:

> My own opinion is, that that early writer against Christianity did … refer to the appearance of Christ to Mary Magdalene, as found in Mark xvi. 9; but that Origen, in answering him, did not exactly apprehend the purport of his objection, from (probably) not knowing or using that section of this Gospel. This would not be the only place in which Origen has misapprehended the force of remarks of Celsus from difference of reading in the copies which they respectively used, or from his not being aware of the facts to which Celsus referred. (251–2)

In my opinion there is a simpler textual explanation for Celsus's derision: this caricatured emotional response—apparently befitting a woman or, possibly, a bewitched man—seems much more like a disparaging reading of the women in Mk 16:8 or Mary Magdalene in Jn 20:11-15 (cf. *Cels.* ii.59), than of Mary Magdalene in the LE, which portrays her without reference to her emotion. See Chapters 2–3 on emotional displays of Mary versus those of the Eleven.

[34] Gk. for uterus is ὑστέρα, whence the term "hysteria" comes. Cf. Plato's reference to the "wandering womb" (*Tim.* 91).

[35] Thus, Josephus reports the practice, contemporary in Judaism at his time, of disallowing women to testify, based on the triviality and rashness of their kind (literally, "race"; διὰ κουφότητα καὶ θράσος τοῦ γένους αὐτῶν), just as slaves were likewise forbidden, on account of the "low birth of their soul" (διὰ τὴν τῆς ψυχῆς ἀγένειαν), which apparently makes them more susceptible to desire for gain or fear of punishment (*Ant.* 4.8.15). Cf. Philo, *Quaest. Gen.* 4.15; Gaius, *Inst.* 104, 109, 144 (cf. 48–9, in the categories of persons, Roman women were usually "subject to the authority of another"); Tacitus, *Annals* 3.34.

[36] Setzer says of the Gospel resurrection accounts, "Discussions of whether or not women's witness was legally valid seem out of place since this is hardly a legal context" ("Excellent Women," 261n8). Richard Bauckham notes that Josephus's explanation of the legal stipulation is not what is important but, rather, the rationale he gives for women's inadmissible testimony: "a version of the common ancient prejudice that women are less rational than men, more easily swayed by emotion, more readily influenced, all too prone to jump to conclusions without thoughtful consideration" (*Gospel Women: Studies of the Named Women in the Gospels* [New York: T&T Clark, 2002], 270).

[37] See earlier on the "trouble with belief." See also Gerald C. Tiffin, "The Problem of Credulity of Women," in *Essays on Women in Earliest Christianity* (ed. Carroll D. Osburn; Joplin, MO: College Press Publishing Company, 1995), 2:408–9.

[38] See Jane F. Gardner's chapter on "The Guardianship of Women," in *Women in Roman Law and Society* (Bloomington: Indiana University Press, 1986), 5–29.

[39] Women in the imperial family exercised some amount of independence; vestal virgins were in a legal limbo status that freed them from the power of their father, but placed them under the (at least technical) jurisdiction of the *Pontifex Maximus* (see Sarah B. Pomeroy, *Goddesses, Whores, Wives, and Slaves: Women in Classical Antiquity* [New York: Schocken Books, 1975], 214).

first witnesses to the empty tomb may have risked dismissal for this reason.⁴⁰ Perhaps aiming for just such credibility, Paul does not include Mary Magdalene or any women in his list of witnesses to Jesus's resurrection, instead listing Cephas first then the "Twelve" (ὅτι ὤφθη Κηφᾷ, εἶτα τοῖς δώδεκα; 1 Cor. 15:5). Paul even lists himself finally as a witness to the risen Jesus, but never credits Mary Magdalene with that role (vv. 5-8).⁴¹

Although the LE provides a version of the resurrection appearances later than most in the NT, Mary Magdalene is placed first among the witnesses. This placement is consistent with the women's visits to the tomb across the (then) proto-canonical Gospels on which it is clear the author relied.⁴² Among those sources, the LE confirms the solo appearance to Mary Magdalene reported by John (20:11-18). The issue is not whether such an insistence could have sparked questions of credibility: as we have seen, it probably did. The point is this: Mary's position of prominence had become so fixed in the Gospel tradition that the second-century author placed her there without apology.

A later phenomenon in a form of Christian apologetics illustrates a telling parallel. Eusebius's *Quaestiones ad Marinum*⁴³ is one of the pieces of evidence most frequently

---

⁴⁰ See Bauckham, *Gospel Women*, 252-67. Judith Lieu presents a modern abuse of the stereotype, which she calls the "sting in the tail": "This disqualification [of female witnesses] even allows modern scholars to contend that the primary resurrection traditions were the appearance narratives, and that the empty tomb traditions found in the Gospels developed later in conjunction with an emphasis on the bodily resurrection, with the presence only of the gullible women as a spurious apologetic for the tradition's late emergence" ("The Women's Resurrection Testimony," in *Resurrection: Essays in Honour of Leslie Houlden* [ed. Stephen Barton and Graham Stanton; London: SPCK, 1994], 35). Lieu does not name the object(s) of her criticism, but is likely referring to Bultmann, at least. He determines the Easter morning account, during which named women reach the tomb to find it empty, "a quite secondary formulation which neither went with the preceding sections of Mark ... nor, in [Bultmann's] view, with the supposed end of Mark which must have recounted the appearance of Jesus in Galilee" (Rudolf Bultmann, *The History of the Synoptic Tradition* [trans. John Marsh; Oxford: B. Blackwell, 1972], 281-2). If Bultmann is Lieu's target, he is not alone; she could also have in mind others who follow his view (e.g., Gerd Lüdemann, *The Resurrection of Jesus: History, Experience, Theology* [Minneapolis: Fortress, 1994], 116).

⁴¹ It is possible that traditions of the women at the tomb were unknown to Paul. If he knew them, one might conclude that the testimony of the "least of the apostles" and "one untimely born" (1 Cor. 15:8, 9) was still more reliable than a woman's.

⁴² Cf. also *Ep. Apost.* 9-11.

⁴³ Clarification of terms is necessary: the *Quaestiones ad Marinum* is the second of the two known parts of *Quaestiones et Responsiones*, composed by Eusebius (on the question of authorship, cf. note 79 in this chapter). Scholars are willing to say that the work has been "lost," but because we are unsure what percentage of the text remains in what we *do* have, it seems better to speak simply of the text as we have it. Although other editions are cited in note 79, J.-P. Migne's edition in the PG is the most widely accessible, so I will refer to his designations: (1) the text known (and published by Mai) from a "most beautiful" (*pulcherrimo codice*) Greek manuscript held at the Vatican (Vat. Palat. 220), containing (a) sixteen question-and-answer pairs addressed to Stephanus (PG 22:879-936), and (b) four question-and-answer pairs addressed to Marinus (PG 22:937-958); (2) "supplements" to the *ad Stephanum*, including excerpts from the catena on Luke by Nicetas of Heraclea, among others (both in Greek and in Syriac) (PG 22:957-982); (3) a lengthy "supplement" to the *ad Marinum* from Nicetas's catena on Luke (PG 22: 983-1006); and (4) "minor supplements" to the *ad Marinum* (PG 22:1007-1016). Claudio Zamagni calls parts 1a and b (as designated earlier) the *"ekloge,"* based on the Greek heading ΕΚΛΟΓΗ ΕΝ ΣΥΝΤΟΜΩ, "selection in summary" (*Eusèbe de Césarée, Questions Évangéliques: Introduction, texte critique, traduction et notes* [SC 523; Paris: Cerf, 2008]). Nicetas of Heraclea's catena on Luke contains a text thought

marshaled in debates over the origins of the LE.[44] Because Eusebius acknowledges manuscripts both with and without the LE (but those without, most "accurate"), his letter is a popular stomping ground for the debate. The preoccupation with Eusebius's testimony for or against the LE has dominated discussion of the *ad Marinum* to such a degree that scholars have overlooked an integral characteristic of the document: namely, women are central figures in nearly every pericope Eusebius discusses in his question-and-answer epistle.

When Marinus asks four overarching questions about the Gospels' resurrection accounts, which Eusebius answers, *all four* feature women. Only Marinus's first question leaves out Mary Magdalene's name. The verses in discussion involve her (Mt. 28:1; Mk 16:1-2, 9); as a result, Eusebius's answer uses her name often.[45] On the other hand, there are other discrepancies among resurrection narratives that call for attention beyond those pericopes that involve women. Although roughly a century later than Eusebius's *Quaestiones ad Marinum* and written in different circumstances, Augustine's more comprehensive *Harmony of the Gospels* (also a different genre: apology proper) does

---

to be from the *ad Marinum* (designated no. 3 here), which is similar in form with, but does not replicate any of the question-and-answer pairs we know from, the Vatican manuscript. However, the two traditions overlap in their presentation of the *ad Stephanum* text, sometimes providing identical wording; where one text is more detailed, it is typically that of Nicetas, which Zamagni judges to be closer to the original Eusebian text (*Questions Évangéliques*, 19–20). Zamagni offers the most information regarding both the relationship and degree of independence between the "*ekloge*" and Nicetas's citation (15–16, 19–21). He summarizes his tentative conclusions, which notably moderate the degree of alteration to Eusebius's original text ascribed to either Nicetas or the compiler of the *ekloge*: "Les deux auteurs ont eu accès indépendamment à l'original eusébien perdu et tant la tradition de l'*eklogè* que celle de Nicétas ont éliminé quelques parties du texte (pas les mêmes), mais sans modifier significativement celles qu'ils ont choisi de rapporter" (21). Contrast John W. Burgon on the abbreviator's work in the *ad Marinum* (*The Last Twelve Verses of Mark: Vindicated Against Recent Critical Objectors & Established* [repr., Oxford: James Parker and Co., 1871], 43). The clarification of what constitutes the Eusebian *Quaestiones et Responsiones* (which Eusebius himself calls ζητημάτων καὶ λύσεων; *Dem. ev.* VII.3) is necessary, because the "supplements" (i.e., nos 2–4 above) are sometimes cited as part of the same document in some critical studies on Eusebius's *Quaestiones* (e.g., Allan E. Johnson, "Rhetorical Criticism in Eusebius' Gospels Questions," *StPatr* 1 [1983]: 35–9); in others, they are excluded from consideration (or unmentioned, as in the case of James Kelhoffer, "The Witness of Eusebius' *ad Marinum* and Other Christian Writings," *ZNW* 92 [2001]: 99–107<).

[44] E.g., William E. Farmer, *The Last Twelve Verses of Mark* (SNTSMS 25; New York: Cambridge University Press, 1974), 3. Farmer somewhat mistakenly calls the text a "fragment" and begins his study of the LE with the *ad Marinum*. In addition to the works by Kelhoffer and Zamagni (see note 40), the reader may consult the first full translation in English: Roger Pearse, ed., *Eusebius of Caesarea: Gospel Problems and Solutions* (trans. David J. Miller and Adam C. McCollum; Ancient Texts in Translation; Ipswich, UK: Chieftain, 2011).

[45] In contrast of the sixteen questions in the *ad Stephanum*, all of which concern some aspect of the genealogy and birth narratives in Matthew and Luke, only five pertain (in question or answer) to women. The difference is, perhaps, unsurprising: each Gospel's post-resurrection accounts feature women in at least one episode, but the vast majority of names in the genealogy belong to males. The gynocentric questions pertain to why Tamar, Uriah's wife, and Ruth appear in the genealogy; these are the subjects of questions 7, 8, and 9, respectively (*Ad Stephanum* 7.1-8; 8.1-4, 9.1-3). Another explanation for the gender imbalance might be that we lack the full series of questions and answers as Eusebius wrote them. Indeed, the text of *Quaestiones* that we have has been called a fragment or, more accurately, an epitome (Kelhoffer, "Witness of Eusebius," 82). Condensation more closely approximates the term *ekloge*/ἐκλογή, which, as Zamagni points out, is the title that heads the document discovered by Cardinal Mai (Zamagni, *Questions Évangéliques*, 21; see also note 76).

not avoid questions concerning women (e.g., *Cons.* III.58) but represents more closely of the percentage of the narrative in which women are found. The *ad Marinum*, in contrast, discloses a greater interest in episodes involving women, whether because of their gender—which, in my opinion, is *the* significant element around which many of the questions cohere—or because of the characters in specific episodes themselves.

Marinus's questions addressed to Eusebius are *internal* to Christianity[46] and have a gendered cause: key components of the resurrection story and, indeed, the historical roots of Christian faith are contingent on the witness of women. Eusebius's *ad Marinum* makes sense within a context of general discomfort with the reliance on women's testimony. The scrutiny is, therefore, more intense regarding the coherence or incoherence of accounts that rely on women. Indeed, as Eusebius comments in his introductory comments to Marinus, he passes by "the middle things" (τὰ μέσα) of the Gospel accounts and cuts "to the things at the end of [the Gospels] *about which everyone always inquires*" (ἐπὶ τὰ πρὸς τῷ τέλει τῶν αὐτῶν πάντοτε τοῖς πᾶσι ζητούμενα).[47] Eusebius's interest in the manuscript representation of Mark's LE is not where Mark should end, or on formal canonical boundaries. His primary concern is to demonstrate the reliability and agreement of the Evangelists' witness. Doing so involves validating women's testimony, regardless of source.

If Mk 16:9-20 had been considered irreconcilable with Mt. 28:1, it is quite possible that Eusebius's first solution (*ad Marinum* I.1)—to excise the questionable passage (Mk 16:9)—might have been acceptable. While removing a portion of the received text (albeit one of dubious provenance) was an option, Eusebius never suggests as a possibility that the women's testimony was unreliable (as Celsus proposed). Neither does he insinuate that later, male witnesses to the resurrected Jesus should be preferred as more trustworthy. Instead, Eusebius's priorities—first, to demonstrate agreement among the Gospels; second, to preserve readings, even when in doubt—serve to uphold the accuracy of the women's witness to both the empty tomb and the risen Christ. In the interest of illustrating harmony among the Evangelists, Eusebius must also defend the Gospels' female witnesses to the resurrection of Jesus. The LE may also demonstrate this impulse nearly two centuries earlier. The author of Mk 16:9-20 ties even more closely the testimony of Mary Magdalene to the ultimate success of the disciples' proclamation of the resurrection.

2.3 "Marian Primacy"

Could the positive attention paid to Mary and the prolonged negative attention toward the Eleven indicate that the LE is attempting to upend a proto-Petrine Primacy that may have been circulating? The implication of such a suggestion is that Mary Magdalene

---

[46] Johnson compares Eusebius's κατασκευή (defense) to contemporary examples and rhetorical handbook guidelines for refutation (ἀνασκευή) and defense: "Each of the 'questions' raised in Eusebius' *Gospel Questions and Solutions* represents one or more of the 'possible weaknesses' or 'topics for refutation' recommended by the rhetorical manuals. Conversely, each of the headings on Hermogenes' outline of refutation is illustrated among Eusebius' questions" ("Rhetorical Criticism," 34).

[47] *Ad Marinum*, prologue (Zamagni, *Questions Évangéliques*, 194–5); emphasis added.

supplants Simon Peter in his position of prominence among the disciples. Indeed, the LE upholds a sort of "Marian primacy," but not in the sense that its converse, "Petrine primacy," is typically understood. Reestablishing Mary Magdalene as a faithful follower and source of reliable testimony is of *first*—that is, *primary*—importance to the author of the LE. But one who searches for a conspiracy to overthrow the place of the eleven male apostles, and especially Peter, within the lines of the LE will be disappointed.

To the degree that the argument presented earlier has demonstrated that in the LE Mary Magdalene is a disciple of great interest and one worthy of emulation, she is indeed primary—that is to say, *preeminent*. But to suggest that the LE's account of post-resurrection intentionally undermines Peter and in his place substitutes Mary is likely an exaggeration for several reasons.

2.3.1 Ways in Which the Long Ending Cannot Be Said to Uphold "Marian Primacy"

First, the perception that Peter is granted primacy among the disciples proceeds from solid statistics: all four Gospels mention Peter so frequently throughout Jesus's ministry that he is undisputedly primary among the disciples.[48] Narratively, Peter is a relatively static persona across the Gospels; that is, he is consistently brazen, both in foibles and triumphs, devotion and inconstancy.[49] The culminating event in this characterization is Peter's denial of Jesus, which is found in all four canonical Gospels (Mt. 26:69-75; Mk 14:66-72; Lk. 22:56-62; Jn 18:15-18, 25-27). While Mary Magdalene is the woman most frequently named in the crucifixion, burial, empty tomb, and resurrection texts,[50] her overall frequency cannot compete with the ubiquity of Peter throughout the Gospels.

---

[48] Simon Peter's name is mentioned at least once in over fifty passages across the canonical Gospels (the greatest concentration of references to Peter by name is in the denial pericope), not to mention Acts and the rest of the NT corpus. Peter's primacy among the disciples as narrated in Gospels is widely acknowledged to the extent that it is often stated without defense (cf. John Y. H. Yieh, "Peter, the Apostle," *NIDB* 4: 475). Explanations to the contrary exist—in fact, in a forthcoming publication, Robert Gundry argues that Matthew denigrates Peter—but such claims are swimming upstream. See Theodore J. Weeden for the classic presentation of the case that Mark "is assiduously involved in a vendetta against the disciples" (*Mark: Traditions in Conflict* [Philadelphia: Fortress, 1971], 50).

[49] The Gospels consistently portray Peter as inconsistent (see also Paul's accusation in Gal. 2:11-14). There is also the popular tendency to harmonize the Gospels so that an action ascribed to Peter in one place is generalized into his biography. One such example is a favorite of Easter pageants and summary retellings of Good Friday's events. The rash incident in Gethsemane by which one among Jesus's retinue cuts off the ear of the high priest's slave appears in each of the four Gospels; but it is attributed to Peter only in John (18:10-11). In the Synoptic Gospels, the perpetrator is anonymous: "one of those with/standing by/about him" (Mt. 26:51; Mk 14:47; Lk. 22:49-50). Mark's account does not make clear that the violent offender is among Jesus's party. Note the lack of specificity in Mark's description: εἷς δέ [τις] τῶν παρεστηκότων ("one [who was] standing by"; 14:47a). R. Alan Culpepper emphasizes the uncertainty in Mark's account (*Mark* [Smyth and Helwys Bible Commentary; Macon, GA: Smyth & Helwys, 2007], 510). This tendency to include details unique to only one Gospel extends far beyond Peter's involvement, of course: in the same episode Jesus is recorded as healing the slave's ear only in Luke's version of the story (22:51), although the happy ending is seldom neglected in popular harmonizations.

[50] See Chapter 2, esp. Table 2.2, the chart of named women.

Second, as much as Peter stands at the forefront of the disciples' activity during Jesus's ministry, his "primacy" *in post-resurrection accounts* is variegated. Thus, the fact that his name does not appear in the LE is not without precedent. Mark's empty tomb scene anticipates Peter's presence: although he does not enter the scene in 16:1-8, he is specifically mentioned in v. 7, when the young man in white commands the women at the tomb to go and tell Jesus's disciples *and Peter* (τοῖς μαθηταῖς αὐτοῦ καὶ τῷ Πέτρῳ) that Jesus will meet them in Galilee. The Intermediate Ending fulfills this expectation: "They [the women] reported briefly to those with Peter [τοῖς περὶ τὸν Πέτρον] everything which was commanded." The LE, on the other hand, does not specify Peter's inclusion, although he would be numbered among the Eleven.

Given Peter's prominence elsewhere in the First Gospel (esp. chs 14–16), it is of particular note that Matthew makes no further mention of Peter by name after his denial of Jesus in 26:75. We can presume that Peter is assumed present whenever the generalized group of "disciples" are mentioned (28:7-9); surely he is amid "the eleven disciples" (οἱ ... ἕνδεκα μαθηταί; 28:16). In contrast to his absence in Mt. 28:1-20, Peter returns to prominence in the post-resurrection narratives of both Luke[51] and John.[52]

As the final and most important reason why Mary's highlighted role in the LE cannot be said to topple Peter from any nascent, contemporary ascendancy among the disciples is that Mary Magdalene's role as the proclaimer of Jesus's resurrection does

---

[51] Luke mentions Peter twice in the episodes subsequent to Jesus's crucifixion. When the women return and report what they learned from the two messengers, Peter is certainly among those ("the Eleven and all the rest"/τοῖς ἕνδεκα καὶ πᾶσιν τοῖς λοιποῖς, 24:9; "the apostles"/τοὺς ἀποστόλους, v. 10) who hear the proclamation and disregard the women's words. Without any stated transition from his disbelief, v. 12 says: "But Peter got up and ran to the tomb, and, stooping down, he looked in and saw only the linens. And he went away, wondering to himself what had happened." According to the report to Cleopas and his fellow disciple, Peter was further favored with an encounter with the risen Lord—albeit offstage (v. 34). The Pauline tradition that places Peter (Cephas, Κηφᾶς) as the first witness to Jesus's resurrection (1 Cor. 15:5) is never presented as a narrative episode in the Fourfold Gospel Canon, although it may be inferred from Luke (24:34). In the fifth-century majuscule Codex Bezae (D), Lk. 24:12 is missing entirely. Text-critically, D is the great exception regarding v. 12, as even P[75] supports the NA[28]'s reading. Nonetheless, the lacuna in a major witness calls attention to some unusual aspects of the verse. Beyond its aforementioned awkward fit with what precedes (i.e., Peter is certainly included by association among the disbelievers, but runs urgently to the tomb to see for himself), some of the wording accords surprisingly with John 20's account of the "other" disciple's inspection of the empty tomb. In Luke, Peter runs (ἔδραμεν) to the tomb (ἐπὶ τὸ μνημεῖον) and "stooping down, he sees only the linen cloths" (παρακύψας βλέπει τὰ ὀθόνια μόνα; 24:12). John recounts that the other disciple outruns (προέδραμεν) Peter, arriving first at the tomb (πρῶτος εἰς τὸ μνημεῖον; 20:4). The other disciple, then, stooping down, sees the linen cloths lying there (παρακύψας βλέπει κείμενα τὰ ὀθόνια; v. 5). Several correlations, such as the terms for "tomb" and "linen cloths," of course, are likely identical because there are only so many ways to denote these items. Peter's *running* in Luke and being *outrun* in John smack of contestants in a "most-loyal-disciple" competition. Peter's departure is accompanied by introspective wondering (πρὸς ἑαυτὸν θαυμάζων τὸ γεγονός) in Luke, whereas in John the other disciple is moved to belief by what he sees (καὶ εἶδεν καὶ ἐπίστευσεν; v. 8), which boosts the perception of rivalry. The absence of Lk. 24:11 in D seems evidence more of a fluke than of the verse's questionable status. If anything, John's account may be aware of the Lukan tradition and pushes Peter gently aside. On the other hand, recognizing Peter as the one to be "dethroned" indirectly bolsters a tradition of Peter's primacy.

[52] Although Jesus appears to the gathered disciples all at once in John, the "other disciple" is the first to have believed (however vaguely *what* he believed is stated). For whatever preference it grants to the "other" or "beloved" disciple (esp. in Jn 20:2-10 and 21:20-22), the Fourth Gospel expresses a great deal of interest in Peter in its final episodes. Much of the narrative focus on Peter concerns his rehabilitation as a disciple worthy of Jesus's trust (21:15-19).

not replace any function that Peter fulfills in the Gospels. He is in focus as a designated recipient of this good news in Mk 16:7; he is not its messenger. Unnamed, Peter and the rest of the Eleven are commissioned to *go* and *tell* (v. 15). The LE tells us that they—not Peter in particular—satisfied Jesus's command (v. 20).

2.3.2 Ways in Which the Long Ending Can Be Said to Uphold "Marian Primacy"

It would be a serious overextension of the evidence to claim that the LE's depiction of Mary is intended to fuel her supersession of Peter's prominence. The expression of her *primacy* as first recipient of Easter tidings is not in competition with or threatening to his, yet one disparity is worth noting. At the point where the author of the LE affixed the "more satisfying" ending to the Gospel of Mark, evidently viewing the women's silence in Mk 16:8 as a failure, the story resumes with Mary. Yet there is no narration of Mary's repenting or being restored as a follower. Rather, she receives Jesus's favor as the first witness to the resurrection without a second reference to any fault on her part. This stands in contrast to the portrait of Peter in John's Gospel: there, Peter undergoes a lengthy reinstatement in John 21. This restoration is painful for Peter, precisely because it involves a threefold undoing of his threefold transgression (Jn 21:7).[53] The LE does not narrate any restorative steps taken by Jesus for Mary Magdalene. At the same time, the form of rehabilitation the Eleven (including Peter) receive in the LE is a sound rebuke (Mk 16:14).

Three things are certain in the LE: the risen Jesus appears first to Mary Magdalene (Mk 16:9); she seizes the opportunity to be the first to bear the news of a living Lord (v. 10); she is the only named disciple to whom the risen Jesus appears (cf. vv. 12-20). No longer caught in a fearful silence (v. 8), she is a bold *evangelist* herself. Compared with Peter, Mary Magdalene occupies a primary position, but does not replace him as a proclaimer.[54]

3. Implications of This Second-Century Continuation of Mark

This approach to the LE engages the text as an ending to Mark. It is an ending that fixes Mark's conclusion more firmly among the Fourfold Gospel as a corroborating witness, even as it engages tensions that persist throughout the uncontested body of the Second Gospel (1:1-16:8). These observations call into question some common

---

[53] Peter "was hurt" (ἐλυπήθη) *because* (ὅτι) Jesus asked him the third time (τὸ τρίτον), "Do you love me?" (Jn 21:17).

[54] A further way in which Mary represents an integral connection between following Jesus and the future activity of the church is her role as both a recipient of Jesus's exorcistic work (16:9) and the ongoing work of exorcism to which the disciples are commanded (16:17; also 6:7, 13). Exorcism and Jesus's command over the spiritual realm is another significant emphasis in the larger Gospel (e.g., 1:23-27; 3:11-12; 5:1-20). While some of these ties have been explored in Chapter 2, this is a significant theme linking Mk 1:1-16:8 and 16:9-20 and worthy of further study.

generalizations in NT scholarship: namely, that diagnosing alterations to NT texts as "spurious" might be sufficient and that early (proto-orthodox) Christianity progressed unflinchingly toward the oppression of women without marked exceptions.

Kelhoffer, whose careful work on the LE has reignited interest in the Markan appendix and has been invaluable in my own research, includes in his summary of findings and implications the following statements:

> It may have been this very type of alteration of Gospel passages about which the pagan critic Celsus ... complained when charging that some Christians "go so far as to oppose themselves and *alter the original text of the Gospel* (μεταχαράττειν ἐκ τῆς πρώτης γραφῆς τὸ εὐαγγέλιον) three or four or several times over, and they change its character to enable them to deny difficulties in the face of criticism" (*Contra Celsum* 2.27). Viewed in this light, such a conspicuous alteration of the ending of the Gospel of Mark offers a striking example of what Bart Ehrman has credibly termed the corruption and continual re-writing of biblical texts by proto-Orthodox believers.[55]

Here I must part ways with Kelhoffer. Alteration of NT texts does not automatically constitute "corruption."[56] Further, if the LE's alteration to the Gospel escapes "criticism," it flies headlong into others, some proffered by Celsus himself. Particularly in light of widely accepted, normative gender expectations and its extension of a negative presentation of Christian heroes, the LE seems far from a panacea.

3.1 The Significance of the Long Ending as Early Reception of Mark's Gospel

The LE's impetus for contrasting Mary Magdalene's trusting proclamation with unfaithful male disciples can be found in the text of Mk 1:1–16:8 itself. Groups of women are named thrice in the last two chapters of the Second Gospel, as the focus shifts from the deserting Twelve to the faithful women. The names in the various brief lists change, but Mary Magdalene (Μαρία ἡ Μαγδαληνή) is referred to consistently and always appears first. These female disciples were among a larger such group from Jesus's Galilean ministry who are first explicitly mentioned in an epilogue to the crucifixion scene (15:40-41). Their reappearance in various nominal configurations mark each subsequent episode of the narrative: women know where Jesus's corpse was laid (15:47); then, they are reasonably taken aback when before dawn they find not their deceased teacher, but a young man at the open tomb (16:1, 5).[57] Mark 16:8 leaves

---

[55] Kelhoffer, *Miracle and Mission*, 480.

[56] This means that I dispute, likewise, Bart Ehrman's characterizations to this effect (see *The Orthodox Corruption of Scripture: The Effect of Early Christological Controversies on the Text of the New Testament* [New York: Oxford University Press, 2011]).

[57] A common reading of 15:47 is that Mark forestalls the charge that the women went to the wrong tomb (C. Clifton Black, *Mark* [ANTC; Nashville: Abingdon, 2011], 338). Adela Yarbro Collins simply explains 15:47 as a Markan addition to earlier passion traditions in order to prepare for the empty-tomb story (*Mark* [Hermeneia; Minneapolis: Fortress, 2007], 779). William L. Lane, on the other hand, determines that it must be "factual," because Jewish culture placed "no value" on women's testimony; thus, Mark would be unlikely to invent such an account (*The Gospel of Mark* [NICNT; Grand Rapids: Eerdmans, 1974], 581). Somewhere between a literary transition and a

open the question: Did the women who brave the gruesome crucifixion of their Lord ultimately disappoint him?

If the added ending, 16:9-20, were merely correcting narrative details potentially damaging to the early Christian movement, one might select different elements from the other Gospels to do a better job. Projecting authorial intent to an otherwise mysterious author is a thorny endeavor, although not an uncommon one.[58] However, by observing what the LE *does* to Mk 16:1-8 and what the LE *adapts* from the eventually canonical traditions of which the author was evidently aware (Jn 20:11-18; Lk. 24:13-35; Mt. 28:18-20), we can with some confidence perceive what problems the twelve-verse expansion serves to resolve. It is noteworthy that the LE's presentation of Mary Magdalene protects the women from a response to Jesus's resurrection that is ultimately faithless. When the "Longer Ending" begins and Jesus appears first (πρῶτος) to Mary Magdalene, it eradicates any possible conclusion that the women failed to convey the news and that the resurrected Jesus never appeared to his followers. The women's silence in 16:8 is broken when 16:9-11 attests to Mary's witness.

The added ending does the male disciples no such favor. They are depicted as weeping and mourning, an emotional response that may illustrate a component of their faithlessness that is elsewhere accorded to women.[59] Moreover, it solidifies and multiplies their instances of unbelief (vv. 11, 13), making explicit Jesus's harsh and repeated judgment of them (twice in v. 14). Moreover, belief and disbelief become even more emphatically serious matters in v. 16. Ultimately, as proven by the success of the mission (v. 20), the formerly disbelieving disciples participate as witnesses to the gospel. These failed disciples are given a chance to change, invested with the authority and commission to proclaim the good news of Jesus's resurrection (v. 15). This second chance for the disciples to get things right with the help of the Lord (τοῦ κυρίου συνεργοῦντος; v. 20) is, effectively, what the LE has begun to narrate by providing renewed opportunity to one of Jesus's devoted female disciples. Lest anyone suspect that the women's faith finally fails (v. 8), the LE gives Mary Magdalene the chance to set the record straight.

D. C. Parker points out the implicit validation afforded the Second Gospel by the added ending:

---

historical certainty lies a valuable observation: Mark and his antecedent tradition are comfortable with investing *women* with the sole corroboration of Jesus's burial site.

[58] Of course, the Evangelists were all initially anonymous, even though tradition has afforded us handy attributions.

[59] The women's mourning at Jesus's crucifixion (Lk. 23:27-28) and Mary Magdalene's tears in Jn 20:11, 13, and 15 at the tomb have been discussed earlier. Another interesting intersection of crying and gender is found in the fragmentary, second-century text of *The Gospel of Mary*: "Then Mary arose, saluted them all, and spoke to her brothers: 'Weep not, be not sorrowful, neither be undecided, for his grace will be with you all and will protect you. Rather, let us praise his greatness, for he has prepared us and made us to be men'" ([alt.] trans. by R. McL. Wilson in *New Testament Apocrypha: Gospels and Related Writings* [ed. Wilhelm Schneemelcher; Cambridge and Louisville: James Clarke/Westminster/John Knox, 1991], 1:393). Near the conclusion of the text, as we have it, Andrew and Peter reject Mary Magdalene's report, lodging objections charged with gender-difference concerns. Peter's protests, in a strange turn, make Mary weep (cf. Bart D. Ehrman, *Lost Scriptures: Books That Did Not Make It into the New Testament* [Oxford: Oxford University Press, 2003], 37).

One other interesting point emerges from this comparison. Both the Intermediate and the Long Ending, with their emphasis on proclamation, provide the Gospel with its own validation. By writing, Mark is obedient to this command, for he enshrines the command within his book. The Short Ending provides no such security for the book. Indeed, quite the reverse, for the women's *silence* means that, within the story, we have no means of knowing that any of it happened.[60]

The LE confirms not merely Jesus's predictions of his fate (Mk 8:31-32; 9:30-32; 10:32-34), but also the young man's message from the undisputed Gospel of Mark (16:6-7). Furthermore, Jesus's confirmation of Mary's message and that of the two unnamed disciples occurs immediately after the report of their actions (vv. 14-20). Jesus's commission, fantastically vast in scope (both of signs and geography), also allows nearly no narrative time to elapse before the narrator authenticates its fulfillment. Yet it is not a generic gospel or resurrection message that the LE confirms. The validity that the LE reinforces is that of the good news in a distinctly Markan way. This "Markan flavor" continues to recognize faith in the least likely places: like turning into a proclaimer one who has just sprinted away in terrified silence (vv. 8-10). Likewise, those who have the greatest access to Jesus are those who resolutely fail to understand. That is, they fail until Jesus finally makes them get it, which Mark's Jesus could absolutely do.[61]

3.2 The Significance of the Long Ending for the Four-Gospel Canon

As Kelhoffer suggests, the fact that a second-century author believed that he or she had the authority to append new material to the ending of Mark indicates that the Gospels were not yet considered inviolate or fixed.[62] Nonetheless, the alteration respects—even to the point of retaining an awkward juxtaposition of sentences—the ending at 16:8. And this is no small matter: this ending at 16:8, which was considered dissatisfying enough to require repair, is left intact.[63] The text as it stood was either sufficiently well known or incipiently sacred that the "fix" took the form of a noticeable addition, rather than the amendment of the text as received.

Most of what the author of the LE added was not novel but relied on other, proto-canonical traditions. In an introductory text on the Greek texts, manuscripts, and translation of the NT, Stanley E. Porter summarizes[64] the situation of the LE:

---

[60] Parker, *Living Text*, 146; emphasis in the original.
[61] This is, of course, an interpretation of Mark's depiction of discipleship that highlights the negative aspects of the Twelve's perception, obedience, and follow-through. There is ample evidence that Jesus's disciples could understand (e.g., 8:29) and sacrificed much in order to follow Jesus faithfully (e.g., 10:28-31). It is especially in comparison with the other Gospels that one can notice Mark's greater willingness to report Jesus's frustration with his closest followers. Mark depicts their obduracy in unveiled terms in ways that, for instance, Matthew and Luke do not (cf. Mk 8:15-21; Mt. 16:5-12, esp. v. 12; and Lk. 12:1). The author of the LE seems well acquainted with other Gospel traditions and, in my view, picks up on the characterization of the disciples as faithless that appears more often in Mark. See Chapter 3 for more on Markan discipleship.
[62] Kelhoffer, *Miracle and Mission*, 479.
[63] Cf. Ibid., 479–80.
[64] In this section Porter relies heavily on the LE chapter of Parker's *Living Text* (cf. 124–74), whose approach to text criticism is foundational for my own.

It was created ... by drawing upon material at least as important and accessible as Mark's Gospel: the three other Gospels and Acts. In other words, the four Gospels and Acts were already apparently considered a collected body of authoritative writings of the church by the early part of the second century, so that when later writers wished to "complete" Mark's Gospel, they drew upon these Gospels.[65]

Porter may overstate the case, but only barely. The author of the LE makes unique combinations of known elements (as argued in Chapter 2) but works within canonical boundaries that are both flexible (permitting addition) and limiting (restricting the nature of the addition).

Beyond the increased emphasis on faith versus disbelief and the emphatic characterizations of the figures that model each attribute, the LE does something else profound. Of the material clearly derived from one of the other Gospels, there is at least one element that, apart from Mark's LE, would be unique to that Gospel. Matthew is no longer the only Gospel with an expansive commission (28:18-20); Mark now has one (16:15-18). Likewise, Luke is not the only Gospel that tells of two disciples in transit who encounter a Jesus they do not recognize (24:13-35); Mark now includes a resurrection appearance of Jesus "in a different form" (16:12-13). John is not the only Gospel that tells of Mary Magdalene's solitary encounter with the risen Jesus (20:11-18); a similar story of Mary as the first witness of the risen Jesus can be found in Mark's ending (16:9-11). Mark 16:9-20 does not simply cobble together a more satisfying ending; it reasserts and confirms important elements drawn from its sources.

In light of this confirmatory aim, the application to Mk 16:9-20 of terms such as *forgery* and *spurious* seem inappropriately disapproving and are arguably beside the point. Such categories, which may be appropriate within the technical context of textual criticism, are freighted with such negative connotations that they should no longer be applied to theological exegesis of a text like Mark's LE.[66] Labeling a text as "spurious" or "forged" casts all of its elements in the light of "heresy" or "falsification," when the shape and content of the second-century addition demonstrates intentions exactly *counter* to that.[67] Matthew D. C. Larsen has come to similar conclusions: "Forgeries fabricate an authentic writing, or perhaps make false authorial claims about a well-known person; adding to an unfinished text, rather, improves upon a text perceived to be open and in some way ambiguous or lacking."[68]

---

[65] Stanley E. Porter, *How We Got the New Testament: Text, Transmission, Translation* (Grand Rapids: Baker, 2013), 101–2.

[66] See, e.g., Kelhoffer, *Miracle and Mission*, 150–4; James Tabor, "The 'Strange' Ending of the Gospel of Mark and Why It Makes All the Difference," n.p.: http://www.biblicalarchaeology.org/daily/biblical-topics/new-testament/the-strange-ending-of-the-gospel-of-mark-and-why-it-makes-all-the-difference/(cited November 2, 2014).

[67] Kelhoffer is not convinced that the author of the LE would have been welcomed by "others in the second century who held views that eventually came to be recognized as orthodox" (*Miracle and Mission*, 480). He considers the question unresolved. Unorthodoxy seems hardly a concern for this text, especially considering the apparently intentional restriction of source traditions in the author's composition (proto-canonical Gospels) coupled with the text's hasty and near-universal acceptance as Mark's ending.

[68] *Gospels before the Book* (New York: Oxford University Press, 2018), 120. Larsen argues further, basing his claims on his treatment of Mk 1:1–16:8 as *hypomnēmata*, or unfinished notes:

Instead of attempting to introduce *novel* stories and theology,[69] the author of the LE worked creatively within existing proto-canonical traditions in a way that confirms other Gospels' accounts, while fitting them to the themes and interests of Mark. Bypassing the negative overtones of "forgery," terms such as "epitome," "homage," or "mosaic" better describe the kind of traditional amalgamation and abbreviation that resulted in the LE.

As long as "spurious" is the designation for this later addition, the LE will not be studied as it functioned for most of its history: as the conclusion to Mark. Because some of the best treatments on the Second Gospel have gone this route—confidently dismissing the Long, Intermediate, and otherwise expanded endings of Mark from consideration—I suspect that it is due not to individual episodes of oversight, but to a systemic oversimplification of the goal of textual criticism. For years, the self-stated job of a text critic was often to reject scribal errors[70] and to uncover the original text of the NT, or at least our best approximation of it.[71] Without a doubt, some text critics are still motivated by such an aim. There has been, however, in other quarters of textual criticism an ideological shift.[72] Eldon Jay Epp provides an excellent summary of the

---

All the new endings of the textual tradition of the Gospel according to Mark may be better understood in the latter category, because they attempt to rework the text we now call the Gospel according to Mark by adding (what was perceived to be) a much-needed proper ending—complete with a resurrected Jesus and all. Stated simply, adding an ending to an unfinished text would be regarded as a proper response to such a text. (idem.)

[69] See, e.g., the aforementioned contrast with the *Gospel of Peter*'s inventiveness (note 10). There, the cross is mobile (*Gos. Pet.* 39) and even seems to speak (42).

[70] Eldon Jay Epp characterizes this practice as "negative" and finds it particularly in Hort's description of the text-critical task (cf. "The Multivalence of the Term 'Original' in New Testament Textual Criticism," *HTR* 99 [1999]: 248n5).

[71] Epp collates a series of quotations from an earlier generation of text critics that demonstrate that, for some, this was the simple goal (ibid., 248–9). Of course, as Epp notes, the approach is not solely confined to the nineteenth and turn of the twentieth centuries; a recent introduction to text criticism also defines the field by the search for autographs (J. Harold Greenlee, *Introduction to New Testament Textual Criticism* [Peabody, MA: Hendrickson, 1995], 11). The focus of textual criticism in English literature has traditionally sought the authoritative version of a text, which is usually (but not always) the original version or manuscript (Ross Murfin and Supryia M. Ray, *The Bedford Glossary of Critical and Literary Terms* [Boston: Bedford, 1997], 399). For an expansion of English literary textual criticism's aims, drawing on the author's work on Byron, see Jerome McGann, *A Critique of Modern Textual Criticism* (Chicago: University of Chicago Press, 1983). As in NT studies, the proliferation of digital technology has called for a reassessment of the purpose of textual criticism within English poetry scholarship (see idem., "Textual Scholarship, Textual Theory, and the Uses of Electronic Tools: A Brief Report on Current Undertakings," *Victorian Studies* 41 [1998]: 609–19).

[72] A similar sense of a broader shift is reflected in Chris Keith's introduction to his work on another famous manuscript variant: "This work joins other recent studies that dwell at the intersection of textual criticism and the history of early Christianity ... the result of calls to employ textual criticism for purposes other than recovering an 'original text'" (*The Pericope Adulterae, the Gospel of John, and the Literacy of Jesus* [Boston: Brill, 2009], 4–5). More than a half-century ago, Kenneth Clark's presidential address, published in the *JBL*, was presented on December 30, 1965, to the annual meeting of the Society of Biblical Literature at Vanderbilt University in Nashville, TN. This address is the selfsame one that spurred William Farmer to reinvestigate Mk 16:9-20 in his *Last Twelve Verses* in 1974 (see ix). Clark ("The Theological Relevance of Textual Variation in Current Criticism of the Greek New Testament," *JBL* 85 [1966]) raises the questions of original and secondary, of spurious and authentic in this way:

multiple ways in which the term "original" has been employed across the breadth of text-critical scholarship.[73] Although the statement of text-critical goals spans a wide spectrum among its practitioners, Epp suggests that "expressing the text critical goal some kind of qualifying phrase, usually along the lines of 'the most likely original text,' is what most in the field have said or still say."[74] It is my contention that, as long as the question put to the LE remains that of "original" versus "spurious," not only is the current body of evidence unable to settle the debate, but the important questions of interpreting the *actual* readings of Mark will remain unasked.

It is clear that Markan commentators need to make sense of an ending at 16:8, the form in which the Gospel's earliest audiences would have encountered the text. But biblical commentators are also responsible to address significant interpretations and receptions, and the reality is that centuries of Markan readers would not have said their final *amen* until they heard recounted the Lord "confirming the word with signs following" (16:20b), rather than the women's silence "for they were afraid" (16:8b).

> It is not our primary concern at this time to determine what is original and what is secondary, but rather to demonstrate the variety of reading and of consequent meaning. It has been remarked that "there are no 'spurious readings' in New Testament manuscripts." The intent of such a statement is only to insist that every variation is genuine in its time and place. Although a variant which is a departure from the original text may be described as spurious, yet every intentional and sensible variant has a claim to authenticity in the history of Christian thought. (2)

To be clear, Clark did not "craft" the discipline's shift, nor is it entirely clear whether his statement bespeaks a methodological perspective or, rather, is merely talking about "our primary concern" in terms of this particular address. His reference to a statement that "there are no 'spurious readings'" comes from Donald Riddle, "Textual Criticism as a Historical Discipline," *AThR* 18 (1936): 221. In favor of the interpretation that Clark agreed with Riddle's methodological assertion is Clark's return to a question of whether or not NT interpreters can speak of an "original" text ("Theological Relevance," 16). In a vision-casting and summary genre like a "presidential address," Clark's statements may be intended to raise questions, rather than to position his suggestions among the answers to those questions. When Farmer took up Clark's suggestion that the question of the Markan ending remained open, Farmer remained within the typical paradigm of authentic versus inauthentic (e.g., *Last Twelve Verses*, 79). Although Riddle and Clark's perspective may speak for only a segment of text critics, their approach has only gained support since Clark's address. For the genesis and spread of this idea, see Epp, "Multivalence," 271–5.

[73] See Epp, "Multivalence." Of especial interest is his analysis of the two benchmark text-critical manuals of our time, the Alands' and Metzger's (251–2). In summary, Epp finds that their methods and aims often remain unstated, defaulting instead to the *praxis* of text criticism. Late in their respective volumes, a statement of a goal—finding the original text of the NT—is eventually made. But elsewhere each author also hedges with caveats like "*most nearly* [emphasis added] conforming to the original" (Bruce M. Metzger and Bart D. Ehrman, *The Text of the New Testament: Its Transmission, Corruption, and Restoration* [4th ed.; New York: Oxford University Press, 2005], xv).

[74] Epp, "Multivalence," 253. He continues,

> It should be clear that this review of handbooks on New Testament textual criticism has yielded little clarity regarding the use or meaning of "original text," and it is for this reason that I have pursued the matter at length—precisely to make the point that over the greater part of two centuries virtually no discussion of this matter is to be found in the very volumes that have been the major guides in the theory and practice of the discipline. (253–4)

Epp subsequently states that there are a few exceptions to this lack of clarity in text-critical theory, with which he deals in more detail.

Interpreters, then, might be surprised to consider what difference such an ending makes to the reading of Mark.[75]

My study attempts to take seriously on a limited scale Epp's general suggestion for "fresh insights" in text criticism: "Recognizing the multivalence of 'original text' ensures that New Testament textual criticism will certainly diminish and possibly relinquish its myopic concentration on an elusive and often illusive target of a single original text."[76] In theorizing about Mark's original (and inaccessible) ending, I do not wish to ignore its many other *actual* endings.

By effectively fusing the text's canonical status with conjectures about the text's history,[77] the conventional approach—in which only the "authentic" ending of Mark deserves interpretation—sidesteps valid and important functions the LE has served. I submit that the question of whether or not the LE *should* be read as scripture be sidelined in favor of an observation of how it functions as an ending. Furthermore, interpreting the LE's narrative reveals how it crystallizes a particular reading of the text to which it became integral.[78] That is, noting the twelve disciples' persistent faithlessness and the overwhelmingly positive portrayals of women in Mk 1:1–16:8 are not available merely to modern readers. Treating the LE both as a conclusion to Mark and a reception of that same Gospel illustrates that these narrative threads stood out to ancient readers as well.

3.3 The Significance of the Long Ending for an NT Critical Commonplace about Women

It has become nearly axiomatic in recent NT studies that the early Christian movement underwent an early and swift decline from an egalitarian, structurally free, and diverse group to a patriarchal at times misogynistic and authoritarian organization bent on uniformity in theology and practice. Indeed, signals of developing restrictions to women's involvement in the early church have been found in the NT texts.[79]

---

[75] Several already do so quite well, of course; two good examples are Black, *Mark*, and Collins, *Mark: A Commentary*.
[76] Epp, "Multivalence," 270.
[77] For an example to the contrary, see Tregelles, *Printed Text*, 257–8; see also a discussion thereof in section 3 of Chapter 1.
[78] Perhaps more significant than reaffirming a particular way of reading Mark or Mark's ending, the LE may be in part responsible for the fact that Mark continued to be *read at all*: "It is quite possible that the 'longer' ending of Mark, with its post-resurrection appearances, 'could have functioned to bring' Mark's gospel into harmony with the fourfold collection,' and in this fashion influenced the canonical process" (Epp, "Issues in the Interrelation of New Testament Textual Criticism and Canon," in *Perspectives on New Testament Textual Criticism: Collected Essays, 1962–2004* [NTSup 116; Boston: Brill, 2005], 635; repr. from *The Canon Debate* [ed. Lee Martin McDonald and James A. Sanders; Peabody, MA: Hendrickson, 2002]; the internal quotation citing Brevard S. Childs, *The New Testament as Canon: An Introduction* [Philadelphia: Fortress, 1984], 51–2).
[79] See note 86 for some pertinent references. See Monika Fander's recent, selective summary of (English- and German-language) feminist evaluations of Mark ("Gospel of Mark: Women as True Disciples of Jesus," in *Feminist Biblical Interpretation: A Compendium of Critical Commentary on the Books of the Bible and Related Literature* [ed. Luisa Schottroff and Marie-Theres Wacker; trans. Lisa E. Dahill et al.; Grand Rapids: Eerdmans, 2012], 626–7).

A preeminent and formative feminist interpreter has depended on just such a trajectory from empowered to repressed women for their reconstructions of early Christian communities.[80]

Judith Lieu's brief but careful treatment of the women in the canonical empty tomb and resurrection narratives (absent the LE) is undertaken without an explicit feminist hermeneutic. Her exploration is surely gynocentric but traces development without assuming access to the prehistory of the texts. Her tone shifts as she approaches her conclusion:

> New Testament tradition has lost all traces of these women on the pages of the history of the early Church, even of Mary Magdalene, whose persistence in the tradition sounds the strongest ring of truth: only the mother of Jesus of those at the cross (in John at least!) reappears in Acts. Are we not encountering the deliberate minimizing of the testimony of the women? The tradition was too resilient to be effaced, but it could be confined; restrained and retained so that the women have a voice, but a voice which declares its own limitations. The resurrection witness of the women is a witness to their own confinement.[81]

For Lieu, this "confinement" can be exemplified in each Gospel tradition, which "(re)asserts the authority of male leadership by propelling the narrative towards its 'proper' climax": Jesus's appearance to and commissioning of exclusively male disciples.[82]

In one of the most popular handbooks on NT textual criticism, Metzger and Ehrman include a section dealing with burgeoning subfields of text criticism in which social-historical contexts and extant manuscripts can be mutually informative.[83] The authors suggest that more work needs to be done with regard to what the manuscript history of the NT reveals about the changing position of women in early Christianity. It is noteworthy, however, that their expectations for what textual variants might reveal are limited, as the following quotation demonstrates, to adverse changes: "The significance of textual problems for assessing *the oppression of women* in early Christianity ... still await[s] an extensive and rigorous analysis."[84] Indeed, the section headings show the one-way expectation. In a chapter subsection entitled "The Use of Textual Data for the Social History of Early Christianity," the authors include six areas in which scholars have utilized text-critical data to contribute to what we know about the social-historical developments in the Christian movement.[85] These categories include: (1) doctrinal disputes of early Christianity, (2) Jewish-Christian relations, (3) the oppression of women in early Christianity, (4) Christian apologia, (5) Christian asceticism, and

---

[80] See Elizabeth Schüssler Fiorenza, *In Memory of Her: A Feminist Theological Reconstruction of Christian Origins* (New York: Crossroad, 1983).
[81] Lieu, "Women's Resurrection Testimony," 42.
[82] Ibid., 41–2.
[83] Metzger and Ehrman, *Text of the New Testament*, 280–99.
[84] Ibid., 290; italics added. This section's closing statement calls for more systematic study of text variants concerning women, a lacuna that my project partially fills. Nonetheless, it is telling that the authors' presumption is that textual changes were only made to the detriment of women.
[85] Ibid., 280–1.

(6) the use of magic and fortune-telling in early Christianity.[86] Notice that the one topic among these six in which the title is *not* expressed neutrally is that of the treatment of women in early Christianity[87]; "oppression" is the assumed experience of women to which text-critical discoveries might contribute and which the authors prescribe.

I do not mean to say that this trajectory of oppression does not exist. In some places and in some texts there are manifest attempts to limit and to control the leadership of women and their expression of faith.[88] The Pastoral Epistles offer key examples, evidencing a regression in the liberties and roles permitted women in comparison to the uncontested Pauline letters.[89] Even within the undisputed Pauline corpus, there are wide variations—perhaps based on divergent local contexts and changed circumstances—in expectations for women believers.[90]

As an alteration of a text in the direction of upholding women's faithful discipleship, it is noteworthy that the second-century amendment of the text that is the LE was the one that became accepted and effectively canonized along with the Gospel to which it was affixed. Had there been a widespread campaign to suppress the involvement of women in Jesus's ministry and the early church, surely such an addition could never have survived, much less become so prevalent.

A textual variant that moves in the direction evidenced by Mark's LE—both corroborating proto-orthodoxy and a nascent Four-Gospel Canon, while not conforming to cultural commonplaces—is not the kind of textual modification that modern interpreters have conditioned themselves to expect. While the LE may be exceptional in the realm of NT text variants, with respect to its length and degree of impact on the text that it alters, it illustrates the point that scribal variations do not "correct" texts in uniform or predictable directions.

4. Conclusion: The Long Ending Canonizes Mary Magdalene's Witness

Attention to the narrative shape and exegetical consequences of the LE, rather than focusing on its textual origins, allows interpreters access to evidence for the problems

---

[86] Ibid., 280–99.

[87] By comparison, the first topic is not formulated as "Heresies in Early Christianity," nor is the sixth "Abuses of Magic."

[88] Lieu's essay "The Women's Resurrection Testimony" highlights the ways in which the Gospels may evidence a willful restriction of women's roles. Metzger and Ehrman cite several Pauline examples (*Text of the New Testament*, 289–90 n. 45–6).

[89] Both 1 Timothy (esp. 2:9-15) and Titus (2:3-5) illustrate a considerable restriction of women's roles even within the canonized Pauline tradition, in contrast to Gal. 3:28, Paul's references to female associates (Euodia and Syntyche who "co-labored" [συναθλέω; Phil. 4:2-3]; Prisca and her husband Aquila [described as συνεργός; Rom. 16:3; cf. 1 Cor. 16:19]; Phoebe who is a patron [προστάτις; Rom. 16:1-2]; Mary who labored [κοπιάω; Rom. 16:6]; Junia, kinsperson and noteworthy among the apostles [ἐπίσημοι ἐν τοῖς ἀποστόλοις; Rom. 16:7]), reservations about marriage (1 Cor. 7), and even instructions on women's mandated head-coverings that assume their praying and prophesying (1 Cor. 11:5).

[90] A case in point is the much-discussed charge that women/wives be silent in church (1 Cor. 14:33b-36) as compared with 11:5, 13, which presupposes female prophecy in the church at worship.

its author sought to address—and, in that process, to restrain our preoccupation with things that may trouble us. Our reading has demonstrated several aspects of the *kind* of ending that the LE provides for Mark. It is a canonically referential ending. It heightens characterizations of both female and male disciples, based on trends in the body of the Second Gospel (thus, Chapters 2 and 3). It is an ending that corrects the faithlessness of the Eleven only after repairing the image of Mary Magdalene's discipleship. These tendencies do not fit comfortably within the boundaries of normal gender expectations in the Greco-Roman world. While this might be an accidental result of the traditions the author of the LE combined, it remains the case that its episodes do not hit the points of conformity to ancient gender norms. Several factors in its portrayal—Mary as reliable proclaimer and model of faithful following, but the Eleven as inappropriately weepy unbelievers—appear to be toying with, perhaps subverting, gender expectations in order to draw attention to the right posture of discipleship.

What the variety of texts from the early centuries of Christianity demonstrate, however, is that perceptions of women's roles were varied. There are exceptions—even significant ones—to any perceptible downturn in women's roles in the Christian movement. The LE is just such an exception. For Mary Magdalene's role is not covered up, passed by, treated as already resolved (in 16:8); it is reintroduced and reinforced. The male disciples are reintroduced, not as the culmination of the church's hope, but rather as culminating a failure of faith that has plagued them throughout the Second Gospel. Jesus vindicates the reliability of Mary's witness, which is equally valid to that of two male disciples. When, at long last, Jesus commissions the Eleven, which the author of the LE presents as their effective redemption, their faithful discipleship confirms the basic pattern of *going and telling* that Mary sets in motion in 16:10.

Appendix

The Many Endings to Mark's Gospel: Introductions, Text, and Translations

Opening one's critical edition of the Greek NT, or most English versions,[1] the end of Mark ch. 16 may appear like a "choose-your-own-adventure" novel. The presentation of Mark's various extant endings ranges from informative to misleading. Even within the most critically accepted editions of the Greek NT, the Nestle-Aland[28] and the UBS[4], the series of brackets housing the various passages found at Mark's conclusion can cause misunderstanding. Tables A.1 and A.2 clarify how Mark's endings are configured across the manuscript tradition. The Intermediate Ending (discussed later in the chapter) is in second position, after 16:8, even though it is far more narrowly attested than the Long Ending (hereafter LE) and appears as "an ending" in its own right in only one extant manuscript. The LE is listed second, as though it were an "option" roughly equivalent to the Intermediate; this obscures the fact that for the majority of church history this is the ending of Mark in nearly every manuscript in circulation. Finally, the Freer Logion is relegated to a footnote, likely because it is known only from one Greek manuscript; yet it is attested by Jerome, which is more than can be said for the Intermediate Ending's patristic support.

Whether one remains thoroughly convinced that the shortest extant ending at 16:8 is the original conclusion to the Second Gospel, or, conversely, is a staunch defender of the *Textus Receptus*, or any view in-between, an awareness of the textual alternatives is indispensable. As Parker emphasizes:

> The fact that we have decided that the Intermediate and Long Endings are secondary does not mean that we have forgotten that they exist, or that we can now read Mark with its Short Ending as though we had never read it with its Long Ending … Thus, even if one insists on a single original text of Mark, one cannot escape the need to be aware of the fact that all the text forms affect our interpretation of it. This fact is true whichever ending one believes to be original. So, while readers of the Bible are in disagreement with regard to the text of Mark which they read, they have this in common—the different forms in which the text exists.[2]

A table comparing the endings of Mark, arranged in parallel columns, is presented in this Appendix.
[1] Among the exceptions are the KJV, Jerusalem Bible, and CEV (which has noticeable, all-capitalized headings to the Long and Intermediate Endings that read "One Old Ending to Mark's Gospel" and "Another Old Ending to Mark's Gospel," respectively).
[2] D. C. Parker, *The Living Text of the Gospels* (New York: Cambridge University Press, 1997), 147.

Indeed, in the case of Mark, interpreters have been granted uncommon insight into *how else* its conclusion was communicated. Rather than trading in conjecture, we are privy to several different ways in which the Gospel according to Mark *actually* ends. Each way has its own emphases and ambiguities. As will become obvious, all endings were not created (or received) equally: the manuscript attestation of each ending or combination of endings is uneven, with some found in very few manuscripts and others widely represented. Instead of the order in which the options are commonly presented in Greek critical editions and English versions, I will follow the order of conjectural dating—as closely as we can tell, as all the endings came into circulation relatively early—starting with the earliest recoverable ending and concluding with the latest. The degree of attestation, along with the chief witnesses for the reading, will be noted within each section.

We suspect that Mark was written sometime around 70 CE and that the LE was added sometime between then and the end of the second century (at which point it is plainly attested by Irenaeus).[3] The LE was likely composed in the first half of the second century (120–150).[4] There remain roughly two centuries of evidentiary silence before the master scribes copied the fine codices Sinaiticus and Vaticanus in the fourth century. These provide the earliest physical evidence we have of any form of Mark's ending, since the Chester Beatty Gospel papyri (P⁴⁵) is missing the ending of the Gospel.

1. The Shortest Ending (= at 16:8)

The oldest and most reliable manuscripts that chiefly render the LE textually suspect are Codex Sinaiticus (ℵ)[5] and Codex Vaticanus (B).[6] Both end the Gospel at v. 8, with the words "for they were afraid" (ἐφοβοῦντο γάρ). These two uncial codices are best dated to the middle- to late-fourth century. Text critics have long counted ℵ and B among the strongest witnesses for an early textual stage in the development of the NT.

2. The Long Ending (= Longer Ending = Mk 16:9-20)

Of the ancient Markan manuscript copies, 99 percent contain the LE. Instead of stopping at 16:8, these copies carry on through 16:20. By sheer volume, this ending

---

[3] Irenaeus, *Haer.* iii.X.6. See James A. Kelhoffer, *Miracle and Mission: The Authentication of Missionaries and Their Message in the Longer Ending of Mark* (Tübingen: Mohr Siebeck, 2000), 169–75. Justin Martyr, in his *Apology* (ca. 150 CE), summarizes the disciples' post-resurrection missionary activity in a way reminiscent of the LE, but his textual source is uncertain (*1 Apol.* I.45; see Kelhoffer, *Miracle and Mission*, 172; Parker, *Living Text*, 132). Likewise, there is a good case to be made that Tatian was aware of Mark's LE and incorporated the majority of it into his Gospel Harmony (ca. 150 CE), but because of the nature of our extant versions we cannot be positive what Tatian's original (likely Syriac) actually included (see Thedor Zahn, *Tatian's Diatessaron* [Erlangen: A. Deichert, 1881], 219).

[4] See Kelhoffer, *Miracle and Mission*, 169–75.

[5] For a more complete description and history of Codex Sinaiticus, see Bruce M. Metzger and Bart D. Ehrman, *The Text of the New Testament: Its Transmission, Corruption, and Restoration* (4th ed.; New York: Oxford University Press, 2005), 62–7.

[6] For a more complete description and history of Codex Vaticanus, see ibid., 67–9.

should be the "winner" among its textual rivals.⁷ And for centuries—more than one millennium—it was the functional "champion" of the competition for the concluding text of Mark.

Such figures are misleading, however, with respect to the text-critical method, as the bulk of the manuscript data comes not from the earliest stages of the Christian movement, but much later. Antiquity trumps number in determining the best or earliest readings, although the latter is a better indicator of practical usage within the early church. Although the ending at 16:8 is represented in our two most ancient (likely fourth-century) uncials (ℵ and B), the LE has its own majuscule witnesses: from the fifth century, A C D, and from later centuries (eighth to tenth) Θ K X Δ Π; as well as witnesses that contain a "variation" on the LE. Lists of manuscript evidence for the endings of Mark often obscure the fact that witnesses for two other ending-arrangements *actually* testify to the LE as well: from the late fourth or early fifth century, W merely expands the LE (with an interpolation between vv. 14 and 15)⁸; from the seventh, eighth, and ninth centuries, L Ψ 099 0112 include the Intermediate Ending (see I.2.iii below) before continuing into the full LE.⁹ Miniscules, too, attest to the LE of Mark: the ninth-century "queen of the cursives," 33; the eleventh-century, 28; and representatives from the Ferrar group of closely related miniscule, f^{13} among others.¹⁰ Further, Latin, Harclean Syriac, as well as many Ethiopic and Bohairic versions,¹¹ contain the LE. The LE is *the Markan ending* in the Majority Text, the Latin Vulgate, and, subsequently, the King James Version, which accounts for its widespread acceptance as the conclusion of the Second Gospel until the modern era.

The critical Greek text and author's translation of Mk 16:9-20

⁹ Ἀναστὰς δὲ πρωῒ πρώτῃ σαββάτου ἐφάνη πρῶτον Μαρίᾳ τῇ Μαγδαληνῇ, παρ᾽ ἧς ἐκβεβλήκει ἑπτὰ δαιμόνια. ¹⁰ ἐκείνη πορευθεῖσα ἀπήγγειλεν τοῖς μετ᾽ αὐτοῦ γενομένοις πενθοῦσι καὶ κλαίουσιν· ¹¹ κἀκεῖνοι ἀκούσαντες ὅτι ζῇ καὶ ἐθεάθη ὑπ᾽ αὐτῆς ἠπίστησαν.

⁹ Now, after he rose early on the first day of the week, he appeared first to Mary Magdalene, out of whom he had cast seven demons. ¹⁰ After-wards she went and reported to those who had been with him, as they were mourning and weeping; ¹¹ And these men, hearing that he was alive and was seen by her, did not believe.

---

[7] The LE is found "in 99 percent of the Greek manuscripts as well as the rest of the tradition" (Kurt and Barbara Aland, *The Text of the New Testament* [2d ed.; Erroll F. Rhodes, trans.; Grand Rapids: Eerdmans, 1989], 292).

[8] See the treatment of the "Freer Logion" in section 5.

[9] An image of the LE of Codex L is available in Aland and Aland, *Text of the New Testament*, plate 29, p. 112.

[10] For descriptions of these and many more important manuscripts, see Metzger and Ehrman, *Text of the New Testament*, 62–94.

[11] The margin of the Harclean Syriac and the referenced Ethiopic and Bohairic mss are also witnesses to the Intermediate Ending (as are L Ψ 099 0112, mentioned earlier as containing both texts).

¹² Μετὰ δὲ ταῦτα δυσὶν ἐξ αὐτῶν περιπατοῦσιν ἐφανερώθη ἐν ἑτέρᾳ μορφῇ πορευομένοις εἰς ἀγρόν· ¹³ κἀκεῖνοι ἀπελθόντες ἀπήγγειλαν τοῖς λοιποῖς· οὐδὲ ἐκείνοις ἐπίστευσαν. ¹⁴ Ὕστερον δὲ ἀνακειμένοις αὐτοῖς τοῖς ἕνδεκα ἐφανερώθη καὶ ὠνείδισεν τὴν ἀπιστίαν αὐτῶν καὶ σκληροκαρδίαν ὅτι τοῖς θεασαμένοις αὐτὸν ἐγηγερμένον οὐκ ἐπίστευσαν. ¹⁵ καὶ εἶπεν αὐτοῖς· πορευθέντες εἰς τὸν κόσμον ἅπαντα κηρύξατε τὸ εὐαγγέλιον πάσῃ τῇ κτίσει. ¹⁶ ὁ πιστεύσας καὶ βαπτισθεὶς σωθήσεται, ὁδὲ ἀπιστήσας κατακριθήσεται. ¹⁷ σημεῖα δὲ τοῖς πιστεύσασιν ταῦτα παρακολ-ουθήσει· ἐν τῷ ὀνόματί μου δαιμόνια ἐκβαλοῦσιν, γλώσσαις λαλήσουσιν καιναῖς, ¹⁸ καὶ ἐν ταῖς χερσὶν ὄφεις ἀροῦσιν κἂν θανάσιμόν τι πίωσιν οὐ μὴ αὐτοὺς βλάψῃ, ἐπὶ ἀρρώστους χεῖρας ἐπιθήσουσιν καὶ καλῶς ἕξουσιν. ¹⁹ Ὁ μὲν οὖν κύριος Ἰησοῦς μετὰ τὸ λαλῆσαι αὐτοῖς ἀνελήμφθη εἰς τὸν οὐρανὸν καὶ ἐκάθισεν ἐκ δεξιῶν τοῦ θεοῦ. ²⁰ ἐκεῖνοι δὲ ἐξελθόντες ἐκήρυξαν πανταχοῦ, τοῦ κυρίου συνεργοῦντος καὶ τὸν λόγον βεβαιοῦντος διὰ τῶν ἐπακολουθούντων σημείων.	¹² After these things, he was revealed in a different form to two of them as they walked into the country. ¹³ And although they went and reported to the rest, neither did those ones believe. ¹⁴ Finally, he was revealed to the Eleven while they were reclining at table, and he upbraided them for their unbelief and hardheartedness, because they did not believe those who witnessed that he had been raised up. ¹⁵ And he said to them, "Going into the whole world, preach the gospel to all creation. ¹⁶ The one who believes and is baptized will be saved, but the one who disbelieves will be condemned. ¹⁷ Now, signs will follow closely those who believe; In my name they will cast out demons, they will speak in new tongues, ¹⁸ they will take up snakes in their hands and, should they drink any poison, it will certainly not harm them, they will lay hands on the sick and they will be well. ¹⁹ So then, after speaking to them, the Lord Jesus was taken up into heaven and sat at the right hand of God. ²⁰ And they went out and preached everywhere, because the Lord was working with them and confirming the word through the signs that were following.

Many of this ending's narrative elements noticeably replicate (or harmonize) pieces from other Gospels' accounts.

3. The Intermediate Ending (= Shorter Ending)

"Intermediate" is the better description of the ending of Mark that is listed first among the current Greek critical editions' (NA²⁸ and UBS⁴) bracketed expansions to Mark 16. It is often labeled the "Shorter Ending," but such nomenclature is misleading because these two sentences of text comprise *the ending* of Mark in only one manuscript (an Old Latin version, discussed later). Aside from this one exception, the Intermediate

The critical Greek text and author's translation of the intermediate ending

Πάντα δὲ τὰ παρηγγελμένα τοῖς περὶ τὸν Πέτρον συντόμως ἐξήγγειλαν. Μετὰ δὲ ταῦτα καὶ αὐτὸς ὅἸησοῦς ἀπὸ ἀνατολῆς καὶ ἄχρι δύσεως ἐξαπέστειλεν δι' αὐτῶν τὸ ἱερὸν καὶ ἄφθαρτον κήρυγμα τῆς αἰωνίου σωτηρίας. ἀμήν.	But they [the women] proclaimed briefly all that they were commanded to those around Peter. Now, after these things Jesus himself sent forth through them, from east to west, the sacred and incorruptible message of eternal salvation. Amen.

Ending acts as a bridge between 16:8 and 16:9-20, often with other editorial notes (see I.2.iv, below), in every other instance in which it appears.

As noted here, in most of the Intermediate Ending's attestations it serves to connect the LE to the women's fear and silence in 16:8. The exception is the African Old Latin Codex Bobiensis (it[k] or k),[12] in which the ending appears on its own and concludes the Second Gospel. Codex Bobiensis is exceptional in two other ways: (1) It is the earliest extant instance of the Intermediate Ending, dating to the fourth or fifth century; and (2) it has a unique addition earlier in the chapter, between vv. 3 and 4.[13]

This intermediary passage continues with greater fluidity from 16:8 than does the LE. That is, in summary, the Intermediate Ending contains: no restatement of time (unlike 16:9); no change of subjects (Mary Magdalene and, though unnamed, Jesus in 16:9)[14]; and Peter, central and named among the recipients of the message (as is expected by 16:7). The first sentence succeeds in gathering the narrative strands that 16:8 left dangling. Its mild adversative δὲ acknowledges a slight contrast from the silence of the women narrated in 16:8 and informs readers, instead, that the women conveyed the whole message (πάντα) to the intended recipients.

---

[12] Bridget Gilfillan Upton's chapter on the "Shorter Ending" collects and explains details on Codex Bobiensis, even arranging a comparison with the NA[27] and the RSV (*Hearing Mark's Endings: Listening to Ancient Popular Texts Through Speech Act Theory* [Boston: Brill, 2006], 171–80).

[13] The conclusion to the women's question to one another in v. 3 ("Who will remove the stone from the door of the tomb [ἐκ τῆς θύρας τοῦ μνημείου;] for us?") ends more concisely, *ab osteo?*, and leads into the following, unparalleled statement: *subito autem ad horam tertiam tenebrae diei factae sunt per totum orbem terrae, et descenderunt de caelis angeli et surgent in claritate vivi Dei; simul ascenderunt cum eo et continuo lux facta est* (NA[28]). Parker translates the variant: "But suddenly at the third hour of the day it became dark throughout the world, and angels descended from heaven and rising in the glory of the living God at once ascended with him, and immediately it became light" (*Living Text*, 125–6). For more on Codex Bobiensis, although lacking discussion of the Markan ending in the manuscript, see Adolphine Henriëtte Annette Bakker, *A Study of Codex Evang. Bobbiensis (k): Part I* (Amsterdam: N.V. Noord-Hollandsche Uitgeversmaatschappij, 1933). See also Gilfillan Upton, *Hearing Mark's Endings*, 171–80.

[14] These first two observations are evident in a narrative comparison of the Intermediate Ending to 16:9, the first verse of the LE. Regarding the comparatively ill fit of 16:9 with the preceding text, Parker observes, "There is no resumption of the theme of fear and silence in verse 8, and Mary Magdalene is introduced afresh in verse 9, as though she were not already on stage" (*Living Text*, 138).

Metzger comments about the Intermediate Ending, "No one who had available as the conclusion of the Second Gospel the twelve verses 9–20, so rich in interesting material, would have deliberately replaced them with a few lines of a colorless and generalized summary."[15] Thus, for the Intermediate Ending's origin, Metzger's hypothesizes a scenario in which the LE was absent. The Intermediate Ending reads like another instance of an attempt to bring closure to an ending of Mark that was considered unsatisfactory. Unfortunately, we have no evidence, except in the aforementioned Old Latin manuscript (*k*), that it functioned in this way. We cannot know whether it was a perceived deficiency of 16:8, the disjuncture or lack of narrative transition between vv. 8 and 9, or perhaps some perceived inadequacy of the LE, less obvious to modern interpreters, that motivated the composition of this brief text. Nonetheless, the second sentence, along with its benedictory ἀμήν (missing in L and Coptic and Ethiopic versions[16]), seems less like a transition and more like a conclusion. Indeed, the absence of "amen" in several manuscripts, in which the LE follows, signals that ancient scribes might have found a concluding "amen" inappropriate when the story continued in 16:9-20. With or without the "amen," however, the summary tone of both sentences, and especially the description of "the sacred and incorruptible message of eternal salvation," smacks of a brief but earnest attempt to craft Mark's grand finale.

4. Textual Obeli, Sigla, and Annotations at the Ending in the Manuscripts

Frequently, scribes used obeli and other markings or notes to signify that the text they were copying was debated at a certain point. These "asterisks" are not, in themselves, another ending for Mark; rather, the symbols and annotations accompany several combinations of Markan endings. One example of symbols functioning on their own is the tenth-century miniscule 274, which includes a symbol F0F8 in the left margin next to the final line of 16:8 (comprising just two syllables, -το γάρ). The line of text itself breaks with a series of symbols and a wide space, after which begins the text of the LE (Ἀναστὰς δέ), which continues uninterrupted. Then, in the lower margin of the page, there are five lines of text: the Intermediate Ending, written in a smaller hand of typically majuscule characters. To the left of these five lines are five symbols in a horizontal row: the same symbol F0F8 that acted as a footnote in the margins of the text above.[17]

Decorations also accompany some scribal notes. The eighth-century Codex Regius (L) includes a line of decorations (best described as tiny squiggles, resembling

---

[15] Bruce M. Metzger, *A Textual Commentary on the Greek New Testament* (2d ed.; Stuttgart: Deutsche Bibelgesellschaft, 1994), 105. As a result of this observation, Metzger takes the Intermediate Ending as evidence in favor of 16:8 being "the earliest ascertainable form" of Mark (ibid.).

[16] An image of the LE of Codex L is available in Aland and Aland, *Text of the New Testament*, plate 29, p. 112.

[17] An image of this page of ms. 274 is available in ibid., 324, fig. 25. The caption's text, however, is somewhat misleading. Instead of showing the full text of 16:6-20 and the Intermediate Ending, the page shown ends in the middle of v. 15 (with a marking after ἅπαντα, which may be the start of the next word, κηρύξατε).

the Arabic numerals "2" or "3") underneath the final lines of 16:8. At the top of the next column, decorations form a box (squiggles form the vertical lines; dashes create the horizontal) around a note that reads, "This also is in circulation." The text of the Intermediate Ending follows. Another decorative box encloses a second note: "This also is in circulation after εφοβουντο γαρ." The text of the LE follows.[18]

The significance of this widespread, yet not universal, phenomenon among scribes is that it illustrates their conservative, or preservationist, tendencies. Even when certain readings were known to be in question, it was considered better to perpetuate than to excise them. This practice is made more explicit in several patristic witnesses to the debate over the LE.

5. The Freer Logion within the Long Ending

In his polemical *Dialogue against the Pelagians*, Jerome sets up as debate between two representative figures, Atticus (the "Christian," who speaks, ostensibly, for Jerome) and Critobulus (the "Pelagian"). Unsurprisingly, Atticus gets far more lines in this dialogue and, by the second book, moves into a monologue in which he cites lines from scripture, gathered by theme, to argue for the inability of humans to live without sin.[19] It is in this context that Jerome (as Atticus) quotes from copies of Mark with which he is familiar:

> In certain copies and especially in Greek codices, according to Mark at the end of his Gospel, is written: *Afterward, while the Eleven were reclining at table, he appeared, and he excoriated them for their disbelief and hardness of heart, because they had not believed those who had seen him risen. And they apologized saying: 'This age of iniquity and disbelief is under Satan, who does not allow the true virtue of God to be understood because of unclean spirits; therefore, reveal your righteousness now.'* If you contradict that, you will certainly not dare to decline this: *The world is situated in wickedness*, (Jerome, *Pelag*. II.15,1–9; emphasis in the original)[20]

The first line of Jerome's Markan quotation is a straightforward translation of Mk 16:14 from the LE. The last line of the excerpt quotes 1 Jn 5:19. But the source of the second line that Jerome attributes to Mark was a mystery to readers of Jerome for most of subsequent history, as the text from which it came was lost. The citation was generally

---

[18] An image of the folio under discussion (113r) is printed in John William Burgon, *The Last Twelve Verses of Mark: Vindicated against Recent Critical Objectors and Established* (Oxford: James Parker, 1871), 126. Burgon's description follows on p. 127. See also Parker, *Living Text*, 127.

[19] John N. Hritzu, the translator of a standard English edition of *Dialogus adversus Pelagianos*, suggests that, compared to his contemporary Augustine, Jerome's attitude was "less hostile" and his motive seems more eager "to win than to condemn the Pelagians" ("Introduction," in *Saint Jerome: Dogmatic and Polemical Works* [FC; Washington: Catholic University of America, 1965], 223).

[20] The line numbering, throughout, and any Latin citations come from the Corpus Christianorum edition of the Latin text (Jerome [S. Hieronymi], *Dialogus Adversus Pelagianos* [Corpus Christianorum; Series Latina LXXX; Pars III, 2; ed. C. Moreschini; Turnhout: Brepols, 1990]).

The critical Greek text and author's translation of the Freer Logion

κἀκεῖνοι ἀπελογοῦντο λέγοντες ὅτι ὁ αἰὼν οὗτος τῆς ἀνομίας καὶ τῆς ἀπιστίας ὑπὸ τὸν σατανᾶν ἐστιν, ὃ μὴ ἐῶν τὰ ὑπὸ τῶν πνευμάτων ἀκάθαρτα τὴν ἀλήθειαν τοῦ θεοῦ καταλαβέσθαι δύναμιν· διὰ τοῦτο ἀποκάλυψον σοῦ τὴν δικαιοσύνη ἤδη, ἐκεῖνοι ἔλεγον τῷ χριστῷ. καὶ ὁ χριστὸς ἐκείνοις προσέλεγεν ὅτι πεπλήρωται ὁ ὅρος τῶν ἐτῶν τῆς ἐξουσίας τοῦ σατανᾶ, ἀλλὰ ἐγγίζει ἄλλα δεινά· καὶ ὑπὲρ ὧν ἐγὼ ἁμαρτησάντων παρεδόθην εἰς θάνατον ἵνα ὑποστρέψωσιν εἰς τὴν ἀλήθειαν καὶ μηκέτι ἁμαρτήσωσιν ἵνα τὴν ἐν τῷ οὐρανῷ πνευματικὴν καὶ ἄφθαρτον τῆς δικαιοσύνης δόξαν κληρονομήσωσιν.[21]	And they [the Eleven] defended themselves saying, "This age of lawlessness and unbelief is under Satan, who does not permit the truth [and] power of God to overtake the unclean things of the spirits; therefore, reveal your righteousness now." And Christ addressed them, "The limit of the years of Satan's authority have been fulfilled, but other dreadful things are drawing near; And for those who sinned I myself was handed over to death, in order that they might return to the truth and no longer sin, so that they might inherit the spiritual and incorruptible glory of righteousness in heaven."
Compared with Jerome, Pelag. II.15.5–8: *Et illi satisfaciebant dicentes: Saeculum istud iniquitatis et incredulitatis sub Satana est, qui non sinit per immundos spiritus ueram Dei apprehendi uirtutem: idcirco iam nunc reuela iustitiam tuam.*[22]	And they apologized saying, "This age of iniquity and disbelief is under Satan, who does not allow the true virtue of God to be understood because of unclean spirits; therefore, reveal your righteousness now."

ignored until an ancient Gospel codex surfaced and was acquired by Charles L. Freer in 1906.

The discovery and subsequent study of the Freer Gospels Codex (or Codex Washingtonianus, W), which dates to the late fourth or fifth century, cast light on this long-dismissed statement of Jerome's.[23] The hand of the scribe of Codex Washingtonianus

---

[21] Jerome, *Pelag.* II.15.5–8. The NA[28] editors include *substantia* rather than *sub Satana*, which they include in parentheses with a question mark. The latter seems far more likely, as Jerome refers to the text of the LE and the first line of the Freer Logion, translated in Latin with great accuracy. Parker also favors the *sub Satana* reading because of its correlation to the Greek text of W (*Living Text*, 128, n. 2). The variant *substantia* would more likely have surfaced later, in a context unfamiliar with the Greek text to which Jerome refers. I presume the NA[28] editors prefer *substantia* because it is the "harder" reading of the two and makes much less sense in the context.

[22] The Greek text is from the Nestle-Aland's textual apparatus (cf. NA[28], p. 176). Parenthetical annotations pointing to editorial uncertainties—e.g., "(+ και *vel* αληθινην *pro* αληθειαν?)" inserted between καταλαβέσθαι and δύναμιν—have been omitted, as I have translated the text the editors preferred.

[23] A statement by Burgon, written in 1871 and quite amusing in retrospect, is written in his characteristically argumentative fashion:

> Jerome, on a point like this [i.e., the attestation of Mk 16:9-20], is entitled to more attention than any other Father of the Church ... endowed with extraordinary Biblical learning, ... his testimony is most weighty. Not unaware am I that Jerome is commonly supposed to be a witness on the opposite side [due to his "mistake"] ... But it ought to be enough to point out that we should not have met with these last twelve verses in the Vulgate, had Jerome held them to be spurious ... He makes the extraordinary statement that in certain of the copies, (especially the Greek), was found after ver. 14 *the reply of the eleven Apostles*, when our Saviour "upbraided them with their unbelief and hardness of heart, because they believed not them which had seen Him after He was risen." To discuss so weak and worthless a forgery,—no trace of which is found in any MS. in existence, and of which nothing whatever is known except what Jerome here tells us,—would be to waste our time indeed. (*Last Twelve*, 28; emphasis in the original)

Table A.1 Synoptic table of the Greek text of Markan endings (excluding obeli)

Shortest Ending, Mk 16:8	Long Ending, Mk 16:8 + 16:9–20	Intermediate Ending + Long Ending, Mk 16:8 + Int. End. + 16:9–20	Intermediate Ending (as in Codex *k*), Mk 16:8 + Int. End.	Long Ending + Freer Logion (as in Codex W), Mk 16:8 + 16:9–14 + Freer Logion + 16:15–20
...⁸ Καὶ ἐξελθοῦσαι ἔφυγον ἀπὸ τοῦ μνημείου, εἶχεν γὰρ αὐτὰς τρόμος καὶ ἔκστασις· καὶ οὐδενὶ οὐδὲν εἶπαν· ἐφοβοῦντο γάρ.	...⁸ Καὶ ἐξελθοῦσαι ἔφυγον ἀπὸ τοῦ μνημείου, εἶχεν γὰρ αὐτὰς τρόμος καὶ ἔκστασις· καὶ οὐδενὶ οὐδὲν εἶπαν· ἐφοβοῦντο γάρ. ⁹ Ἀναστὰς δὲ πρωῒ πρώτῃ σαββάτου ἐφάνη πρῶτον Μαρίᾳ τῇ Μαγδαληνῇ, παρ᾽ ἧς ἐκβεβλήκει ἑπτὰ δαιμόνια. ¹⁰ ἐκείνη πορευθεῖσα ἀπήγγειλεν τοῖς μετ᾽ αὐτοῦ γενομένοις πενθοῦσι καὶ κλαίουσιν· ¹¹ κἀκεῖνοι ἀκούσαντες ὅτι ζῇ καὶ ἐθεάθη ὑπ᾽ αὐτῆς ἠπίστησαν. ¹² Μετὰ δὲ ταῦτα δυσὶν ἐξ αὐτῶν περιπατοῦσιν ἐφανερώθη ἐν ἑτέρᾳ μορφῇ πορευομένοις εἰς ἀγρόν· ¹³ κἀκεῖνοι ἀπελθόντες ἀπήγγειλαν τοῖς λοιποῖς· οὐδὲ ἐκείνοις ἐπίστευσαν. ¹⁴Ὕστερον δὲ ἀνακειμένοις αὐτοῖς τοῖς ἕνδεκα ἐφανερώθη καὶ ὠνείδισεν τὴν ἀπιστίαν αὐτῶν καὶ σκληροκαρδίαν ὅτι τοῖς θεασαμένοις αὐτὸν ἐγηγερμένον οὐκ ἐπίστευσαν. ¹⁵ καὶ εἶπεν αὐτοῖς· πορευθέντες	...⁸ Καὶ ἐξελθοῦσαι ἔφυγον ἀπὸ τοῦ μνημείου, εἶχεν γὰρ αὐτὰς ἔκστασις· καὶ οὐδενὶ οὐδὲν εἶπαν· ἐφοβοῦντο γάρ. Πάντα δὲ τὰ παρηγγελμένα τοῖς περὶ τὸν Πέτρον συντόμως ἐξήγγειλαν. Μετὰ δὲ ταῦτα καὶ αὐτὸς ὁ Ἰησοῦς ἀπὸ ἀνατολῆς καὶ ἄχρι δύσεως ἐξαπέστειλεν δι᾽ αὐτῶν τὸ ἱερὸν καὶ ἄφθαρτον κήρυγμα τῆς αἰωνίου σωτηρίας. [ἀμήν] ⁹ Ἀναστὰς δὲ πρωῒ πρώτῃ σαββάτου ἐφάνη πρῶτον Μαρίᾳ τῇ Μαγδαληνῇ, παρ᾽ ἧς ἐκβεβλήκει ἑπτὰ δαιμόνια. ¹⁰ ἐκείνη πορευθεῖσα ἀπήγγειλεν τοῖς μετ᾽ αὐτοῦ γενομένοις πενθοῦσι καὶ κλαίουσιν· ¹¹ κἀκεῖνοι ἀκούσαντες ὅτι ζῇ καὶ ἐθεάθη ὑπ᾽ αὐτῆς ἠπίστησαν. ¹² Μετὰ δὲ ταῦτα δυσὶν ἐξ αὐτῶν περιπατοῦσιν ἐφανερώθη ἐν ἑτέρᾳ μορφῇ πορευομένοις εἰς ἀγρόν· ¹³ κἀκεῖνοι ἀπελθόντες ἀπήγγειλαν τοῖς λοιποῖς· οὐδὲ ἐκείνοις ἐπίστευσαν.	...⁸ Καὶ ἐξελθοῦσαι ἔφυγον ἀπὸ τοῦ μνημείου, εἶχεν γὰρ αὐτὰς τρόμος καὶ ἔκστασις· καὶ οὐδενὶ οὐδὲν εἶπαν· ἐφοβοῦντο γάρ. Πάντα δὲ τὰ παρηγγελμένα τοῖς περὶ τὸν Πέτρον συντόμως ἐξήγγειλαν. Μετὰ δὲ ταῦτα καὶ αὐτὸς ὁ Ἰησοῦς ἀπὸ ἀνατολῆς καὶ ἄχρι δύσεως ἐξαπέστειλεν δι᾽ αὐτῶν τὸ ἱερὸν καὶ ἄφθαρτον κήρυγμα τῆς αἰωνίου σωτηρίας. ἀμήν.	...⁸ Καὶ ἐξελθοῦσαι ἔφυγον ἀπὸ τοῦ μνημείου, εἶχεν γὰρ αὐτὰς τρόμος καὶ ἔκστασις· καὶ οὐδενὶ οὐδὲν εἶπαν· ἐφοβοῦντο γάρ. ⁹ Ἀναστὰς δὲ πρωῒ πρώτῃ σαββάτου ἐφάνη πρῶτον Μαρίᾳ τῇ Μαγδαληνῇ, παρ᾽ ἧς ἐκβεβλήκει ἑπτὰ δαιμόνια. ¹⁰ ἐκείνη πορευθεῖσα ἀπήγγειλεν τοῖς μετ᾽ αὐτοῦ γενομένοις πενθοῦσι καὶ κλαίουσιν· ¹¹ κἀκεῖνοι ἀκούσαντες ὅτι ζῇ καὶ ἐθεάθη ὑπ᾽ αὐτῆς ἠπίστησαν. ¹² Μετὰ δὲ ταῦτα δυσὶν ἐξ αὐτῶν περιπατοῦσιν ἐφανερώθη ἐν ἑτέρᾳ μορφῇ πορευομένοις εἰς ἀγρόν· ¹³ κἀκεῖνοι ἀπελθόντες ἀπήγγειλαν τοῖς λοιποῖς· οὐδὲ ἐκείνοις ἐπίστευσαν. ¹⁴Ὕστερον δὲ ἀνακειμένοις αὐτοῖς τοῖς ἕνδεκα ἐφανερώθη καὶ ὠνείδισεν αὐτῶν τὴν ἀπιστίαν αὐτῶν καὶ σκληροκαρδίαν ὅτι τοῖς θεασαμένοις αὐτὸν ἐγηγερμένον οὐκ ἐπίστευσαν.

εἰς τὸν κόσμον ἅπαντα κηρύξατε τὸ εὐαγγέλιον πάσῃ τῇ κτίσει. 16 ὁ πιστεύσας καὶ βαπτισθεὶς σωθήσεται, ὁ δὲ ἀπιστήσας κατακριθήσεται. 17 σημεῖα δὲ τοῖς πιστεύσασιν ταῦτα παρακολ–ουθήσει· ἐν τῷ ὀνόματί μου δαιμόνια ἐκβαλοῦσιν, γλώσσαις λαλήσουσιν καιναῖς, 18 καὶ ἐν ταῖς χερσὶν ὄφεις ἀροῦσιν κἂν θανάσιμόν τι πίωσιν οὐ μὴ αὐτοὺς βλάψῃ, ἐπὶ ἀρρώστους χεῖρας ἐπιθήσουσιν καὶ καλῶς ἕξουσιν.

19 Ὁ μὲν οὖν κύριος Ἰησοῦς μετὰ τὸ λαλῆσαι αὐτοῖς ἀνελήμφθη εἰς τὸν οὐρανὸν καὶ ἐκάθισεν ἐκ δεξιῶν τοῦ θεοῦ. 20 ἐκεῖνοι δὲ ἐξελθόντες ἐκήρυξαν πανταχοῦ, τοῦ κυρίου συνεργοῦντος καὶ τὸν λόγον βεβαιοῦντος διὰ τῶν ἐπακολουθ–ούντων σημείων.

14 Ὕστερον δὲ ἀνακειμένοις αὐτοῖς τοῖς ἕνδεκα ἐφανερώθη καὶ ὠνείδισεν τὴν ἀπιστίαν αὐτῶν καὶ σκληροκαρ–δίαν ὅτι τοῖς θεασαμένοις αὐτὸν ἐγηγερμένον οὐκ ἐπίστευσαν. 15 καὶ εἶπεν αὐτοῖς· πορευθέντες εἰς τὸν κόσμον ἅπαντα κηρύξατε τὸ εὐαγγέλιον πάσῃ τῇ κτίσει. 16 ὁ πιστεύσας καὶ βαπτισθεὶς σωθήσεται, ὁ δὲ ἀπιστήσας κατακριθήσεται. 17 σημεῖα δὲ τοῖς πιστεύσασιν ταῦτα παρακολ–ουθήσει· ἐν τῷ ὀνόματί μου δαιμόνια ἐκβαλοῦσιν, γλώσσαις λαλήσουσιν καιναῖς, 18 καὶ ἐν ταῖς χερσὶν ὄφεις ἀροῦσιν κἂν θανάσιμόν τι πίωσιν οὐ μὴ αὐτοὺς βλάψῃ, ἐπὶ ἀρρώστους χεῖρας ἐπιθήσουσιν καὶ καλῶς ἕξουσιν.

19 Ὁ μὲν οὖν κύριος Ἰησοῦς μετὰ τὸ λαλῆσαι αὐτοῖς ἀνελήμφθη εἰς τὸν οὐρανὸν καὶ ἐκάθισεν ἐκ δεξιῶν τοῦ θεοῦ. 20 ἐκεῖνοι δὲ ἐξελθόντες ἐκήρυξαν πανταχοῦ, τοῦ κυρίου συνεργοῦντος καὶ τὸν λόγον βεβαιοῦντος διὰ τῶν ἐπακολουθ–ούντων σημείων.

κἀκεῖνοι ἀπελογοῦντο λέγοντες ὅτι ὁ αἰὼν οὗτος, τῆς ἀνομίας καὶ τῆς ἀπιστίας ὑπὸ τὸν σαταναν ἐστιν, ὁ μὴ ἐῶν τὰ ὑπὸ τῶν πνευμάτων ἀκάθαρτα τὴν ἀλήθειαν τοῦ θεοῦ καταλαβέσθαι δύναμιν· διὰ τοῦτο ἀποκάλυψον σοῦ τὴν δικαιοσύνη ἤδη, ἐκεῖνοι ἔλεγον τῷ χριστῷ. καὶ ὁ χριστὸς ἐκείνοις προσέλεγεν ὅτι πεπλήρωται ὁ ὅρος τῶν ἐτῶν τῆς ἐξουσίας τοῦ σατανᾶ, ἀλλὰ ἐγγίζει ἄλλα δεινά· καὶ ὑπὲρ ὧν ἐγὼ ἁμαρτησάντων παρεδόθην εἰς θάνατον ἵνα ὑποστρέψωσιν εἰς τὴν ἀλήθειαν καὶ μηκέτι ἁμαρτήσωσιν ἵνα τὴν ἐν τῷ οὐρανῷ πνευματικὴν καὶ ἄφθαρτον τῆς δικαιοσύνης δόξαν κληρονομήσωσιν.

15 καὶ εἶπεν αὐτοῖς· πορευθέντες εἰς τὸν κόσμον ἅπαντα κηρύξατε τὸ εὐαγγέλιον πάσῃ τῇ κτίσει. 16 ὁ πιστεύσας καὶ βαπτισθεὶς σωθήσεται, ὁ δὲ ἀπιστήσας κατακριθήσεται. 17 σημεῖα δὲ τοῖς πιστεύσασιν ταῦτα παρακολ–ουθήσει· ἐν τῷ ὀνόματί μου δαιμόνια ἐκβαλοῦσιν, γλώσσαις λαλήσουσιν καιναῖς, 18 καὶ ἐν ταῖς χερσὶν ὄφεις ἀροῦσιν κἂν θανάσιμόν τι πίωσιν οὐ μὴ αὐτοὺς βλάψῃ, ἐπὶ ἀρρώστους χεῖρας ἐπιθήσουσιν καὶ καλῶς ἕξουσιν.

19 Ὁ μὲν οὖν κύριος Ἰησοῦς μετὰ τὸ λαλῆσαι αὐτοῖς ἀνελήμφθη εἰς τὸν οὐρανὸν καὶ ἐκάθισεν ἐκ δεξιῶν τοῦ θεοῦ. 20 ἐκεῖνοι δὲ ἐξελθόντες ἐκήρυξαν πανταχοῦ, τοῦ κυρίου συνεργοῦντος καὶ τὸν λόγον βεβαιοῦντος διὰ τῶν ἐπακολουθ–ούντων σημείων.

Note: The text of endings without conventional numbering is distinctively underlined, to differentiate them from their preceding verses.

Table A.2 Synoptic table of the author's English translation of Markan endings (excluding obeli)

Shortest Ending (AT)	Long Ending (AT)	Intermediate and Long Ending (AT)	Intermediate Ending alone, as in Codex k (AT)	Long Ending with Freer Logion, as in Codex W (AT)
...⁸ And, going out quickly, they fled from the tomb, for trembling and amazement had seized them. And they said nothing to anyone, for they were afraid.	...⁸ And, going out quickly, they fled from the tomb, for trembling and amazement had seized them. And they said nothing to anyone, for they were afraid. ⁹ Now, after he rose early on the first day of the week, he appeared first to Mary Magdalene, out of whom he had cast seven demons. ¹⁰ Afterwards she went and reported to those who had been with him, as they were mourning and weeping; ¹¹ And these men, hearing that he was alive and was seen by her, did not believe. ¹² After these things, he was revealed in a different form to two of them as they walked into the country. ¹³ And although they went and reported to the rest, neither did those ones believe.	...⁸ And, going out quickly, they fled from the tomb, for trembling and amazement had seized them. And they said nothing to anyone, for they were afraid. But they proclaimed briefly all that they were commanded to those around Peter. Now, after these things Jesus himself sent forth through them, from east to west, the sacred and incorruptible message of eternal salvation. [Amen] ⁹ Now, after he rose early on the first day of the week, he appeared first to Mary Magdalene, out of whom he had cast seven demons. ¹⁰ Afterwards she went and reported to those who had been with him, as they were mourning and weeping; ¹¹ And these men, hearing that he was alive and was seen by her, did not believe. ¹² After these things, he was revealed in a different form to two of them as they walked into the country. ¹³ And although they went and reported to the rest, neither did those ones believe.	...⁸ And, going out quickly, they fled from the tomb, for trembling and amazement had seized them. And they said nothing to anyone, for they were afraid. But they proclaimed briefly all that they were commanded to those around Peter. Now, after these things Jesus himself sent forth through them, from east to west, the sacred and incorruptible message of eternal salvation. Amen.	...⁸ And, going out quickly, they fled from the tomb, for trembling and amazement had seized them. And they said nothing to anyone, for they were afraid. ⁹ Now, after he rose early on the first day of the week, he appeared first to Mary Magdalene, out of whom he had cast seven demons. ¹⁰ Afterwards he went and reported to those who had been with him, as they were mourning and weeping; ¹¹ And these men, hearing that he was alive and was seen by her, did not believe. ¹² After these things, he was revealed in a different form to two of them as they walked into the country. ¹³ And although they went and reported to the rest, neither did those ones believe. ¹⁴ Finally, he was revealed to the Eleven while they were reclining at table, and he upbraided them for their unbelief and hardheartedness, because they did not believe those who witnessed that he had been raised up.

¹⁴ Finally, he was revealed to the Eleven while they were reclining at table, and he upbraided them for their unbelief and hardheartedness, because they did not believe those who witnessed that he had been raised up. ¹⁵ And he said to them, "Going into the whole world, preach the gospel to all creation. ¹⁶ The one who believes and is baptized will be saved, but the one who disbelieves will be condemned. ¹⁷ Now, signs will follow closely those who believe; In my name they will cast out demons, they will speak in new tongues, ¹⁸ they will take up snakes in their hands and, should they drink any poison, it will certainly not harm them, they will lay hands on the sick and they will be well.

¹⁹ So then, after speaking to them, the Lord Jesus was taken up into heaven and sat at the right hand of God. ²⁰ And they went out and preached everywhere, because the Lord was working with them and confirming the word through the signs that were following.

¹⁴ Finally, he was revealed to the Eleven while they were reclining at table, and he upbraided them for their unbelief and hardheartedness, because they did not believe those who witnessed that he had been raised up. ¹⁵ And he said to them, "Going into the whole world, preach the gospel to all creation. ¹⁶ The one who believes and is baptized will be saved, but the one who disbelieves will be condemned. ¹⁷ Now, signs will follow closely those who believe; In my name they will cast out demons, they will speak in new tongues, ¹⁸ they will take up snakes in their hands and, should they drink any poison, it will certainly not harm them, they will lay hands on the sick and they will be well.

¹⁹ So then, after speaking to them, the Lord Jesus was taken up into heaven and sat at the right hand of God. ²⁰ And they went out and preached everywhere, because the Lord was working with them and confirming the word through the signs that were following.

And they defended themselves saying, "This age of lawlessness and unbelief is under Satan, who does not permit the truth [and] power of God to overtake the unclean things of the spirits; therefore, reveal your righteousness now." And Christ addressed them, "The limit of the years of Satan's authority have been fulfilled, but other dreadful things are drawing near: And for those who sinned I myself was handed over to death, in order that they might return to the truth and no longer sin, so that they might inherit the spiritual and incorruptible glory of righteousness in heaven."

¹⁵ And he said to them, "Going into the whole world, preach the gospel to all creation. ¹⁶ The one who believes and is baptized will be saved, but the one who disbelieves will be condemned. ¹⁷ Now, signs will follow closely those who believe; In my name they will cast out demons, they will speak in new tongues, ¹⁸ they will take up snakes in their hands and, should they drink any poison, it will certainly not harm them, they will lay hands on the sick and they will be well.

¹⁹ So then, after speaking to them, the Lord Jesus was taken up into heaven and sat at the right hand of God. ²⁰ And they went out and preached everywhere, because the Lord was working with them and confirming the word through the signs that were following.

Note: The text of endings without conventional numbering is distinctively underlined, to differentiate them from their preceding verses. AT: author's translation.

Appendix

(W, also known as the Freer Gospels Codex) is a lovely, slanting majuscule. Although the final pages of Mark's Gospel (fourth in the codex's order: Matthew, John, Luke, and Mark, as in P[45]) show signs of damage, they are extremely legible. The Codex represents our only Greek manuscript in which the text Jerome translates into Latin—and more—follows v. 14. The insertion is called the "Freer Logion."

The text of Mark 16 in W shows no awareness that the LE's suitability is debated. There is, at most, a gap the width of two letters between εφοβουντο γαρ and αναστασ, the first word of 16:9. A space of similar length marks a "paragraph" break before v. 12. The Freer Logion's expansion of the LE, lacking any annotation or siglum, follows v. 14 after a slightly more pronounced space, perhaps the width of five to six letters of text. The insertion concludes at κληρονομησωσιν; at v. 15 the LE resumes after a medium-sized space in the text. As previously stated, this copy of the ending of Mark is the only manuscript, in Greek or any version, that includes this text. One might consider the Logion a unique variant introduced by the scribe of W, although Jerome expresses awareness of the reading *in certain manuscripts* (*In quibusdam exemplaribus*; Pelag. II.15.1).

Bibliography

Aland, Kurt. "Der wiedergefundene Markusschluß? Eine methodologische Bemerkung zur textkritischen Arbeit." *Zeitschrift für Theologie und Kirche* 67 (1970): 1–13.
Aland, Kurt and Barbara. *The Text of the New Testament*. Translated by Erroll F. Rhodes. 2d ed. Grand Rapids: Eerdmans, 1989.
Alford, Henry. *The Greek Testament*. 4 vols. Boston: Lee and Shepard, 1874.
Anderson, Gary A. "The Penitence Narrative in the *Life of Adam and Eve*." *Hebrew Union College Annual* 63 (1992): 1–38.
Attridge, Harold W. "An 'Emotional' Jesus and Stoic Tradition." Pages 77–92 in *Stoicism in Early Christianity*. Edited by Tuomas Rasimus et al. Grand Rapids: Baker, 2010.
Bakker, Adolphine Henriëtte Annette. *A Study of Codex Evang. Bobbiensis (k): Part I*. Amsterdam: N.V. Noord-Hollandsche Uitgeversmaatschappij, 1933.
Bauckham, Richard. "Salome the Sister of Jesus, Salome the Disciple of Jesus, and the Secret Gospel of Mark." *Novum Testamentum* 33 (1991): 245–75.
Bauckham, Richard. *Gospel Women: Studies of the Named Women in the Gospels*. New York: T&T Clark, 2002.
Beavis, Mary Ann. "Women as Models of Faith in Mark." *Biblical Theology Bulletin* 18 (1988): 3–9.
Betsworth, Sharon. *The Reign of God Is Such as These: A Socio-literary Analysis of Daughters in the Gospel of Mark*. Library of New Testament Studies Monograph Series 422. New York: T&T Clark, 2010.
Bickerman, E. J. "The Date of Fourth Maccabees." Pages 275–81 in *Studies in Jewish and Christian History*. 2 vols. Arbeiten zur Geschichte des antiken Judentums und des Urchristentums 9. Leiden: Brill, 1976.
Birch, Andreas. *Variae Lectiones ad Textum IV Evangeliorum*. Copenhagen: C. G. Prost, 1801.
Black, C. Clifton. *Mark*. Abingdon New Testament Commentaries. Nashville: Abingdon, 2011.
Black, C. Clifton. *The Disciples according to Mark: Markan Redaction in Current Debate*. 2d ed. Grand Rapids: Eerdmans, 2012.
Black, David Alan, ed. *Perspectives on the Ending of Mark*. Nashville: Broadman and Holman, 2008.
Blank, Josef. "Frauen in den Jesusüberlieferungen." Pages 9–91 in *Die Frau im Urchristentum*. Edited by Karl Rahner and Heinrich Schlier. Quaestiones disputatae 95. Freiburg: Herder, 1983.
Bode, Lynn. *First Easter Morning: The Gospel Accounts of the Women's Visit to the Tomb of Jesus*. Rome: Biblical Institute Press, 1970.
Bovon, François. *Luke 1*. Hermeneia. Translated by Christine M. Thomas. Minneapolis: Fortress, 2002.
Bow, Beverly. "Sarah 2." Pages 152–3 in *Women in Scripture: A Dictionary of Named and Unnamed Women in the Hebrew Bible, the Apocryphal/Deutero-canonical Books, and the New Testament*. Edited by Carol Meyers. Boston: Houghton Mifflin, 2000.

Bridges, Carl B. "The Canonical Status of the Longer Ending of Mark." *Stone-Campbell Journal* 9 (2006): 231–42.
Brower, Kent. *Mark: A Commentary in the Wesleyan Tradition*. New Beacon Bible Commentary. Kansas City: Beacon Hill, 2012.
Bruce, F. F. "The End of the Second Gospel." *The Evangelical Quarterly* 17 (1945): 169–81.
Buch-Hansen, Gitte. "The Emotional Jesus: Anti-Stoicism in the Fourth Gospel?" Pages 93–114 in *Stoicism in Early Christianity*. Edited by Tuomas Rasimus et al. Grand Rapids: Baker, 2010.
Bultmann, Rudolf. *The History of the Synoptic Tradition*. Oxford: B. Blackwell, 1972. Translated by John Marsh. Translation of *Geschichte der synoptischen Tradition*. Göttingen: Vandenhoeck & Ruprecht, 1957.
Bultmann, Rudolf. *The Gospel of John: A Commentary*. Translated by G. R. Beasley-Murray, R. W. N. Hoare, and J. K. Riches. Philadelphia: Westminster, 1971.
Bultmann, Rudolf. *Die Geschichte der synoptischen Tradition*. 10th ed. Göttingen: Vandenhoeck & Ruprecht, 1995.
Burgon, John W. *The Last Twelve Verses of Mark: Vindicated against Recent Critical Objectors & Established*. Oxford: James Parker, 1871.
Burkett, Delbert. *Rethinking Gospel Sources: From Proto-Mark to Mark*. New York: T&T Clark, 2004.
Burridge, Richard A. *What Are the Gospels? A Comparison with Graeco-Roman Biography*. 2d ed. Grand Rapids: Eerdmans, 2004.
Catchpole, David. "The Fearful Silence of the Women at the Tomb: A Study in Markan Theology." *Journal of Theology for Southern Africa* 18 (1977): 3–10.
Charlesworth, James H. *The Good and Evil Serpent: How a Universal Symbol Became Christianized*. New Haven: Yale University Press, 2010.
Childs, Brevard S. *The New Testament as Canon: An Introduction*. Philadelphia: Fortress, 1984.
Church of God (Cleveland, Tenn.), The. "Signs Following Believers." No pages. Cited August 10, 2012. Online: http://www.churchofgod.org/index.php/pages/doctrinal-commitments.
Church of God in Christ, The. "What We Believe." No pages. Cited August 10, 2012. Online: http://www.cogic.org/our-foundation/what-we-believe/.
Clark, Kenneth W. "The Theological Relevance of Textual Variation in Current Criticism of the Greek New Testament." *Journal of Biblical Literature* 85 (1966): 1–16.
Cohick, Lynn. *Women in the World of the Earliest Christians: Illuminating Ancient Ways of Life*. Grand Rapids: Baker, 2009.
Collins, Adela Yarbro. *Mark*. Hermeneia. Minneapolis: Fortress, 2007.
Conway, Colleen. *Behold the Man: Jesus and Greco-Roman Masculinity*. New York: Oxford University Press, 2008.
Covington, Dennis. *Salvation on Sand Mountain: Snake Handling and Redemption in Southern Appalachia*. Boston: Addison Wesley, 1994. Repr., Cambridge, MA: Da Capo Press, 2009.
Croy, N. Clayton. *The Mutilation of Mark's Gospel*. Nashville: Abingdon, 2003.
Culpepper, R. Alan. *Mark*. Smyth and Helwys Bible Commentary. Macon, GA: Smyth & Helwys, 2007.
Dannemann, Irene. *Aus dem Rahmen fallen: Frauen im Markusevangelium: eine feministische Re-vision*. Berlin: Alektor-Verlag, 1996.
De Boer, Esther. *Mary Magdalene: Beyond the Myth*. Translated by John Bowden. London: SCM Press, 1997.

De Jong, Matthijs J. "Mark 16:8 as a Satisfying Ending to the Gospel." Pages 123–49 in *Jesus, Paul, and Early Christianity: Studies in Honour of Henk Jan de Jonge*. Edited by Rieuwerd Buitenwerf, Harm W. Hollander, and Johannes Tromp. Novum Testamentum Supplements 130. Boston: Brill, 2008.

Denyer, Nicholas. "Mark 16:8 and Plato, *Protagoras* 328D." *Tyndale Bulletin* 57 (2006): 149–50.

Dewey, Joanna. "Women in the Gospel of Mark." *Word and World* 26 (2006): 22–9.

Dibelius, Martin. *From Tradition to Gospel*. Translated by Bertram Lee Woolf. Revised ed. Cambridge: James Clarke, 1971.

DiCicco, Mark. "What Can One Give in Exchange for One's Life? A Narrative-Critical Study of the Widow and Her Offering, Mark 12:41–44." *Currents in Theology and Mission* 25 (1998): 441–9.

Driggers, Ira Brent. *Following God through Mark: Theological Tension in the Second Gospel*. Louisville: Westminster John Knox, 2007.

Edwards, James R. "Markan Sandwiches: The Significance of Interpolations in Markan Narratives." *Novum Testamentum* 31 (1989): 193–216.

Ehrman, Bart D. *Lost Scriptures: Books That Did Not Make It into the New Testament*. Oxford: Oxford University Press, 2003.

Ehrman, Bart D. *The Orthodox Corruption of Scripture: The Effect of Early Christological Controversies on the Text of the New Testament*. New York: Oxford University Press, 2011.

Ehrman, Bart D. *Forgery and Counterforgery: The Use of Literary Deceit in Early Christian Polemics*. New York: Oxford University Press, 2012.

Elliott, J. K. "Text and Language of the Endings to Mark's Gospel." *Theologische Zeitschrift* 27 (1971): 255–62.

Epp, Eldon J. "The Multivalence of the Term 'Original' in New Testament Textual Criticism." *Harvard Theological Review* 99 (1999): 245–81.

Epp, Eldon J. "Issues in the Interrelation of New Testament Textual Criticism and Canon." Pages 595–639 in *Perspectives on New Testament Textual Criticism: Collected Essays, 1962–2004*. Supplements to Novum Testamentum 116. Boston: Brill, 2005. Repr. from pages 485–515 in *The Canon Debate* (ed. Lee Martin McDonald and James A. Sanders; Peabody, MA: Hendrickson, 2002).

Evans, Craig. *Mark 8:27–16:20*. Word Biblical Commentary. Vol. 34b. Nashville: Thomas Nelson, 2001.

Fander, Monika. *Die Stellung der Frau im Markusevangelium: Unter besonderer Berücksichtigung kultur- und religionsgeschichtlicher Hintergründe*. Altenberge, Germany: Telos-Verlag, 1989.

Fander, Monika. "Frauen in der Nachfolge Jesu: Die Rolle der Frau im Markusevangelium." *Evangelische Theologie* 52 (1992): 413–32.

Fander, Monika. "Gospel of Mark: Women as True Disciples of Jesus." Pages 626–44 in *Feminist Biblical Interpretation: A Compendium of Critical Commentary on the Books of the Bible and Related Literature*. Edited by Luise Schottroff and Marie-Theres Wacker. Translated by Lisa E. Dahill et al. Grand Rapids: Eerdmans, 2012. Translation of *Kompendium Feministische Bibelauslegung*. 2d ed. Gütersloh: Chr. Kaiser Gütersloher Verlagshaus, 1999.

Farmer, William R. *The Last Twelve Verses of Mark*. Society for New Testament Studies Monograph Series 25. New York: Cambridge University Press, 1974.

Farrer, Austin. *A Study in St. Mark*. London: Dacre Press, 1951.

Foster, Paul. "The *Gospel of Peter*." Pages 30–42 in *The Non-canonical Gospels*. Edited by Paul Foster. London: T&T Clark, 2008.

Foursquare Church, The. "Divine Healing." No pages. Cited August 10, 2012. Online: http://www.foursquare.org/about/what_we_believe/spirit_filled_life.

Gardner, Jane F. *Women in Roman Law and Society*. Bloomington: Indiana University Press, 1986.

Gaventa, Beverly Roberts and Patrick D. Miller, eds. *The Ending of Mark and the Ends of God: Essays in Memory of Donald Harrisville Juel*. Louisville: Westminster John Knox, 2005.

Gilfillan Upton, Bridget. *Hearing Mark's Endings: Listening to Ancient Popular Texts through Speech Act Theory*. Boston: Brill, 2006.

Greenlee, J. Harold. *Introduction to New Testament Textual Criticism*. Peabody, MA: Hendrickson, 1995.

Griesbach, J. J. *Novum Testamentum Graece: Cum Selecta Lectionum Varietate*. 2 vols. Leipzig: G. J. Göschen, 1803.

Griesbach, J. J. "Pentecostes festos dies pie celebrandos civibus indicit academia Ienensis." Pages 471–86 in *Opuscula Academica*. Vol. 2. Edited by Johann Philip Gabler. Jena: Fr. Frommanni, 1824.

Griesbach, J. J. "Commentatio qua Marci Evangelium totum e Matthaei et Lucae commentariis decerptum esse monstratur." Pages 68–102 in *J. J. Griesbach: Synoptic and Text-Critical Studies 1776–1976*. Edited by Bernard Orchard and Thomas R. W. Longstaff. New York: Cambridge University Press, 1978.

Gummere, R. M., trans. *Seneca: Ad Lucilium Epistulae Morales*. 3 vols. Loeb Classical Library. Cambridge, MA: Harvard University Press, 1918–25.

Gundry, Robert H. *Mark: A Commentary on His Apology for the Cross*. Grand Rapids: Eerdmans, 1993.

Hannah, Darrell D. "The Four-Gospel Canon in the *Epistula Apostolorum*." *Journal of Theological Studies* 59 (2008): 598–633.

Hare, Douglas R. A. *Mark*. Westminster Bible Companion. Louisville: Westminster John Knox, 1996.

Hartman, Lars. "Mark 16:1–8: The Ending of a Biography-Like Narrative and of a Gospel." *Theology & Life* 30 (2007): 31–47.

Hearon, Holly. *The Magdalene Tradition: Witness and Counter-Witness in Early Christian Communities*. Collegeville, MN: Liturgical Press, 2004.

Helton, Stanley N. "Churches of Christ and Mark 16:9–20." *Restoration Quarterly* 36 (1994): 32–52.

Hemelrijk, Emily A. *Matrona Docta: Educated Women in the Roman Elite from Cornelia to Julia Domna*. New York: Routledge, 1999.

Hennecke, Edgar and Wilhelm Schneemelcher, eds. *New Testament Apocrypha*. 2 vols. Translated by R. McL. Wilson. Philadelphia: Westminster, 1963.

Hills, Julian. *Tradition and Composition in the* Epistula Apostolorum. Harvard Dissertations in Religion. Minneapolis: Fortress, 1990.

Hornschuh, Manfred. *Studien zur Epistula Apostolorum*. Patristische Texte und Studien 5; Berlin: de Gruyter, 1965.

Horton, Charles, ed. *The Earliest Gospels: The Origins and Transmission of the Earliest Christian Gospels—The Contribution of the Chester Beatty Gospel Codex P*[45]. Journal for the Study of the New Testament: Supplement Series 258. New York: T&T Clark, 2004.

Hritzu, John N. *Saint Jerome: Dogmatic and Polemical Works*. Fathers of the Church. Washington: Catholic University of America, 1965.

Hug, Joseph. *La Finale de L'Évangile de Marc: Mc 16,9-20*. Paris: J. Gabalda, 1978.
Hurtado, Larry W. *Mark*. New International Biblical Commentary. Peabody, MA: Hendrickson, 1989.
Hurtado, Larry W. "The Women, the Tomb, and the Climax of Mark." Pages 427–50 in *A Wandering Galilean: Essays in Honour of Seán Freyne*. Edited by Zuleika Rodgers. Supplements to Journal for the Study of Judaism 132. Boston: Brill, 2009.
Ilan, Tal. *Lexicon of Jewish Names in Late Antiquity: Part I, Palestine 330 BCE–200 CE*. Tübingen: Mohr Siebeck, 2002.
Iverson, Kelly R. "A Further Word on Final Ga/r (Mark 16:8)." *Catholic Biblical Quarterly* 68 (2006): 79–94.
Johnson, Allan E. "Rhetorical Criticism in Eusebius' Gospels Questions." *Studia Patristica* 1 (1983): 33–40.
Johnson, E. Elizabeth. "Who Is My Mother? Family Values in the Gospel of Mark." Pages 32–46 in *Blessed One: Protestant Perspectives on Mary*. Edited by Beverly Roberts Gaventa and Cynthia Rigby. Louisville: Westminster John Knox, 2002.
Johnson, Luke Timothy. "The Not-So-Empty Tomb (Luke 24:1–11)." Pages 139–45 in *The Living Gospel*. New York: Continuum, 2004.
Joynes, Christine E. "Wombs and Tombs: The Reception History of Mark 16:1–20." Pages 226–43 in *From the Margins 2: Women of the New Testament and Their Afterlives*. Edited by Christine E. Joynes and Christopher C. Rowland. Sheffield: Sheffield Phoenix, 2009.
Joynes, Christine E. "The Sound of Silence: Interpreting Mark 16:1–8 through the Centuries." *Interpretation* 19 (2011): 18–29.
Juel, Donald H. *A Master of Surprise: Mark Interpreted*. Minneapolis: Fortress, 1994.
Juel, Donald H. *The Gospel of Mark*. Interpreting Biblical Texts. Nashville: Abingdon, 1999.
Juel, Donald H. "A Disquieting Silence: The Matter of the Ending." Pages 1–13 in *The Ending of Mark and the Ends of God: Essays in Memory of Donald Harrisville Juel*. Edited by Beverly Roberts Gaventa and Patrick D. Miller. Louisville: Westminster John Knox, 2005.
Juel, Donald H. *Shaping the Scriptural Imagination: Truth, Meaning, and the Theological Interpretation of the Bible*. Edited by Shane Berg and Matthew L. Skinner. Waco, TX: Baylor University Press, 2011.
Keith, Chris. *The Pericope Adulterae, the Gospel of John, and the Literacy of Jesus*. Boston: Brill, 2009.
Kelhoffer, James A. *Miracle and Mission: The Authentication of Missionaries and Their Message in the Longer Ending of Mark*. Tübingen: Mohr Siebeck, 2000.
Kelhoffer, James A. "The Witness of Eusebius' *ad Marinum* and Other Christian Writings." *Zeitschrift für die neutestamentliche Wissenschaft und die Kunde der älteren Kirche* 92 (2001): 78–112.
Kelhoffer, James A. "A Tale of Two Markan Characterizations: The Exemplary Woman Who Anointed Jesus's Body for Burial (14:3–9) and the Silent Trio Who Fled the Empty Tomb (16:1–8)." Pages 85–98 in *Women and Gender in Ancient Religions: Interdisciplinary Approaches*. Edited by Stephen P. Ahearne-Kroll et al. Wissenschaftliche Untersuchungen zum Neuen Testament. Tübingen: Mohr Siebeck, 2010.
Kenyon, F. G. *Handbook to the Textual Criticism of the New Testament*. 2d ed. Grand Rapids: Eerdmans, 1912.
Kermode, Frank. *The Genesis of Secrecy: On the Interpretation of Narrative*. Cambridge, MA: Harvard University Press, 1979.

Kinukawa, Hisako. *Women and Jesus in Mark: A Japanese Feminist Perspective*. Maryknoll, NY: Orbis, 1994.

Kittel, G. and G. Friedrich, eds. *Theological Dictionary of the New Testament*. Translated by G. W. Bromiley. 10 vols. Grand Rapids: Eerdmans, 1964–76.

Klauck, Hans-Josef. *4 Makkabaërbuch. Jüdische Schriften aus hellenistisch-römischer Zeit* 3.6. Gütersloh: Mohn, 1989.

Koester, Helmut. *Ancient Christian Gospels: Their History and Development*. London: SCM, 1990.

Koester, Helmut. "Written Gospels or Oral Tradition?" *Journal of Biblical Literature* 113 (1994): 293–7.

Kraemer, Ross Shepard. *Her Share of the Blessings: Women's Religions among Pagans, Jews, and Christians in the Greco-Roman World*. New York: Oxford University Press, 1992.

Kuske, David P. "Textual Criticism Brief: Mark 16:9-20." *Wisconsin Lutheran Quarterly* 102 (2005): 58–9.

Lachmann, Karl. "Rechenschaft über seine Ausgabe des Neuen Testaments." *Theologische Studien und Kritiken* 3 (1830): 817–45.

Lane, William L. *The Gospel of Mark*. New International Commentary on the New Testament. Grand Rapids: Eerdmans, 1974.

Larsen, Matthew D. C. *Gospels before the Book*. New York: Oxford University Press, 2018.

Larson, Jennifer. "Paul's Masculinity." *Journal of Biblical Literature* 123 (2004): 85–97.

Lieu, Judith. "The Women's Resurrection Testimony." Pages 34–44 in *Resurrection: Essays in Honour of Leslie Houlden*. Edited by Stephen Barton and Graham Stanton. London: SPCK, 1994.

Lincoln, Andrew T. "The Promise and Failure: Mark 16:7, 8." *Journal of Biblical Literature* 108 [1989]: 283–300.

Linnemann, Eta. "Der (wiedergefundene) Markusschluß." *Zeitschrift für Theologie und Kirche* 66 (1969): 255–87.

Long, Thomas. "Empty Tomb, Empty Talk." *Christian Century* 118 (2001): 11.

Lüdemann, Gerd. *The Resurrection of Jesus: History, Experience, Theology*. Minneapolis: Fortress, 1994.

Lunn, Nicholas P. *The Original Ending of Mark: A New Case for the Authenticity of Mark 16:9-20*. Eugene, OR: Pickwick, 2014.

Luz, Ulrich. *Matthew 21–28*. Hermeneia. Minneapolis: Fortress, 2005.

Magness, J. Lee. *Sense and Absence: Structure and Suspension in the Ending of Mark's Gospel*. SBL Semeia Studies. Atlanta: Scholar's Press, 1986.

Malbon, Elizabeth Struthers. "The Poor Widow in Mark and Her Poor Rich Readers." *Catholic Biblical Quarterly* 53 (1991): 589–604.

Malbon, Elizabeth Struthers. *In the Company of Jesus: Characters in Mark's Gospel*. Louisville: Westminster John Knox, 2000.

Marcus, Joel. *Mark*. 2 vols. The Anchor Yale Bible 27-27A. New Haven, CT: Yale University Press, 2002, 2009.

Marshall, Christopher D. *Faith as a Theme in Mark's Narrative*. Society for New Testament Studies Monograph Series 64. New York: Cambridge University Press, 1989.

Martin, Dale. *Sex and the Single Savior: Gender and Sexuality in Biblical Interpretation*. Louisville: Westminster John Knox, 2006.

McDill, Matthew D. "A Textual and Structural Analysis of Mark 16:9–20." *Filología Neotestamentica* 27 (2004): 27–43.

McGann, Jerome. *A Critique of Modern Textual Criticism*. Chicago: University of Chicago Press, 1983.

McGann, Jerome. "Textual Scholarship, Textual Theory, and the Uses of Electronic Tools: A Brief Report on Current Undertakings." *Victorian Studies* 41 (1998): 609–19.

Metzger, Bruce M. *A Textual Commentary on the Greek New Testament*. 2d ed. Stuttgart: Deutsche Bibelgesellschaft, 1994.

Metzger, Bruce M. and Bart D. Ehrman. *The Text of the New Testament: Its Transmission, Corruption, and Restoration*. 4th ed. New York: Oxford University Press, 2005.

Meyers, Carole, et al., eds. *Women in Scripture: A Dictionary of Named and Unnamed Women in the Hebrew Bible, the Apocryphal/Deuterocanonical Books, and the New Testament*. Grand Rapids: Eerdmans, 2001.

Middleton, J. Richard and Michael J. Gorman. "Salvation." Pages 45–61 in vol. 5 of *The New Interpreter's Dictionary of the Bible*. Edited by Katharine Doob Sakenfeld. 5 vols. Nashville: Abingdon, 2006–9.

Migne, J.-P., ed. Patrologia graeca. 162 vols. Paris, 1857–86.

Miller, Susan. "'They Said Nothing to Anyone': The Fear and Silence of the Women at the Empty Tomb (Mk 16.1–8)." *Feminist Theology* 13 (2004): 77–90.

Miller, Susan. *Women in Mark's Gospel*. Journal for the Study of the New Testament: Supplement Series 259. New York: T&T Clark, 2004.

Miller, Susan. "The Woman Who Anoints Jesus (14:3–9): A Prophetic Sign of the New Creation." *Feminist Theology* 14 (2006): 221–36.

Mirecki, Paul Allan. "Mark 16:9–20: Composition, Tradition and Redaction." ThD diss., Harvard, 1986.

Mitchell, Joan L. *Beyond Fear and Silence: A Feminist-Literary Approach to the Gospel of Mark*. New York: Continuum, 2001.

Moore, Stephen. "Mark and Empire: 'Zealot' and 'Postcolonial' Readings." Pages 193–205 in *The Postcolonial Biblical Reader*. Edited by R. S. Sugirtharajah. Oxford: Blackwell Publishing, 2005.

Moore, Stephen D. and Janice Capel Anderson. "Taking It Like a Man: Masculinity in 4 Maccabees." *Journal of Biblical Literature* 117 (1998): 249–73.

Moore, Stephen D. and Janice Capel Anderson, eds. *New Testament Masculinities*. Semeia Studies 45. Atlanta: Society of Biblical Literature, 2003.

Moreschini, C., ed. *S. Hieronymi*, Dialogus Adversus Pelagianos. Corpus Christianorum. Series Latina LXXX. Pars III,2. Turnhout: Brepols, 1990.

Murfin, Ross and Supriya M. Ray. *The Bedford Glossary of Critical and Literary Terms*. Boston: Bedford, 1997.

Nongbri, Brent. "The Use and Abuse of P^{52}: Papyrological Pitfalls in the Dating of the Fourth Gospel." *Harvard Theological Review* 99 (2005): 23–48.

Nongbri, Brent. *God's Library: The Archaeology of the Earliest Christian Manuscripts*. New Haven, CT: Yale University Press, 2018.

Norton, Andrews. *The Evidences of the Genuineness of the Gospels*. 6th ed. Boston: American Unitarian Association, 1877.

Oakeshott, Philip. "The Wrong Conclusion: Mark 16:1–8 and Literary Theory." *Theology* 113 (2010): 105–13.

O'Day, Gail R. "John 7:53–8:11: A Study in Misreading." *Journal of Biblical Literature* 111 (1992): 631–40.

Parker, D. C. *The Living Text of the Gospels*. New York: Cambridge University Press, 1997.

Parrot, Douglas M., ed. *Nag Hammadi Codices III, 3–4 and V, 1: Eugnostos and the Sophia of Jesus Christ*. Leiden: Brill, 1991.

Pearse, Roger, ed. *Eusebius of Caesarea, Gospel Problems and Solutions:* Quaestiones ad Stephanum et Marinum. Translated by David J. D. Miller and Adam C. McCollum. Ipswich, UK: Chieftain, 2011.

Penner, Todd and Caroline Vander Stichele. *Contextualizing Gender in Early Christian Discourse: Thinking beyond Thecla.* London: T&T Clark, 1999.

Pervo, Richard I. *Dating Acts: Between the Evangelists and the Apologists.* Santa Rosa, CA: Polebridge, 2006.

Pesch, Rudolf. *Das Markusevangelium.* 2 vols. Freiburg: Herder, 1984.

Pomeroy, Sarah B. *Goddesses, Whores, Wives, and Slaves: Women in Classical Antiquity.* New York: Schocken Books, 1975.

Porter, Stanley E. "Verbal Aspect and Discourse Function in Mark 16:1–8: Three Significant Instances." Pages 123–37 in *Studies in the Greek Bible: Essays in Honor of Francis T. Gignac, S.J.* Edited by Jeremy Corley and Vincent Skemp. Washington, DC: Catholic Biblical Association of America, 2008.

Porter, Stanley E. *How We Got the New Testament: Text, Transmission, Translation.* Grand Rapids: Baker, 2013.

Riddle, Donald. "Textual Criticism as a Historical Discipline." *Anglican Theological Review* 18 (1936): 220–33.

Robinson, Maurice A. "The Long Ending as Canonical Verity." Pages 40–79 in *Perspectives on the Ending of Mark: 4 Views.* Edited by David Alan Black. Nashville: Broadman and Holman, 2008.

Robinson, Maurice and William G. Pierpont. *The New Testament in the Original Greek According to the Byzantine/Majority Textform.* Atlanta, GA: Original Word, 1991.

Sandys, J. E. *A History of Classical Scholarship.* 2d ed. 3 vols. Cambridge: Cambridge University Press, 1906–8.

Schmidt, C. *Gespräche Jesu mit seinen Jüngern nach der Auferstehung: Ein katholisches-apostolisches Sendschreiben des 2. Jahrhunderts.* Leipzig: Hinrichs, 1919. Repr. Hildesheim: G. Olms, 1967.

Schmithals, Walter. "Der Markusschluß, die Verklärungsgeschichte und die Aussendung des Zwölf." *Zeitschrift für Theologie und Kirche* 69 (1972): 379–411.

Schottroff, Luise. "Maria Magdalena und die Frauen am Grabe Jesu." *Evangelische Theologie* 42 (1982): 3–25.

Schüssler Fiorenza, Elizabeth. *In Memory of Her: A Feminist Theological Reconstruction of Christian Origins.* New York: Crossroad, 1983.

Selvidge, Marla J. *Woman, Cult, and Miracle Recital: A Redaction Critical Investigation on Mark 5:24–34.* Lewisburg, PA: Bucknell University Press, 1990.

Setzer, Claudia. "Excellent Women: Female Witness to the Resurrection." *Journal of Biblical Literature* 116 (1997): 259–72.

Shepherd, Thomas R. "Narrative Analysis as a Text Critical Tool: Mark 16 in Codex W as a Test Case." *Journal for the Study of the New Testament* (2009): 77–98.

Smith, Daniel A. *Revisiting the Empty Tomb: The Early History of Easter.* Minneapolis: Fortress, 2010.

Smyth, Herbert Weir. *A Greek Grammar for Colleges.* New York: American, 1920.

Spencer, F. Scott. *Dancing Girls, Loose Ladies, and Women of the Cloth: The Women in Jesus's Life.* New York: Continuum, 2004.

Stein, Robert H. "The Ending of Mark." *Bulletin for Biblical Research* 18 (2008): 79–98.

Streeter, B. H. *The Four Gospels.* London: Macmillan, 1924.

Stuckenbruck, Loren T. "Prayers of Deliverance from the Demonic in the Dead Sea Scrolls and Related Early Jewish Literature." Pages 146–65 in *The Changing Face of*

Judaism, Christianity, and Other Greco-Roman Religions in Antiquity. Edited by Ian H. Henderson and Gerbern S. Oegema. *Jüdische Schriften aus hellenistisch-römischer Zeit* 2. Munich: Gütersloher, 2006.

Stuckenbruck, Loren T. "Jesus' Apocalyptic Worldview and His Exorcistic Ministry." Pages 68–84 in *The Pseudepigrapha and Christian Origins: Essays from the Studiorum Novi Testamenti Societas*. Edited by Gerbern S. Oegema and James H. Charlesworth. New York: T&T Clark, 2008.

Stuckenbruck, Loren T. "The Human Being and Demonic Invasion: Therapeutic Models in Ancient Jewish and Christian Texts." Pages 94–123 in *Spirituality, Theology, and Mental Health: Multidisciplinary Perspectives*. Edited by Christopher C. H. Cook. London: SCM Press, 2013.

Sugirtharajah, R. S. "The Widow's Mites Revalued." *Expository Times* 103 (1991): 42–3.

Swartley, Willard M. "The Role of Women in Mark's Gospel: A Narrative Analysis." *Biblical Theology Bulletin* 27 (1997): 16–22.

Tabor, James. "The 'Strange' Ending of the Gospel of Mark and Why It Makes All the Difference." No pages. Cited November 2, 2014. Online: http://www.biblicalarchaeology.org/daily/biblical-topics/new-testament/the-strange-ending-of-the-gospel-of-mark-and-why-it-makes-all-the-difference/.

Talbert, Charles H. *What Is a Gospel? The Genre of the Canonical Gospels*. Philadelphia: Fortress, 1977.

Tannehill, Robert. "Introduction: The Pronouncement Story and Its Types." *Semeia* 20 (1981): 1–13.

Taylor, Vincent. *The Gospel According to St. Mark*. London: Macmillan, 1959.

Thackeray, H. St. J. et al., trans. *Josephus*. 10 vols. Loeb Classical Library. Cambridge, MA: Harvard University Press, 1926–65.

Thomas, J. C. "A Reconsideration of the Ending of Mark." *Journal of the Evangelical Theological Society* 26 (1983): 405–19.

Thomas, John Christopher and Kimberly Ervin Alexander. "'And the Signs Are Following': Mark 16:9–20—A Journey into Pentecostal Hermeneutics." *Journal of Pentecostal Theology* 11 (2003): 147–70.

Thompson, Mary R. *The Role of Disbelief in Mark: A New Approach to the Second Gospel*. New York: Paulist, 1989.

Tiffin, Gerald C. "The Problem of Credulity of Women." Pages 401–42 in *Essays on Women in Earliest Christianity*. Edited by Carroll D. Osburn. Vol. 2. Joplin, MO: College Press Publishing Company, 1995.

Tregelles, Samuel Prideaux. *An Account of the Printed Text of the Greek New Testament*. London: Samuel Bagster, 1854.

Trompf, Gary. "The Markusschluss in Recent Research." *Australian Biblical Review* 21 (1973): 15–26.

Trzebiatowska, Marta and Steve Bruce. *Why Are Women More Religious Than Men?* Oxford: Oxford University Press, 2012.

Twelftree, Graham H. *In the Name of Jesus: Exorcism among Early Christians*. Grand Rapids: Baker Academic, 2007.

Tyson, Joseph B. "The Blindness of the Disciples in Mark." *Journal of Biblical Literature* 80 (1961): 261–8.

Van der Horst, P. W. "Can a Book End with γάρ: A Note on Mark 16:8." *Journal of Theological Studies* 23 (1972): 121–4.

Volgers, Annelie and Claudio Zamagni, eds. Erotapokriseis: *Early Christian Question-and-Answer Literature in Context*. Contributions to Biblical Exegesis and Theology 37. Dudley, MA: Peeters, 2004.

Wall, Robert W. "A Response to Thomas/Alexander, 'And the Signs Are Following' (Mark 16:9–20)." *Journal of Pentecostal Theology* 11 (2003): 171–83.

Walsh, P. G. ed. and trans. *Apuleius: The Golden Ass*. Oxford World's Classics. New York: Oxford University Press, 2008.

Weeden, Theodore J. *Mark: Traditions in Conflict*. Philadelphia: Fortress, 1971.

Weir, Heather and Nancy Calvert-Koyzis, eds. *Strangely Familiar: Protofeminist Interpretations of Patriarchal Biblical Texts*. Atlanta: SBL, 2009.

Williams, Craig A. *Roman Homosexuality: Ideologies of Masculinity in Classical Antiquity*. New York: Oxford University Press, 1999.

Williams, Joel F. "Literary Approaches to the End of Mark's Gospel." *Journal of the Evangelical Theological Society* 42 (1999): 21–35.

Williams, Travis. "Bringing Method to the Madness: Examining the Style of the Longer Ending of Mark." *Bulletin for Biblical Research* 20 (2010): 397–418.

Wire, Antoinette Clark. *The Case for Mark Composed in Performance*. Biblical Performance Criticism 3. Eugene, OR: Cascade, 2011.

Witherington, III, Ben. *Women in the Ministry of Jesus: A Study of Jesus' Attitudes to Women and their Roles as Reflected in His Earthly Life*. Society for New Testament Studies Monograph Series 51. New York: Cambridge University Press, 1984.

Wright, Addison G. "The Widow's Mites: Praise or Lament?—A Matter of Context." *Catholic Biblical Quarterly* 44 (1982): 256–65.

Yieh, John Y. H. "Peter, the Apostle." Pages 475–80 in vol. 4 of *The New Interpreter's Dictionary of the Bible*. Edited by Katharine Doob Sakenfeld. 5 vols. Nashville: Abingdon, 2006–9.

Zahn, Thedor. *Tatian's Diatessaron*. Erlangen: A. Deichert, 1881.

Zamagni, Claudio. *Eusèbe de Césarée, Questions Évangéliques: Introduction, texte critique, traduction et notes*. Sources chrétiennes 523. Paris: Cerf, 2008.

Author Index

Aland, Barbara 5 n.2, 56 n.12, 147 n.7, 147 n.9, 150 n.16
Aland, Kurt 5 n.2, 23 n.108, 47, 56 n.12, 140 n.73, 147 n.7, 147 n.9, 150 n.16
Alexander, Kimberly Ervin 8 n.14, 24–5, 25 nn.113–17, 26 n.118, 26 n.120
Alford, Henry 12 n.30, 32 n.152, 33
Anderson, Gary A. 126 n.24
Anderson, Janice Capel 105 n.66, 106 n.72, 107 n.76, 108 nn.82–3
Apuleius 125–7
Attridge, Harold W. 68 n.55, 105 n.67
Augustine 130–1

Bakker, Adolphine Henriette Annette 149 n.13
Bauckham, Richard 62 n.31, 62 n.33, 77 nn.83–84, 110 n.89, 128 n.36, 129 n.40
Beavis, Mary Ann 77 n.84, 120 n.3
Betsworth, Sharon 77 n.80, 77 n.84
Bickerman, E. J. 105 n.66
Birch, Andreas 6 n.9, 7, 8 n.13, 27
Black, C. Clifton 21 n.95, 30 n.140, 35, 89 nn.1–2, 89 n.8, 97 n.37, 135 n.57, 141 n.75
Black, David Alan 8 n.14, 18 n.71, 19 n.72, 20 n.87, 21, 53 n.8
Blank, Josef 77 n.83
Bode, Lynn 77 n.83
Bovon, Francois 62 n.34, 63 nn.35–6
Bow, Beverly 65 n.46
Bridges, Carl B. 8 n.14, 24 n.111
Brower, Kent 114 n.101
Bruce, F. F. 12 n.29
Bruce, Steve 124 n.13
Buch-Hansen, Gitte 68 n.55
Bultmann, Rudolf 28, 62 n.33, 64 n.41, 82 n.102, 129 n.40
Burgon, John W. 8 n.13, 10–16, 18–19, 22 n.98, 24 n.111, 26 n.119, 32, 47, 130 n.43, 151 n.18, 152 n.23
Burkett, Delbert 8 n.14

Burridge, Richard A. 6 n.6

Calvert-Koyzis, Nancy 123 n.8
Catchpole, David 31 n.143, 37 n.191, 76 n.75
Charlesworth, James H. 41 n.206, 65 n.46
Childs, Brevard S. 141 n.78
Church of God (Cleveland, Tenn.) 12 n.31, 24 n.112
Church of God in Christ, The 24 n.112
Cicero 124 n.14
Clark, Kenneth W. 14, 139 n.72, 140 n.72
Cohick, Lynn 127 n.30
Collins, Adela Yarbro 5 n.2, 30 n.140, 56 n.12, 62 n.31, 83 n.105, 83 n.107, 84 nn.109–10, 135 n.57, 141 n.75
Conway, Colleen 108 n.83
Covington, Dennis 114 n.101
Croy, N. Clayton 8 n.14, 9 n.18, 28–30, 30 n.137, 34 n.160, 47
Culpepper, R. Alan 132 n.49

Dannemann, Irene 77 n.84
De Boer, Esther 60 n.31
De Jong, Matthijs J. 8 n.14, 34 n.160
Denyer, Nicholas 8 n.14
Dewey, Joanna 77 n.84
Dibelius, Martin 62 n.33, 63 n.37, 82 n.102
DiCicco, Mark 77 n.84, 83 n.104
Driggers, Ira Brent 89 n.6

Edwards, James R. 78 n.85
Ehrman, Bart D. 5 n.5, 18 n.69, 28 n.127, 29, 96 n.35, 135–6, 140 n.73, 142, 143 n.88, 146 n.5, 147 n.11
Elliott, J. K. 109
Epp, Eldon J. 14 n.39, 47 n.240, 139–41
Eusebius 1 n.1, 2 n.3, 3, 5 n.4, 7 n.9, 15–17, 20 n.82, 31 n.145, 32 n.154, 123 n.9, 124 n.12, 129–31
Evans, Craig 8 n.14, 28 n.127

Fander, Monika 77 n.84, 78 n.89, 141 n.79
Farmer, William R. 14–20, 130 n.44, 139 n.72, 140 n.72
Farrer, Austin 31–3
Foster, Paul 96 n.34
Foursquare Church, The 24 n.112

Gaius 127 n.30, 128 n.35
Gardner, Jane F. 128 n.38
Gaventa, Beverly Roberts 8 n.14, 36 n.177, 37 n.185, 49 n.2
Gilfillan Upton, Bridget 8 n.14, 42, 149 nn.12–13
Gorman, Michael J. 81 n.96
Greenlee, J. Harold 139 n.71
Griesbach, J. J. 6 n.9, 7, 12 n.30, 27 n.124
Gummere, R. M. 106 n.70
Gundry, Robert H. 28 n.127, 34 n.164, 132 n.48

Hannah, Darrell D. 97, 99–100
Hare, Douglas R. A. 53 n.10, 114 n.101
Hartman, Lars 8 n.14, 38
Hearon, Holly 77 n.83
Helton, Stanley N. 24 n.111
Hemelrijk, Emily A. 127 n.30
Hennecke, Edgar 96 n.35, 99
Hills, Julian 96 n.35
Hornschuh, Manfred 97 n.43
Horton, Charles 1 n.2
Hritzu, John N. 151 n.19
Hug, Joseph 57 n.17, 66 n.49, 72 n.66, 116 n.112
Hurtado, Larry W. 8 n.14, 37, 38 nn.192–3, 49 n.2, 76 n.75, 94 n.23, 114 n.101

Ilan, Tal 62 n.32
Irenaeus 146 n.3
Iverson, Kelly R. 8 n.14, 34 n.160

Jerome 3, 5 n.3, 7 n.10, 20 n.82, 97 n.37, 145, 151–2, 157
Johnson, Allan E. 130 n.43, 131 n.46
Johnson, E. Elizabeth 60 n.31, 62 n.31, 76 n.79
Johnson, Luke Timothy 60 n.30
Josephus 65 n.46, 83 n.105, 101 n.54, 102 n.56, 107–8, 128 nn.35–6
Joynes, Christine E. 8 n.14, 27 n.122
Juel, Donald H. 31 n.141, 33 nn.158–59, 35–7, 49

Justin Martyr 146 n.3
Juvenal 127 n.30

Keith, Chris 139 n.72
Kelhoffer, James A. 6 n.9, 7–8, 14 n.38, 15 n.44, 15 nn.46–7, 16 n.47, 18, 19 n.76, 23–4, 27, 39–42, 46–7, 53 nn.7–9, 55, 56 n.14, 58 n.20, 64 n.41, 72 n.66, 77 n.84, 96 n.33, 99, 101 n.53, 109, 113 n.97, 113 n.99, 116 n.112, 127 n.31, 130 nn.43–5, 135, 137, 138 nn.66–7, 146 nn.3-4
Kenyon, F. G. 6 n.8
Kermode, Frank 33 n.159, 35 n.172
Kinukawa, Hisako 77 n.84, 82 nn.100–101, 84 n.110, 85 n.113
Klauck, Hans-Josef 105 n.66
Kraemer, Ross Shepard 71 n.63, 125 n.16
Kuske, David P. 8 n.14

Lachmann, Karl 9 n.19, 30, 31 n.145
Lane, William L. 97 n.37, 116 n.109, 135 n.57
Larsen, Matthew D. C. 23 n.105, 138
Larson, Jennifer 108 n.83
Lieu, Judith 129 n.40, 142, 143 n.88
Lincoln, Andrew T. 33 n.160, 34 n.161, 37
Linnemann, Eta 8 n.13, 23 n.108
Long, Thomas 70 n.61
Ludemann, Gerd 129 n.40
Lunn, Nicholas P. 22–3, 8 n.14
Luz, Ulrich 56 n.14

Magness, J. Lee 34–5
Malbon, Elizabeth Struthers 76 n.75, 76 n.78, 78 n.84, 89 n.7
Marcus, Joel 28 n.126, 30 n.140, 35, 66 n.51
Martin, Dale 108 n.78
McDill, Matthew D. 8 n.14, 23 n.108
McGann, Jerome 139 n.71
Metzger, Bruce M. 5 n.1, 5 n.5, 18 n.69, 28 n.127, 29, 57 n.15, 140 n.73, 142, 143 n.88, 146 n.5, 147 n.10, 150
Meyers, Carole 65 n.46, 71 n.63
Middleton, J. Richard 81 n.96
Migne, J.-P., ed. 15 n.47, 16 n.47, 129 n.43
Miller, Patrick D. 8 n.14, 36 n.177, 37 n.185, 49 n.2
Miller, Susan 77 n.84, 78 n.84, 78 n.86, 82 n.100, 83 n.104
Mirecki, Paul Allan 23 n.108, 39, 57 n.17, 63–4, 72–3, 111

Mitchell, Joan L. 75 n.74, 76 n.74, 77 n.84, 81 n.95
Moore, Stephen D. 105 n.66, 106 n.72, 107 n.76, 108 nn.82–3
Moreschini, C. 151 n.20
Murfin, Ross 139 n.71

Nongbri, Brent 1 n.2, 55 n.11
Norton, Andrews 30 n.139

Oakeshott, Philip 8 n.14, 34 n.164
O'Day, Gail R. 32 n.154
Origen 125, 127, 128 n.33

Parker, D. C. 5 n.2, 14 n.39, 43 n.216, 47 n.240, 56 n.12, 123 n.10, 136, 137 n.60, 137 n.64, 145, 146 n.3, 149 nn.13–14, 151 n.18, 152 n.21
Parrot, Douglas M., ed. 97 n.36
Pearse, Roger, ed. 16 n.47, 130 n.44
Penner, Todd 108 n.83
Pervo, Richard I. 55 n.11
Pesch, Rudolf 60 n.31
Pierpont, Williams G. 18 n.69
Philo 128 n.35
Plato 8 n.14, 128 n.34,
Plotinus 34 n.160
Pomeroy, Sarah B. 128 n.39
Porter, Stanley E. 8 n.14, 137–8

Ray, Supriya M. 139 n.71
Riddle, Donald 140 n.72
Robinson, Maurice A. 8 n.14, 18–22

Sandys, J. E. 16 n.50
Schmidt, C. 99
Schneemelcher, Wilhelm 96 n.35, 99, 136 n.59
Schottroff, Luise 78 n.84
Schussler Fiorenza, Elizabeth 87 n.122, 142 n.80
Selvidge, Marla J. 78 n.84
Seneca 102 n.56, 104 n.65, 106 n.70
Setzer, Claudia 58 n.21, 70 n.61, 111 n.94, 127 n.30, 128 n.36
Shepherd, Thomas R. 8 n.14, 64–6
Smith, Daniel A. 3 n.5, 8 n.14, 94 n.21, 95–6
Smyth, Herbert Weir 92 n.16

Spencer, F. Scott 77 n.80, 77 n.83
Stein, Robert H. 8 n.14, 27, 28 n.127
Stichele, Caroline Vander 108 n.83
Strabo 127 n.30
Streeter, B. H. 16 n.50
Stuckenbruck, Loren T. 65 n.46
Sugirtharajah, R. S. 78 n.84, 83 n.104, 84 n.108
Swartley, Willard M. 77 n.84, 83 n.104

Tabor, James 138 n.66
Tacitus 128 n.35
Talbert, Charles H. 6 n.6
Tannehill, Robert 82 n.102
Taylor, Vincent 60 n.31, 82 n.102, 83 n.104
Tertullian 94 n.20
Thackeray, H. St. J. 101 n.54, 107 n.77
Thomas, John Christopher 8 n.14, 24–5, 26 n.118, 26 n.120
Thompson, Mary R. 89 n.4
Tiffin, Gerald C. 128 n.37
Tregelles, Samuel Prideaux 11 n.25, 12 n.30, 19, 31–33, 47–48, 128 n.33, 141 n.77
Trzebiatowska, Marta 124 n.13
Twelftree, Graham H. 66
Tyson, Joseph B. 89 n.5

Van der Horst, P. W. 34 n.160
Volgers, Annelie 124 n.12

Wall, Robert W. 26 n.120
Walsh, P. G. 125 n.18, 126 nn.20–1
Weeden, Theodore J. 132 n.48
Weir, Heather 123 n.8
Williams, Craig A. 107 n.78, 108 n.78, 108 n.83
Williams, Joel F. 37, 47
Williams, Travis 8 n.14, 21–3
Wire, Antoinette Clark 8 n.14, 45–7
Witherington, III, Ben 77 n.83, 83 n.104
Wright, Addison G. 78 n.84, 83 n.104

Yieh, John Y. H. 132 n.48

Zahn, Thedor 146 n.3

Zamagni, Claudio 15 n.44, 15 n.46, 16 n.47, 124 n.12, 129 n.43, 130 nn.43–5, 131 n.47

Ancient Index

Old Testament

Genesis
18:12	97
18:15	34 n.161
37:34-35	103
46:29	103 n.61

Exodus
4:1-5	41 n.206
7:8-13	41 n.206

Numbers
5:11-31	53 n.8

Deuteronomy
34.8	103
6:5	84 n.109

Joshua
Chs. 3–5	126 n.24

Judges
11:39	35 n.167
21:2	103 n.61

1 Samuel
1:10	103 n.61

2 Samuel
13:36	103 n.61
19:2	103
19:3	103 n.62
19:5-7	103 n.62

2 Kings
4:1-7	35 n.167
20:3	103 n.61

2 Chronicles
Book	35

Ezra
10:1	103 n.61

Nehemiah
1:4	103
8:9	103

Psalms
LXX 117:22a	70 n.59
118:22	70

Song of Songs
Book	35

Isaiah
6:9-10	90 n.10, 111 n.91
30:19	103 n.61
38:3	103 n.61
44:18	111 n.91

Jeremiah
5:21	111 n.91
22:10	103 n.61

Lamentations
1:2	103 n.61
1:4	103 n.61

Ezekiel
12:2	111 n.91
24:17	103 n.61

Daniel
Ch. 3	106 n.71
10:19	106 n.71

Jonah		7:23	105, 106 n.69
Book	35	8:16	106 n.69,
		10:14	106 n.69,
Deuterocanonical Books		13:9	106 n.71,
		13:10	106, 106 n.69
Tobit		15:4	106, 108 n.80
3:7-8	65 n.46	15:4b	106 n.73
3:7-19	65 n.46	15:5	106
3:14-15a	65 n.46	15:5-6	106 n.73
3:16-17	65 n.46	15:10	106 n.69
7:6	103 n.61	15:18-19	106
		15:20b	106
1 Maccabees		15:23	106, 106 n.69
9:20	104	15:28	107
9:21	104	15:30	106 n.69, 107
12:52	103 n.61	16:1	107
		16:1-2, 5-13	107 n.75
Wisdom of Sirach		17:23-24	106 n.69
7:34	103 n.61, 104 n.63		
22:11-12	104 n.63	New Testament	
28:17	104 n.63		
		Matthew	
Baruch		5:24	58 n.18
4:8	104	6:30	115 n.104
4:11	103 n.61, 104	6:33	58 n.18
4:12	104	7:5	58 n.18
4:16	104	8:12	103 n.60
4:21	104	8:26	115 n.104
4:23	103 n.61, 104	9:2-5	65 n.46
		9:20-22	82
Prayer of Azariah (Additions to Daniel)		10:2-4	58
1:28-68	106 n.71	13:14-15	90 n.10
		13:18	90 n.10
4 Maccabees		13:30	58 n.18
Book	104 n.64	13:42	103 n.60
1:4	106 n.69	13:50	103 n.60
1:6	106 n.69	14–16	133
1:7-8	105	14:22-23	58 n.19, 90 n.10
1:11	106 n.69	14:28-31	90 n.10
1:18	106 n.69	14:30-31	90 n.10
2:23	106 n.69	14:31	115 n.104
5:11	70 n.61	14:33	90 n.10
5:23	106 n.69	16:12	90 n.10
5:31	106 n.69	16:13-23	58 n.19
6:5-11	105 n.67	16:14	109
6:21	106 n.69	16:17-19	58 n.19
7:1-5	105	16:21-23	90 n.10
7:5	105 n.68,	16:23	109
7:20	105	16:5-12	137 n.61

16:6	90 n.10	28:17	94, 100, 112
16:8	115 n.104	28:18	112
16:9	90 n.10	28:18-20	25 n.115, 136, 138
17:20	115 n.104	28:19	54, 112
17:23	90 n.10	28:19-20	53
19:4	111 n.91	28:20	25 n.115, 112
19:7	111 n.91		
19:8	111	Mark	
19:8b	111 n.91	Ch. 1	21
19:13-21	111 n.91	1:1	6, 28 n.129
19:30	58 n.18	1:1–16:8	4, 9, 23, 36, 43, 50, 75, 76 n.74, 78, 88, 93, 114, 116, 134–5, 138 n.68, 141
20:10	58		
20:16	58 n.18		
20:17-19	89 n.9		
21:42	70		
22:13	103 n.60	1:1–16:20	39–46
24:51	103 n.60	1:2	28 n.129
25:30	103 n.60	1:3	102 n.57
26:7	85	1:7-8	77 n.81
26:8	89 n.9	1:21-27	65 n.46
26:51	132 n.49	1:23	102 n.57,
26:56	89 n.9	1:23-27	65 n.46, 134 n.54
26:69-75	89 n.9, 132	1:27	65 n.46
26:75	102, 133	1:30-31	78 n.88
27:46	102	1:33	21 n.90
27:55-56	56 n.14	1:34	21 n.90, 65 n.46
27:56	60, 61	1:35	21 n.90
27:61	61	1:39	65 n.46
Ch. 28	99 n.46	1:41	53 n.8, 78 n.87
28:1	16, 56 n.14, 57, 60–1, 74, 98, 130–1	1:44	75 n.74
		2:3-12	79
28:1-20	133	2:5	78 n.87, 81 n.97, 116 n.109
28:7	93 n.19		
28:7-9	133	2:5-9	65 n.46
28:8	54, 67	2:6	116
28:8b	67	2:8	116
28:8-10	90	2:9-11	81 n.97
28:8-9	57	3:5	111 n.91, 116
28:9	58 n.21, 67, 74	3:10-12	65 n.46
28:9-10	28 n.127, 57 n.16, 75	3:11-12	65 n.46, 134 n.54
28:10	68, 68 n.53, 93 n.19, 98	3:13	83 n.107
		3:13-14	89 n.3
		3:13-19	51
28:11	68 n.54	3:14	52 n.6, 80 n.91, 92 n.13
28:11-15	96		
28:15	68	3:14-15	21 n.91
28:16	68, 68 n.53, 93 n.19, 96, 133	3:18	80 n.91
		3:22	65 n.46
28:16-17	23 n.108, 54	3:23	83 n.107
28:16-20	28 n.127	3:23-27	65 n.46

Ancient Index

3:28	84 n.110	6:1-16	66 n.50
3:31-35	76	6:2b-4	82
3:34	78 n.87	6:3	60 n.31
3:35	81	6:5	53 n.8, 55, 82
4:10	51, 89, 92 n.15	6:5-6	78 n.87
4:11	89 n.3, 115	6:6	66 n.50, 82
4:11-12	115	6:7	53 n.8, 83 n.107, 134 n.54
4:12	111 n.91		
4:13	89, 115	6:7-13	21 n.91
4:38-41	89	6:12-13	65 n.46
4:40-41	76 n.77	6:13	53 n.8, 55, 134 n.54
Ch. 5	96 n.35	6:19	77
5:1-13	65 n.46	6:22	77
5:1-20	134 n.54	6:25-26	77
5:15, 33, 36	34 n.162	6:28	77
5:18	51, 77 n.81	6:37	89
5:19-20	66 n.51, 75 n.74, 77 n.81	6:45-52	90 n.10
		6:49	102 n.57
5:21-24a	81	6:49-50	89
5:21-43	78 n.85	6:50	34 n.162
5:22-23	79	6:51b-52	89, 90 n.10
5:22-24a	77 n.81	6:52	111 n.91, 115, 115 n.106
5:23	81 n.99		
5:24	79	7:14	83 n.107
5:24b-34	78	7:18	115, 115 n.106
5:25	79	7:24-30	65 n.46, 78 n.89
5:25-26	80	7:24–8:38	21 n.91
5:25-27	80	7:25-30	82
5:25-34	75 n.74, 79, 81 n.96, 82	7:27	58 n.18, 78 n.89
		7:29	120 n.3
5:26	80	7:32-37	75 n.74
5:27-29	82	8:1	83 n.107
5:27b	79	8:4	89
5:28	80	8:11-12	53 n.8
5:29	79–80	8:12	84 n.110
5:30	79	8:14-21	89
5:30-33a	80	8:15	90 n.10
5:30-34	116 n.109	8:15-21	137 n.61
5:31	80 n.93	8:16	116
5:33	34 n.162, 75 n.74, 80	8:16-21	76 n.77
5:34	78 n.87, 79, 81 nn.96, 99, 82, 120 n.3	8:17	109, 111 n.91, 115
		8:17-21	90 n.10, 115
5:34a	81	8:17b	90 n.10
5:35-43	81	8:18	111 n.91, 115 n.106
5:36	34 n.162	8:21	90 n.10, 115 n.106
5:38	102 n.57	8:25	53 n.8
5:38-39	102, 102 n.57	8:27	37
5:38-43	78 n.88	8:29	89 n.3, 115, 137 n.61
5:42	81 n.99	8:31	27, 36, 69, 70

8:31-32	137	10:43-44	84 n.107
8:31-33	90 n.10	10:46-52	66 n.51
8:32	89	10:47-48	82
8:32-33	115	10:51	82
8:33	109	10:52	51, 66 n.51, 77 n.81,
8:34	83 n.107, 84		81 n.96, 82
	nn.107, 110	11:15-19	70
8:35-37	85 n.112	11:22	115 n.107
9:1	84 n.110	11:22-23	115
9:6	89, 115, 115 n.106	11:23	84 n.110, 115 n.107
9:17-18	115	11:27	70
9:17-27	77 n.81	11:27-33	70
9:17-29	65 n.46	11:28	70
9:18-19	76 n.77, 89	11:30	77 n.81
9:19	115	11:31	70
9:24	115, 115 n.105	12:10	70
9:28	89	12:30	84 n.109
9:30-32	137	12:34	77 n.81
9:31	27, 36	12:41-44	78
9:32	89, 90 n.10, 115,	12:41a	83
	115 n.106	12:41b	83
9:33	116	12:43	83
9:33-34	89	12:43-44	83, 120 n.3
9:36	85 n.111	12:44	82, 84, 85, 86 n.120
9:38	55	Ch. 13	86 n.117
9:41	84 n.110	13:10	122
10:2-12	111 n.91	13:22	53 n.8
10:4	111 n.91	14:1-11	86
10:5	111, 116	14:2-9	85 n.111
10:6	111 n.91	14:3	85
10:13	89	14:3-9	78, 85, 87, 102 n.58
10:13-16	115	14:4	89 n.9
10:14	85 n.111	14:5	86
10:15	84 n.110	14:6	85–87, 102 n.58
10:21	84 n.108	14:6-9	120 n.3
10:22	84 n.108	14:7	86
10:28	89 n.3	14:8	87
10:28-31	116, 137 n.61	14:8a	85 n.116
10:29	84 n.110	14:9	84 n.110, 86, 102 n.58
10:31	58 n.18	14:10-11	86 n.121, 115
10:32	34 n.162, 51, 92 n.15	14:11b	86 n.121
10:32-34	89 n.9, 137	14:16	89 n.3
10:33	36	14:17	67 n.52
10:34	27	14:18	84 n.110, 86 n.117
10:35	84 n.109	14:25	84 n.110
10:35-40	89	14:27	115
10:38	115, 115 n.106	14:28	10, 21 n.88, 27,
10:39	115		28 n.126
10:42	83 n.107, 84 n.107	14:29	85 n.112

Reference	Pages
14:29-31	115
14:30	84 n.110
14:31	85 n.112
14:34	102
14:36b	102
14:37-41	89
14:47	132 n.49
14:50	67 n.52, 75, 85, 89, 91 n.12, 93, 115–16, 121–2
14:50-51	121
14:50-52	89 n.9
14:52	91 n.12, 122
14:62	55
14:66-69	77
14:66-72	67 n.52, 85 n.112, 89 n.9, 93, 115, 121, 132
14:68-69	82 n.100
14:68b	85 n.112
14:72	38 n.192, 67 n.52, 69, 75, 91 n.12, 102, 102 n.57
Ch. 15	85
Chs. 15–16	59 n.25
15:21	79 n.91
15:29-30	70
15:29-32	70
15:31	70
15:32	70
15:34	102, 102 n.57, 115
15:40	38 n.192, 44 n.221, 51, 59 n.25, 60–1, 62 n.32, 63, 65, 67
15:40-41	64, 75, 101, 115, 116 n.110, 135
15:40–16:8	37
15:40–16:20	74
15:41	51, 87
15:42-46	77 n.81
15:43	79 n.91
15:44	84 n.107
15:46-47	101
15:47	44 n.221, 59 n.25, 60–1, 62 n.32, 63, 65, 67, 75, 135
Ch. 16	6, 25 n.115, 21
16:1	44 n.221, 49 n.1, 56–7, 59, 61, 62 n.32, 63, 67, 74, 135
16:1-2	130
16:1-4	98
16:1-8	3, 9, 21, 38, 49–50, 56, 59 n.25, 64, 65, 91 n.12, 101, 116 n.110, 121, 133, 136
16:1-20	43
16:2	44, 49 n.1, 56 n.14
16:3	149
16:4	149
16:5	49, 135
16:6	12, 51–2, 75 n.73
16:6-7	137
16:6-20	150
16:7	10, 36, 27, 28 n.126, 51–2, 67, 74, 91 n.12, 93, 123, 133–34, 149
16:7-8	37, 43, 76 n.74
16:8	1–6, 7 n.11, 8 n.14, 9–10, 12–16, 19, 21 n.88, 22, 26–39, 42, 43 n.216, 44 n.221, 45–9, 51–2, 56, 57 n.15, 59, 64–5, 67, 74, 75 n.74, 76, 88, 94, 101, 116 n.110, 119–20, 122–3, 123 n.10, 124, 127, 128 n.33, 134–7, 140, 144–7, 149–51, 153
16:8b	38 n.192, 140
16:8-9	56
16:8-10	137
16:9	2, 6 n.9, 10 n.21, 16, 17 n.59, 21 n.90, 31 n.146, 43–4, 48, 51–3, 56–7, 59, 61–4, 67, 90, 93–5, 104, 121–2, 128 n.33, 130, 134, 149–50, 157
16:9-10	64–5, 67
16:9-11	43 n.219, 50, 56, 59 n.25, 67, 69, 75 n.71, 82, 90, 99 n.46, 101, 104, 119, 123, 127 n.31, 136, 138
16:9-11	57, 59 n.25, 68–9, 72–4
16:9-14	51–2, 91

16:9-20	1–4, 5 nn.1–2, 6–12, 13 n.34, 14–26, 27 n.124, 31–3, 35, 38–9, 43, 46–7, 49 n.3, 50, 54–5, 57 n.15, 94, 105, 119, 128 n.33, 131, 134 n.54, 136, 138, 139 n.72, 146, 147–50, 152 n.23, 153–6	16:15	5 n.3, 50 n.4, 76, 91, 97, 108 n.85, 109, 112 n.95, 113–14, 120–3, 136–7, 147, 150, 157
		16:15-16	43 n.219, 72 n.66
		16:15-18	43, 50, 53, 93–4, 138
		16:15-20	7 n.12, 23 n.108
		16:16	10, 13, 24 n.111, 31 n.146, 39, 76, 113, 116, 121, 127, 136
16:10	52, 56, 69, 76 n.74, 91, 92 n.14, 93, 100 n.49, 101–2, 103 n.61, 104, 109, 120–2, 127, 134, 144	16:16a	127 n.31
		16:16b	11 n.23, 127 n.31
		16:17	21 n.90, 22, 24 n.112, 66, 134 n.54
		16:17a	40, 127 n.31
16:10b	101	16:17-18	1, 3, 10, 17 n.60, 24–26, 49, 53 n.8, 76, 114, 116 n.109
16:10-11	2, 10, 43, 88, 94, 101		
16:10-14	91		
16:11	50, 52, 67, 70, 72, 91, 91 n.12, 92, 94–5, 100–1, 101 n.52, 109, 136	16:17-20	12 n.31
		16:17b-18	39–40
		16:18	8, 41 n.206, 108 n.85, 114 n.101
16:11b	127 n.31	16:18a	7 n.12, 40, 41 n.206
16:12	22, 57 n.17, 71, 87, 91–5, 122, 137 n.61, 157	16:18b	7 n.12, 9, 41, 53 n.8
		16:18-19	116 n.111
		16:19	7 n.9, 13, 20, 39, 43, 45, 53, 76, 93, 114
16:12-13	43, 43 n.219, 50, 53, 64, 72–3, 75, 82, 88, 101, 109, 120 n.1, 138		
		16:19-20	43 n.219, 50, 72 n.66
		16:20	5, 6, 9–10, 12 n.31, 17–18, 22, 36 n.180, 39, 42–3, 76, 93, 109, 108 n.85, 114, 116, 120–3, 134, 136
16:12-20	134		
16:13	10, 62, 72, 70 nn.60, 62, 91 n.12, 92, 94, 100–101, 109, 121–2, 136		
		16:20a	43
16:13b	127 n.31	16:20b	43, 140
16:13-14	71, 92		
16:14	5 n.3, 43, 43 n.219, 50, 52, 57 n.17, 69, 70 n.60, 71, 72 n.66, 74–5, 88, 90–4, 97, 100 n.49, 101, 102 n.58, 109, 111, 113, 122, 127, 134, 136, 147, 151, 157	Luke	
		1:2	60 n.30
		1:39-56	70 n.61
		Ch. 2	97
		5:20-23	65 n.46
		6:25	102
		7:36-50	102 n.58
		7:38	85 n.113
16:14b	127 n.31	7:39	89 n.9
16:14-15	25 n.117, 52	7:44	85 n.113, 102 n.58
16:14-18	50 n.4	7:50	81 n.96, 102 n.58
16:14-20	120, 137	Ch. 8	59 n.29, 63

8:2	62 n.34, 63, 74, 88	24:10-11	75 n.71
8:2b	54, 63	24:11	54, 57 n.16, 70, 74, 94, 95, 98, 111, 112, 133 n.51
8:2-3	59, 62		
8:11	90 n.10		
8:42b-48	82	24:12	133 n.51
9:22	69, 90 n.10	24:13	71, 96
9:22b	69 n.57	24:13-27	109
9:45	90 n.10	24:13-32	54
10:19	53 n.8	24:13-33a	53
12:1	90 n.10, 137 n.61	24:13-35	72, 74, 94 n.20, 136, 138
12:28	115 n.104		
12:59	83 n.105	24:15	71 n.64
13:16	81 n.98	24:16	71, 109
13:28	103 n.60	24:18	71
13:30	58 n.18	24:22	109
14:28	58 n.18	24:22-23	110 n.89
14:31	58 n.18	24:24	74, 109
15:22	58 n.18	24:25	74, 109–11
17:19	81 n.96	24:25-26	74
18:31-33	69, 69 n.58	24:25-27	50, 94, 96, 120 n.4
18:33b	69 n.57	24:26	110
18:34	89 n.9	24:27	110
20:17	70	24:28	110
22:49-50	132 n.49	24:31	71
22:51	132 n.49	24:33	54, 93 n.19, 95 n.25, 96
22:54-62	89 n.9		
22:56-62	132	24:33-35	54
22:62	102	24:33-36a	72
22:69	55	24:34	72, 95 n.25, 133 n.51
23:27	60, 101, 101 n.55	24:35	90
23:27-28	136 n.59	24:36	72, 88
23:27-31	60	24:37	110 nn.88, 90
23:28	60, 101	24:37-43	96
23:49	60	24:38	110 n.88
23:55	60	24:38-39	110
23:55-56	60	24:39	110 n.90
24:1	56 n.14, 57, 60	24:39-40	98, 110nn.88, 90
24:1-11	60	24:39-43	112
24:3	60	24:41	110 n.88
24:4	59–60, 69	24:41-43	110 n.90
24:5	60	24:45	110 n.88
24:7	69 n.57,	24:46-69	112
24:8	69, 69 n.58,	24:47	54, 112
24:8-9	57, n.16	24:48	112
24:8-10	95	24:49	93 n.19, 112
24:9	54, 60, 133 n.51	24:50	96
24:9b-12	28 n.127	24:51	13, 53, 55
24:10	57, 59–61, 63, 74, 98, 133 n.51		

Ancient Index

John
- Ch. 1 — 97
- 3:18b — 55
- 7:53–8:11 — 32 n.154, 48 n.241
- 9:2 — 65 n.46
- 11:35 — 68
- 12:4 — 89 n.9
- 13:15 — 83 n.103
- 14:12 — 40, 55
- 18:10-11 — 132 n.49
- 18:15-18 — 132,
- 18:16-27 — 89 n.9
- 18:25-27 — 132
- 19:25 — 59 n.25, 60, 61
- 19:26 — 61
- Ch. 20 — 57–8, 69
- 20:1 — 54, 56 n.14, 58, 58 n.22, 60–1, 98, 120 n.2,
- 20:1-2 — 53, 59 n.25, 74
- 20:1-18 — 58
- 20:2 — 58 n.22, 68 n.56
- 20:2-10 — 133 n.52
- 20:3-10 — 50
- 20:4 — 58, 133 n.51
- 20:5 — 133 n.51
- 20:6 — 58 n.22
- 20:8 — 58, 95 n.29, 133 n.51
- 20:11 — 54, 61, 68, 101, 136 n.59
- 20:11-8 — 53
- 20:11-15 — 128 n.33
- 20:11-18 — 57, 68, 120 n.2, 129, 136, 138
- 20:11-19 — 59 n.25
- 20:11 — 54, 98
- 20:13 — 54, 68, 68 n.56, 98, 101, 136 n.59
- 20:14 — 54, 68 n.56
- 20:14-15 — 59
- 20:14-16 — 95
- 20:14-17 — 58
- 20:15 — 68, 98, 101, 136 n.59,
- 20:15b — 68,
- 20:16 — 61
- 20:17 — 68, 98, 112,
- 20:18 — 54, 61, 74–5, 90, 95 n.24
- 20:18a — 68
- 20:18b — 68
- 20:19 — 88, 93 n.19
- 20:22 — 112
- 20:23 — 112
- 20:24 — 112
- 20:24-25 — 94,
- 20:24-29 — 54, 100
- 20:25 — 98
- 20:26 — 88, 93 n.19
- 20:27 — 98
- 20:27b — 74 n.69
- 20:27-29 — 96
- 20:29 — 95 n.29
- Ch. 21 — 28
- 21:1 — 96
- 21:1-2 — 93 n.19
- 21:1-14 — 28 n.126
- 21:7 — 134
- 21:15-17 — 112
- 21:15-19 — 96, 123 n.7, 133 n.52
- 21:17 — 134 n.53
- 21:18-23 — 96
- 21:20 — 112
- 21:20-22 — 133 n.52

Acts
- Book — 35
- 1:2 — 55,
- 1:2 — 13
- 1:8 — 25 n.115, 112
- 1:9 — 13
- 1:11 — 55
- 1:22 — 55
- 1:26 — 54
- 2:4 — 55
- 2:4-13 — 53 n.8
- 2:11 — 55
- 2:14 — 54
- 3:12–4:3 — 120 n.4
- 7:55-56 — 55
- Ch. 9 — 96 n.32
- 12:1-2 — 123 n.9
- 12:1-19 — 96 n.32
- 12:12 — 11 n.26
- 12:25 — 11 n.26
- 12:25–28:31 — 96 n.32
- 13:13 — 11 n.26
- 15:37-40 — 11 n.26
- 28:1-10 — 41 n.206

28:3-6	53 n.8	James	
		4:9	102
Romans		5:14	83 n.106
15:18-19	24 n.112	5:14-16	24 n.112
16:1-2	143 n.89		
16:3	143 n.89	1 John	
16:6	143 n.89	5:19	151
16:7	143 n.89		
		3 John	
1 Corinthians		11	83 n.103
Ch. 7	143 n.89		
11:13	143 n.90	Revelation	
11:5	143 nn.89, 90	18:2	103
12:10	53 n.8,	18:10	103
12:28	58 n.18	18:11	103
12:30	53 n.8,	18:15	103
14:33b-36	143 n.90	18:16	103
15:3-7	58 n.19	18:17	103
15:5	58 n.19, 97 n.36, 129, 133 n.51	18:19	103
15:5-8	129	Other Ancient References	
15:8	129 n.41		
15:9	129 n.41	Apuleius, *The Golden Ass* [*Metam.*]	
16:19	143 n.89	4.28	125 n.19
		4.34	125
Galatians		5.5	125 n.20
2:11-14	132 n.49	5.9-11	125
3:28	143 n.89	5.11	126 n.20
		5.15	127 n.30
Ephesians		5.28–6.22	125
1:1	13	6.1	126
		6.17	126
Philippians		6.21	126
3:17	83 n.103	6.22-24	126
4:2-3	143 n.89		
		Augustine, *Harmony of the Gospels* [*Cons.*]	
1 Thessalonians		III.58	131
1:17	83 n.103		
		Cicero, *De divinatione*	
2 Thessalonians		II.xv.36	124 n.14
3:7	83 n.103		
		Epistula Apostolorum	
1 Timothy		Work	22 n.104, 97, 97 n.42, 113 n.97, 116
2:9-15	143 n.89	1–6	97 n.41, 99
Hebrews		1–11	98
2:4	24 n.112	3	97
3:17	83 n.103	4	99
		9	100

9–10	97 n.44, 108 n.84	104	128 n.35
9–11	100 n.47, 129 n.42	109	128 n.35
10	99 n.46, 100	144	128 n.35
10–11	97 n.37	190–1	127 n.30
11	93 n.18, 96 n.35, 100, 112		

The Gospel of Mary
Work   22 n.104, 136 n.59

11–12	95 n.29, 123 n.7		
11–51	99		
12	96 n.35, 112		

The Gospel of Peter
Work   22 n.104, 28 n.126, 139 n.69

12–14	96		
14	96 n.35	11.43–9	96
15	96 n.32	39–41	123 n.10
16–18	96		
17	99 n.45		

Infancy Gospel of Thomas

		6:3	99
Eugnostos		14:2	99
Work	96 n.36, 97 n.36		

Irenaeus, *Adversus haereses*

Eusebius, *Demonstratio evangelica*
VII.3   15 n.46, 130 n.43

iii.X.6   146 n.3

Eusebius, *Historia ecclesiastica*

Jerome, *Adversus Pelagianos dialogi III*

III.1.2	123 n.9	II.15.1–9	151
III.23.3-4	123 n.9	II.15.1	157
III.31.2-4	123 n.9	II.15.5–8	97 n.37
III.39	32 n.154	II.15.5–8	152

Eusebius, *Quaestiones ad Marinum*
(in *Quaestiones et Responsiones*)

Jerome, *Epistula ad Hedybiam*
Work   7 n.10, 20 n.82

Work	5 n.4, 7. 9, 14–15, 16 n.47, 20 n.82, 124 n.12, 129 n.43, 130–1

Josephus, *Jewish Antiquities*
4.8.15   128 n.35

I	1, 17 n.59
I.1	131

Josephus, *Jewish War*

2.155	83 n.105

Eusebius, *Quaestiones ad Stephanum*
(in *Quaestiones et Responsiones*)

6.395	101 n.54
7.185	65 n.46

7.1-8	130 n.45	7.337–38	107 n.77
8.1-4	130 n.45	7.339	102 n.58
9.1-3	130 n.45	7.351–57	108 n.81
		7.8–9	107

Eusebius, *Quaestiones et Responsiones ad Stephanum et Marinum*

Justin Martyr, *First Apology*

Work	15, 16 n.47	I.45	146 n.3

Juvenal, *Satirae*
6.511–91   127 n.30

Gaius, *Institutiones*
48–9   128 n.35

Letter of Aristeas
250-251a   124 n.15
252   124 n.15

Life of Adam and Eve
3:1   126 n.23
6:1   126 n.25
6:1-2   126 n.25
6:2   126 n.25
6:3   126 n.25
9:1   126
9:2   126
9:3-4   126 n.26
10:1-2   126
10:3-4   126 n.27
18:1   126 n.28
21:2   127
26:2   127 n.29

Origen, *Contra Celsum*
Work   17 n.56, 125 n.17
2.27   135
2.55   127
2.59   128 n.33

Philo, *Questions and Answers on Genesis*
4.15   128 n.35

Plato, *Timaeus*
91   128 n.34

Plotinus, *Enneades*
5.5   34 n.160

Seneca, *Epistulae morales*
XCIX.2   102 n.56
CXIV.24   106 n.70

Seneca, *Ad Lucilium*
63.1-2, 11, 14   104 n.65

Sophia of Jesus Christ
Work   96 nn.35, 36

Strabo, *Geographica*
7.3.4   127 n.30

Tacitus, *Annals*
3.34   128 n.35

Tertullian, *Adversus Marcionem*
4.43   94 n.20

Subject Index

anachronism 19–20, 23, 35, 43, 123, 138
angelic figure 49, 51–2, 65 n.46, 67–8, 75 nn.71, 73, 97–9, 101, 126–7, 137, 149 n.13
anointing woman 85–7
anonymity 59–60, 75–88, 93, 134, 136 n.58
ascension 13, 39, 45, 50, 53, 68, 96, 114
Augustine 130–1, 151 n.19
aurality 41–6, 75 n.74
authenticity 6–27, 31 n.146, 32 n.152, 37, 43, 46–7, 114 n.101, 131, 138–41
authorial intention 1–5, 9, 19–20, 27, 29, 32–3, 47–8, 136–8
authorship 19–20, 23 n.105, 46–7, 53 n.10,

baptism 10, 13, 39, 112–13
Bartimaeus 51, 66 n.51, 77 n.81, 82
belief. *See* faith/faithfulness
bodily. *See* embodiment

canon 23, 25 n.117, 26 n.120, 32, 37, 137–41, 144
canonicity 12, 23, 26 n.120, 32, 47–8, 113–14 n.101, 141
Celsus 125, 127–8, 131, 135
Church of God (Cleveland, TN) 12 n.31, 24 n.112
Codex Sinaiticus (א) 2, 5, 13 n.36, 31 n.150, 56 n.12, 123, 146
Codex Vaticanus (B) 2, 5–7, 13 n.36, 27, 31, 56 n.12, 60 n.31, 123, 146
commission. *See* mission
credulity. *See* gullibility
crucifixion. 38 n.192, 51, 59–62, 70, 79 n.91, 85, 98, 101
crying. *See* grieving

daughter(s) 35 n.167, 60, 65 n.46, 76–9, 81, 101–2
demon-possession 51, 62–7, 113–14, 134 n.54

disbelief. *See* faith/faithfulness, lack of
disciples
    discipleship 37, 44, 67, 76–7, 78 n.86, 87–91, 112, 117, 119–24, 127, 137, 144
    female disciples 1–4, 26, 37–9, 46, 49–51, 59–64, 67, 69, 75–88, 91–2, 116 n.110, 119–20, 122–4, 130, 135–6, 141–4
    male disciples 4, 52, 67–9, 71–5, 77, 78 n.86, 89–117, 119–23, 132–3, 135–6, 142, 144
divine passive 71, 90 n.10, 109
doubt
    of Jesus/his resurrection 44, 54, 74 n.69, 90 n.10, 94–5, 97–8, 100, 110 n.88, 115–16
    regarding Markan ending. *See* authenticity

Eleven, the 2, 10, 44, 50–2, 67–9, 73–5, 88, 91–5, 109–14, 119–22, 134, 144
Elijah 20–1
Elisha 20–1, 35 n.167
embodiment 65 n.46, 80–1, 83 n.105, 96 n.35, 98–100, 105 n.67, 110, 112, 129 n.40. *See also* Jesus; as resurrected
emotions 68 n.55, 69, 101–8, 119, 124 n.15, 128 nn.33–6, 136,
Eusebius 1 nn.1, 3, 5 n.4, 15–17, 20 n.82, 27 n.124, 31 n.145, 32 n.154, 123 n.9, 124 n.12, 129–31
evangelism. *See* proclamation
evangelist. *See* proclamation
Eve 126–7
exemplary. *See* paradigmatic
exorcism. *See* demon-possession

faith/faithfulness
    lack of 44, 89–101, 104, 109–17, 135–8,
    presence of 10, 44, 50–2, 59 n.24, 66–75, 78–82, 95 n.29, 119–27, 135, 144
fear (of the women at tomb). *See* silence (of the women at tomb)

Subject Index

female disciples. *See under* disciples
flight (of the women at tomb). *See* silence (of the women at tomb)
following. *See* disciples; discipleship
forgery. *See* spurious(ness)
form criticism 62 n.33, 64 n.41
Four-Gospel Canon 1–3, 45, 53, 56 n.14, 119, 132, 133 n.51, 134, 137–41, 143
Freer Logion. *See under* Markan Endings; Freer Logion

gender
  grammatical 68 n.54, 71, 73, 92, 101 n.52
  gender-stereotypes 1–4, 44, 46–7, 69–70, 77–80, 83, 85 n.113, 101–8, 111, 120, 122, 124–31, 135, 136 n.59, 141–4
  masculinity 2, 100, 101 n.54, 102, 105–8, 119
genre 6, 16 n.47, 19–20, 34, 38 n.195, 124 n.12, 130
gnostic/ism 96
Great Commission 53, 137–8, 142
grieving 20 n.86, 67 n.52, 68–9, 90 n.10, 93, 98, 100–8, 116, 119, 136, 144
gullibility 122, 124–8, 129 n.40

hard-heartedness 3, 74, 92–3, 109–11, 116, 122, 127
harmony/izing (among Gospels) 12 n.31, 17, 31 n.147, 45, 49, 52–5, 95–6, 124, 129–32, 141 n.78, 146 n.3, 148
Herod/ias 62, 77

implied audience 35, 38, 43–5, 63, 75–6 n.74
inspiration 11, 13 n.34, 18 n.69, 20 n.87, 23, 25, 26 n.120, 32–3, 39, 47
intercalation 78–82
Intermediate Ending. *See under* Markan Endings; Intermediate Ending
Irenaeus 31 n.145, 146

Jairus 77 n.81, 78 n.85, 79–81, 102
Jerome 3, 5 n.3, 7 n.10, 145, 151–2, 157
Jesus
  approval by 73–5, 77 n.81, 78, 81–2, 86–7, 120
  censure by 5 n.3, 52, 83 n.104, 91–4, 109–13, 115, 120, 134
  as resurrected 1, 51–2, 56, 67–76, 94, 104, 109, 113, 120 n.4, 123, 129–31
Joanna 60–3, 95
John the Baptist 77 n.81, 102 n.57
Joseph of Arimathea 77 n.81, 79 n.91

lexical coherence. *See* Long Ending; vocabulary
literary methods 14, 27, 30–1, 33–9, 48, 75 n.74, 77 n.80
Long Ending
  canonical status 1–3, 5–8, 13 n.34, 23, 24 n.111, 26 n.120, 32, 47–8, 75, 114 n.101, 131, 138, 141
  innovation within 49–53, 73–5, 87–8, 94, 114 n.102, 138–9
  as the original ending of Mark 14–26, 47, 145–8
  vocabulary 18, 20–3, 46, 53–5, 56 n.14, 63, 70 n.60, 102

Majority Text 5, 18–19, 86 n.116, 147
male disciples. *See under* disciples
manuscript evidence 1, 5–7, 9, 13 n.34, 15, 23, 25 n.117, 48 n.241, 49 n.3, 55 n.11, 56, 57 n.15, 59 n.27, 76 n.76, 131, 145–57
Mark
  the Evangelist 11, 19–20, 22 n.100, 32 n.152, 47, 123 n.10,
  as literary whole 26–7, 32–3, 35–6, 39–40, 42–3, 45, 47–8, 75, 119, 134, 139, 143–4
  theology of 9, 13–14, 18, 29, 33, 45, 47–8, 50, 75 n.74, 76–8, 88, 95, 102, 113, 119, 123, 134 n.54, 139
Markan Endings
  ending at 16:8 7 n.11, 8 n.14, 9, 13–4, 19, 26–39, 47, 75 n.74, 119, 137, 140, 145–7
  ending at 16:8 as unfinished 29–30, 35, 49, 123 n.10
  Freer Logion 3, 5, 12, 25 n.117, 97, 113, 145, 151–7
  Intermediate Ending 3, 5, 10 n.21, 42 n.215, 43 n.216, 57 n.15, 59, 76, 123, 133, 137, 145, 147–51

longer ending. *See* Long Ending
lost ending theories 2 n.3, 9, 13, 17–18, 27–30, 46
purposeful removal 2, 15 n.45, 19–20, 31 n.147, 131
shorter ending. *See* Markan Endings; Intermediate Ending
terminology (within this study) 5, 91 n.11, 146–52, 157
Mary Magdalene 1–4, 10, 44, 48–88, 90–2, 95, 98–101, 104–5, 109, 111–12, 114, 117, 119–24, 127–38, 143–4
Mary the mother of James and/or Joses 49, 51, 60–1, 63, 95, 121–2
Mary, Jesus's mother 76, 142
masculinity. *See under* gender, masculinity
mission 37 n.187, 42, 50, 52–3, 66, 76, 91, 96 nn.31–2, 109, 112–6, 120–2, 136–7, 144
mother(s) 60 n.31, 76–7, 104–8, 142
mourning. *See* grieving

naming 10 n.21, 46, 51, 58 n.19, 59–65, 67, 71, 74–6, 87, 130, 132

oral performance. *See* aurality
Origen 17, 125, 127, 128 n.33
orthodoxy 1, 19, 31, 135, 138 n.67, 143

paradigmatic 1, 66, 71–3, 83–8, 106, 109, 117, 119–20, 127, 144
passion. *See* crucifixion; or *see* emotions
patristic-era attestation 1 n.2, 2 n.4, 7 n.9, 9, 14–18, 23, 31 n.145, 32 n.154, 39, 46, 131, 145–6, 151–2, 157
Paul/Pauline tradition 40–1, 58 nn.18–19, 83 n.103, 96 n.32, 99, 129, 132 n.49, 133 n.51, 143
Pentecostal hermeneutics 24–6
Pericope Adulterae (John 7:53–8:11) 32 n.154, 48 n.241, 139 n.72
Peter 3, 10, 19 n.72, 28 n.126, 32 n.152, 50, 58, 67, 77, 85 n.112, 89 n.9, 90 n.10, 93, 95–6, 102, 109, 112, 115, 123 n.9, 129, 131–4, 136 n.59, 149
physicality. *See* embodiment
poison-drinking 1, 7 n.12, 8, 17, 19 n.76, 24–5, 40–2, 50, 53, 108 n.85, 114 n.101

proclamation 67–70, 75, 92–4, 108 n.85, 109, 111, 114, 116, 119–22, 127–31, 134–6, 144
proto-canon/ical 3, 47, 53, 129, 137, 138 n.67, 139, 143
proto-feminist/ism 2, 123
psyche 125–6

reader-response 37–8, 42–4
reception 9 n.17, 32, 42–3, 135–7, 140–1
redaction criticism 18, 53–5, 57 n.17,
resurrection 1–4, 10, 20–1, 27–9, 34, 36, 43–4, 47–79, 87–8, 91, 93 n.19, 94–102, 110 n.90, 111 n.91, 112–14, 119–20, 123–4, 127–33, 142
Road to Emmaus 52–3, 71–4, 94–5, 109, 110 n.89

Salome 49, 51, 60 n.31, 61, 62 n.32, 97 n.44, 121–2
salvation/saving 13, 70, 78 n.85, 79–82, 84 n.109, 104, 113, 116, 121, 123 n.10, 124
scribal practices 3 n.5, 4, 16–18, 20 n.80, 27 n.124, 28 n.129, 30, 31 n.147, 45, 47, 49 n.3, 113, 143, 146, 150–2, 157
signs 3, 7 n.12, 8, 10, 12 n.31, 17, 24–6, 39–42, 49–50, 53, 65–6, 113–14, 116, 120, 137, 140
silence (of the women at tomb) 6, 9, 30–1, 33–8, 44, 49, 51, 56–7, 59, 64, 67, 76 nn.74–75, 88, 94, 101, 119–24, 134–7, 140, 149
Simon Peter. *See* Peter
snake-handling 1, 7 n.12, 8, 17, 19 n.76, 24–5, 40–2, 53, 108 n.85, 114
Society of Biblical Literature xi, 14, 139 n.72
spurious(ness) 9–13, 16, 29, 31–2, 38–9, 129 n.40, 134–5, 138–40, 152 n.23,
Stoicism 68 n.55, 104–6, 108
stylistic considerations 20–2, 23 n.108, 31, 33–5, 46, 93–4
Susanna 63
Synoptic comparison/theory 6 n.9, 18 n.63, 20, 54–5, 57, 64 n.41, 82, 89–90, 102, 111, 132 n.49, 153–56
Syrophoenician mother 78 n.89, 82

testimony. *See* witness
textual criticism 1, 5–9, 13–15, 17 n.56, 29, 30 n.137, 32 n.153, 113 n.99, 133 n.51, 138–43, 145–57
timing (of resurrection appearances) 1 n.1, 16, 51, 56–8, 124

unfaithfulness. *See* faith/faithfulness, lack of

weeping. *See* grieving
widow 2, 78, 82–5, 86 nn.119–20, 87, 104, 108 n.82
witness 50–2, 58, 62, 68–70, 74–6, 85, 87–8, 90–4, 100, 109, 111–12, 116, 119, 123–32, 135–7, 142, 143 n.88, 144
woman with a hemorrhage 75 n.74, 78–82
women in the NT 77, 143 n.89. *See also* disciples, female disciples